Lost in the New West

Lost in the New West

Reading Williams, McCarthy, Proulx and McGuane

Mark Asquith

BLOOMSBURY ACADEMIC
NEW YORK • LONDON • OXFORD • NEW DELHI • SYDNEY

BLOOMSBURY ACADEMIC
Bloomsbury Publishing Inc
1385 Broadway, New York, NY 10018, USA
50 Bedford Square, London, WC1B 3DP, UK
29 Earlsfort Terrace, Dublin 2, Ireland

BLOOMSBURY, BLOOMSBURY ACADEMIC and the Diana logo
are trademarks of Bloomsbury Publishing Plc

First published in the United States of America 2022
This paperback edition published in 2023

Copyright © Mark Asquith, 2022

Cover design: Namkwan Cho
Cover image © Getty Images

All rights reserved. No part of this publication may be reproduced or transmitted in any form or by any means, electronic or mechanical, including photocopying, recording, or any information storage or retrieval system, without prior permission in writing from the publishers.

Bloomsbury Publishing Inc does not have any control over, or responsibility for, any third-party websites referred to or in this book. All internet addresses given in this book were correct at the time of going to press. The author and publisher regret any inconvenience caused if addresses have changed or sites have ceased to exist, but can accept no responsibility for any such changes.

A catalog record for this book is available from the Library of Congress.

A catalogue record for this book is available from the British Library.

ISBN:	HB:	978-1-5013-4952-2
	PB:	978-1-5013-7223-0
	ePDF:	978-1-5013-4954-6
	eBook:	978-1-5013-4953-9

Typeset by Integra Software Services Pvt. Ltd.

To find out more about our authors and books visit www.bloomsbury.com and sign up for our newsletters.

To the Balham Book Club, my reminder of why we read.

CONTENTS

Acknowledgements viii

Introduction: 'Where's the All-American Cowboy At?' 1

1 *Butcher's Crossing's* Lost Vision: Williams's Cowboy Outsider 25

2 Lost between Borders: McCarthy's Vanishing Cowboys 47

3 Lost in the Hyperreal: Proulx's Broken Cowboys 95

4 Lost in the Shadow of the Crazies: McGuane's Dislocated Cowboys 145

Conclusion: Where's the All-American Cowboy Going? 193

Bibliography 211
Index 237

ACKNOWLEDGEMENTS

I would like to thank the editorial team at Bloomsbury: Haaris Naqvi for taking on the project in the first place; Amy Martin for overseeing the project; and Akash Udayakumar for his work on the manuscript. I would like to thank Susan Kollin whose perceptive reading and constructive advice made this a much richer book.

I would like to thank Gregory Evans for his support during life-saving coffee breaks at the BL and my wife for her continued patience. I would also like to acknowledge the indirect part played by a group of friends – Justin and Laurence Shinebourne, Nicolas and Veronique Raynaud, Richard Griffiths, Wilder Gutterson, Catherine Pedamon, Isabelle Lesay and Olivier Wolfe, who make up the Balham Book Group. This is an Anglo-French group whose perceptive reading and heated arguments are a reminder of why we read.

Introduction: 'Where's the All-American Cowboy At?'

Getting lost in the West is easy because it is always new and impossible to pinpoint on a map. Western historian Donald Worster confided in 'New West, True West' that even after years of studying scholarly work on the region 'I could not put my finger on the map and say, "There is the West" since that meaning of the word has become bewildering.'[1] Perhaps a map is not the best place to start: How do you find your way around a region that includes the Rocky Mountains, the Great Plains, the Pacific North West, the Arizona Desert, Alaska and Hawaii? But the notion of the West is more 'bewildering' than its geography. For Frederick Jackson Turner – the first great regional historian – 'The Problem of the West' is we're never quite sure which West we are talking or writing about. Amy Hamilton reminds us that even when writers have sought consensus – such as the first issue of the flagship *Western American Literature* in 1966 – some argued that 'the word "West" does not describe a geographical entity so much as it names an idea [that] has something to do with the romantic ideal of America's destiny' whilst others pointed to 'a vast unsettled wilderness, a region, real or imaginary, "out there" in the mountains, forests, plains, and deserts'.[2] Ironically, both hedge even when establishing the parameters of West as geography or symbol: the first conceptual approach is immediately closed by an appeal to American destiny; the latter slips in an 'imaginary' to preface the 'out there'. 'Out there' or 'in here', it is this ambivalence that writers, particularly those under consideration in this study, have been grappling with, exposing and exploiting in their construction of the West in their work.

Like the 'West', the concept of the 'New West' is problematic and has a long and troubling history. A despairing Charles Wilkinson warned in

---

The question 'Where's the all-American Cowboy at?' is posed by Billy Parham right at the beginning of McCarthy's *Cities of the Plain* (p. 3).

the University of Colorado's seminal *Atlas of the New West* (1997) that 'Old West, New West, it is hard terrain to read. One prevails this week, the other the next ... so you can say New West – and we do – because it has become common parlance and because it collects a rough set of ideas in a way that is often useful. But use the term gingerly'.³ The chapters that follow – exploring the land, infrastructure, people and cultural practices – are full of maps that codify everything from the region's dams, roads, Native American reservations and writers' homes – but remain elusive in defining what binds them together to make up a cohesive vision of the New West. To some extent the phrase is tautological for the West has always promised newness. For Leslie Fiedler, even as the first settlers arrived on the East coast (the Western limit of their world), their eyes were straying towards a New West, which both threatened and promised with the allure of a New Eden.⁴ Thus, the vision of renewal within a Western paradise is the thread connecting the first settlers in their prairie schooners; patients, like Theodore Roosevelt, sent West for the clean air; Okies fleeing the dust bowl; Jack Kerouac's psychedelic road trip; Lycra-clad mountain bikers in search of rugged adventure and those seeking retirement in carefully curated ranchettes. In each iteration the West remains 'new' – whether conceived of as a location, a state of mind, advertising propaganda or a label deployed by historians and scholars of Western literature. The historian Joseph Taylor has sought to establish the 'New West trope' against more clearly defined cultural epochs by reviewing the use of the phrase in Library of Congress titles.⁵ He has identified four in the last 135 years. There are clearly more depending on the angle of entry – the romantic or extractive or Post 911 or Digital West – but his chronology provides a useful contextual framework when considering the authors in this study.

The first is the transcontinental West of rail boosterism recorded in works like Samuel Bowles's *Our New West* (1869) and Charles Brace's *The New West* (1869). Both present the West as a well-connected business opportunity whilst simultaneously reconceptualizing it through the lens of the European sublime as a wilderness awaiting contemplation.⁶ It is a 'wilderness' awaiting the canvases of the Hudson River painters and the ploughs of Yeoman Adams. As early as the 1890s, Frederick Jackson Turner drew down the curtain on this age of expansion ushering in a New West constructed on the notion of the 'Frontier'. Turner really understood the narrative power of symbolism, weaving the wagon train, plough and log cabin into an iconography that celebrated the new American virtue of rugged independence.⁷ What he proposed was radical: no longer was the real America to be found on the East Coast, or even in the Southern states, but in the West. We might add, in the past. Slippery and problematic, his 'Frontier thesis' (a term that announced its academic credibility) entered the American consciousness and a region recognized for its emptiness was reconfigured in terms of borders – the most important being between 'civilization' and 'savagery' and between the single voice of the white conqueror and the diverse voices of those silenced 'others'. The West became both geographical location and a process of nation building in which effete Easterners were broken down and remade as Americans. For Richard Slotkin this process became a 'regeneration through violence'[8] – not the genocidal violence against hostile Indians (screened out and aestheticized) but a broader Darwinian survival of the fittest underpinned by the concept of Manifest Destiny.[9]

The creation of the Frontier West was ably aided and abetted by what Christine Bold has derisively called 'The Frontier Club' – men like the impresario Buffalo Bill Cody, the painter Frederic Remington, the future president Theodore Roosevelt and the Dime novelists Owen Wister and Zane Grey. Their West is that of the Western: an ethnically pure space (all favoured Jim Crow laws) free from technology and assertive women, where they were free to create new identities in accordance with the hyper-masculine role model provided by the cowboy.[10] Cody's Wild West Extravaganza presented the West not as an empty wilderness awaiting cultivation from earnest Adams, but a landscape full of Indians waiting to be scripted into a more murderous drama dominated by brave scouts and the US cavalry. Significantly, like Turner, Cody presented his West as 'history' – a claim based upon his deployment of authentic props (buckskins, battle axes, stagecoaches) combined with actual participants (his 'Custer's last stand' used Native Americans who had fought in the actual battle). For Cody, if the actors are real, so is this version of events, a logical blurring exemplified by his dual role as army scout and theatrical impresario, often wearing the same uniform for both.[11] For Slotkin, Cody's collapsible arena becomes the ultimate 'mythic space in which past and present, fiction and reality, could co-exist'. With no script or cohesive plot and 'actors' who never emerge from role, the departing audience will have been aware that their experience differed from that when consuming a play.[12] It is precisely this blurring of 'fact' and 'fiction' through the codification of a set of narrative codes and behaviours that has shaped our confused reaction to the region ever since.

For those not lucky enough to get a ringside seat, the exploits of the stars of Cody's arena – Daniel Boone, Billy the Kid, Cody himself – were replicated in the Dime Western. Cheap paper and improved printing techniques offered the opportunity for the dissemination of new stories to a brand-new audience of office-bound young men. The West was a popular subject, partly because its heyday (1860–90) aligned with the chronology of settlement, but also because the industrialized slaughter of the Civil War found Americans looking West in search of a new pastoral narrative of bravery and conquest. The Western was the ideal subject because, as Richard Etulain has argued, it offered a window on a simpler, more natural national past for a society wary of the threats of industrialization and urbanization.[13] For Jane Tompkins, its success is reducible to questions of gender: 'The Western doesn't have anything to do with the West as such. It is about men's fear of losing this mastery, and hence their identity, both of which the Western tirelessly reinvents.'[14] And 'tirelessly reinvents' it does, as the same stock characters (sheriff, gunslinger) are presented in familiar landscapes (desert, saloon) engaged in familiar activities (shootouts, cattle drives), accoutred with the same visual signifiers (guns, spurs) making it, according to Claude Levi-Strauss, the 'structuralist form *par excellence*'.[15] This made it easy for young Eastern readers to follow the plots (whether young clerks on lunch breaks or teenage boys under the bed covers) and Eastern writers (all major publishers were headquartered in New York) to churn out stories on an industrial scale (the celebrated Prentiss Ingraham authored over 600 novels) without having set foot in the West (the much-feted Gilbert Patten earned his sobriquet 'Wyoming Bill' from having once travelled through the state on a train).[16] The lack of first-hand experience meant that authors relied on an increasingly codified set of caricatures, symbols and events, transforming the West of the Western into what Jean Baudrillard would characterize as the perfect example of a *simulacrum* – not a copy of something real, but something that becomes real (or hyperreal) in its own right.[17]

Riding the hyperreal Frontier are liminal figures like Kit Carson, Wyatt Earp and Jesse James, who are at once historical figures and fictional characters; it is these 'real' cowboys that were transformed into 'reel' cowboys in the early days of cinema. The familiarity of conventions combined with the genre's emphasis on actions over words made the Western ideal for silent cinema. The Dime West also transformed easily to countless B movie staples designed to fill up the cinema double bill, before being transformed into widescreen success by Gary Cooper, Erol Flynn and John Wayne. By the 1950s Dime Westerns were selling at an annual rate of 35 million copies; Westerns constituted 34 per cent of the features produced by the big studios and eight of the top ten TV shows were Westerns – including *Bonanza* (1959–65), *Wagon Train* (1957–65) and *Maverick* (1957–62).[18] There is a didacticism about such shows, the simplified racial and gender relations underpinned by a good vs evil storyline designed to acculturate young boys into a masculine world parents feared lost in the suburbs. Thus, though family audiences in the 1950s may have gone through two world wars, the Great Depression and entered the nuclear age, they will have been reassured by cultural semiotics with which Cody would have been familiar.

The Western cowboy hangs over the West like a fast-drawing guardian angel: even as we enter Taylor's third New West of urbanization, mass-industrialization and the New Deal, Bruce Grant's *The Cowboy Encyclopaedia: The Old and the New West from the Open Range to the Dude Ranch* (1951) makes clear that most Americans (including those living in the West) still conceived of the West in terms of the 'Frontier' and cowboys.[19] The first real challenge to this vision came from the work of the 'New Historians' – Donald Worster's *Rivers of Empire* (1985), Patricia Limerick's *The Legacy of Conquest* (1987) and Richard White's *It's Your Misfortune and None of My Own* (1991). The 1989 'Trails: Towards a New Western History' symposium in Santa Fe effectively brought the curtain down on the Turnerian Frontier – the Frontier being, in Limerick's words, the dreaded 'F Word' which is shorthand for 'the place where white people get scarce'. For Turner's 'Creation myth' is really just 'a tale explaining where its [white] members came from and why they are special, chosen by providence for a special destiny'.[20] If an account of Western conquest is to make sense, she argues, then it is essential to stop seeing it as a frozen region 'with Indian people and Hispanics waiting like stage furniture for the play to begin when the white men came out'.[21] The New Historians offered a postmodern vision of Western history, in which ideology and myth give way to plurality and complexity, and the linearity of an imposed voice of authority gives way to the many voices left out by Turner – the Native Americans, ethnic minorities, women – which, when heard, often reveal uncomfortable and contradictory histories. Their focus on the West as a 'place' as opposed to 'process' resonated comfortably with the prevailing anti-imperialism, anti-capitalism, anti-militarism rhetoric of academia; their West ceases to be conceived of as a playground of white masculinity, becoming instead a polyphonic zone of competing stories recounting a history of oppression, and also, as Krista Comer has noted, emancipation for those seeking to challenge feminist, racial and queer cultural norms.[22]

Although the New Historians were successful in critiquing the simplicity of the Turnerian Frontier, their regional approach was challenged by poststructuralist critics in the 1990s who sought to decouple the West from geographical considerations which they felt were tainted by patriarchal and nationalist politics. For poststructuralists, the New West is unmoored from the geographical Frontier and the idea of a 'true' West is replaced by the West conceived as a signifier endlessly repeated and reinterpreted globally. When Sal Paradise stumbles upon Cheyenne's 'Wild West Week' whilst *On the Road* (1957) he is horrified: 'In my first shot at the West I was seeing to what absurd devices it had fallen to keep its proud tradition.'[23] It is an indictment of both his dreams and the regional commodification of the myth, but to postwestern critics the kitsch demonstrates 'a set of tropes that, despite their misrepresentations, aim at making a coherent set of arguments regarding the meaning of the West'.[24] They are on display in the deployment of easily identifiable signifiers – tomahawks and war paint – in the first ever screen Western 'Captured by Indians' (1899) which is filmed, not in Wyoming, but in a Lancashire Mill town in the UK; the same symbols and tropes are deployed 130 years later to foreshadow a similar captive narrative in South Korean director Bong Joon-ho's Oscar-winning *Parasite* (2019).[25] When the 'typical' Western landscape is more likely to be found in Italy or Alberta, and cowboy codes have morphed into *Homeland* and *Breaking*

Bad, in what sense can we identify an actual place? Neil Campbell in his *The Cultures of the American New West* (2000) calls for reimagining the West not as a region but as both 'process' and 'geographies' that are contingent, and mobile:

> Efforts to define the West inevitably reduce its complexities and smooth out its contradictions by transforming cultural processes into natural ones, history into myth. To view the West otherwise is to see it as several spaces simultaneously, overlapping, in contact and exchange, as 'third space'. In this sense, the New West is always relational, dialogic, engaged in or capable of reinvention – and, therefore, contradictory, irreducible, and hybrid.[26]

Campbell rejects the notion of the West as 'a fixed, permanent graphical and ideological fact' in order to shift our attention to a 'New West' that embraces the urban, global and virtual. Figuratively, he rejects the West as a space conceived in terms of linear growth out of rootedness (symbolized by the tree) and conceives of it instead as symbolized by the complex underground horizontal root system of the rhizome.[27] The 'rhizomatic West' is 'a third space' made up of competing dialogues, the most important of which is that of the contemporary West with its mythical past. It is a dynamic environment which acknowledges that nostalgia for the Old West and the lives lived by contemporary Westerners are not fixed in a relationship of historical influence, but bleed into each other.[28]

The reduction of the West to free-floating signifier helps make sense of an urban West of trailer parks, methane mines, Korean cowboy shirts and coarse fishing, but it also leaves it dangerously unmoored. Nina Baym's 2006 review of a number of works of postwestern literary scholarship noted that authors' discussion of portability was often hedged by a curious identification with a 'real' place that exists – a place identified as 'the West'.[29] The regional approach of the New Historians has re-emerged in the scholarship of 'Settler Colonial' theorists. However, they have rejected the approach predicated on American exceptionalism in favour of a transnational comparative model that places the West within the context of colonial projects in countries as diverse as Australia, Ireland and Israel. As Thomas Dunlap has argued, 'In Anglo settler countries assumptions, ideas, and goals were far more common than the myth of American exceptionalism allows.'[30] What makes this approach so significant is its focus on the shared narratives of dispossession. Patrick Wolfe, an influential theorist in the field, argues that unlike other colonialists who were driven by enslavement and resource extraction, settler colonialists are focussed on justifying their erasure of indigenous peoples by narratives, institutions, treaties and the word of God. Thus, 'The Frontier' rejected by the New Historians re-emerges as a device that is both conceptual and spatial: it is a social fiction (or a 'performative representation') that allowed an invasion to occur.[31] And because the 'invasion is a structure not an event' it is wrong to seek to identify one celebrated and colourful Frontier era in the past. As Tom Lynch makes clear, there should be no post in postcolonialism: rather the Frontier is given new meanings through new literary traditions and rhetorical tropes into the future.[32] For settler colonial theorists it becomes one of many rhetorical manoeuvres – to which might be added the transformation of the land into 'wilderness' landscape; the labelling of indigenous peoples as nomads; the importance of naming and mapping – that allows for the production of a settler mythology, which, whether in Australia, New Zealand or the West, creates political and cultural legitimacy.[33]

The purpose of this thumbnail sketch is to demonstrate just how easy it is to get lost in a West that can't decide whether it's a region defined by its aridity; an idealistic direction of travel; a political paradigm endorsed through the ideologies of 'Manifest Destiny' and the 'Frontier'; a romantic 'wilderness' (another Anglo-Imperial construct) promising self-identification; or a free-floating cultural signifier comprising of kitsch symbols. For writers seeking to engage with the West, this identity problem is exacerbated by the long shadow cast by the Western: we may struggle defining what or where the West is but recognize the simplicity of the genre that has come to define it. It is no accident that *Shane* is mediated through the admiring gaze of a young Joey Starrett: this is its audience. Engaging seriously with the West, therefore, implies dealing with what William Kittredge identifies as the 'insidious trap' of the narrative modes making up the Western.[34] John Williams, one of the writers under examination in this study, complained that 'the West has been the victim of a bad and cheap mythologizing over the years' and there has been no flowering of serious Western literature to rival its Southern counterpart.[35] When he arrived at the University of Denver on the GI Bill in the 1950s, he came under the influence of the academic publisher Alan Swallow who was trying to reclaim the West and the Western on behalf of serious art through his small-scale publishing house ('Sage Books' imprint).[36] 'We used to talk a lot,' Williams recalls, the upshot being *Butcher's Crossing* (1960) – his attempt to rescue the Western from prime-time TV and to do 'something serious for the West'.[37] It is, however, as his own experiences proved, an exercise fraught with difficulty. For Kittredge, doing 'something serious' meant reconfiguring the Western to reveal the 'real' story of the West. However, as Limerick and the New Historians discovered in their attempts to overturn Turner, there is no distinction between the 'real West' and the 'fake West': they are 'Siamese twins sharing the same circulatory system' which is 'cultural' rather than historical.[38] Thus, though Kitteridge's Cord Series of novels – with such titles as *The Nevada War* (1982) and *Brimstone Basin* (1986) – offered a feminist, self-reflexive subversion of the genre, his loyal readership took them at face value and accused him of selling out.³⁹ Similarly, Larry McMurtry, self-appointed scourge of the mythical West, thought that his *Lonesome Dove* (1985) was the ultimate 'anti-western', but to his horror his readers accepted it 'as a reinforcement of the myth.'⁴⁰

Williams offered a different approach: a bildungsroman (though the spiritual evolution of his protagonist is questionable) written in the form of a Western (he deploys familiar Western characters and tropes) that uses the cultural dislocation of the central protagonist to draw the reader into a critical appraisal of the genre and the mythology upon which it is constructed. Essentially, he makes a virtue of being lost in a New West. His passive protagonist arrives in the New West with his head full of an idealized Old West, which makes him naive and tragic; the shattering of his optimism combined with the fragmentation of his fragile identity becomes an analogue of the West as a whole. It is a narrative model replicated in the work of Cormac McCarthy, Annie Proulx and Thomas McGuane whose youthful protagonists (always young men) find themselves lost in the 'Many Lives of the New West' outlined by Taylor. They are ambivalent agents of Manifest Destiny on the Tex/Mex border of the 1850s; naive settlers lured West by a misappropriated 'pioneer rhetoric'; wannabe cowboys escaping New Deal America in favour of Old West Mexico; alienated burger flippers who dream of being Shane; young men torn by a love of the land and a desire to make it pay. Their experiences allow the writers to engage with questions of race, gender and identity and the possibility of forging a meaningful life in a rapidly changing environment whose older myths and stories no longer provide adequate answers. They are, in short, lost in a New West as lost as themselves.

II

The Western Literature Association's monumental *A Literary History of the American West* (1987) has one small paragraph devoted to *Butcher's Crossing* (there are separate chapters on A. B. Guthrie, Vardis Fisher and Frank Waters). The entry is brief but perceptive:

> Its youthful eastern protagonist joins a buffalo hunt in a high Colorado valley; following a wasteful slaughter, he suffers a snowbound winter and returns to town to discover that the entire venture has been made futile by the failure of the hide market. These events are given philosophical dimension by the fact that the protagonist enters upon his experience expecting to find God and bliss in the wilderness but finds instead vacuity and meaninglessness. The novel thus figures forth, against the senseless destruction of the buffalo, the evolution of the American mind from the

transcendentalism of the nineteenth century to the existentialism of the twentieth.[41]

In his tale of a young man (William Andrews) who travels West in search of 'wildness' only to be confronted by the brutality of the last great buffalo hunt, Williams sets out to dismantle a founding myth and also, through his existential pondering, our expectations of the genre. It is written as a Western: it deploys all the familiar Western archetypes (gnarled mountain men, drunken camp tenders, the prostitute with a heart of gold) engaged in familiar rituals (dangerous river and desert crossings, buffalo hunting) set against a grandiose landscape, but filters them through the detached sensibility of a young boy whose growth from childish optimism to cynicism becomes a means of critiquing both mythology and genre. This process begins with his critique of the Turnerian myth of regeneration through violence (in this novel there is simply violence) that centres on the trading post of 'Butcher's Crossing'. Williams went through a number of titles – *A Naked World*, *Lost Horizon* and *The Crossing* – all of which suggest an existentialist meditation rather than a Western, before settling on the name of the settlement. This becomes, as the gerund implies, not an outpost of civilization, but a launch pad for brutal violence. Read within a settler colonial context, it is a site flourishing outside the state's official borders because the buffalo hunting that it sustains coincides with a broader expansionist project of indigenous erasure. Williams places the outpost within a transnational hide trade facilitated by a network of shrewd business operatives who are contemptuous of the romance of the mountain men under their employ. But this is not the West that Andrews – his head full of nineteenth-century transcendentalism – and, by extension, the reader either want or see.

Williams targets not only Turner, but the spiritually endorsed ideas he blames for projecting a generation of naive young men West in search of themselves. He notes that the novel 'developed from my notions of what would happen if the Emersonian ideals that were in vogue in the East in the late nineteenth century were put to some kind of test in the *real* kind of nature that the Easterners were so romantic about'.[42] 'Emersonian ideals' mixed Calvinist teleology, Kantian metaphysics, Wordsworth's romanticism and Eastern philosophy to posit the physical world as the manifestation of the mind of the creator. Church worship was replaced by a unity with the 'Over-Soul' accessed through contemplation amidst the trees. Williams's scepticism is made clear through the novel's two epigraphs – the first, from Emerson's *Nature* (1850), is an exaltation of the natural world, which is contrasted with a quote from Herman Melville's *The Confidence Man*, which warns that such idealism is more likely to leave one freezing to death on the prairie.

Williams's suspicion of Emerson is conjoined with a more generalized complaint that the earliest Western writers deployed simple binary codes that appealed to the Calvinist sensibilities of their New England readers. In his essay 'The "Western": Definition of the Myth' (1961) he complains that the wilderness is a stage upon which cowboys (his election demonstrated by the virtue of his actions) take on Indians (Williams's preferred term) in a traditional good vs evil binary. Meanwhile, in mountain man sagas such as A. B. Guthrie's *The Big Sky* (1947) and Frederick Manfred's *Lord Grizzly* (1954), he complains that the land is presented as an enemy against which their protagonists are forced to do battle in order to survive. Such a struggle makes sense, he argues, only if the traditional 'voyage into the wilderness' is understood not as an epic of endurance but as 'a voyage into the self, experimental, private and sometimes obscure'.[43] There are shades of *Moby Dick* in this formulation: the desert wilderness, the snow that traps the hunters and the white skin of the skinned buffalo, becoming, like the skin of the white whale, a blankness that offers an opportunity for an exploration of self. There are also shades of the existentialist focus on 'identity' and 'meaninglessness' that was being popularized in America by the visit of Sartre, Beauvoir and Camus in the immediate post-war period. Articles appeared in lifestyle magazines such as *Vogue* and *Harper's Bazaar*, whilst more considered articles by luminaries such as Hannah Arendt appeared in *Nation* and *The Partisan Review*.[44] Williams was a fan: his ill-fated first novel, *Nothing but the Night* (1948), is a psychological novel in the style of Camus's *The Outsider* (1942). His central protagonist is the archetypal 'outsider' confronting difficulty in assigning meaning to his actions and forging an identity from the face he sees in the mirror. In *Butcher's Crossing* this character becomes Andrews, the young son of a Calvinist minister who heads West in search of meaning and identity only to be confronted with barbarity and existential emptiness.

An existential Western was always going to be a risk. The marketing department at Panther Books didn't know how to market it and chose a conventional front cover which showed a cowboy and settler woman in front of a wagon train with the puff: 'Through blinding heat across an unyielding land they trekked. Men in search of a burning vision.'[45] Critics didn't know how to review it, one contemporary warning readers expecting the traditional 'shoot-em-up Western' that they will be disappointed because there is 'enough symbolism and philosophic thought to make it as modern a narrative as you found in Camus or Sartre'.[46] Williams's editor, Marie Rodell, warned her fragile author: 'Brace yourself for a bad shock next Sunday [*The New York Times*] has reviewed *Butcher's Crossing* as a western ... and the idiot who writes the column has of course no small inkling of what the book is about.'[47] He didn't, but damned the book to oblivion by describing the reading experience as like being 'hauled by a snail through a pond of molasses'.[48] The book was a flop that sold fewer than 5,000 copies;

that is, until its reappraisal in the light of the phenomenal success of the recently republished *Stoner* (1965). Picking over the novel in 2007, Morris Dickstein wrote in the *New York Times* that *Butcher's Crossing* was 'the first and best revisionist western' that 'paved the way for Cormac McCarthy'.[49] It is a view echoed by Brett Easton Ellis's acknowledgement that 'It may be one of the more literary westerns I've read, but it *is* a western – and a precursor to what Cormac McCarthy would do with the genre, especially in his blood-soaked and hallucinatory *Blood Meridian*'.[50] In *The Guardian*, John Plotz writes:

> Critics have singled out movies of the early 1970s (*Butch Cassidy and the Sundance Kid, The Outlaw Josey Wales, McCabe and Mrs. Miller, Jeremiah Johnson*) and some novels of the early 1980s (especially Cormac McCarthy's *Blood Meridian*) as the first wave of 'revisionist westerns.' But back in 1960, without McCarthy's lurid baroque extravagances, without any cool Hollywood soundtrack, John Williams wrote what may be the perfect *anti*-western.[51]

Butcher's Crossing is indeed the perfect *anti*-Western in that, according to Fiedler's definition, it 'gives new life and new significance to the old formula'.[52] It also shares an umbilical relationship with *Blood Meridian*. McCarthy's story of a group of bloody scalp hunters operating on the Tex/Mex borders in the 1850s is, like Williams's novel, a clear revisionist exposure of the mindless violence underpinning Turnerian expansionism. In both novels there is no moral centre and there is no heroic central character deconstructed, but an ambivalent young man (in McCarthy's case 'The "Kid"' whose epithet challenges the mythical Billy through his 'taste for mindless violence'). As 'revisionist' Westerns they make 'visible' the violence hidden beneath the blinkered vision of Turner, sanctioned and sanitized by Manifest Destiny and aestheticized by Hollywood. There is a focus on detached vision in both novels: we are invited to 'see' without feeling, the authors deliberately refusing to editorialize or explain and withholding censure or moral judgement. These are Westerns – they deploy familiar Western archetypes engaged in a classic Western narrative – but Williams's tone of detached meditation and McCarthy's baroque declamation means that they don't read or sound like Westerns. Furthermore, there is a tendency to disruption of expectations signalled by their epigraphs, which, in their citation of contrasting and chaotic references – Emerson, Paul Valery, Melville, the *Yuma Daily Sun* – seek to both elevate and problematize the intellectual scope of the books. There is at their centre a group of hunters led by a demonic 'Ahab-like leader' whose blinkered and bloody pursuit of the elusive prey (whether skins or scalps) is transformed into an exploration of the soul. Both writers treat character as a means of exploring wider themes; for all Andrews' introspection he hardly breathes, appearing little more than a place marker with a supporting cast of Western archetypes designed to explore Williams's existentialist preoccupations. Likewise, McCarthy's characters seem to be constructed from an amalgam of the historical and literary and to be so thinly drawn that, as Dana Phillips has noted, McCarthy 'seems to have largely dispensed with the concept of character in fashioning his material'.[53] There is no interiority (McCarthy is dismissive of the psychological novels of Henry James.[54]) and since, with the exception of the Judge, they spit as often as they speak, the reader's quest for motive remains conjectural. And, finally, both novels provide no closure (McCarthy's epigraph from Paul Valery cures the reader of hopes of divine justice), just an emptiness reflected in the barren landscape through which the riders journey. Thus, the oft repeated 'They rode on' – which could apply to both novels – becomes less a discourse marker than a statement of evasion.

Blood Meridian and *Butchers Crossing* open with a Westward escape and end two years after the extinction of the buffalo, which becomes a potent symbol of the historic closure of the Frontier. The former formalizes this event through the image of the cowboy sinking fence posts in order to run cattle on the land that the hunters in the novel have so brutally emptied; thus McCarthy introduces the paradox that he will explore throughout *The Border Trilogy* (which begins a hundred years after *Blood Meridian*): the fencing that makes the cowboy's job possible also curtails the free range that is central to his identity. 'The border story', A. Carl Bredahl Jr. reminds us, is 'the most common story in western writing' because it identifies 'a place of transition rather than demarcation', which can be conceived as a 'new frontier [that] describes ... an area of continual opening'.[55] Whether opening or closing, the border story offers a postmodern vehicle that records the existential anguish of characters caught in the liminal space between optimism and nostalgia. And this is the postmodern anxiety suffered by the young cowboy questors at the centre of *The Border Trilogy*. They are disenfranchised ranch sons lost in Taylor's third New West of powerful women, oil, interstates and barbed wire, who spend their time trying to re-create the West that McCarthy had comprehensively demolished in *Blood Meridian*. For them, the West becomes a portable signifier relocated to Mexico, which they treat as a blank slate (problematic behaviour discussed later). Here they are able to appropriate the narrative conventions, cultural signifiers and tropes of the cowboy safely away from constraints of the urban and, above all, feminine. Their dream is signalled by their fastidious costumery (the Western is in the thrall of spectacle), the pastiche dialogue learned from Hollywood B movies and the continually recycled plots and character archetypes.

That their quests fail is secondary to their performance of a set of highly stylized codes, which are celebrated and critiqued in equal measure. This is done intra-textually through a range of Mexican mentors who mock their idealistic appropriation of dead myths. They, in their turn, are placed in opposition to a variety of Texan characters who remain in awe of the boys' romantic idealism. This narrative commentary is reinforced meta-textually through McCarthy's irony. The three-book structure, Robert Jarrett notes, allows McCarthy to recycle narrative events (Grady's love affairs; Billy's knife fight) with a gentle parodying that demonstrates their gradual disillusionment with the Western dream.[56] It isn't satire but a sub-textual critique signalled by the ironic shading of set-piece Western scenes (the river crossing, the release of the girl from 'Mexican bandits', the 'gunfight' (discussed in full in Chapter 2)). It is reinforced further by the repetition of theatrical metaphors (the puppet shows alluded to by the Duena (*APH*, 240), or the performance of *Pagliacci* (a 'play within a play') watched by Billy (*C* 230)). Indeed, Rick Wallach argues that McCarthy's minimalist use of visual grammar deliberately draws attention to the text's orality, as if the boys have already been scripted into a play within a play or one of the Mexican songs that punctuate the narrative.[57] The cumulative effect guides the reading strategy of *The Trilogy* in which we are made aware that we are consuming a Western novel and also its interpretive performance by two young men; a process that leads to the genre's gentle deconstruction

In some ways, Grady and Parham would not look out of place if they rode into Proulx's Wyoming. Indeed, Elaine Showalter has noted that Proulx 'writes about cowboys, ranchers, and drifters in ways that ... puts her version of the American West next to that of Cormac McCarthy'.[58] 'Next to' but not always consistent with, for despite McCarthy's best revisionist intentions, he seems, like McMurtry, to have been stifled by a deep-seated imaginative sympathy for the mythological West. This is not the case with Proulx, a middle-aged woman impervious to the allure of regional male bravado. The New West under inspection in her work is that surrounding her Wyoming *Bird Cloud* home. Proulx's neighbours are no longer family ranchers but 'the heirs to fortunes in "Ciba-Geigy, Anschutz, Wal-Mart, Campbell's Foods."'[59] They are baby-boomers who, as Limerick has observed, 'bought the Gene Autry lunch box and the Roy Rogers chaps and the Hopalong crayons', and who now have bought the whole ranch.[60] For isolated ranchers struggling to make ends meet, the pressure to 'sell up' and 'sell out' is overwhelming, thus condemning them to the role of support actors in somebody else's Western fantasy. The New West has evolved into what Jack Lessinger has theorized as a 'Penturbia' and what Tim Robbins describes as a 'Last Refuge' for incomers in search of the 'wild lonesome'. Modern westering and settlement is more likely to involve pensioners seeking a slower pace of life; fishermen enamoured by the cowboy aesthetic of *A River Run's through It*; New Age hippies seeking alternative Native American lifestyles; thrill-seekers riding the high lonesome on titanium mountain bikes; and tech entrepreneurs in log 'ranchettes' with good connection and a horse in the paddock and a 4X4 in the driveway.[61] As the corner store closes down to re-open as themed cowboy café and bait shop we have entered the hyperreal with both insiders and outsiders performing a highly stylized reproduction of Western identity. Proulx's interest is in those young men (and occasionally women) trapped in the service of the hyperreal: they are young men waiting in themed restaurants whilst measuring themselves against the unachievable models of masculinity represented by the cowboy. Wallace Stegner notes, 'A lot of clerks and soda jerks in western cities are partly what fact and history have made them, and partly what the romantic imagination and traditional stereotypes tell them to be.'[62] And the more the 'imagined' West overwhelms the real locality and regional culture gives way to stereotypes, the more they find themselves dependent, both economically and psychologically, on a myth which they privately begin to suspect.

Like McCarthy, Proulx positions herself as an 'historian' of the West. She edited the geographical and ethnological work *Red Desert: History of a Place* (2009) and has provided the forewords to a number of historical works and photographic collections. Her methodology is guided by the New Historicism of the eighties and also an older *Annales* tradition that informed the academic approach of her aborted PhD in Renaissance Studies. She was drawn to communities living within a cultural tradition defined by a particular landscape, that start 'to experience the erosion of traditional ways, and attempt to master contemporary, large-world values'.[63] This methodology informed her first novel, *Postcards* (1992), which explored the post-war collapse of the New England dairy industry, and also *The Shipping News* (1993), which focussed on the demise of the Newfoundland fishing industry. 'Writing about the American West', she argues, 'is just like writing about the American East or wherever' – it's just another region under threat, as its cowboys and ranchers come to terms with the economic, environmental and mythical disintegration that surrounds them.[64] Her *Wyoming Trilogy* presents a playfully postmodern rather than realist approach, signalled by the tagline to *Close Range* – 'Reality's never been of much use out here'. The 'here' in question is conceptually aligned with Campbell's 'thirdspace' – a site that flattens the distinction between New and Old, fake and real in favour of competing narratives and dialogues (a form of Bakhtinian polyphony), the most important being the region's conversation with its own past.[65] Her 'rhizomatic Wyoming' acknowledges that nostalgia, and the lives lived by contemporary Westerners are not fixed in a relationship of historical influence, but bleed into each other. This blurring is enhanced by her adoption of the modes and syntactical tropes of journalistic reportage balanced with historical notation and flights of magic realism (a genre that advertises the blurring of fiction and reality) that reminds us of its constructedness. Real historical events, locations and people (enforced intra-textually through the postmodern ploy of detailed 'acknowledgements') share narrative space with fictional creations leading us, in a manner that is playful rather than pompous, to interrogate the process of mythmaking and what constitutes the West.

Proulx observes that 'if you get the landscape right, the characters will step out of it, and they'll be in the right place'.[66] Her landscape consists of easily recognizable Western signifiers – hoodoos, buttes and gulches – which elevate her Wyoming to the hyperreal. The characters stepping out of this fantasy West are descendants of Sherwood Anderson's *Winesburg, Ohio* (1919) filtered through the *Dirty Realism* of Jayne Phillips and Pam Houston via McMurtry's *Texasville* (1987). They are grotesques forced into the kitsch reproduction of Western identity signalled by their parodic names – Pake Bitts, Chay Slump, Dirt Sheets – living on faux Western ranches – 'The Harp', 'The Coffee Pot' – in hyper-stylized Western towns – Woolybucket, Elk Tooth, Cowboy Rose.[67] These caricatures provide the Western chorus against which Proulx develops her realist protagonists: vulnerable young men whose search for authenticity and identity brings under critical scrutiny the Western codes by which they live their lives. Her 'settler stories', for example, chart the settlement of the New West from the era of the prairie schooner to the SUV, exposing how the myth of the 'lone pioneer' was exploited by railroad and real estate companies. Her indictment of reckless adolescent fantasy is amplified by her focus on the reluctant wives they drag behind them whose suffering remains unalleviated by the glamour of Western mythology. They, unlike the female characters of either Williams or McCarthy, are fully rounded and active participants in the deconstruction of their own marginalized existence. In other stories, Proulx's protagonists are a means of critiquing a wide range of New Western concerns, notably the struggle between ranchers and environmentalists over the region's ecological heritage; the impact of globalization on local identity and Western values; and the place of women in the Western story. She is particularly concerned with the psychological damage caused by a macho but sexless mythology that reduces complex emotions to plaintive song lyrics and privileges relationships between men and their horses above those with women. In other stories, and particularly *That Old Ace in the Hole* (2002), it is the land that moves centre stage. For McCarthy the land is nothing more than a baroque stage upon which theatrical acts of depravity are committed; for Williams it is a blankness that facilitates an inner journey; for Proulx, by contrast, the land emerges as victim of the wrong story. Through the simple expedient of having her naive young protagonist listen to the stories of a gallery of assorted Texans, Proulx explores how settler communities take possession and domesticate their surroundings through symbolism, ritual and narrative. Such stories vindicate indigenous erasure and validate community as they chart how the West was won (in which *Exodus* and Eden dominate), was lost (through intensive methods) and how, through re-wilding projects, it will be redeemed.

Proulx's *Wyoming Stories* are about those left behind: the losers in a global economy clinging onto a cowboy myth that validates their existence whilst contorting them into new shapes. McGuane's *Deadrock* stories, by contrast, are about those young men who get away to build alternative lives only to return emotionally unfulfilled with the hope that the West will perform its traditional function of putting them back together again. Thus, Turner is once again turned on his head and a genre concerned with striking out to find an identity is replaced with the native who returns to do the same. Robert Adams complained in *The New York Review of Books* that the *Deadrock novels* all tell the same story.[68] They do: it is McGuane's story. The feted Hollywood screenwriter whose 'Captain Beserko' period of marriages, drugs and fast cars is brought to an abrupt halt by a high-speed crash and family tragedy, which is then followed by a move to Livingston, Montana, and the ranch life that he had first experienced as a boy.[69] It is an autobiographical experience that echoes the familiar literary trope of the prodigal's return, which allows for the scrutiny of the role of place in forging identity.[70] Thomas Hardy presented the archetype in *The Return of the Native* (1879), in which the return from the bright lights of Paris to a life of furze cutting on Egdon Heath becomes a means of exploring the young protagonist's existential malaise. It is a model taken up by Hemingway, whose damaged returnees are those scarred by war who find a world of domesticity unequal to their psychological needs. It is also the plight of the Native American victims in Leslie Marmon Silko's *Ceremony* (1977) and Louise Erdrich's *Love Medicine* (1984) who are seeking solace through the landscape and 'ceremonies' of their ancestors. In *Rock Springs* (1987), fellow Montana writer, Richard Ford, introduces a number of characters struggling with a childhood trauma (death, a sexual encounter or a parental argument) that can be alleviated only by the return home. Barbara Kingsolver's *Animal Dreams* (1990) feminizes this otherwise insistently masculine trope through the experiences of Codi, a lost soul who spends fourteen years on the road before returning to the ironically named Grace (Arizona) to look after her sick father and put her life back together. She hopes to 'step off the bus and land smack in the middle of sense and belonging' but quickly realizes that her dreams of integration are nothing but a 'hopeful construction'.[71]

Codi's malaise is shared by McGuane's returnees who hope to find a sense of belonging within a Western context only to find a region suffering an identity crisis as acute as their own. McGuane is determined to question what we mean by 'the West' – rejecting not only the West of 'cowboys and Indians' but also 'the pompous backward-looking revisionist West of Wallace Stegner, Vardis Fisher, and even A. B. Guthrie' in which men have horse trouble but never order pizza.[72] His postmodern construction is revealed in the Introduction to William Allard's aptly entitled collection *Vanishing Breed, Photographs of the Cowboy and the West* (1982):

> The West, whatever that is, is still there, believe it or not, in its entirety. It is the leading chimera of our geography. The dead windmills lost behind the high wire of the missile range, the stove-up cowboy at the unemployment office, the interstate that plunges through the homesteads, all bring aches to an American race memory ... The West vanished for the Indian and the drover; it vanished for the cowboy. Simultaneously it reappeared in all the same places, and in movies and rodeos. It's like fire. Hollywood, calf tables, and depreciation schedules can't kill it.[73]

This is typical McGuane – the mockery lubricates the dryly serious and adds nuance whilst the scripted diffidence ('whatever that is') is both flippant and demanding critical scrutiny. Campbell's rhizomatic West is replaced with a set of combustible cultural signifiers – landscapes, homesteads and vanishing Indians – making up a hopeful, if misguided, race memory. It lives in a set of symbols (Stetsons, Saloons and windmills), archetypes and ritualistic tropes independent of both geography and history that help to produce a particular identity. Because it is fictional it is indestructible, overshadowing every iteration of the New West and those attempts to tell a different Western story.

Deadrock (a play on McGuane's Livingston home) is a cliché of a Western town nestling beneath the aptly named Crazy Mountains. The mountains should act as a site of spiritual regeneration, but are emblematic of Deadrock men struggling for self-definition in the shadow of a hyper-masculine mythology. Like Anderson grotesques (McGuane, like Proulx, lists Sherwood Anderson as an influence[74]) his characters are trapped in a performance of a highly stylized version of a Western identity. They are both proud Westerners with superior values to corporate America, and exhausted characters in a degraded landscape clutching at warn out myths. His ranchers are descendants of the men who carved out the country and brutal patriarchs obsessed with land inheritance; his Indians (McGuane's preferred term) are gnomic prophets and alcoholic drifters; his cowboys are custodians of the Old West and big-belted, wife-beating drunks. This is the Deadrock to which his protagonists return, desperate to embrace the landscape, windmills and heroism of the old West, but constrained by an environment in which the 'borders' are more likely to be herbaceous than transformative. Absence has also made them culturally sophisticated – they read the Classics and display a range of culinary skills – which means that their romanticism is tempered by an alertness to the vulgarity of cowboy kitsch. This ambivalence makes them both tragic and ridiculous, a cross between Hamlet (a continual inter-textual reference) and Buster Keaton.[75] The typical McGuane protagonist is aptly represented by Patrick Fitzpatrick in *Nobody's Angel* (1981): an ex–

Cold War tank commander who returns West to cure himself of a 'sadness for no reason' by saving the family ranch in the manner of Gary Cooper before riding off into the sunset with his very own Calamity Jane. However, despite his performance of highly stylized Western behavioural tropes, in which others are reduced to stage props, his highly developed sense of irony means he is unable to take himself seriously. Only the land – in which his protagonists ride, hunt and fish – provides an opportunity for them to embrace the West unironically. Yet even here they are torn between nostalgia for a landscape that confirms their cowboy identity and their desire to make it pay in a global economy.

The *Deadrock novels* offer variations on Western themes reassessed through a gentle mockery that lays open the pathos beneath. In *Something to Be Desired* (1984) Lucien Baker is a 'cowboy outsider' who understands the disparity between myth and reality, opening up a kitsch cowboy-themed spa in a knowingly ironic play on the West's reputation for putting people back together. Throughout the novel, McGuane opens up for ridicule the divergence between the West Lucien cherishes and projects to his customers and the ersatz version in which he participates, which becomes, as his sulphurous name implies, a postmodern hell. In *Keep the Change* (1989), McGuane seems troubled by the way in which the Western landscape and its rituals become part of an exclusively hyper-masculine legacy handed down from fathers to sons. Difficult filial relations are central to all the *Deadrock novels* (indeed they are the catalyst for the movement West for almost all the young protagonists in this study) and are a domestic version of the conflict between the hard-nosed business practice and romanticism played out in the West as a whole. In *Nothing but Blue Skies* (1992) Nathaniel Lewis claims that 'McGuane seems intent on nothing less than a re-examination of the myth of the American West' through his depiction of the 'sweeping vision of the post-Reagan West, a landscape blighted by environmental, economic, and spiritual frailties', all of which are played out through the personal struggles of his central protagonist.[76] The novel says nothing about blue skies; it is about the land and those unworthy people, like the central protagonist, who own it, and those, like the cowboys whom he employs, who understand it. *The Cadence of Grass* (2002) ushers in a sea change in McGuane's fictional approach as the troubled young male protagonist gives way to a woman. A number of Proulx's *Wyoming Stories* centre on female protagonists who endure a feminized version of the alienation suffered by her lost young men (discussed in Chapter 4). None, however, are as strong and conflicted as McGuane's Evelyn Whitelaw. She is, as her name suggests, a latter-day Eve struggling in an Anglo patriarchy, torn between the models of femininity endorsed by her glamorous sister and her nostalgia for an Old West in which she can never participate fully. McGuane's most arresting decision, however, is to roll up the traditional Old/New, male/female, realism/magic realism binaries into a single character: Donald Aadfield. Donald is a cross-dressing mountain man desperate to explore contemporary farming methods but trapped within the traditions of the parental ranch. In many ways, he is a personification of the complexity facing all McGuane's young men who find themselves lost in the cultural practices of a West that seems as lost as themselves.

In the cross-dressing Donald we have moved a long way from Will Andrews; furthermore, there seems to be little of Williams's narrative austerity in the gentle mockery, occasional flights of magical realism and screwball comedy of McGuane and Proulx. However, they share a preoccupation with masculine identity, allowing the disillusion of their protagonists to draw the reader into a new and potentially critical relationship with the familiar narratives and props of the mythical West. Their West is forever new because it is continually being brought into existence as an imaginative space that will provide the rugged independence and spiritual fulfilment that they find lacking in a New West dominated by the urban, the interstate, manners, technology and assertive women. They gain their cultural validation through a specific landscape that they can embrace unironically and the performance of a set of narrative tropes and codes that become the means of the authors' revisionist interrogation. They all have difficulties with women, the result of conforming to genre in which the latter are idealized into silence. When, despite the horrors of the buffalo hunt and the futility represented by the piles of burning hides, Andrews rides out of Butcher's Crossing determined to continue West, he dramatizes the indestructibility of a myth that supports and contorts the lives of contemporary Westerners. Like Shane, Andrews doesn't come back. If he did, then Deadrock would be just the kind of highly stylized Western town he would wash up in, propping up the bar in one of the numerous themed restaurants, boring the customers – John Grady, Jack Twist and Patrick Fitzpatrick – with tales about the last great buffalo hunt that he undertook as a kid, before he, like Billy Parham, accepts an invitation to play a version of himself on screen.

Notes

1 Donald Worster, 'New West, True West: Interpreting The Region's History', *Western Historical Quarterly* 18: 2 (April 1987), 141–56 (p. 143).
2 The first is Jim Fife, the latter Don Walker. Quoted in Amy T. Hamilton and Tom J. Hillard, 'Before the West Was West: Rethinking the Temporal Borders of Western American Literature', *Western American Literature* 47: 3 (Fall 2012), 286–307 (p. 289).
3 Charles Wilkinson, 'Paradise Revisited', in William Riebsame and James Robb (eds.), *Atlas of the New West* (New York: Norton, 1997), 15–45 (p. 18).
4 Fiedler, 'The World without a West', in *The Return of the Vanishing American* (London: Paladin, 1968), pp. 32–3.

5   Joseph Taylor, 'Many Lives of the New West', *Western Historical Quarterly* 35: 2 (Summer 2004), 141–65.
6   Bowles, *Our New West: Records of Travel between the Mississippi River and the Pacific Ocean* (Hartford Connecticut: Hartford publishing, 1869), v.
7   See James R. Grossman (ed.) *The Frontier in American Culture: An Exhibition at the Newberry Library – Essays by Richard White and Patricia Nelson Limerick* (California: University of California Press, 1994), p. 9.
8   Slotkin, *Regeneration through Violence: The Mythology of the American Frontier, 1600–1860* (Norman: University of Oklahoma Press, 1973), p. 17.
9   Slotkin, *The Fatal Environment: The Myth of the Frontier in the Age of Industrialization, 1800–1890* (New York: Atheneum, 1985), p. 15.
10 Bold, *The Frontier Club: Popular Westerns and Cultural Power, 1880–1920* (Oxford: Oxford University Press, 2013), p. 2; see also Robert Shulman's 'Introduction' to *The Virginian* (Oxford: Oxford University Press, 1998), p. xxiii; Peggy and Harold Samuels, *Frederic Remington: A Biography* (New York: Doubleday, 1982), p. 141.
11 Henry Nash Smith, *Virgin Land: The American West as Symbol and Myth* (Cambridge: Harvard University Press, 1950), p. 108.
12 Slotkin, *Gunfighter Nation: The Myth of the Frontier in Twentieth Century America* (New York: Harper, 1992), p. 69.
13 Etulain, 'The Historical Development of the Western', in Etulain, and Michael T. Marsden, eds., *The Popular Western: Essays toward a Definition* (Bowling Green, OH: Bowling Green University Popular Press, 1974).
14 Tompkins, *West of Everything: The Inner Life of Westerns* (Oxford: Oxford University Press, 1992), p. 45.
15 See Jim Kitses, *Horizons West: The Western from John Ford to Clint Eastwood* (1969) (London: Thames and Hudson and British Film Institute, 2007), p. 11.
16 See Gary Scharnhorst, '"All Hat and No Cattle": Romance, Realism, and Late Nineteenth Century Western American Fiction', in Nicolas Witschi (ed.), *A Companion to the Literature and Culture of the American West* (Oxford: Blackwell Publishing, 2011), 281–96 (p. 283).
17 Baudrillard, *America* (London: Verso, 1989), p. 32.
18 Wyn Wachhorst, 'Come Back, Shane! The National Nostalgia', *Southwest Review* 98: 1 (2013), 12–25 (p. 18); JoAnn Conrad, 'Consuming Subjects: Making Sense of Post-World War II Westerns', *Narrative Culture* 2: 1 (Spring 2015), 71–116 (p. 71).
19 Quoted in Taylor, 'Many Lives', p. 148.
20 Limerick, *The Legacy of Conquest* (New York, London: Norton, 1987), p. 322.
21 In conversation with Jim Robbins, *Last Refuge: The Environmental Showdown in Yellowstone and the American West* (New York: Morrow and Co., 1993), pp. 254–5.
22 Comer, 'Exceptionalism, Other Wests, Critical Regionalism', *American Literary History* 23: 1 (2011), 159–73 (p. 161).
23 Kerouac, *On the Road* (1957) (Harmondsworth: Penguin Modern Classics, 2000), p. 30.
24 See Alex Trimble Young and Lorenzo Veracini, '"If I am Native to Anything": Settler Colonial Studies and Western American Literature', *Western American Literature* 52: 1 (Spring 2017), 1–23 (p. 5).

25 The early film shows local actors (women with headdresses and tomahawks) playing Indians attempting to take a baby girl from a woman before two cowboys (with Stetsons and kerchiefs) appear, shoot the attackers dead and save the family. Available at the BFI website: https://player.bfi.org.uk/free/film/watch-kidnapping-by-indians-1899-1899-online [accessed 11 October 2020].
26 Campbell, *The Cultures of the American New West* (Edinburgh: Edinburgh University Press, 2000), p. 164.
27 Campbell, *The Rhizomatic West: Representing the American Westin a Transnational, Global, Media Age* (Lincoln: University of Nebraska, 2008), p. 35.
28 Campbell, *Cultures*, pp. 20–3.
29 Nina Baym, 'Old West, New West, Postwest, Real West', *American Literary History* 18: 4 (Winter, 2006), 814–28 (p. 816).
30 Dunlap, *Nature and the English Diaspora: Environment and History in the United States, Canada, Australia, and New Zealand* (Cambridge: Cambridge University Press, 1999), p. 48.
31 Patrick Wolfe, *Settler Colonialism and the Transformation of Anthropology: The Politics and Poetics of an Ethnographic Event* (London: Cassell, 1999), p. 165.
32 Lynch, '"Nothing But Land": Women's Narratives, Gardens, and the Settler-Colonial Imaginary in the US West and Australian Outback', *Western American Literature* 48: 4 (Winter 2014), 374–99 (p. 377).
33 See Alex Trimble Young, 'The Rhizomatic West, or, the Significance of the Frontier in Postwestern Studies', *Western American Literature* 48: 1/2 (Spring, Summer 2013), 115–40 (p. 128).
34 Kittredge, *Owning It All: Essays* (Port Townsend, WA: Graywolf Press, 1987), p. 171.
35 Bryan Wooley, interview with John Williams, *The Denver Quarterly* 20: 3 (1985–6), 11–31(pp. 16–17)
36 According to the critic Allen Tate, Swallows was 'one of the genuine heroes of contemporary literature'. 'My Debt to Alan Swallow', *The Denver Quarterly* 2 (Spring 1967), p. 43.
37 Ibid., Wooley, interview.
38 Limerick, *The Real West* – Catalog of an exhibition sponsored by the Colorado Historical Society and Denver Art Museum (Denver: Civic Center Cultural Complex, 1996), 13–22 (p. 13).
39 Kittredge, *Owning it All*, p. 171.
40 Interview with Mervyn Rothstein, *The New York Times* (1 November 1988); Mark Horowitz, 'Larry McMurtry's Dream Job', *New York Times on the Web*. http://www.nytimes.com/books/97/12/07/home/article2.html. [accessed 9 August 2020].
41 Levi S. Peterson, 'The Rocky Mountains', in the Western Literature Association's, *A Literary History of the American West* (1987) (Fort Worth: Texas Christian University Press, 1987), p. 842.
42 Ibid., Woolley interview (Woolley's italics), p. 16.
43 Williams, 'The "Western": Definitions of the Myth', in Irving Deer and Harriat A Deer (eds.), *The Popular Arts: A Critical Arts* (New York: Charles Scribner's and Sons, 1967), 98–111 (pp. 100, 101).

44 Arendt, 'French Existentialism', *Nation* 162 (February 1946), 226–8; 'What is Existentialism?' *Partisan Review* 13 (1946), 34–56.
45 *Butcher's Crossing*, Panther Books (1963)
46 Stanton Peckham, 'D. U. Professor Produces Fine Novel of the West', *The Sunday Denver Post* (clipping undated), John Williams Papers, MC716: Box 27, folder 2.
47 Letter: Rodell to Williams, March 29, 1960. John Williams Papers MC716: Box 4.
48 Anonymous short review, *New York Times* (3 April 1960), John Williams Papers MC716: Box 27, folder 2.
49 Dickstein, *New York Times Book Review* (June 2007); https://www.nytimes.com/2007/06/17/books/review/Dickstein-t.html [accessed 15 January 2020].
50 Ellis, 'Review of *Butcher's Crossing*', *The Guardian* (31 October 2014). http://www.theguardian.com/books/2014/oct/31/john-williams-butchers-crossing-great-literary-western-stoner [accessed 4 September 2016].
51 Plotz, '*Butcher's Crossing*: An Appreciation of John Williams's Perfect Anti-western', *The Guardian* (3 August 2016) https://www.theguardian.com/books/2016/aug/03/butchers-crossing-an- [accessed 6 May 2017].
52 See Christine Bold, *Selling the Wild West: Popular Western Fiction, 1860 to 1960* (Bloomington, IN: Indiana University Press, 1987), p. 156.
53 Phillips, 'History and the Ugly Facts of Cormac McCarthy's *Blood Meridian*', *American Literature* 68: 2 (1996), 433–60 (p. 441).
54 See Richard B. Woodward, 'Cormac McCarthy's Venomous Fiction', *New York Times* (19 April 1992), p. 31.
55 Bredahl, *New Ground: Western American Narrative and the Literary Canon* (Chapel Hill: University of North Carolina Press, 1989), p. 99.
56 Robert L. Jarrett, 'McCarthy's Sense of an Ending', in James D. Lilley (ed.), *Cormac McCarthy: New Directions* (Albuquerque: University of New Mexico Press, 2002), 313–41 (p. 325).
57 Wallach, 'Theater, Ritual, and Dream in the Border Trilogy', in Wade Hall and Rick Wallach (eds.), *Sacred Violence: A Reader's Companion to Cormac McCarthy* (El Paso: Texas Western Press, 1995), 159–174 (p. 171).
58 Showalter, *A Jury of her Peers: American Women Writers from Anne Bradstreet to Annie Proulx* (New York: Alfred A. Knopf, 2009), p. 508.
59 Proulx, *Bird Cloud: A Memoir* (London: Fourth Estate, 2011), p. 127.
60 Limerick, quoted in Jack Hitt, 'Where the Deer and the Zillionaires Play', *Outside Magazine* (October 1997), 122–234 (p. 232).
61 Lessinger, 'Creating Penturbia', in *Penturbia: Where Real Estate will Boom After the crash of Suburbia* (Seattle, Washington: SocioEconomics, Inc., 1991), 236–44 (pp. 239–40); Ibid., Robbins, *Last Refuge*, p. 212.
62 Stegner, *The Sound of Mountain Water* (1969) (Harmondsworth: Penguin Books, 1997), p. 20.
63 Anon., 'An Interview with Annie Proulx', *Missouri Review*, 22: 2 (Spring 1999), pp. 84–5 https://www.missourireview.com/article/an-interview-with-annie-proulx/ [accessed 4 July 2020].
64 Christopher Cox, 'An Interview with Annie Proulx', *The Paris Review* 188 (Spring 2009) http://www.theparisreview.org/interviews/5901/the-art-of-fiction-no-199-annie-proulx [accessed 4 September 2019].
65 See Campbell, *The Rhizomatic West*, pp. 32–7; *Cultures*, pp. 20–3.

66 John Skow, 'On Strange Ground', *Time Magazine* (17 May 1999) http://content.time.com/time/magazine/article/0,9171,990992,00.html [accessed 29 August 2020].
67 See Alan Weltzien for an excellent discussion of Proulx's use of caricature in 'Annie Proulx's Wyoming: Geographical Determinism, Landscape, and Caricature', in Alex Hunt (ed.), *The Geographical Imagination of Annie Proulx: Rethinking Regionalism* (Lanham: Lexington Books, 2009), 99–112 (p. 100).
68 Robert Adams, 'Cornering the Market', *New York Review of Books* 39: 20 (3 December 1992) 14–16 (p. 14).
69 Interview with Christine June, *Bloomsbury Review* 20: 4 (June/August 2000), 13–14. Repr. In Beef Torrey (ed.), *Conversations with Thomas McGuane* (Jackson: University of Mississippi Press, 2007), 157–65 (p. 158).
70 See Robert Rebein for an excellent discussion of all the novels mentioned. *Return of the Native: The place of American fiction after Postmodernism*, unpublished PhD dissertation (University of New York, 1995), p. 87.
71 Kingsolver, *Animal Dreams* (New York: Harper Collins, 1990) pp. 184, 12, 149.
72 Interview with Gregory L. Morris, in Gregory Morris (ed.), *Talking Up a Storm: Voices of the New West* (Lincoln, Nebraska: University of Nebraska Press, 1994), p. 210. See also David Abrams interview with Thomas McGuane, *The Montana Pioneer* (December 2010) https://montanapioneer.com/an-interview-with-thomas-mcguane/ [accessed 11 September 2019].
73 Allard, *Vanishing Breed* (Boston: Little Brown, 1982), pp. 6–7.
74 Eric Larsen, 'A Literary Quilt of Faded Colors', *Los Angeles Times Book Review* (17 September 1989), p. 3.
75 *Nobody's Angel*, p. 217. See also Interview with Renaud Monfourny (1990) reprinted in Torrey *Conversations*, 134–42 (p. 139); Interview with Jim Schumock (1999) reprinted in Torrey *Conversations*, 147–56 (p. 154); Richard Stengel, 'Hurtin' Cowboy', *Time Magazine* (26 April 1982).
76 Lewis, 'Review', *Western American Literature* 28: 3 (Fall 1993), 283–4 (p. 283).

1

Butcher's Crossing's Lost Vision: Williams's Cowboy Outsider

At one stage in his life, John Williams found himself lost on a wild frontier. His notebooks recount how whilst flying missions in the China-Burma-India theatre during the Second World War, he was shot down and had to scramble through the jungle to safety with four injured crewmen. The experience proved traumatic, his wife recalls that 'the war never went away' – but he also never published a book about it.[1] The manuscript he was working on when he died, *The Sleep or Reason*, was his response and, as his titular reference to Goya implies, it was to be less a war story than the story of how war allows those demons to emerge that brutalize soldiers and degrade society.[2] The book had its origins in the aborted novel *The Tent*, which concerns a four-man team of soldiers sent deep into the Burma jungle to erect a radio mast. On paper the mission seems straightforward, but once they enter 'the tent' of the impenetrable jungle, their quest becomes less physical than existential.[3] They are led by a naive and idealistic corporal named Ferguson, a Williams archetype whose youthful optimism is brought crashing down by contact with a reality that refuses to be seized cartographically. His four-man patrol comprises different strategies for dealing with their situation: Brenan, a religious fanatic, finds meaning in prayer; Hauser, a vital but cynical character, dreams of sex; Nichols idealizes his new wife.[4] It would have been a richly layered exploration of his experiences, but Williams abandoned the novel complaining that it was 'too immediately close to what I had done' – an ambiguous admission that highlights the rawness of the memories whilst reminding us that he had explored these themes twenty years earlier in *Butcher's Crossing*.[5] It is fitting, perhaps ironically so, that Williams should choose the Western form – a genre that blurs the distinction between myth and reality, because Williams's biographer, Charles J. Shields, can find no evidence for the actual event – concluding rather ruthlessly: 'Call it lying, but writers call it creating fiction.'[6] Whatever the 'reality' the similarities are striking: the four-man teams are paralleled, with Williams's ramshackle Burmese crew poured into a traditional Western mould: Brenan is transformed into Charlie Hoge – an ancient Bible bashing, alcoholic camp-tender who offers sibylline premonitions; the cynical Hauser is mirrored by the team's skinner, Schneider, a foul-mouthed sensualist who, as his job implies, is only interested in surfaces; the idealistic Ferguson is prefigured by William Andrews, the naive optimist whose focalizing consciousness transforms him into the critical 'outsider'. As such he becomes the ideal recorder of the horrors he encounters, turning Emersonian optics inside out to reveal an ambivalent, rather than a benevolent, nature. Through his eyes Williams scrutinizes the shortfall between ideal and reality that marks their movement into the West, warning the reader that the much-feted interior journey is just as likely to end in darkness as light.

As suggested in the Introduction, Williams's desire 'to do something serious' for the West meant questioning Emersonian poetics. Williams was critical, noting wryly that whilst his acolyte, Henry Thoreau, was espousing the virtues of Walden Pond, he 'used to go into town nearly every weekend to get a home cooked meal'.[7] In *Butcher's Crossing* this role is taken up by Andrews, Williams making it clear through reference to a backstory in which he escapes the chapel of his Harvard college to find solace in the woods in the way prescribed in Emerson's most famous essay, *Nature*:

> There in some small solitude, standing on bare ground, he felt his head bathed by the clean air and uplifted into infinite space; the meanness and the constriction he had felt were dissipated in the wildness about him. A phrase from a lecture by Mr. Emerson that he had attended came to him: I become a transparent eyeball. Gathered in by field and wood, he was nothing; he saw all; the current of some nameless force circulated through him ... Through the trees and across the rolling landscape, he had been able to see a hint of the distant horizon to the west; and there, for an instant, he had beheld somewhat as beautiful as his own undiscovered nature.
>
> (45–6)

The optimism is uplifting; however, the paraphrase ensures that Andrews has not escaped the droning voices for the 'solitude' of nature but is simply ventriloquizing Emerson amidst the trees. Furthermore, Andrews's bid for autonomy is not helped by Emerson's contradictions: how can he be nothing and yet see all? What can a transparent eyeball with no retina see? As the ill-conceived figure suggests, Emerson never managed to resolve the idealist paradox in which the world seems to both exist and be a creation of the senses. He was content with the contradiction because it suggested an enlarged perspective. For Williams, however, this vacillation is symptomatic of an entirely unsustainable approach to man's relationship with the natural world, which is what he seeks to critique in the novel. In the end it is the 'dead eyes' of Charlie Hoge rather than Emerson's greedily romantic 'transparent eyeball' that offer a more appropriate lens through which to record the emptiness of their Western adventure.

Throughout the opening chapters of the novel, Williams artfully reconfigures the existentialist figure of 'the outsider' to participate in the deconstruction of both the Emersonian 'eyeball' and more familiar Western tropes. He takes the archetypal Frontier settlement – which for Turner would offer a fragile outpost of civilization amidst savagery – and transforms it through the name 'Butcher's Crossing' into the state of transition implied by the gerund and a launch pad for brutality. He takes the traditional emblem of the prairie schooner with its Turnerian implications of liberty, hope and new beginnings and transforms it into the cramped wagon in which Andrews is only aware of where he has been. Turnerian nostalgia is deftly illustrated through the image of Andrews travelling into the future whilst looking in the 'rear-view mirror'. Andrews himself challenges the conception of the Western hero, offering a postmodern version of identity. He arrives on the page with little backstory, brought into being through a present tense assemblage of details that emphasize his youth, newness to the land and visual myopia. Even when not the observer he remains the focalizing consciousness (he is present in every scene in the novel), his air of detachment augmented by narrative ambivalence. In a congratulatory letter to Williams, Robert Heilman commended what he identified as his 'technical method', which is to relate 'the visible palpable event, the photographable event so to speak, and to let it stand as a symbol for all psychic or spiritual events that accompany it'.[8] When, for example, Andrews arrives, we are told 'his boot struck the earth, a round puff of dust flew up, surrounding his foot; it settled on the new black leather and on the bottom of his trouser leg, making their colors nearly the same' (11). We are drawn to a seemingly trivial object of focus through a detachment that will later attend the brutal descriptions of Miller's shooting or Schneider's clinical skinning. In this case the ocular precision parodies Emersonian notions of man merging with nature, as when this newly upholstered 'tenderfoot' comes into direct contact with the land, he does not unite with it, rather, it covers him with dust. Once in town he becomes the archetypal 'outsider' – a mirror-gazer, balcony voyeur and blind auditor as alienated from his own body as the world around him. In a scene that prefigures the hunters' snow entrapment later in the novel (when they are forced to sew themselves into buffalo hides), Andrews lies in his hotel room watching the curtains gently billowing and conceiving of himself suspended inside an enormous, pulsing beast waiting to be born (15).

The midwife in this process is supposed to be McDonald, recommended by Andrews's father because he 'came west, and made a life for himself' (18). He represents an economics of Western development built around the lucrative hide market, and, as such, enables Williams to widen his critique of

Emersonian idealism through a consideration of the socio-economic realities underpinning Western expansion. In his presentation, Williams seems to have in mind men like J. N. Dubois or Charles Rath (who established the important trading centre of Rath City on the southern plains) who encouraged independent hunters into company teams.[9] Anthony Hutchison has argued that he is a representative of the unfettered capitalism advocated by the mid-century 'Young America' movement, which traces its roots to the conceptual validation of Manifest Destiny and, more troublingly, Emerson's most politically Conservative 1844 lecture 'The Young American'.[10] Throughout the narrative, Williams draws attention to this conceptual irony through his reconfiguration of visual metaphors: for McDonald 'men with vision' are not those in search of the Over Soul, but those making smart investments (20). His economic model is underwritten by capital investors and insider dealing and he encourages Andrews to 'Look' at the emptiness as an investment opportunity that only requires him 'to sign [his] name to a piece of paper at the state Office' (20). It is the antithesis of Andrews's vision: the ideal of communing with nature reduced to the purchase of empty space processed through documentation. Williams reinforces this deadening effect through the scattered bills of sale that cover the floor of McDonald's office, the paper equivalent to which the buffalo has been reduced. McDonald accepts Andrews as a potential investor but is contemptuous of those people living off the land 'not knowing what to do with it' into which category fall the usual victims of Manifest Destiny – Native Americans, Mexicans – and those independent hunters whose professionalism is occluded by romanticism (19). For Andrews, who is offered a job as book keeper, the only way to keep his vision alive is by looking beyond McDonald:

> He paused and let his gaze go past McDonald, away from the town, beyond the ridge of earth that he imagined was the river bank, to the flat yellowish green land that faded into the horizon westward. He tried to shape in his mind what he had to say to McDonald. It was a feeling; it was an urge that he had to speak. But whatever he spoke he knew would be but another name for the wildness that he sought. It was a freedom and a goodness, a hope and a vigor that he perceived to underlie all the familiar things of his life, which were not free or good or hopeful or vigorous. What he sought was the source and preserver of his world, a world which seemed to turn ever in fear away from its source, rather than search it out, as the prairie grass around him sent down its fibred roots into the rich dark dampness, the Wildness, and thereby renewed itself, year after year.
>
> (21)

Andrews has to 'gaze' (which suggests a lack of focus consistent with the 'transparent eyeball') beyond the real Westerner in front of him to 'see' the riverbank that takes on the imaginative border between civilization and 'Wildness'. The above passage was an addition to the completed typescript just before submission, suggesting that Williams, just like his character, was having difficulty expressing what it is that they are looking for.[11] The language drifts from the linguistically simplistic to the conceptually opaque (whatever could he mean by the awkward allusion to 'the source and preserver of his world'?) which seems reflective a young mind grasping at ideals beyond experience. It is also ruggedly organic, the roots driving into the 'rich dark dampness' of a buried 'Wildness' contrasting with his memory of the 'evenly spaced elms' and 'plotted fields' of his Boston home: a nature which appears to have had the vitality sucked out of it (21–2). The scene also acts as the first warning of the dangers of Andrews's particular brand of idealism. For when he is led by 'a subtle magnetism in nature' to walk to the edge of the town (a formulation that paraphrases Thoreau's endorsement of walking as a means of unifying with the Over-Soul) he expects to find a vast river 'between himself and the wildness and freedom that his instinct sought' and is disappointed to find instead a 'muddy trickle over flat rocks' (48).[12] It is the first of many such disappointments.

McDonald is not the man to introduce Andrews to the 'wildness' he seeks, but Miller is – a hard-eyed non-conformist, who offers the vision of one last glorious buffalo hunt in a hidden valley (27). However, from the beginning it is clear that the expedition exists as a childish ideal (the valley landscape belongs to the realm of fairy tale), which allows Williams to interrogate the motives of all participants whilst simultaneously re-evaluating a number of familiar Western tropes. There is a dream-like quality about their meeting; Williams wakes from a dream and this time the 'subtle magnetism' takes him to a cliché of a cowboy saloon. There is an insistence on a yellow filter that adds a 'slow fluidity to the scene': Outside yellow street lights glint on the eyeballs of tethered horses, whilst a blacksmith's hammer beats; inside the lamps pick out the yellow face of a disinterested bar-tender, whilst poker chips chink (27). The carefully staged central group – the archetypal mountain man, one-armed side kick, and prostitute with heart of gold – are picked out through their cured leather skin, flaxen hair and white neb of a stump (there are undertones of Ahab's stump in this last detail). The whiskey flows but conversation is limited as there is a suitably cowboy mistrust in language; at one stage Miller upbraids Andrews, 'you sure talk easy, son' (31). It is a deliberate contrast with McDonald's evasive loquaciousness, which signals the importation of an Eastern understanding of words *and* contracts over a Western belief in words *as* bonds. All, however, is not as it seems. Miller is already an anachronism: his insistence on hunting alone rather than as part of a team outfitted by a hide dealer like McDonald is part of mountain man nostalgia, which is why, as his suit implies, he is out of work (33). What he offers Andrews, therefore, in his promise of a last great hunt is not a business proposition, but a validation of their shared romanticism. We are told that it arranges itself in Andrews's mind 'like the loose stained bits of glass in a kaleidoscope' – a suitably childish metaphor that complements the dream-like yellows that dominate *Butcher's Crossing* (39).

From the moment they leave the settlement, the journey to the valley – which includes a desert crossing and the discovery of buffalo skeletons and an abandoned homestead – becomes both a private odyssey and a means of scrutinising a number of Western tropes. The titles of a number of recent Western novels – Cormac McCarthy's *The Crossing* (1984), Guy Vanderhaeghe's *The Last Crossing* (2002), Wallace Stegner's *Crossing to Safety* (2007), Louise Erdrich's *Tracks* (2009) and Barry Lopez's *Crossing Open Ground* (2013) – attest to the transformative power of crossing the Western landscape. And for Jane Tompkins the typical Western crossing involves the desert; it promises toil and pain and spiritual elevation, testing hardiness, intelligence and self-discipline whilst giving 'the hero a sense of himself'.[13] This 'self' is always the same: a man whose hardness reflects the hardness of his environment; a heroic figure revealed in a pan shot of the lone cowboy riding briskly through Monument Valley. And yet there has always been an ambiguity to this figure: has he mastered his environment or is he dwarfed by it? Is he lonesome or simply alone? Anthony Mann was posing just such questions in the 'psychological Westerns' he was directing throughout the period Williams was writing the novel. The long opening shot of Will Lockhart (James Stewart) in *The Man from Laramie* (1955) shows an isolated character set against a barren wilderness, who becomes, through the Noire expressionist camera angles, a symbol of psychic emptiness rather than hardy self-reliance.[14] His *Man of the West* (1958) – another title that forces us to focus on a man set against his surroundings – is not heroic in the traditional sense, but a reformed outlaw, Link Jones, whose journey through ghost towns (the ultimate symbol of broken dreams) and the desert reflects a desolate journey to his empty core.[15] Such figures seem to resonate with Williams whose novel deconstructs the psychological impact of those hours in the saddle. In a note-to-self whilst working on the manuscript he wrote, 'Establish monotony of trip, and unreality still within that monotony', before setting out 'The Meaning of the Journey':

A. Monotony, 1) Release from self. 2) Chaos of self.
B. The new life – meaningless of detail, which imposes artificial meaning on journey – getting up, riding, eating, ritualistic business.
C. External changes in men 1) Andrews – much physical change. 2) Miller – some physical, much inner. 3) Schneider – little change, except negative. 4) Hoge – almost none.
D. The meaning of the journey.[16]

From the outset, the journey is existential rather than cartographical. Although it is clear that Williams had in mind a particular location (his files are full of maps of the region covered in the novel[17]), there are no place names referenced in the descriptions and all the usual geographical markers that enable the reader to find their way around a Western – named rivers, mountains with Native American names, hoodoos, buttes and gulches – are ignored in favour of flat emptiness. In this way the Turnerian notion of the desert as a crucible for breakdown and reconstruction is pushed to its existential limits:

> It seemed to him [Andrews] that the land rather than the horse moved beneath him like a great treadmill, revealing in its movement only another part of itself.
> Day by day the numbness crept upon him until at last the numbness seemed to be himself. He felt himself to be like the land, without identity or shape, sometimes one of the men would look at him, look through him, as if he did not exist.
>
> (78)

Though Andrews's body appears stationary, there is movement of a different kind. As the weather toughens his skin and muscle replaces soft fat 'he thought at times that he was moving into a new body, or into a real body that had lain hidden beneath layers of unreal softness and whiteness and smoothness' (86). The self becomes an act of cartography in which old borders are relinquished in favour of a 'true' identity. Yet, once again the warning signs are here. Miller is presented as a cowboy with an intuitive grasp of the land, but the more we see him crawling around on all fours sniffing for water, the more Williams seems to be warning of the dangers of assuming an alignment between 'instinct' and moral ascendancy (104).

As the journey progresses, further Western shibboleths come under examination: the mountains are the only verticals in a land of horizontals that draw them on like some 'giant lodestone' and stand in juxtaposition to their discovery of a railroad line (106). The line exists – it is part of the mapped geography of the region included in Williams's collection of maps entitled 'Cow Country, Railroads and Indian Troubles 1865–1885'.[18] However, within the context of the novel it acts as a reminder of both modernity and the economic reality underpinning their quest. Where Miller strokes it with genuine admiration and bemusement, working it into his romantic vision, the more commercially astute Schneider recognizes that where there are railroads, there are no buffalo. He is right: railroads increased access for hunters to unsettled portions of the buffalo's habitat (many national magazines, such as *Harper's Weekly* and *Leslie's Illustrated* initially presented hunting to Eastern audiences as an easily accessible addition to a tourist itinerary[19]) whilst also providing a means of shipping hides back East in bulk.[20] Williams refuses to extrapolate, allowing the railroad line to exist as a symbol that prepares us for the end of the novel by reinforcing the hunters' irrelevance; for all Miller's instinctive grasp of the land, he could have arrived more quickly and safely at his destination if he had simply taken the train.

A similar act of narrative revision takes place when the party stumble upon a deserted settler claim. The narrator notes that the implements designed to bring the land under control – the 'wooden plow' and the 'wagon wheel' – lie discarded and rotting in the dust, whilst the prairie has reclaimed the cultivated plot (69). These are the casualties of Manifest Destiny, representatives, as Miller gloatingly reports, of the many who have tried it, but 'pull out when it gets a little bad' (70). There is no room for the 'plow' in Miller's wilder conception of the West, so his voice carries a 'thin edge of satisfaction' (69). By the novel's close, Andrews's experiences lead him to intuit a similar fate for Butcher's Crossing: 'Soon there would be nothing here ... the prairie grass would slowly creep upon the roadway. Even now, in the light of the early sun, the town was like a small ruin' (273). A similar message of doom is encoded in the depiction of their discovery of the bones of a Native American buffalo hunt. It is a symbolic moment, which elides the extermination of the Indigenous Peoples with the buffalo that had been their life source. Tasha Hubbard argues that the strategic and systematic slaughter of buffalos constitutes genocide – 'destroy the buffalo and one destroys the foundation of the Plains Indigenous collectivity and their very lives' – but Williams does not venture into this territory.[21] Native Americans are absent from his West. Practically, he has dated the expedition to 1878, just after the Kansas/Colorado region had been cleared of both buffalo and indigenous tribes. Indeed, buffalo shooting was an economic activity engaged in by maverick groups tacitly endorsed by government as a means of solving the 'Indian question' through starvation.[22] Williams's marginalization of Native American characters is not unusual in a genre in which, despite their threatened presence, they rarely appear. John Cawelti makes clear that their role in the traditional Western is to represent a form of savagery vanishing in the face of white progress and civilization.[23] Williams, however, reverses this formulation, allowing Miller to offer, in a rare moment of reflection, open admiration for the resourceful way in which Native Americans used buffalo bones to make jewellery and children's toys. All he can do with the bones is swing them 'as if it were a club' – a symbolic enactment of the violence that he will unleash upon the valley and to which the indigenousness peoples have already been subjected. When we do meet a small group of Native Americans, they are isolated stragglers, shapeless women and 'wizened old men' – refugees from violence who, according to Miller, 'ain't worth shooting anymore' (85). At one stage, they had been an admired part of his architecture of the West, but now they, like the buffalo and ironically the men who hunt them, are stragglers from a bygone age.

The most significant element of both national myth and genre construction that Williams confronts in his account is, of course, the slaughter of the buffalo – an event that, according to the historian John Hanner, was 'one of the more spectacular events in American history'. In little more than a decade (1871–83) roughly 10 million animals were exterminated by commercial hunters, largely for their hides – the white flesh left to rot on the prairies.[24] Williams seems to have been helped in his conceptualization of the novel through the publication of a number of buffalo-themed novels in the mid-1950s, namely Mari Sandoz's *The Buffalo Hunters* (1954), Milton Lott's *The Last Hunt* (1954) and Wayne Gard's *The Great Buffalo Hunt* (1955). Sandoz's novel is part of her ethnographic work (she also published *The Cattlemen* (1958) and *The Beaver Men* (1964)) and mixes fiction and reportage (she includes Western heroes Like Buffalo Bill Cody) in a way that both celebrates and critiques the fate of the animals and the impact of the removal on Native Americans. Lott's novel, crowed *The New York Times*, is 'the real thing, a gritty, tough, exciting story reeking with the pungent smells of dead buffalo and of dirty men'.[25] Unfortunately, this 'reeking' authenticity condemned Richard Brooks's 1956 film of the novel to a box office flop, leaving the director to muse 'the Western and its gun play is like a musical – it's fantasy and it should be kept as such'.[26] Williams consulted these works, and seems to have found in Lott's four-man team – an experienced hunter grown sick of the trade, a young firebrand, a 'half-breed' with an intuitive grasp of the land, and, most strikingly, an old skinner with a hand-carved wooden leg – the archetypes through which to explore his own more existential journey.[27] For though there are points of contact (such as Sandoz's description of Charlie Hart who led a hunting gang in Kansas in the mid-1870s that killed 3,500 animals.[28]), Williams's interest is existential rather than environmental and ethnological. There is no outrage, as with Sandoz, at the quantity of the slaughter; nor, as with Lott's novel (which includes a subplot in which an 'Indian' horse thief is skinned and his captured wife forced to tan the hide), is there a clear elision of the fate of buffalo and the Native Americans. Nor does Williams deploy a familiar Eden mythology to show the garden despoiled by serpent-like young Adams. Rather, Williams is focussed on the dehumanization of process through a form of narrative levelling that leaves the preparation of food, feeding of horses, casting of shot and slaughter of buffalo on a continuum. We are told that Andrews:

> Came to see Miller as a mechanism, an automaton, moved by the moving herd; and he came to see Miller's destruction of the buffalo, not as a lust for blood or a lust for the hides or a lust for what the hides would bring, or even at last the blind lust of fury that toiled darkly within him – he came to see the destruction as a cold, mindless response to the life in which Miller had immersed himself. And he looked upon himself, crawling dumbly after Miller upon the flat bed of the valley … and did not know who he was or where he went.
>
> (137)

Miller, the Emersonian 'natural man', is supposed to be merging with the Over-Soul, but here there is a deadening effect on both hunter and hunted. Optics are revealing of motive; the record of Miller's mechanized behavior indicates that he is not motivated by profit, sport or blood lust: he hunts because he believes that he has outlived his purpose and seeks validation from one last kill. He later tells Andrews in partial explanation of his behaviour: 'All a man can do is not think about them, just plow into them, kill them when he can, and not try to figure anything out' (168). The slaughter is not designed to horrify but change the way we conceive of violence and its place in both genre and history. Narratively, whilst the hunters have slaughtered, they have been transformed into beasts; whilst they have emptied the valley of life, they too have been emptied of life, the evacuation being so thorough that nothing remains but violence. At this stage of his development, Andrews is only dimly aware of this truth; he does not know who he is and why he is crawling around after Miller, but he has grasped that it is only the report of the rifle and the piles of hides that give meaning to their days.

Williams explores these existential themes further through the snow entrapment endured by the hunters when they are ironically forced to sew themselves into the hides of the slaughtered buffalo. The imagery is once again pre-natal with Andrews eventually born into a new world that is oppressive in its blankness: 'He opened [his eyes] upon a brilliance that seared them over for an instant with a white hotness' (183). One of Williams's preparatory prompts makes clear his desire to 'get at the meaninglessness of the landscape, the monotony of the activity, the whiteness' – as a means of emphasizing the crisis facing the hunters.[29] There are shades of *Moby Dick* in this formulation, and just as Ishmael's attempts to plumb the mystery of 'The Whiteness of the Whale' lead to a reductive cataloguing that leaves him marvelling at the conflicting resonances of its sleek beauty and funereal emptiness (the very opposite of his companion Queequeg's heavily tattooed skin), the overriding sense is of existential terror. In Williams's case, the snow figuratively challenges Emerson's transparent eyeball, for Andrews is literally blinded by blankness and forced to wear hide blinkers that transform him into 'a vague shape that did nothing, that had no identity' (202). Hoge can only face such an existential blankness by escaping into booze and the Bible, Schneider engages in imaginary conversations with a prostitute, Miller thrives, but only at the expense of narrowing his vision to that of the valley which he inhabits. Andrews continues in his role as outsider: he may have lost his early optimism, but he is yet to develop alternative strategies that impose meaning on either his surroundings or actions that suggest the development of moral conscience. Williams highlights Andrews's malaise through his numbed reaction to his last sight of the valley upon which the hunters have wrought such destruction. A more didactic Western text may have deployed the imagery of Paradise lost, or, like Colonel Richard Dodge's eyewitness account of buffalo hunting in the mid-1870s (re-released by Anchor Books when Williams was working on his manuscript), attempted to prompt a moral reaction through horror: 'The air was foul with the sickening stench, and the vast plain, which only a short twelvemonth before teemed with animal life, was a dead, solitary putrid desert.'[30] For Williams, however, the final view of the valley is recorded through Andrews's ambivalent eyes:

> Andrews looked back upon the valley which in a few minutes would be gone from his sight. At this distance, the new growth of grass was like a faint green mist that clung to the surface of the earth and glistened in the early morning sun. Andrews could not believe that this same valley had been the one he had seen pounding and furious with the threshings of a thousand dying buffalo; he could not believe that the grass had once been stained and matted with blood; he could not believe that ... a few weeks ago it had been stark and featureless under a blinding cover of white.
> (213–4)

Vision is once again prominent in a scene that, as Jack Brenner notes, pastiches Emerson's paean to spring in *Nature* in which the poet encourages us to observe that as 'the snow-banks melt, and the face of earth becomes green before it, so shall the advancing spirit create ornaments along its path ... it shall draw beautiful faces, warm hearts, wise discourse, and heroic acts around its way, until evil is no more seen'.[31] The hunters' experiences contradict such sentiments; their faces have been ravaged, their discourse transformed into primitive grunts and their heroic acts have been mass slaughter. Nevertheless, nature remains ambivalent rather than a source of moral censure, the grass growing between the corpses whatever the moral outrage perpetrated by man. That nature should not aid Andrews's moral education is reinforced by his catalogue of doubts. Seeing is believing and we are repeatedly reminded that what he doesn't see 'he could not believe'. The only real lesson to be learned, and that he fails to extrapolate, is that nature, unlike their hunting camp or Butcher's Crossing itself, endures.

The final Western set-piece given an existentialist treatment is the traditional river crossing, in Williams's version of which Schneider is speared and killed by a stray log and they lose all their hides (225). The scene could have been taken from a John Ford film: man pitted against an immense, unforgiving environment; his swollen pride reflected through the pathetic fallacy of the swollen river. John Milton, reviewing the novel in the *Minneapolis Sunday Tribune* in 1960, reads the death of Schneider as part of an allegory through which Williams explores how the hunters face nature in different ways: 'Miller assaults nature and is repulsed; Hoge fears nature and is spiritually destroyed; Schneider ignores nature and is physically destroyed; Will Andrews accepts, absorbs, learns nature's lessons and survives.'[32] It is a perceptive reading, but insists on an externality against which solid characters are pitted. For Williams, however, the river, as it has throughout the novel, acts as a boundary, a symbol of man's imaginative capacity and a metaphor which contrasts with the static blankness of both the desert and winter landscape. Here, the accident could symbolize nature's revenge and the difficulty of the 'butchers crossing' back to civilization, but the narrative resists such simple moralizing. Rather, the log represents one of those unforeseen random life-changing events that make us aware of the contingency of the universe, which is why Schneider, who has always ridden with his hat drawn low over his eyes, fails to see it. His death is an existentialist fable worthy of Sartre: living in a continuous present may relieve us of the 'angst' of self-creation, but it is no protection from the randomness of a meaningless universe, a realization glimpsed only at the moment of death.

The Andrews who returns to Butcher's Crossing has seen much but seemingly learned little. It is left to McDonald, the hide buyer, to offer some explanation, which in turn opens up the interpretative centre of the book. In his final novel, *Augustus* (1971), Williams's dying emperor identifies three stages of a man's life: the optimism of youth; the tragedy of middle age, and the comedy of old age when the individual recognizes the mockery of circumstance.[33] In *Augustus* (1971) the stages are encompassed by one man, but in *Butcher's Crossing* it is McDonald who is the victim of life's cruel comedy and who is tasked with enlightening the hunters. His role is made explicit by his ironic laughter: 'McDonald laughed, and his laughter choked in a fit of coughing. "My God, man. Ain't you got eyes? ... Can't you look at it straight?"' (246–7). The motif of the transparent eyeball has come full circle with McDonald's denouncement of all those who saw the West as sustaining either economic or romantic visions. His lesson for Miller is that an intuitive grasp of the landscape and a capacity to endure the harshness of winter is no insurance against the violence of economics: 'You go your own way, stinking the land up with what you kill. You flood the market with hides and ruin the market, and then you come crying to me that I've ruined you ... You're no better than the things you kill' (248–9). It is a simple lesson in the laws of supply and demand, which reminds both hunters and readers that Butcher's Crossing maybe an outpost in the Wild West, but its existence is dependent on it being woven into a web of interconnected capitalist transactions. Like Miller, McDonald rues his blindness, claiming his 'instinct' only works in a specific environment – 'it was coming. If I'd been back east, I would have knowed it' – and has been exposed by the crossing into the unfamiliar (247). His recognition amplifies the truth intuited by Schneider, that like the buffalo and the Native Americans they themselves are stragglers, part of an older West made irrelevant by economics. Miller's anguished riposte – 'Get out of this country. It doesn't want you' – summons a collective, romanticized vision of the West of which he is both participant and archetype and which has been consigned to the realms of nostalgia (249).

McDonald's message to Andrews is more abstract and as a consequence his language becomes more personal and reflective:

> You always think there's something to find out ... Well, there's nothing ... You get born, and you nurse on lies, and you get weaned on lies, and you learn fancier lies in school. You live all your life on lies, and then maybe when you're ready to die, it comes to you – that there's nothing, nothing but yourself and what you could have done ... I forgot what I learned a long time ago. I let the lies come back. I had a dream, too, and because it was different from yours and Miller's, I let myself think it wasn't a dream. But now I know, boy. And you don't. And that makes all the difference.
> (250, 1)

There is no benevolent Emersonian Nature drenched with God-given significance (the fancy lies taught in school), no grand plan and no 'self' waiting to be discovered. He chides himself for allowing the West to foster hope, not the romantic hope of finding meaning, but the commercial hope of making money. Because it was rooted in the reality of human activity, he considered it different, but now he acknowledges its similarity. There is simply emptiness, a determination to make sense of it and an identity that changes with circumstance. Recognition of this state of affairs links the shocked look on Schneider's face with 'the hollow glint in Charley Hoge's eyes' and the blankness of Miller when shooting the buffalo (272). All reveal the terror of those who have glimpsed the contingency of the universe, that where Emerson's transparent eyeball 'is nothing but sees all' his characters see that all is nothing.

One area of Andrews's evolution that has remained a blank thus far is his sexual development, which in Williams's conception of the novel becomes another frontier to be crossed. In the subplot involving Andrews's wide-eyed love affair with a barroom prostitute, Francine, Williams sets out to critique repressive narratives, particularly the 'virgin/whore' binary, which serve to keep his lost young men (and his interest remains phallocentric) in a state of arrested development. The sexual identities of the patrol in his aborted novel *The Tent* are instructive: Hauser is like Schneider, a man of vital energy but loose morality who spends his time visiting brothels. Life is reduced to the satisfaction of primal urges; all else Hauser dismisses as a failure to look life in the eye. None of the others join him: Brenan, like Charley Hoge, is too busy in confession imagining the sins of the flesh; Ferguson is too sexually naive and torn by guilt. His prurience is shared by Nichols, a recently married volunteer, who keeps a picture of his wife wrapped in a condom in his breast pocket; it is a practical measure (it keeps it dry), but clearly symbolic of both his sexual integrity and his repression.[34] Significantly, we are guided to find a distorted heroism in Hauser's carnality, which, though a form of denigration, nevertheless treats women as flesh and blood rather than ideals. Andrews, like Ferguson, is a prude; the son of a genteel Boston Unitarian minister, he has been brought up with a deep suspicion of 'wild nature', whether the dark woods or his own lust. Elsewhere in his writing, Williams draws attention to the suspicion of the physical world exhibited by the early Puritan church: 'That which exists in nature tends to be in conflict with that which exists in God's mind – hence our half-conscious aversion to sexuality, to bodily matters, to spontaneity, and to those shapes of flux and change that we must observe in natural processes.'[35] Hence, he extrapolates the dilemma facing the early settlers who knew that lust was a sin whilst simultaneously acknowledging that sex was all around them in the shape of fecund nature. This is the territory explored by Nathaniel Hawthorne, a stern critic of Puritanism, particularly the repressed desire of *The Scarlet Letter* and stories like 'Young Goodman Brown'. Unfortunately, Emerson is of little help when it comes to sex. It exists for him on a Neo-platonic, rather than a practical, level; submersion in the Over-Soul implies a sexless return to the androgynous state of the Platonic ideal before the division into male and female; a unified state personified in Adam before the creation of Eve from one of his ribs. If Andrews had been reading Walt Whitman things might have been different. Where for Emerson the body is a springboard to higher thoughts, Whitman worships 'the spread of my own body' and transforms it into a creed. In the fifth part of 'Song of Myself' – which explores different notions of selfhood – the metaphor of the transparent eyeball gives way to a sexual encounter in which the self is absorbed in the flesh of another and finds transcendence through annihilation.[36]

Unfortunately, Andrews's reading of Dime novels will have been of little use when it comes to women. For all their swagger, cowboys make poor role models when it comes to relationships with women. It is as if, to paraphrase William Dale Jennings, such texts 'would have us believe that erectile tissue was completely missing in the metabolism of the West'.[37] Perhaps not missing but redirected through suggestive metaphors into the mastering of the virgin landscape, expertise with a Colt 45 and horse breaking. The West of the Western is constructed through the erasure of women, and when they do appear they occupy a series of marginalized archetypes: 'pioneer angels' (who conquer the West armed with a broom and shotgun); 'virtuous schoolmarms' (the Virginian's Molly, whose goodness is presented by her surrogate motherhood); 'Indian Princesses' (the erotic dark other), 'wild cats' (Calamity Jane, Annie Oakley, Belle Starr – women who conform to masculine stereotypes) and 'soiled doves' (the prostitute whose trade ensures the continued independence of the cowboy). A number of revisionist works have sought to unpack such simplistic binaries: Jon Sander's movie *Painted Angels* (1997), for example, follows the lives of the girls who service an array of unwashed mountain men and slovenly railroad workers before their aging bodies give out and they descend into a life of drug abuse and poverty. Perhaps most daringly is Jonathan Nolan's remake of Michael Crichton's 1973 book and film, *Westworld* for HBO. 'Westworld' is a Bill Cody, Disney-style theme park in which android 'hosts' are programmed to act out typical Western narratives to entertain paying visitors. In each episode, viewers are reminded of the constructed nature of their experience by a constant alternation between the performance of scripted Western storylines (in which the same dialogic tropes are repeated) and the lab in which these narrative arcs are programmed.[38] The original had malfunctioning cowboy gunslinger (Yul Brynner) running amok and killing guests, but the more thoughtful remake gives over more time and consideration to the role of the female characters. Dolores Abernathy, for example, is the beautiful, innocent ranch daughter who awakes every day to a world reminiscent of *The Little House on the Prairie* but is programmed into a narrative in which she is ritualistically violated. When offered a gun for self-protection by another character, she is physically unable to pull the trigger because her role is that of virginal victim. When she shares these experiences with the prostitute, Maeve, her gradual awakening to her role invites us to question the role of women in both the series and the genre as a whole. We sympathize with Dolores who has been programmed into a narrative for male gratification, but, as the traditional 'virgin/whore' binary gives way to a new woman/machine dichotomy, we are reminded that within the genre this is the only narrative available for Maeve.

At first sight, Williams's Francine seems a cliché excavated from his radio youth; a Miss Kitty (the beautiful saloon proprietor who helps Marshall Matt Dillon bring law and order to Dodge City) from the long-running radio (and later TV series) *Gunsmoke*.[39] There is no hint in her presentation of the entrapment, drug addiction, violence, unsafe abortions and sexual diseases (rampant and potentially fatal in the nineteenth century[40]) that constituted the life of the Frontier prostitute according to the historical accounts assembled by Anne Butler and Ona Siporin in *Uncommon Common Women (1996)*, and by Jay Moynahan in *Ladies of Negotiable Virtue* (2010), and Jan Mackell's 'Soiled Doves' (2013): 'The ranks of the West's poor and uneducated supplied the region's boom era of the nineteenth century. Women entered the profession at an early age ... could not read or write and had few opportunities to extricate themselves from their lives.'[41] This is not Francine. However, her presentation is not a failure of revisionist nerve on Williams's behalf; rather, in a novel focused on the superficialities of skin and flesh, she is a potent symbol of sexual objectification. She is introduced to us by Miller, who depicts her not as a person but, like the buffalo, a commodity in his mythological West:

> A whore in Boston, and a whore in Butcher's Crossing; now, there's two different things ... In Butcher's Crossing, a whore is a necessary part of the economy. A man's got to have something besides liquor and food

to spend his money on, and something to bring him back to town after he's been out on the country. In Butcher's crossing, a whore can pick and choose, and still make a right smart amount of money; and that makes her almost respectable. Some of them even get married; make right good wives, I hear, for them that want wives.

(29–30)

For Miller, both he and Francine are in the skin game; her profession is a product of supply and demand economics around which he has constructed a compelling narrative of equality. It is a seductive account and partially true; historians who identify the appalling working conditions also acknowledge that it offered women a degree of economic independence 'female companionship, a decorous lifestyle, the promise of monetary gain and a modicum of female agency'.[42] However, exoneration is not Williams's intention here. Francine is not presented as a shrewd businesswoman in the mould of Mrs Miller in *McCabe and Mrs Miller* (1971) and Williams's Miller is no McCabe but a psychopathic fantasist who is proved wrong about everything bar his capacity for destruction. Williams's interest in Francine, as it is throughout the novel, is the body that gains meaning through its objectification, a process controlled by cultural constraints. To the hunters, the buffalo is the ultimate 'other', the body only taking on meaning within an economic context when it is skinned, and the hides transformed into bills of sale. The bodies left behind are essentially without meaning. Likewise, Francine's body only takes on meaning for her customers through commercial transactions, episodes from which she mentally absents herself.

In Williams's sexual subplot, Francine becomes a place marker measuring the butchers crossing of psychological and culturally endorsed borders of behaviour, which comes to reflect Andrews's engagement with the West as a whole. Initially, he is the love-struck romantic, his stuttered 'she doesn't look like – a –' recording an amputated act of self-censorship that prepares us for his desire to dislocate Francine from her profession (29). It is a censoriousness in which the narrator freely participates, presenting the couple as childish lovers: Andrews taking genteel strolls arm in arm with a 'girl' (the pronoun usage is insistent); Andrews staring into her large, pale and curiously detached eyes; or Andrews observing the 'minute beads of sweat that stood out distinctly above her full upper lip and caught in the sunlight like tiny crystals' – the sweat of commodified sexual exertion transformed into beauty under the idealized gaze of her lover (29, 43). Such is his youthful idealization that he cannot sleep with her, Williams dramatizing his psychological turmoil in a scene in which he flees from her naked body when she offers herself to him. Williams prepares us for this reaction through the carefully contrived symbolism of the room, for not only is it reminiscent of his own home, but it is decorated with 'framed engravings of woodland scenes' that remind us that he prefers his 'wild' nature sanitized and framed.

A bizarre and suggestive scene, it has a precursor in the earlier *Nothing but the Night*, in which an equally young and naive protagonist is depicted standing before the naked body of a prostitute. Here she is objectified as 'a living statue, a motionless poem of light and flesh, of shadowing breast and ivory thigh' – an image at once lyrically idealized and sexually charged (*NN* 114). She is both angel and prostitute, a dialectic with which the protagonist has been struggling in his Proustian relationship with his mother, which he attempts to exorcize by beating up the prostitute. Andrews's horror is less dramatic, but derives from his recognition of her profession: on the street he is able to conceive of Francine as the innocent victim of economic circumstance, one of the 'brightly dressed and mysterious' women he passed in the streets in Boston, whom, an early manuscript version makes clear, 'he had imagined with a kind of excitement'.[43] However, standing before her naked form he is unable to rid himself of the image of the 'hundreds of men, steadily streaming in and out'. As a consequence, he flees (63).

In crude terms, it will take the buffalo hunt to destroy his idealism and make him comfortable around flesh. Unfortunately, this gives rise to scenes that, though symbolically consistent in their layering of Andrews's mind/body struggle, seem clumsily misogynistic in their degradation. One such is a dream that elides the white flesh of a degutted calf with that of Francine. In Williams's original conception, he sought to draw attention to the obvious chauvinism by having the calf's blood stain the banknotes which Andrews later presents to Schneider for wages: thus, the timidity of Andrews around flesh is contrasted with Schneider's determination to 'hire myself a little German girl for a couple of days' (150). The published version is less overt, Williams focusing instead on the shared whiteness of flesh and snow as indicative of blankness and therefore meaninglessness, a symbolic link made clear when he eventually sleeps with her:

> She was a presence which assuaged a need in him ... and when he opened his eyes, meeting the eyes of Francine open and wide and unfathomable below him, again he was almost surprised that she was there. Afterwards, he remembered the look in her eyes and wondered what she was thinking, what she was feeling, in the close moments of their passion ... And finally this wondering drew his mind and his eye away from the center of his self and focused them upon Francine.
>
> (257)

Eyes, as they have been throughout the book, are once again central. There is none of the fleshy eroticism of those sexual literary pioneers Williams most admired, D H Lawrence and Henry Miller; his chapter breaks do not work as they do in Lawrence to heighten the sexual climax, but as a discrete curtain to be drawn over events to protect the reader's sensibilities. Williams takes his cue from Sartre and particularly Beauvoir, according to whom sex releases the individual from the tyranny of 'subjectivity' as they see themselves from the perspective of the 'other'.[44] It is, as Beauvoir concedes, an unashamedly phallocentric theory; the passive female is only present to bring the male into a greater understanding of himself. However, there is at least in the acknowledgement of the necessity of the woman in this act of male self-creation, a small step towards equality.[45] This is the evolution – guided by the temporal discourse markers 'presence', 'afterwards' 'and finally' – that Andrews undergoes that enables him to avoid the egotism of Schneider and the self-destructive impulse of Miller. Where the solipsistic Andrews of the early chapters was a passive recipient of sensations (his voyage into the unknown a catalogue of saddle sores), his erotic encounter with Francine makes him wonder about the lives of others. Central to his brooding curiosity is the 'look in her eyes' which reveals the emptiness shared by the hunters as she mentally removes herself from the encounter to become, like the buffalo, the body in a commercial transaction. His loss of idealism is signalled by his capacity to think of her male customers 'without resentment' since he too has become one of the faceless strangers who traipse through her bedroom (262). It is reinforced by the inclusion of a scene late in the novel in which Andrews meets with another prostitute, not the 'soiled dove' of his Western imagination, but a whisky-swilling working girl whose skin (once again the emphasis is on flesh) 'hung in loose folds on her face' (243). She is not wide-eyed but has 'small black eyes that moved stiffly behind puffed eyelids' appraising him 'quickly' and 'expertly' (242). She is a cliché of a different type (the snake-like temptress), her 'fallen' status suggesting a different and equally damning indictment of male sexual narratives.

The novel ends with Andrews's ride into the sunset, which, in accordance with Williams's strategy throughout the novel, becomes a Western cliché to be disrupted. The catalyst is Miller's magnificently staged bonfire, a futile gesture through which he mocks a universe that appears to be laughing at him. As the flames illuminate the brothel, we are reminded that the buffalo hides, like the bodies of the prostitutes, are no longer needed in the West (Francine too is packing up to leave). For Miller, the economic worth of the hides is secondary to their value in defining him as a cowboy, which is what he becomes in the cliché of his silhouetted horse rearing against the flames (269). For McDonald, the hides have only ever had economic value, but even though they are now valueless he still resents the bonfire, not on grounds of waste, but because, as he explains to Andrews, 'they were mine' (268). His belief in possession as an end in itself, detached from utility, economics, morality and even common sense, anticipates the fetishization of ownership that will transform Frontier settlements like Butcher's Crossing into successful economic propositions. This is everything Andrews rejects: and yet as he emerges phoenix-like from the ashes to perform a clichéd ride West we are told that: 'A thin edge of the sun flamed above the eastern horizon. He turned again and looked at the flat country before him, where his shadow lay long and level, broken at the edges by the crisp new prairie grass' (274). Andrews may be heading West, but his fleshy experiences with both buffalo and Francine have left him unencumbered by its romantic potential; he understands that no meaning nor new identity awaits him, only a different way of seeing.

Notes

1. Alan Prendergast, 'Sixteen Years After his Death, Not-so-famous Novelist John Williams is Finding his Audience', *Westword* (2010) http://www.westword.com/news/sixteen-years-after-his-death-not-so-famous-novelist-john-williams-is-finding-his-audience-5110462 [accessed 4 September 2016].
2. Williams interview with Bryan Woolley, *Denver Quarterly* 20: 3 (1985–6), 11–31 (pp. 24–5).
3. Williams, typed manuscript of *The Tent MC 716,* University of Arkansas Special Collections, John Edward Williams Papers, MC716: *Box 29 Folder 2*. The date scribbled on the front page of the manuscript is August 1978.
4. Williams, *The Tent MC 716,* John Williams Papers, MC716: *Box 29 Folder 2,* p. 34.
5. See Dan Wakefield, 'John Williams, Plain Writer', *Ploughshares* 7: 3/4 (October 1981), 9–22 (p. 21).
6. Shields, *The Man Who Wrote the Perfect Novel: John Williams, Stoner, and the Writing Life* (Austin: University of Texas Press, 2018), p. 35.
7. Ibid., Woolley interview, p. 16.
8. Heilman to Williams (31 August 1965), John Williams Papers MC716: Box 30, folder 3.
9. See Wayne Gard, *The Great Buffalo Hunt* (1959) (Lincoln, Nebraska: Bison Books, 1971), pp. 90–1, 231–4.
10. See Anthony Hutchison, 'Young America and the Anti-Emersonian Western: John Williams's *Butcher's Crossing*', *Western American Literature* 55: 3 (Fall 2020), 237–60.
11. Williams, typed manuscript, John Williams Papers MC716: Box 10, folder 1 (p. 15).
12. Thoreau, 'Walking' (1863). Quoted Carl Bode (ed.) *The Portable Thoreau* (New York: Penguin, 1982), pp. 602–3. For excellent reading of this relationship see Jack Brenner, '*Butcher's Crossing*: The Husks and Shells of Exploitation', *Western American Literature* 7: 4 (February 1973), 243–59 (p. 249).
13. Tompkins, *West of Everything*, p. 81.
14. See Kitses, *Horizons West*, p. 162.
15. See Philip French, 'Anthony Mann's Western Masterpiece', *The Guardian* (5 April 2015) https://www.theguardian.com/film/2015/apr/05/man-of-west-review-philip-french-classic-dvd-anthony-mann-western-masterpiece [accessed 3 March 2020].

16 Handwritten plan, John Williams Papers, MC716: Box 30, folder 3.
17 See John Williams Papers, MC716: Box 9, folder 7.
18 John Williams Papers MC716: Box 9, folder 7.
19 M. Scott Taylor, 'Buffalo Hunt: International Trade and the Virtual Extinction of the North American Bison', *The American Economic Review* 101: 7 (December 2011), 3162–95 (pp. 3162–63).
20 John Hanner, 'Government Response to the Buffalo Hide Trade 1871–1883', *The Journal of law and Economics* 24: 2 (October 1981), 239–71 (pp. 242, 45).
21 Hubbard, 'Buffalo Genocide in Nineteenth Century North America: "Kill, Skin, and Sell"', in A. Woodford (ed.), *Colonial Genocide in Indigenous North America* (Durham, NC: Duke University Press, 2014), p. 294.
22 See David D. Smits, 'The Frontier Army and the Destruction of the Buffalo: 1865–1883', *Western Historical Quarterly* 25: 3 (Autumn 1994), 312–38 (pp. 317, 326).
23 See John Cawelti, *Six Gun Mystique Sequel* (Madison: University of Wisconsin Press, 1999), p. 22.
24 Hanner, 'Government Response to the Buffalo Hide Trade 1871–1883', 239–71 (p. 239).
25 Orville Prescott, 'Books of The Times', *New York Times* (13 October 1954), p. 29.
26 Paul Mayersberg, *Hollywood, the Haunted House* (London: Allen Lane, Penguin, 1967), p. 121.
27 Williams's handwritten preparatory notes, John Williams Papers, MC716: Box 9, folder 27;
28 Sandoz, *The Buffalo Hunters: The Story of the Hide Men* (1954) (Lincoln, London: University of Nebraska Press, 1978), pp. 244, 254.
29 Handwritten notes: John Williams Papers MC716: Box 30, folder 3.
30 Dodge, *The Plains of the Great West and their Inhabitants* (1876) (New York: Archer House, 1959), pp. 142, 133.
31 Ibid., Emerson, *Nature* (1849), in Poirier (ed.) *Ralph Waldo Emerson*, p. 36; Ibid., Brenner, '*Butcher's Crossing*', p. 254.
32 John Milton 'Butcher's Crossing Tells How 4 Men Face Nature', *Minneapolis Sunday Tribune* (3 March 1960). John Williams Papers MC716: Box 27, folder 2.
33 John Williams, *Augustus* (1971) (London: Vintage, 2003), pp. 284–5.
34 Ibid., Williams, *The Tent*, pp. 33, 28.
35 Williams, 'Henry Miller: The Success of Failure', *The Virginia Quarterly Review* 44: 2 (spring 1968), 225–45 (p. 236).
36 Whitman, 'The Song of Myself,' in *Leaves of Grass* (1855); the 1892 edition is available at https://www.poetryfoundation.org/poems/45477/song-of-myself-1892-version [accessed 12 May 2021].
37 Jennings, *The Cowboys* (New York: Bantam Books, 1972), p. 224.
38 Elizabeth Mullen, "Not Much of a Rind on You": (De)Constructing Genre and Gender in *Westworld*, '*TV Series* 14' (2018); https://journals.openedition.org/tvseries/3304 [accessed 20 September 2020].
39 Radio series ran from 1952–61; T V from 1955–75.

40 Mackell, 'Soiled Doves: An Overview of Good Girls Gone Bad in the American West', *True West* (September 30, 2013) https://truewestmagazine.com/soiled-doves-good-girls-gone-bad/ [accessed 1 August 2020].
41 Butler and Siporin, *Uncommon Common Women: Ordinary Lives of the West* (Logan, UT: Utah State University Press, 1996), p. 93.
42 See Karen Jones and John Wills, *The American West: Competing Visions* (Edinburgh: Edinburgh University Press, 2009), p. 136; Jan Moynahan, *Ladies of Negotiable Virtue: An account of Pioneer Prostitutes* (Spokane, Wash: Chickadee Pub., 2010) p. 1.
43 Typed manuscript fragment: John Williams Papers MC716: Box 30, folder 3.
44 See Jean Paul Sartre, *Being and Nothingness* (1943), trans. Hazel Barnes (London: Routledge, 2003), p. 391.
45 Beauvoir, *The Second Sex* (1947), trans. C. Borde and S. Malovany-Chevallier (London: Jonathan Cape, 2009), p. 167.

2

Lost between Borders: McCarthy's Vanishing Cowboys

'See the child' begins McCarthy's bloody and hallucinatory *Blood Meridian*, an exhortation that guides us to his narrative strategy throughout both this novel and the *Border Trilogy*. Many readers of the novel are drawn towards visual metaphors: Campbell observes that these works 'peer into the abyss of Western American History and bear fictional witness to its terrifying and spectacular events', whilst Sara Spurgeon claims that *Blood Meridian* presents us with a 'perverted ... mythic structure few besides McCarthy have dared to gaze at unflinchingly'.[1] There is a focus on 'vision' in McCarthy's 'revisionism' as we are invited to watch the growth into maturity of a young man whose rite of passage becomes an analogue of our engagement with the West. 'The Kid', like Andrews before him, appears on the page as an object of scrutiny; he will be our passive witness to unspeakable horrors, a 're-visioning' that makes visible the violence hidden beneath the blinkered vision of Turner.[2] The present tense is unnerving, as is its use throughout the novel, and has the effect of de-historicizing the historical record so that we are witness of events as they occur. The phrasing is an ironic echo of Alexander Pope's *Essay on Man* – 'Behold the child, by Nature's kindly law / Pleased with a rattle, tickled with a straw', which McCarthy reinforces through a later reference to Wordsworth's aphoristic: 'All history present in that visage, the child the father of the man' (a formulation that appeals to the development of the human spirit through contact with the pastoral in accordance with 'Nature's Holy Plan').[3] McCarthy's *Essay on Man*, like *Butcher's Crossing*, sets out to overturn such romantic sensibilities and replace Wordsworthian benevolence with Darwin's 'Nature red in tooth and claw'.

This wasn't always McCarthy's intention. Early manuscript drafts suggest a more conventional Western based on the kind of extensive historical research encouraged by the New Historians.[4] McCarthy read over three hundred books; the most important was Samuel Chamberlain's *My Confession: Recollections of a Rogue* (1850), an eyewitness account of the atrocities committed by the Glanton Gang on the Texas–Mexico border in the 1850s.[5] It provided him with the key events and characters and legitimized the narrative perspective of a teenage runaway. A curious document with a tautological title that advertises its authenticity whilst alliteratively transforming it into a Dime novel, it fits in with McCarthy's postmodern approach to narrative as an inter-textual patchwork: as he has claimed in interview – 'Books are made from other books'.[6] In *Blood Meridian* the marginal character of Captain White articulates a xenophobia that mimics the speeches of the real-life expansionists John O'Sullivan and William Swain; more centrally, the historical figure of Judge Holden is transformed into a character pastiche, part Milton's Satan (underlined by the inscription 'In Arcadia et Ego' on his rifle), part Melville's Ahab and Conrad's Colonel Kurtz (McCarthy adding to one of the Judge's speeches 'the horror, the horror? See H of Darkness'[7]). He is the dark personification of the Turner thesis, in whom the notion of 'regeneration through violence' is transformed through the syntactical tropes of the baroque into a pornographically excessive 'hymn of violence'.[8] His determination to author himself into being through his notebooks combined with his highly stylized rhetorical performance effectively draws attention to the inherent theatricality of Western mythology. And just as during the writing process the character of the Judge grew to dominate the theatrical space, Chamberlain's teenage runaway was transformed into the figure of the ambivalent outsider. The 'Kid', whose epithet challenges the mythical Billy through his 'taste for mindless violence', becomes a thinly drawn and morally ambivalent central protagonist (3). The description of him fighting 'all races, all breeds. Men whose speech sounds like the grunting of apes' draws attention to an atavistic behaviour, which, like that into which Williams's snow-trapped scalp hunters fall, is a direct challenge to Emerson's primitivism. He is simply further along the devolutionary scale. Narratively he functions much like Will Andrews – an Emersonian 'transparent eyeball' whose unfocussed gaze 'sees all' in the 'optical democracy' of McCarthy's borderlands (247). For both novels ask explicitly and implicitly what happens when the universalizing eye – whether that of the narrator or characters – gazes upon the brutal; what happens when the 'wild and barbarous' terrain that draws on both men proves horrifying rather than liberating, a crucible of existential doubt rather than masculine affirmation (4).

The journey of the scalp hunters like that of the hide hunters is presented as conjectural; we are continually reminded that theirs is a voyage into the unknown where 'all was darkness without definition' (100) and that 'they wasnt no name to it. It was just a wilderness' (32). And though they are always in the saddle they never seem to get anywhere:

The horses trudged sullenly the alien ground and the round earth rolled beneath them silently milling the greater void wherein they were contained. In the neuter austerity of that terrain all phenomena were bequeathed a strange equality ... and in the optical democracy of such landscapes all preference is made whimsical and a man and a rock become endowed with unguessed kinships.

(247)

Williams observed that though his hunters appear to be moving through space 'it seemed to [Andrews] that the land rather than the horse moved beneath him like a great treadmill' meaning that they were actually moving into newer versions of themselves (*BC* 78). In McCarthy's 'optical democracy' (reinforced through parataxis in which nothing is presented in a state of subordination) everything is equal and nothing meaningful or significant: but where for Emerson an optical democracy might confer unity, for the scalp hunters all is sameness, leaving the riders trapped in an epistemological void. This levelling is both horizontal (flat desert) and vertical (historical) emphasized through the record of human history – the pictographs, bleached bones, dried seas and mummified remains – through which they ride.[9] The borderland becomes an iteration of Campbell's 'third space' in which the scalp hunters, rather than moving into newer versions of themselves, become conduits of older more savage versions of humanity 'ornamented with human parts like cannibals' (189).[10] History becomes a jumble that erupts into the narrative in the Comanche attack on Captain White's filibusters. It is, like the descriptions of the mechanical felling of the buffalo in *Butcher's Crossing*, a scene we are invited to spectate rather than experience. It is narrated through the Kid's eyes, the ambivalent tone of his polysyndeta – 'everywhere there were horses down ... and he saw a man who sat charging his rifle ... and he saw men kneeling who tilted ... and he saw men lanced ... and he saw the horses of war trample down the fallen' – offering a direct refutation of both Turner's regeneration through violence and the moral ascendency conferred by Emerson's transparent eyeball (53).[11]

In McCarthy's *Essay on Man*, the role of witness is debased and those with spiritual insight are, like the Tarot reader who divines the Kid's clemency, blindfolded. The Kid rides through a landscape that is not a metaphor of something else, but brutally actual and populated by others in the act of blind apprehension: a bush 'hung with dead babies' their heads turned 'to stare eyeless at the naked sky' (57); a dead Apache warrior left 'to scrutinize with his drying eyes the calamitous advance of the sun' (110); a 'convocation' of severed heads '[that] glared blindly out of their wrinkled eyes' (220); and flies walking 'on [the] shrunken eyeballs' of Mexican villagers massacred in the sanctuary of their church (61). The horror is blinding leaving concepts like good and evil part of a discourse that seems somehow entirely inappropriate to the narrative of the novel. We, like Sheriff Ed Tom Bell's attempts to understand the motives of killer Anton Chigurh in *No Country for Old Men* (2005), are left to reject the evidence of our senses: '*They say the eyes are the windows of the soul. I don't know what them eyes was the windows to and I guess I'd as soon not know*' (McCarthy's italics, NC, 4).

The worlds of *Butcher's Crossing* and *Blood Meridian* cannot be brought under control because in its optical democracy there is no transcendence, man is simply a part of a bloody Darwinian process. They both, however, have their prophets. In the former, it is MacDonald who chastises the innocent Andrews for his failure of understand the events he has witnessed: 'McDonald laughed, and his laughter choked in a fit of coughing. "My God, man. Ain't you got eyes? ... Can't you look at it straight?"' (*BC* 246–7). Nihilistic despair gives way to rueful laughter at what he finally apprehends as life's dark comedy. Despite delivering the novel's central epistemological message, McDonald is a marginal character. This is not the case for McCarthy's Judge Holden, who grew out of all proportion to dominate the narrative. Like McDonald he recognizes the emptiness of the hunters' desire for some explanation of the lives to which they are committed – 'Your heart's desire is to be told some mystery' – and his answer is equally dismissive: 'The mystery is that there is no mystery' (252). He is, however, determined to fill up the void through the assertion of self. It is no accident that we first meet him in the tent of a revivalist preacher, whom he falsely accuses of being an imposter, before enthroning himself as the prophet of a new religion. His power is essentially rhetorical as he ranges from Classical mythology, Enlightenment philosophy and biblical declamation, a process that draws attention to the importance of narrative, which includes the mythology of the Western, in ordering human experience into a meaningful existence.[12] Thus, stories, rather than the ritual slaughter of Williams's hunters (the report of the rifle and the number of hides), emerge as the primary epistemological tool available to assemble human experience in defiance of meaninglessness. Central to this process are the Judge's books, which are full of pressed flowers and geological, botanical and zoological sketches through which he authors his own existence. Since he claims that 'whatever in creation exists without my knowledge exists without my consent' there is nothing worth saving outside his books (18, 204, 124). Thus, he is the antithesis of Emerson's poet; his eyes do not recreate the world through his poetic sensibility to reveal god; rather, he substitutes the world with his books and becomes god.

The Judge is the perfect guide to the world of *Blood Meridian*; his ersatz intellectualism, at once profound and ridiculous, challenges the scholarly theatricality of Turner's Frontier thesis, replacing regenerative with nihilistic violence. Furthermore, a poetry-declaiming, nimble-footed, hairless, pederast offers a narrative challenge to our expectations as readers of what constitutes a Western character. His smiling presence – he is perched on a rock smiling in the middle of the desert when the scalp hunters first come across him – envelops the narrative, transforming the traditional hard riding Western trope into something absurd (125). As such he becomes part of McCarthy's strategy of continually destabilizing our reading experience by presenting a Western and also its comically grotesque deconstruction.[13] McCarthy allows the Judge to draw attention to this narrative feature through a speech delivered to the assembled scalp hunters:

> Had you not seen it all from birth and thereby bled it of its strangeness it would appear to you for what it is, a hat trick in a medicine show, a fevered dream, a trance be-populate with chimeras having neither analogue nor precedent, an itinerant carnival, a migratory tent show whose ultimate destination after many a pitch in many a mudded field is unspeakable and calamitous beyond reckoning.
> (245)

The world we have already observed through the eyes of the Kid is not 'bled of' but it 'bleeds strangeness'. In McCarthy's borderlands dancing and Carnival are ubiquitous, making literal the existential absurdity that surrounds the behaviour of the hunters whilst simultaneously disrupting expectations. The inhabitants of the towns of Bexar and Chihuahua are presented in Carnival – dancing girls with painted faces, clowns juggling rats, itinerant magicians and blind fortune-tellers (22). Their theatricality is presented as another order of madness of the scalp hunters, who themselves are bedecked in scapulars of ears. They are, as Sara Spurgeon observes, 'dark versions of classic Western heroes from the Deer-slayer and Daniel Boone to Buffalo Bill'.[14] The Comanche attack on Captain White's filibusters is transformed from Western mode to carnival horror, in which the attackers, having clothed themselves from a child's dressing up box, appear as a 'company of mounted clowns' – death hilarious! (53). In this context, it is ironic that the severed head of Captain White should end up in a large jar performing the function of a sightless fairground attraction. A description late in the novel of the Kid escaping Mexican troops is presented using the tropes and discursive practices familiar to the Western genre (he even has a sidekick), until McCarthy introduces the Judge, naked beneath a parasol of skins trailing an imbecile on a lead, who crashes into the narrative like a disruptive carnival act (297).[15]

The Kid, like Andrews, is both participant in and witness to this bloody carnival, which leads us to ask whether he evolves in Turnerian fashion or remains 'a troubling Peter Pan whose inner life remains a closed book'.[16] Vereen Bell argues that 'part of the book's horror derives from the fact that there are no ordinary characters to allow us to maintain a sense of objectivity'. There is no Ishmael or Marlowe to comment on the horrors, but the Judge, who is both Ahab and Kurtz and 'who is frightening because his horrible acts are rationalised by his own philosophy of nihilistic violence'.[17] To some extent this is true; the Kid, like Andrews, goes through a series of rebirths, but remains passive rather than seeming to evolve. His bloody fight with a barman is followed by the description of him 'wad[ing] out into the river like some wholly wretched baptismal candidate' (27); following the massacre of Captain White's regiment, 'he went forth stained and stinking like some reeking issue of the incarnate dam of war herself' (55). In each case there seems to be no reflection and moral growth, rather a descent into wretchedness. Yet where Andrews's clichéd ride into the sunset indicates the presence of a 'butcher crossing' westward who is capable of participating in another buffalo blood bath, McCarthy hints at something more promising. His means of exploration, interestingly, is the aftermath of a buffalo hunt (he even dates it as 1878) – an apocalyptic scene of devastation in which piles of bleached white bones are scavenged by ragged men. McMurtry includes similar imagery in *Lonesome Dove* when Gus and Call ride into a buffalo graveyard cared for by the simpleton outcast, Aus Frank, who spends his time assembling the bones into vast, surreal pyramids. Gus concedes that Aus 'has plenty to work with, for ... bones stretched far across the plain' and recalls when he and Call were rarely out of sight of the vast milling herds. Thus, the pyramids are an indictment of mindless destruction and visible lament for a lost world. Aus blames the bankers for encouraging such rapacious activity, but the irony is not lost on Gus that it is their clearance of the wilderness that has made such exploitation possible: 'That's what we done, you know. Kilt the dern Indians so they wouldn't bother the bankers.'[18] In McCarthy's scene we join the aftermath, when one of the hunters articulates similar sentiments to the Kid:

> [He] told him of the buffalo and the stands he'd made against them, laid up in a sag on some rise with the dead animals scattered over the grounds and the herd beginning to mill and the riflebarrel so hot the wiping patches sizzled in the bore and the animals by the thousands and tens of thousands and the hides pegged out over actual square miles of ground and the teams of skinners spelling one another around the clock and the shooting and shooting weeks and months ... and the meat rotting on the ground and the air whining with flies and the buzzards and ravens and the night a horror of snarling and feeding with the wolves half crazed and wallowing in the carrion ... We ransacked the country. Six weeks. Finally found a herd of eight animals and we killed them and come in. They're gone. Ever one of them that God ever made is gone as if they'd never been at all.
>
> (316–17)

Sara Spurgeon observes of this scene that 'here is the new covenant, this hunter and those like him proselytes of the new order the Judge has helped bring into being in which man's relationship to the wilderness is one of butchery on a scale scarcely imaginable'.[19] Spurgeon is surely correct here; where Andrews's last glimpse of the valley upon which the hunters have wrought such carnage guides us to the green grass sprouting between the corpses (symbol of an ambivalent or even benevolent nature) here the hunter recalls the 'whining', 'snarling' and 'wallowing in the carrion' that reflects the horror of a Darwinian natural order.[20] Glanton's hunters are part of this Darwinian order whilst participating in a brutal economic capitalism in which scalps become bloody commodities in a free market exchange. Their cynicism is underlined by their replacement of Native American scalps with those they were paid to protect; their moral disintegration is emphasized by their decision to continue scalping for no economic reward. Their killing is vindicated by both economics and Turnerian myth creation: violence has been necessary to clear the land and create the hardy individuals who are capable of reflection; now the killing has been replaced by cleaning, as the bone pickers cart off the bones to be made into fertilizer to encourage future growth. This Turnerian conclusion is supported by the epilogue, in which the bloody sun of the 'Blood Meridian' gives way to a new dawn in which a team drive holes into the 'rock which God has put there' in order to fence the free range and bring 'restraint', 'prudence' and 'reflectiveness' to the bone covered prairie (337).

And yet McCarthy is clearly troubled by such a conclusion, for where Glanton never shows remorse, the hunter's speech closes with a tone of lament; an acknowledgement, like that of Gus and Call, that something godly is gone forever because they 'ransacked the country'. It is further challenged symbolically through the introduction of the simpleton child, Elrod – a leering version of the Kid's younger self. This is a novel that sets out to disrupt the romantic assertion that 'the child is the father of the man', which is what the Judge does in his convoluted story of the harness maker who murders the traveller and buries him secretly. The violent act creates two child victims: the traveller's son who will forever martyr the 'frozen god' of his father and fall into distracted inaction; the son of the murderer who is brutalized through the confession of the father and, like the Kid, goes West and becomes 'a killer of men' (145). In yet another inversion of Emerson, the West is transformed from a geography of hope to a sanctuary for murderous orphans presided over by the Judge as surrogate father. This is the role he offers for the Kid – 'Dont you know that I'd have loved you like a son?' – providing parenting that is Darwinian ('At a young age ... [children] should be put in a pit with wild dogs' (307)) rather than Wordsworthian and therefore more, he argues, in keeping with the demands of the West. In the West of the Judge 'moral law is an invention of mankind for the disenfranchisement of the powerful in favour of the weak' and the Kid is to be reproached for possessing 'a flawed place in the fabric of [his] heart' because '[he] alone reserved in [his] soul some corner of clemency for the heathen' (250, 299). In the world of *Blood Meridian* clemency is a betrayal of the Judge's will to power and the only heart that we see is the shrivelled exhibit kept by an old slaver in a box (19). As befitting his marginal status, the scope of the Kid's moral compass is displayed by inaction rather than action, as with his inability to kill the wounded Shelby or the Judge (when advised to do so by Tobin when he has the chance) (206–10, 285). However, his refusal to kill the orphan Elrod, who baits him by refusing to accept that he is a real cowboy, demonstrates the development of a moral restraint ironically worthy of a fictional cowboy. That it is fleeting, and Elrod dies, reinforces the sense created throughout the text that violence is not purgative or regenerative but simply generative of more violence. It is therefore ironic that where Andrews' ride into the sunset demonstrates that, despite the brutality of his experience, the Western dream endures, the Kid should end up murdered in a jakes for displaying a modicum of sensitivity judged incompatible with the Darwinian West.

II

Blood Meridian ends with the image of the cowboy sinking fence posts in order to run cattle on the land that the hunters in the novel have so brutally emptied; thus, McCarthy introduces the paradox that the fencing that makes the cowboy's job possible curtails the free range that is central to his identity.[21] It is one of many borders (geographical, psychological, genre and sexual) that he will explore throughout *The Border Trilogy*, the most prominent being that which demarcates the heroic West of the imagination from the West in which his protagonists actually live. What constitutes a 'real' cowboy is central to the *Trilogy* – the question hanging over it aptly expressed by Parham's searching 'Where's the All-American Cowboy At?' (3). McCarthy's young protagonists share a postmodern anxiety concerning 'authenticity' and find themselves trapped in a hall of mirrors unable to differentiate between copies and originals. This entrapment is emphasized through Grady's formative relationship with mirrors; his reflection, like that of Andrews before him, is an important means of monitoring his appearance for the visual signifiers that sustain his mythological self. The mirror presents the material with its counterpart: the tangible lost in a self-reflexive engagement with its spectral image. It is announced in the novel's opening image of the reflected candle in the room in which John Grady's grandfather lies dead; it presents a very different manifestation of the 'optical democracy' that shaped the perceptions of the characters of *Blood Meridian*:

> The candleflame and the image of the candleflame caught in the pierglass twisted and righted when he entered the hall and again when he shut the door ... behind him hung the portraits of forebears only dimly known

to him all framed in glass and dimly lit ... Lastly he looked at the face
so caved and drawn among the folds of funeral cloth ... That was not
sleeping. That was not sleeping.

(3)

McCarthy's parataxis means that there is no subordination of detail;
everything participates in the same reality, which is, as the reflected twisting
candle flame suggests, struggling to differentiate between copy and original.
The 'dimly known' forebears are frozen behind glass, whilst the grandfather,
who represents Grady's last tie with the fabled old West, is neither dead nor
'not sleeping' but living in Grady's imagination. Grady's West is characterized
by the pictures of horses that adorn the walls. However, his Grandfather's
pragmatic insistence that they are 'picturebook horses' alerts us to the fact
that this West is a stylized copy of a copy that has existed in the realm of
nostalgia for a considerable time (16). There are already oil companies in the
yard, and the setting sun of *Blood Meridian* has been transformed into the
headlamp of a distant train 'boring out of the east like some ribald satellite
of the coming sun' (3). Such imagery, as Leo Marx argues, is archetypal of
Eden corrupted by the machine's entry into the garden. McMurtry uses it
at the beginning of *Horseman, Pass By* (1961) in which the meditations
of the young Lonnie Bannon on the beauty of his grandfather's ranch are
interrupted by the sound of a distant train. The scene is paradigmatic: his
grandfather's West is 'passing by', a process hastened by the necessity of
putting down his diseased herd (a potent symbol of the decayed vision that is
passing). For McCarthy, the twisting candle flame and shuddering headlamp
bring not illumination but a sense of alienation, transforming Grady into the
allegorical outcast. Taking her cue from the serpent, Gail Moore Morrison
reads him as Adam expelled from the paradise of his parental ranch;[22] Charles
Bailey reads novel as a courtly romance in which Grady is the knight-errant
who wanders in the wilderness, falls in love with an unattainable princess,
tames horses, goes into combat, but eventually loses the woman he loves;[23]
Daniel Cooper Alarcon, Megan Riley McGilchrist and Sarah Spurgeon
focus on the 'pretty horses' of the child's lullaby to posit a coming of age
tale in which Grady's maturation depends upon the recognition of the tragic
consequences that arise when one tries to carry this childish vision into the
real world.[24] He is, as the pretty horses imply, a teenager lost in a world that
seems different to the one his imagines.

Grady's attempts to reconnect with the West of his imagination become
McCarthy's means of re-examining the metanarrative upon which Western
mythology is constructed.[25] This process begins with McCarthy's playful
evocation of the blood red sun of *Blood Meridian* as Grady saddles up and
rides into the past via the old Comanche road:

The sun sat blood red and elliptic under the reefs of bloodred clouds
before him. He rode ... when the shadows were long and the ancient

road was shaped before him in the rose and canted light like a dream of the past where the painted ponies and the riders of that lost nation came down out of the north with their faces chalked and their long hair plaited ... all of them pledged in blood and redeemable in blood only.

(5)

He rides West in a cliché of cowboy resolution, but though it evokes the noble Western tradition, it is doomed to end in failure. Lonnie takes a similar ride, thus becoming the figurative 'horseman passing by' – taking his grandfather's horse, significantly named Stranger, and galloping over the aptly named 'Idiot Ridge' before being thrown before a fence: an apt symbol of his imprisonment within the closed range. Grady's ride is similarly symbolic: he cannot actually see the road; what he 'sees' is his vision which he colours with his own expectations. In *Blood Meridian* the blood red sun was a phallus suggestive of a panorama of masculine violence; for Grady, the landscape remains a superficial mixture of colour and chaos recoverable through the inflected lens of Hollywood. The Native Americans, as they do throughout McCarthy's work, appear as little more than screens upon which his characters can project their own fantasies. They offer representations or simulations of, to use Gerald Vizenor's term, 'Indianness' – a condition that has nothing to do with actual Native Americans and more to do with an Anglo desire for an 'authentic' connection to the past.[26] Seen through Grady's eyes, they are reminiscent of the authentic ethnic Other existing on the other side of what Fiedler described as that 'endlessly retreating frontier of innocence'.[27] It is Grady's 'innocence' that summons up the ghosts, McCarthy's deliberately overwritten references to being 'pledged' or 'redeemed' in blood is suggestive of the Turnerian rhetoric deployed to exonerate their extermination, language that Grady accepts and retools to emphasize their spiritual transcendence. Like Miller in *Butcher's Crossing*, Grady seems blissfully unaware of the irony that the Native Americans were removed to make way for the ranch he so covets, and that now he, like them, is vanishing from the landscape that bears their imprint.

'Throughout the novel,' as Meg King has observed, 'Grady is compared to the Comanches in order to capture the way in which he represents a culture threatened with extinction.'[28] His father, Wayne, grasps the irony, but his act of self-identity – we're 'like the Comanches was two hundred years ago' – is a nostalgic call for a lost way of life constructed on a contentious alignment of marginalization and suffering experienced by both groups (25). Wayne's words echo the sentiments verbalized by real ranchers confronted by an array of 'hostile' forces – federal agencies, corporate agribusiness, suitcase ranchers, nutritionists, environmentalists and pushy Easterners – during the period McCarthy was writing the novel. As one Montana rancher quipped: 'I have become, for all practical purposes, an Indian.'[29] Sally Robinson makes clear why this manoeuvre is problematic, arguing that 'while the identity politics of the dominant shares many assumptions and rhetorics with the identity politics of the marginalized, the two politics are not, and never can be, fully commensurate'.[30] There is always, as with arguments for 'reverse racism' or 'reverse sexism', an asymmetric power relationship embedded within Anglo hegemony that proves irreversible. Philip Deloria contends in his *Playing Indian* (1999) that imaginative identification with Native Americans emerges from 'the context of a postmodernism that emphasized relativism and openness' to transform the term 'Indian' to a cultural signifier of 'individual freedom'.[31] Notions of 'individuality' and 'freedom' are at the root of McCarthy's deployment, as they are also in McMurtry's *Lonesome Dove* (1985). In the latter, Gus McCrae complains that in murdering the 'Indians' they have 'killed off most of the people that made this country interesting to begin with' and that 'we'll be the Indians, if we last another twenty years' stuck on a reservation with all the other 'old rowdies'.[32] Wayne, like McCrae, is emblematic of the cowboy's decline; when he shares with his son the gossip of Shirley Temple's divorce, he is really focussing our attention on the fact that all the great American icons are breaking up – the cowboy included. In response he constructs a hyper-stylized performance of a cowboy identity, which is gently undermined by McCarthy's narrator. The rides that he takes with his son may read like excerpts from 'The High Country', but his backstory makes clear that he married into the ranch; real economic power lies in the hands of his recently divorced wife, allowing him to play out his cowboy fantasies. Hence, there is an air of artifice around their behaviour that makes them ridiculous:

> Two horsemen passed outside in the road and they studied them. His father stirred his coffee a long time. There was nothing to stir because he drank it black. He took the spoon and laid it smoking on the paper napkin and raised the cup and looked at it and drank. He was still looking out the window although there was nothing there to see.
>
> (24)

All the usual cowboy props are present – coffee, cigarettes, the endless landscape – but they inhibit, rather than encourage, emotional intimacy. Father and son may scrutinize and envy the horseman passing by, but theirs is a world of 'paper napkins' in which spoons, rather than Colts, 'smoke' and absent women pull the financial strings.

Women are powerful but peripheral in the *Trilogy*. They are either matriarchs who endure through apotheosis; motherly figures who keep the boys filled up with hearty meals; sultry senioritis worthy of cowboy quest: or trouble. Much of the dialogue in the novels reveals a pejorative misogyny supported and contested by the central protagonists. Politically, it is as if the impact of second and even first-wave feminism and the new historicism of the mid-1980s had passed McCarthy by. McMurtry, by contrast, was calling out the genre's sexism as early as the 1960s, claiming that for too long Western writers had kept their gaze averted from the subtleties of language and tone of the feminine experience.[33] 'I love to write about women', he has stated, and critics have praised his presentation of strong and complex female characters, who defy the conventional Western stereotypes.[34] We need only consider the strong-minded Lois and Jacy Farrow (*The Last Picture Show* (1966)); the sexually liberated Molly Taylor whose name signals her revisionary status (*Leaving Cheyenne* (1962)); and Katie Garza, the emancipated love interest for Billy the Kid who defiantly upsets male convention by killing the hero (*Anything for Billy* (1988)). They are not character-types we find in McCarthy; his strong women signal their independence by removing themselves from their partner's Western fantasy leaving him to focus on his real concern: the crisis of Anglo-American masculinity. Even when central to the plot – as with Grady's two love interests – McCarthy's women, as both Susan Kollin and Michael Johnson have noted, 'lack full-blown realization' and are little more than 'side-show attractions' locked in cliché.[35] This, however, is not a failure of art: they are clichés because we see them through Grady's eyes, a myopic perspective forged in a childhood dominated by the idealized Western tropes symbolized by the picture of 'All the Pretty Horses'. Such revisionism does not depend upon the inclusion of more realistic characters; it critiques from the inside, a risky strategy, as Lee Clark Mitchell has observed, since it re-inscribes the narrative conventions and gender tropes that it seeking to critique.[36] Our reading strategy, therefore, depends on our awareness of Grady's unreliability and discomfort around women. His evasiveness, ridiculously stylized chivalry and occasional bouts of overt misogyny (in which the narrator actively participates) become McCarthy's means of exposing a cowboy code that is antithetical to the feminine.

Grady's mother is a case in point: she has no connection with the mythological past and has moved to the city to become a professional actor. Wayne is unable to understand her restlessness; his analysis of their relationship is puerile in its superficiality – 'She liked horses. I thought that was enough' – and ironic in its diagnosis: 'I thought she'd outgrow some of the notions she had but she didn't. Maybe they were just notions to me' (24). It is the father and son who should be outgrowing antiquated notions of gender identity, not the newly enfranchised mother. The family lawyer, unencumbered by the prevailing cowboy mythology, is more progressive in his tentative suggestion that 'she's a young woman and my guess is she'd like to have a little more social life than what she's used to' (17). Grady proves equally clueless, his psychological limitations dramatized by his wanting to see one of her theatrical performances because 'he'd the notion that there would be something in the story itself to tell him about the way the world was' (21). It is the first of many scenes designed to draw attention to the importance of performance: Grady is lost because his mother's behaviour, both on and off stage, does not conform to the limited roles assigned to women in the Western genre of his imagination. This confusion is compounded when the next morning he witnesses her on the arm of a man in a suit rather than cowboy boots. His response is to retreat into a narrative over which he has control when, during the drinks interval, he assumes the classic pose of a cowboy ('one boot jacked back against the wall behind him') and smokes roll ups whilst we are told 'he was not unaware of the glances that drifted his way from the theatregoers' (21). This self-reflexive pose is typical of a genre in the thrall of spectacle, in which performance offers a mask that prevents engagement, particularly with women. McCarthy explores this feature further in the richly symbolic but otherwise inexplicable scene in which Grady's girlfriend leaves him for a boy with a car. He meets her in town on his way to get 'a broken bridle bit welded' (another symbol showing his loss of control) and engages in an exchange that wavers between truculence and silence: 'He stood back and touched the brim of his hat and turned and went on up the street. He didnt look back but he could see her in the windows of the Federal Building across the street standing there and she was still standing there when he reached the corner and stepped out of the glass forever' (29). He is a poseur: his actions are designed to be chivalric but are emotionally inarticulate. The mirrored buildings remind us of the pier glass and that he is happier as an observer of his own performance, which is reflected and therefore inauthentic. However, as he walks out of the frame it appears that he has ceased to be part of a reflected cowboy dream and become, in his mind at least, part of the real thing.

Becoming part of the real thing means hitching up with Grady Rawlins and, in time honoured fashion, lighting out for territory. In their mind's eye 'they rode out on the round dais of the earth which alone was dark and no light to it and which carried their figures and bore them up into the swarming stars so that they rode not under but among them and they rode at once jaunty and circumspect ... like young thieves in a glowing orchard' (30). Narratively, we seem to be back in the sublime world of *Blood Meridian* and *Butcher's Crossing*, but here the kitsch imagery – 'swarming stars', 'glowing orchards' – combined with the simple syntactical connections draw attention to the childish rhetorical construction. It is an idealized scene (the term 'dais' reinforcing the theatricality) created by the boys to play out bandit dreams with a combination of jaunty delusion and circumspection. For, as the imagery of thieves in the orchard suggests, their imaginary West has already fallen. Where Andrews and the Kid faced an endless wilderness, the boys are forced to lead their horses through 'a midden of old truckdoors and transmissions and castoff motorparts' (32). It appears a meta-theatrical nod to the opening scene of *Lonely are the Brave* (1962) – the film in which they are starring rather than the *Shane* they had hoped. This film version of Edward Abbey's *Brave Cowboy* (1956) shows Jack Burns (Kirk Douglas) crossing a busy road and riding through a scrapheap of old cars. We instinctively admire and pity him, the virtuous innocent whose spiritual imprisonment is signalled by his constant need to cut fences and whose rugged independence and simple loyalties are combined with a hopelessness with women. When he is struck and killed by a lorry carrying toilets, it seems in its pathos and absurdity a striking symbol of the cowboy's place in the contemporary West in which he remains the ridiculous object of nostalgia. McCarthy's 'brave cowboys' aren't cowboys at all, but innocents abroad whose youth is underlined by their packed lunches and their simplistic reading of the cheap oil company map that they buy to guide them on their way:

> There were roads and rivers and towns on the American side of the map as far south as the Rio Grande and beyond that all was white.
> It dont show nothin down there, does it? said Rawlins.
> No.
> You reckon it aint never been mapped?
> There's maps. That just aint one of em. I got one in my saddlebag.
> Rawlins came back with the map and sat on the ground and traced their route with his finger. He looked up.
> What? said John Grady.
> There aint shit down there.
>
> (34)

Through the maps that pepper the Trilogy, McCarthy draws attention to the constructedness of space. To Rawlins the blankness of the map is an opportunity for self-construction along Western lines; an interpretation reinforced by Grady's map, which, in a clearly symbolic manoeuvre, is kept in his saddlebag. However, Grady's gnomic observation that 'There's maps' draws attention to the arbitrary nature of the signs that confer signification; for where for the boys the blankness signifies the 'wilderness' that allows for cowboy dreams of the 'lonesome drifter', the reader understands that it expresses aggressive capitalist economics according to which those regions without oil don't exist.[37] Maps are contentious documents in McCarthy's West; even the otherwise omniscient character of The Judge in *Blood Meridian* is forced to acknowledge their limitations as he scratches one in the earth in his attempts to find the Delawares abducted by a bear (*BM* 138). They are nothing more than a 'decoration' according to scornful local Mexican villagers viewing a similar map drawn for Billy and Boyd in *The Crossing*, 'a picture of a voyage' to be pissed away by the local dogs (*C* 184). In effect, it is not by knowing the symbols on the map that one knows the country; rather, the map is a translation of the culturally organic into the static. Quijada, the ranch foreman Billy and Boyd meet later in the novel, is one of the many guides who make this clear whilst simultaneously indicating the dangers of their quest:

> The world has no name ... The names of the cerros and the sierras and the deserts exist only on maps. We name them that we do not lose our way. Yet it was because the way was lost to us already that we have made those names. The world cannot be lost. We are the ones.
>
> (C 387)

We are lost in the world that is lost to us, which we recreate and navigate through the act of arbitrary naming that imposes cultural dominance. Quijada's life is an enactment of such mapping. He is part Yaqui, representative of a people which has suffered a history of cultural displacement, who has filled up the blankness by transforming himself into the archetypal cowboy complete with 'John B Stetson hat and a pair of expensive latigo boots' (251). He understands the importance and arbitrariness of cultural signification and that an identity, whether personal or regional, is imposed rather than discovered, which is why maps describe a journey rather than help to plot a route.

The oil company map reflects economic cultural imperialism and is therefore an apt symbol for a couple of fantasists who want to replace the blankness of oil speculation with cowboy fun and games without troubling themselves with the regional geography. Blake Allmendinger complains that McCarthy's Mexico is a regrettable cliché, which it is because its geography and people are presented as nothing more than stage props for Grady's unrolling Western drama.[38] It conforms to the 'infernal Paradise' presented in the work of Malcolm Lowry (*Under the Volcano* (1946)) and D H Lawrence, a meeting place of Old and New governed by binaries such as beautiful/desolate, civilized/cruel, dreamlike/bloody and peopled by exotic inhabitants frozen in time.[39] Thus, his protagonists shuttle between the paradise of the Hacienda and the infernal Saltillo prison; the mountains and lakes of the country and the brothels of Juraz. The Mexicans they meet are either aristocrats like Don Hector and the Duena, or 'bandidos' like the pimp, Eduardo; they are either good natured peasants who provide a backdrop of exotic colour, or psychopaths like the Captain who arrests them. This duality extends to the reading experience, according to which we are made aware that we are consuming a Western novel and also its interpretive performance by two wide-eyed young men, a process that leads to the genre's gentle deconstruction. This dual narrative is signalled intra-textually by the ironic shading of set-piece Western scenes – river crossings, gun fights, hold ups and barroom brawls. When, for example, the boys stop at a village to take a drink, they are observed by a girl 'reading a comic book' who 'looked up at them and looked at the comic book and then looked up again': the contents of the book have been made real, as the boys take their behavioural cue from the book (49). With a repertoire of codified gestures, they act out a classic barroom whiskey scene with fruit juice: 'I dont know what that shit is ... But it tastes pretty good to a cowboy. Let us have three more here' (50). The girl's untranslated Spanish is easily incorporated into Grady and Rawlins's role play, whilst their B-movie banter is a deliberately overplayed pastiche verging on parody. For the narrative voice in this scene, like many in *the Trilogy*, is characterized by a troubling tone that leaves us, in Judith Butler's terms, uncertain where they stand in relation to the performativity of the subject.[40] We see such positioning again when the boys are brought face to face with a motley group of buffalo hunters. The free indirect discourse presents them as both authentic hunters 'their hats marbled with grease and sweat, their boots mended with raw cowhide' and a 'a rough lot' dressed in ragged 'outfits' who fail to live up to Grady's expectations of cowboy glamour. There is an edge of mockery in his pose – 'John Grady smoked and watched them' – and his only interest in them is as a barometer of his own authenticity, both as models and judges (61).

Grady's cowboy vision remains conjectural and therefore powerful; Rawlins, by contrast, is presented as increasingly suspicious of their role-playing, particularly in relation to their young sidekick, Blevins. A character reminiscent of Elrod, the simpleton bone picker from *Blood Meridian*, he performs the similar function in not allowing Grady to evolve. A crack-shot in an outsized Stetson and on an outsized horse, he has taken his name from a radio evangelist thereby adding transcendence to Grady's idealist dream. This contrasts with Rawlins's more pragmatic recognition of the limits of their play-acting, which forces him into the role of cynical commentator of Blevins's behaviour. When, for example, Blevins seeks to explain where Comanches would lay traps in the old days, Rawlins demands 'what in the putrefied dogshit would you know about the old days?' (57). When Blevins warns of an approaching group of riders – 'If we can see them they can see us' – it is Rawlins who exclaims 'What the hell is that supposed to mean?' (61). Even Blevins's impressive piece of cowboy gunplay (shooting a billfold as it is thrown into the air) is prompted by Rawlins's knowing question: 'You ready, Annie Oakley?' (55). Blevins's narrative function is made clear by McCarthy in the dramatically symbolic scene in which during a thunderstorm he is stripped Lear-like down to his essentials. He explains his fear by the curious history of a cowboy ancestor who was killed by a lightning bolt that welded the buckle of his belt shut, and another who was struck with a bolt that melted the fillings in his teeth and soldered his jaw shut (68). In this parody of the genre, these men are literally transformed into taciturn, big buckled lonesome cowboys in the crucible of the West. The reduction of Blevins, by contrast, is pathetic: he loses his horse and pistol and, stripped of his cowboy props, he becomes what he really is: a vulnerable young boy in baggy underwear in a dangerous environment.

McCarthy underlies this vulnerability in the very next scene when they meet a group of horsemen; now they do not salute the boys as fellow cowboys, but they offer to buy Blevins.

The Hacienda of Our Lady of the Immaculate Conception (a bitingly ironic name) is presented as the cowboy paradise that the boys have been seeking: 'This is how it was with the old waddies, aint it?' notes Rawlins with an unusually apposite question mark (96). However, all is not as it seems: it runs a thousand head of cattle and has a private plane, which means that it has more in common with the industrialised ranches left behind than the boys would care to admit. Furthermore, whilst Grady (whose own family ranch was 1,800 acres) takes his meals in the hacienda, Rawlins is in the bunkhouse, maintaining a class distinction that their shared cowboy camaraderie hides. Its central activity is horse breaking, an activity in which Grady excels and which provides McCarthy with a rich seam of narrative metaphor by which he carefully deconstructs a series of Western clichés. Grady's expertise, Spurgeon notes, highlights the paradox that his days spent hobbling and corralling horses deploying the signifiers of cowboy identity – spur, lasso, whip – consign the revered wildness essential to his identity to the realm of his dreams.[41] Furthermore, these particular horses aren't wild, but descendants of a breeding program which have since gone wild, which is analogous to the position in which the boys find themselves. It is, however, when it comes to the interior landscape, that the Western is at its most childish and the cowboys' relationship with his horse most suspect. In the Classic Western, the absence of women means that the horse provides the ear for emotional outpourings otherwise forbidden to the taciturn cowboy; more menacingly, control over a horse is easily translated into self-mastery and the control of others, particularly women. Such subtext, notes Tompkins, is made laughably apparent in a scene from Zane Grey's bestselling novel *Wildfire* (1917), in which the hero is depicted riding through a burning forest to save the girl he loves, who is strapped naked to the back of another horse.[42] McCarthy's unpicking of such ridiculousness begins with *All the Pretty Horses* of the title, which warns us of the centrality of storybook horses to their Western dreams. Thus, when at one stage Rawlins announces that 'A goodlookin horse is like a goodlookin woman ... They're always more trouble than what they're worth' McCarthy makes clear that he knows he is quoting second-hand dialogue; a feature that reminds us that the storybook Westerns responsible for his acculturation maintain a dubious relationship between pretty horses and pretty women (89). It is one such storybook fantasy that is brought to life in the character of Alejandro who literally rides into the text amidst a hyperbolically described cowboy paradise:

> A young girl came riding down the road and passed them and they ceased talking. She wore English riding boots and jodhpurs and a blue twill

hacking jacket ... and her black hair was loose under [her hat] and fell halfway to her waist and as she rode past she turned and smiled and touched the brim of her hat with her crop and the valqueros touched their hatbrims one by one down to the last of those who'd pretended not even to see her as she passed.

(94)

The boys are our focalizing agents and the attention to detail is forensic – a detailing of her riding gear (of which they approve) and her hair (Grady also falls in love with Magdalena's long black hair). Rawlins's comment – 'Did you see that little darling?' – conflates his admiration of both horse and rider, thereby reminding us of an uncomfortable cowboy cliché that McCarthy deconstructs through the romance with Grady. The affair is narrated from Grady's perspective, hence the aura of trashy pulp fiction (and also racial cleansing in which McCarthy freely participates[43]) that attends the description of Alejandro at the dance ('her neck as pale as porcelain' (123)), or in the lake ('She was so pale in the lake she seemed to be burning' (141)). This becomes more sinister when he is aligned with the stallion brought onto the range by Alejandro's father, Don Hector, to inseminate the herd. Up to this point his chosen method of horse breaking through whispering has suggested a more consensual relationship and therefore a purer vision of the cowboy myth, but his words to the stallion – 'I rule the mares ... it is I who brings you the mares from the mountains, the young mares, the wild and ardent mares' – reveals the sexual impulse gone awry in a form of control that foreshadows the pimping activities of Eduardo in *Cities of the Plain* (128). Such descriptions justify Rawlins's accusation that Grady is after the 'spread' rather than the girl, just another an Anglo-Turnerian imperialist dusted with cowboy glamour. However, McCarthy turns this Turnerian narrative on its head through Alejandra's demand that she be allowed to ride the stallion bareback. In stepping out of the role of silent, sultry senorita, she figuratively steps into an alternative narrative of spoilt schoolgirl enjoying a bit of cowboy rough. As she takes the reins, she also pushes their relationship from the realms of 'pretty horses' to those with 'veins pulsing under the wet hide' as she orchestrates their sexual liaisons (129). Significantly, to get down to the actual business of sex, the cowboy needs to get off his horse.

Don Hector and the Duena Alfonsa are amongst the adult mentors located throughout the Trilogy, whose function is to warn the boys of the dangers of their naive idealism and, in this particular instance, their disapproval of the relationship with Alejandro. The exchange with Don Hector brings Mexico into focus, not as a cartographical blank, but a country with its own history, mythology and sense of modernity. Bloodlines and breeding are all that matter to him, whether in horses, love and politics, which is why he admires Grady's method of taming horses by shaping rather than breaking their essential character. However, though Don Hector is happy to import a stallion to strengthen his breeding program, he is unwilling to extend the same privilege to Grady with regard his own daughter. For him the horse is not a symbol of a lost past, but part of a future that increasingly refuses to conform to Grady's idealism. Duena Alfonso is different because through both her gender and history, McCarthy introduces a competing and diverse narrative of romantic self-realization in the form of the 1910 Mexican Revolution. She is a romantic who has witnessed the catastrophe caused when dreams – which 'have an odd durability for something not quite real' – shatter on contact with reality. She was the youthful lover of one of the revolution's chief architects, Gustavo Madero, but was exiled to Paris by parents keen to protect their bloodlines, just as he was importing notions of social justice from the same city. Thus, McCarthy links the naivete of romantic lovers with a wider idealism, making clear that Grady, like Madero, must stop trying to impose alien myths upon a foreign country with its own history and mythology. Her broader lesson is that Grady, like those idealistic Mexicans, must reject the myths upon which he has constructed his life and accept the presence of other equally powerful narratives.

Grady's refusal to listen leads to his expulsion from the Hacienda (a second Fall) and the second half of the novel in which his narrative control is continually challenged by others who threaten him on both a physical and mythological level. Truth becomes narrative, a postmodern proposition that McCarthy makes intra-textually through the offer of the captain who arrests Grady for horse theft, to 'make the truth' of his confession before others do; it is a cynical proposal entirely at odds with Grady's belief that 'there is but one truth' (168). The captain's truth, like Grady's, is performative: he is continually assuming poses 'as if perhaps he'd admired [them] somewhere in others' and even has a sidekick who 'looked like an extra in a stage play reciting his only lines' (167, 261). He presents himself as 'the one when I go someplace then there is no laughing' – a figure like Eastwood's 'The Man with no Name' with whom Grady could sympathize (181). However, his confession that he earned his reputation by beating up a prostitute who humiliated him should act as a warning that he is not following a cowboy script in which respect is earned by cowboy nobility, but one governed by terror. Throughout his experiences in the Saltillo prison, Grady finds the 'truth' of his cowboy narrative under assault: when, on their journey there, Blevins is summarily executed, Grady is shocked, not because he cares for the victim, but because this behaviour doesn't happen in cowboy films. The same is true of his knife fight. Fighting, observes Lee Clark Mitchell, is central to the Western because it allows the protagonist to be literally deconstructed and rebuilt in accordance with a highly prescriptive version of cowboy masculinity: a form of regeneration through violence.[44] McCarthy's dining hall fight achieves the opposite aim, breaking down the theatricality of the cowboy performance to expose the bloody violence beneath. To the other diners, the fight is part of the spectacle with which the Western seems in thrall; seen from their perspective, the blood is a thing of beauty, emerging like a 'red boutonniere blossoming on the left pocket' of the hired assassin, and when it is all over they leave 'like theatre patrons anxious to avoid the crush'. For Grady, however, the experience has been viscerally different; the blood is not the theatrical variety but the kind that 'sloshed in his boots' (201).

At such a moment McCarthy seems to be manoeuvring his protagonist into greater self-understanding; but this, like Andrews's snow entrapment in *Butcher's Crossing*, or the immediate aftermath of the kid's bloody fight with the barman in *Blood Meridian*, proves false: the mythical glamour is overwhelming. His convalescence deconstructs another genre staple in which after a display of virtuous violence the cowboy is put back together by a female love interest. In the scenes of Billy the Kid tended by Rio (Jane Russell) in Howard Hughes's *The Outlaw* (1941), Georgiana ministering to Cal in William Berke's *Code of the West* (1947), or Angie Lowe to Hondo in John Farrow's *Hondo* (1953), men are confirmed as heroic and women admiring carers whose tenderness is hedged with the erotic. Both aesthetically and psychologically, Grady's hallucinatory convalescence has more in common with that of Captain Willard (Martin Sheen) at the hands of Marlon Brando's Colonel Kurtz in Coppola's *Apocalypse Now* (1979). Both provide exclusively male environments in which the drifting consciousness combines with paternal promptings to open up a form of introspection and the potential for rebirth. It is now that Grady's thoughts centre on the terrible experiences suffered by his father in a Japanese prisoner of war camp, tales of violence that he had always blocked out because they were incompatible with his hyper-masculine Western identity.

However, despite the potential for spiritual growth he decides to think 'about horses and they were always the right thing to think about', which suggests that although he now understands his father's pain, he wants, as the simple syntax suggests, to remain a child (204). Thus, upon his release, he is presented, like Andrews during the ride West at the close of *Butcher's Crossing*, displaying a peculiar mix of childish self-awareness. This is reinforced by McCarthy's presentation of Grady's reflections on events in Mexico in the form of a story told to a group of inquisitive and appreciative children: 'He told them how they (Grady and Rawlins) had come from another country, two young horsemen riding their horses, and that they had met with a third who had no money nor food to eat nor scarcely clothes to cover himself' (243). Significantly, he doesn't tell his story: the detached third person delivery suggests that he is already in the process of being immortalized in a communal 'corrido' – which is, of course, Grady's hope. In such songs, the cowboy overcomes all obstacles to get the girl, or he dies gloriously in his attempt. Grady has failed on both counts. Furthermore, his self-insertion into his own myth flies in the face of Alejandro's earlier attempt to cure Grady of his romanticism by showing him the spot where her grandfather (Gustavo Madero) had been murdered, a moment when, the narrator observes, 'there was no mother to cry. As in the corridos. Nor little bird that flew. Just the blood on the stones' (253). This is how idealism ends: in blood not songs. Grady ignores such warnings, McCarthy underlining his deafness by depicting him departing from Alejandro in the convertible car of an opera singer: he is determined to remain the operatic centre of his own tragic story (255).

Grady's return to Mexico, ostensibly in search of his lost horse, is calibrated to transform the reader's perception of his idealistically heroic status to that of the stubborn victim of his own narrative. The decision itself replaces introspection with a cliché of Western resolution in which the narrator happily participates:

> He sat the horse in the crossroads and by the light of the full moon read the names of towns burned into crateslats with a hot iron and nailed to a post ... He sat a long time. He leaned and spat. He looked toward the darkness in west. The hell with it, he said. I aint leavin my horse down here.
>
> (257)

As with all the momentous decisions in the novel, adherence to narrative – in this case since he can't have the girl, he'll have the horse – reinforced by a charade of cowboy gestures prevents Grady from either thinking or evolving. Where he was nonplussed by his mother's stage presence at the beginning of the novel, in the drama he creates in Mexico he knows all the lines and it is the supporting cast who are desperately trying to remember theirs. When, for example, he waits in the office of the captain who arrested him for horse theft, he adopts the stylized pose of boots on the desk, pistol at the ready, whilst the narrator adds the shading of the augmented-diegetic sound of the pistol cock and the maid who puts 'her hands over her ears and closed her eyes' (258). The captain, we are told, 'hadn't been told to put his hands up but he'd put them up anyway' in compliance with the familiar script, whilst his sidekick 'looked like an extra in a stageplay reciting his only lines' (259, 60). Throughout the encounter, McCarthy's detached third-person narration conjoined with parataxis and reported, rather than direct speech, combines to give the impression of participants performing in a tired narrative. This is particularly the case in the final gun battle, the heroic presentation of which is designed as a contrast with the squalid knife fight. The Mexican participants remain anonymous (mere stage props), it is the horses that are named and are given vivid personalities. They become the 'pretty horses' of cowboy folklore. When Grady is shot, his mount 'reared onto its hind legs' in typical cowboy fashion; when in full flight with the captain we are told the 'horse stood twisting like a circus horse and the captain must have sawed back on Redbo's reins' (269). The modal verb reminds us of our position as observer of this circus show and the degree to which the action is precipitated by our culturally endorsed expectations: the captain must have fallen back, and the horse reared because that's what they do in Westerns.

Does Grady evolve at all? There are moments, such as when awaking from a grubby bar fight following his rejection by Alejandro, when he is presented as more introspective. As he studies his swollen face in a mirror trying to piece together the events of the night before, we are told that his attacker had 'stood much as Rawlins had stood when last he saw him ... Who'd come to ruin no man's house. No man's daughter' (255). The identity of his assailant is secondary to his similarity to Rawlins, which prompts Grady to reflect that where his friend had ruined nothing, he had, through his affair with Alejandra, destroyed everything. In another example he shoots a doe and is struck by the combination of beauty and blood which he elides with 'Alejandra and the sadness he'd first seen in the slope of her shoulders which he'd presumed to understand and of which he knew nothing' (282). Now he does know: the world is beautiful, but at its core there is sadness, which is why he chooses to distance himself from it. Thus, it is in sadness and guilt rather than heroism that he becomes the lone rider of his dreams; a part of the mythology that all men admire but which only the lonely will follow. And it is this admiration that prevents him from evolving.

When he rides by a wedding in the town of Los Picos, we see him from the perspective of a 'man sitting alone on one of the benches' who 'raised one hand to the pale rider passing' (285). We are guided to feel pity for the wedding party – the suit is too big for the groom and the bride is embarrassed. They are stiff and formal, prematurely aged; this is the fate that Grady has narrowly avoided through a choice that the old man now salutes. McCarthy repeats the point when Grady rides into Langtry and asks a couple of men bent over a pickup truck the date. The narrative speculates that they feel themselves in the presence of a more authentic version of masculinity than that suggested by their socket-wrench: 'He must have appeared to them some apparition out of the vanished past because he jostled the other with his elbow and they both looked' (287). And their admiration is amplified by a complicit narrator watching them watching him as he rides away. Most damaging, however, is the judgement of the judge who tries him for horse theft. Like Judge Holden, his judgement is narrative rather than moral, claiming when Grady has delivered his account: 'I don't believe anybody could make up the story you just now got done tellin us' (288). However, it is the prosecution's claim of 'mistaken identity' that is most illuminating. For though Grady's cowboy identity validates a 'story' in which he is the only moral actor, he is not a real cowboy but a boy trapped in an imaginary performance of a fictional genre. In many ways, therefore, the judge's exoneration comes less from Grady's innocence than his respect for a life lived indebted to living a storybook pretence.

Like Andrews, Grady has become the lonesome cowboy of his imagination, a role that McCarthy pastiches through his dramatization of the traditional cowboy ride into the sunset. The chiasmus in 'The desert he rode was red and red the dust he raised' syntactically returns us to the beginning of the novel and Grady's ride along the imaginary Comanche ghost road. As the dust and sun 'coppers' his face, McCarthy visually reinforces Grady's resemblance to the displaced Native Americans, not the vanishing race of his imagination, but the straggling old men crouching amongst the pump jacks who appear like refugees from *Butcher's Crossing* (301). Grady, like Andrews before him, is riding West with a vision narrowed by the experiences that the novel has narrated. Where previously the young Adam had 'ten thousand worlds for the choosing' he now just has 'the world to come' (302). And even this remains conjectural, for as the mirror imagery throughout the novel has made clear, he is trapped within a historical narrative that makes movement forward impossible.

III

At the heart of *The Crossing*, as with *Butcher's Crossing*, lies the act of crossing borders to makes oneself anew. The Parham family, we are told, had quit the bones of sister and grandmother to ride South, Billy carrying baby Boyd in the bow of his saddle naming 'to him features of the landscape and birds and animals in both Spanish and English' (3). Like Adam in a new Eden, his act of naming confers meaning, but the dual labelling intimates an existential anxiety. For McCarthy, the act of naming confirms Billy's unacknowledged participation in a wider colonial project in which despite his romantic belief that 'you could ride clear to Mexico and not strike a crossfence' the land has been linguistically subjugated (3). John Steinbeck's narrator of *East of Eden* (1952) claims that 'when the Spaniards came they had to give everything a name. This is the first duty of an explorer – a duty and a privilege'.[45] Within the context of the novel, his 'Adam *Trask*' singularly fails in this *task* and consequently fails to create an Eden. Steinbeck goes on to note that 'the names of places carry a charge of the people who named them, reverent or irreverent, descriptive, either poetic or disparaging' and 'the Americans had a greater tendency to name places for people' where the Spanish named after Saints, geographical features, or 'the way the expedition felt at the time'.[46] Wallace Stegner explores the power of naming in his essay 'A Sense of Place' written just a couple of years before McCarthy's novel, in which he notes: 'Once, as George Stewart reminded us in *Names on the Land*, the continent stretched away westward without names. It had no places in it until people had named them, and worn the names smooth with use.' Thus, Daniel Boone killing a bear at a specific spot was not significant until it was remembered as Bear Run in a cultural narrative comprising of 'history, ballads, yarns, legends, or monuments'.[47]

For Stegner, Stewart understood that the process of naming allows us to understand both the land and ourselves, so that we can only know who we are when we know where we are. To critics like Elizabeth Cook-Lynn, Stegner's 'sense of place' is legitimized solely by discourse which enacts a linguistic emptying ('the continent stretched away westward without names') that effectively precedes and masks the more brutal military erasure.[48] The idea that nothing is understood until it is named depends upon a conceptual understanding and linguistic apparatus that is Anglo-centric. McCarthy intervenes in this contentious area through Billy's act of dual naming, which enacts Anglo conquest whilst simultaneously acknowledging the porosity of linguistic borders. Significantly, he uses Spanish labels – a language, as lexicographer Jay Arthur has noted, better suited to the aridity of the Western landscape than a language designed to describe temperate England.[49] There are, however, no Native American names. Thus, as with Grady's night ride, the physical removal of the indigenous population is reinforced by their linguistic erasure. Indeed, Tom Lynch points to the evidence accumulated by Barry Lopez's *Home Ground: Language for an American Landscape* (2006) to conclude that whilst Anglo settlers have appropriated Hispanic words – 'canyon', 'mesa', 'playa' – and woven them into their conceptualization of a strange geography, they have been poor in borrowing indigenous terms, allowing the language, like the figure of the 'Indian' itself, to 'vanish'.[50]

For Billy, as for Grady, finding an identity in the New West means looking back to the Old West, which he naively hopes to achieve by seeing through the eyes of others. Optics are once again central to McCarthy's symbolic structure, but not the mirrors that announce Grady's self-reflexive entrapment, or the Kid's witnessing of the barbarity that challenges Emersonian romanticism. The eyes that interest Billy belong to the wolf that he frees and the 'Indian' he discovers outside his parents' homestead; eyes which he romantically believes have looked upon the vanishing West. In the latter's 'antique eyes' he sees himself 'twinned' and wandering, lost in a maze illuminated by a sinking red sun – what is, in effect, the world of the novel that follows (6). They contrast with his father's blue eyes, which are 'very beautiful half hid away in the leathery seams of his face. As if there were something there that the hardness of the country had not been able to touch' – the eyes of a man who works the land but is not part of it (16). In rendering the Native American simply a cipher for white concerns, Kollin argues that once again McCarthy seems guilty of the kind of marginalization that plagues the genre as a whole.[51] Thus, Billy's 'Indian' is transformed into a Vizenorian symbol of 'Indianness' – a condition that has nothing to do with the Native American in front of him and everything to do with his desire for an 'authentic' connection to the past.[52] Louis Owens observes that 'the American Indian in the world of consciousness is a treasured invention, a gothic artefact evoked... out of the dark reaches of the continent to replace the actual native, who, painfully problematic in real life, is supposed to have long since vanished'.[53] The Indian becomes a gothic invention without an original, representative of a form of cultural authenticity in the process of 'vanishing' (a euphemistic trope that removes the brutality of erasure). However, Billy's Indian (unlike Grady's Comanche) has not vanished and entered the realm of nostalgia, but is a tattered remnant who is sinisterly alive and will later return to murder his family. It's just that Billy, unlike the reader, cannot see this – a myopia that will characterize the childishness of his engagement with the West throughout the novel. His blindness is exposed intra-textually by the bizarre story of a brave revolutionary soldier who has his eyes sucked out by a vindictive guard. As his eyes shrivel on their stalks, it becomes a grotesque dramatization of an idealized world (a world worth fighting for) in the act of vanishing, which is analogous to the position of McCarthy's young cowboys.[54]

The wolf section of the novel (published by *Esquire* under the title 'The Wolf Trapper') has antecedents in Jack London's *Call of the Wild* (1903) and, more pertinently, William Faulkner's classic story 'The Bear'. Faulkner's is a coming of age tale in which the protagonist's invitation to join the bear hunters is a coded initiation to the world of men. Faulkner challenges the familiar narrative through the intervention of a half Native American mentor who encourages the boy to observe rather than kill the bear, which functions as an embodiment of the wilderness. Thus, Barcley Owens notes, 'the bear quest transforms the boy into a man who empathizes with his quarry more than with the hunters'.[55] McCarthy's wolf functions in a similar manner – 'books are' after all 'made from other books' – but in his retelling the emphasis is on the wolf as symbol of the West's relationship with its past. Old Mr. Johnson, the respected disseminator of cowboy folklore in *Cities of the Plains*, equates their passing with the loss of the values of the West in general: 'When things are gone they're gone. They aint coming back ... I didn't know that you could poison that' (*COP*, 126). 'Poisoning' is presented as an illegitimate form of pest control because it removes the wolf whilst destroying the mythological legacy. McCarthy has already 'poisoned' its legacy in *Blood Meridian* by allowing it to become a venerated part of a Darwinian ecosystem that exonerates the predation of the scalp hunters. In a novel in which emotion is rare, only the howl of the wolf causes the hunters to 'smile' in mutual recognition (*BM*, 129,117). In *The Crossing*, however, it has been brought back again through an exclusively masculine nostalgia. Billy's father acknowledges the need to protect his cows, but determines to use those trappers who sustain the wolf's folkloric status. Mr Echols is a softened version of Judge Holden, the dusty contents of his cabin – the jars that contained 'the inward parts of the beast' and traps that looked like an 'Astrolabe or sextant' – represent an attempt to make sense of the wolf, which has the effect of elevating it to a mythological status (22). This is reinforced by the ersatz mysticism of Don Arnulfo who likens the wolf to a snowflake: 'If you want to see it you have to see it on its own ground. If you catch it you lose it' (46). The declamatory register, the untranslated Spanish and the conflation of direct and indirect speech allow McCarthy to record that 'the boy didn't know if he understood or not'. He doesn't, since Billy interprets the invocation to cross over and 'see it on its own ground' as an invitation to return the wolf to Mexico, which becomes the West of his imagination. The wolf slots into simple symbolic binaries that distinguish Old from New West, Wild vs Civilized, Cowboy vs Homesteader – its release from entrapment figuratively releasing Billy from a world from which he feels alienated into something new. However, this is another act of misguided idealism and of the two, it is the wolf who proves more maturely adaptive to circumstance. She has already overcome the old binaries that once shaped her behaviour and abides by 'the new protocols' that allow her to defy borders by crossing into new territory; an act that contrasts with the unreflective pull of nostalgia that characterizes Billy's momentous decision to release her (25). He chooses the wolf and the vanishing world to which he believes she has been witness; a world, ironically, that she had rejected by coming north in search of community and a future for her children.

Returning the wolf is presented as a 'boys' own adventure' in which Billy engages in the performative rituals he associates with the cowboy. Through them McCarthy unpicks some of the ironies of the West's relationship with its past and particularly its blindness (optics remain important) to other cultural practices. In the American leg, the wolf evokes a combination of fear, pity and nostalgia, dramatized symbolically through Billy's stop-off at one particular ranch. At first there is fear as the rancher sets his dogs on the trespassers; then, wisecracking mutual respect; finally pity as the rancher instructs his wife to fix up the wolf before restraining her with a 'dog collar with the rancher's name' (72). The Wild West is feared, mastered, possessed and re-animated by nostalgia. When Billy leaves, the rancher leans on his gate watching the wolf disappearing into the darkness, her bandaged foot appearing as some 'pale djinn'. He is, like Billy's father, trapped in a domesticated and restrictive world envying those ghosts of a childishly nostalgic past.

Once in Mexico, however, the wolf is woven into a more complex set of competing narratives, which undermine Billy's simple story of redemption through release. She becomes the fairy-tale monster who, according to one witness, had 'eaten many schoolchildren', and to another the pet of 'a young boy who had run away naked into the woods' (102). She is also put on display as an exhibit in a fairground booth, which reminds us of the economic exploitation missing from Billy's symbolic projection. Finally, she becomes part of a wolf-baiting spectacle, which balances our pity with a stinging critique of Billy's idealism. It is Billy's fantasy, along with the wolf, that is tethered to the stake in this scene. The list of increasingly threatening dogs, ending in the diabolical Airedales, reminds us of the brutality recorded in *Blood Meridian* that has been expunged from Billy's West. Furthermore, McCarthy's careful detailing of the local notaries decked out in the 'gaudy attire' of 'spangles' and 'silver braid' suggests the presence of an alternative, equally childish narrative (the clothes seem to have come from a child's dressing up box) in which the wolf performs a vital symbolic function (106). This point is made clearly by the young son of the hacendado (dressed in a similarly gaudy braided jacket and sash) who reminds Billy that though the 'wolf knew nothing of boundaries' they had both crossed one when they entered Mexico, which is a country with his own culture and traditions: 'You think that this country is some country you can come here and do what you like' (119). From the minute they crossed the border Billy's fantasy has relied on his ability to ignore the country he is in (at one stage a band of pilgrims is scattered as their pack-mules take fright at the wolf (84)), but in the wolf-pit he is forced to face it. When Billy leaves the ring, he abandons the wolf to their narrative. However, his return and execution of the wolf is both an act of humanity and a symbolic attempt to take back control by figuratively drawing to a close this particular version of his Western story.

Having killed the wolf Billy takes her place and escapes to the mountains to be reborn as 'the child he never was' (129). Once again, the symbolism of rebirth and identity construction is conjoined with the presence of a particular landscape:

> He crossed through a high pass where the way was so narrow that the rocks bore old scars of wagonhubs and below the pass were scattered stone cairns, the mojoneras de muerte of that country where travelers had been slain by Indians years before ... Along the face of the stone bluffs were old pictographs of men and animals and suns and moons as well as other representations that seemed to have no referent in the world although they once may have. He sat in the sun and looked over the country to the east ... that was once seafloor and the small pieced fields and the new corn greening in the old lands of the Chichimeca where the priests had passed and soldiers passed and the missions fallen into the mud ... all of it waiting like a dream for the world to come to be, world to pass. He saw a single vulture hanging motionless in some high vector that the wind had chosen for it. He saw the smoke of a locomotive passing slowly downcountry over the plain forty miles always.
>
> (134–5)

The landscape is a palimpsest of Western signifiers – stone cairns, wagon trails, fallen missions, sites of Indian massacres, ancient pictographs and the residue of ancient inland seas. Looking east Billy registers a world of ephemerality existing only in a dream of nostalgia which points both forward to the world of modernity (symbolized by the distant smoke of the locomotive) and backward (the motionless vulture). In such surroundings he is able to contextualize his own recent acts within a heroic Western tradition; he sings his father's songs and becomes the 'pale rider' of his own quest. And yet, though Billy's reflections are rooted in greening corn and cowboy ballads, the language in which they are expressed reveals a postmodern anxiety concerning authenticity and simulation that seems to have more in common with Baudrillard than either history or Hollywood. He, like the ancient drawings, seems to 'have no referent in the world' but instead be trapped like the vulture in 'some high vector' in an artificially resurrected system of signs that are not 'imitations' but a substitution of 'the real for the real itself'.[56] The success of his rebirth, therefore, like that of Grady and Andrews before him, becomes dependent upon his ability to decode the signs upon which he constructs his identity.

Unfortunately, Billy, like Grady, is a very bad semiotician. When he watches a group of itinerant players perform Pagliacci (a 'play within a play' about an opera company of clowns) he is unsure whether the behaviour of the mules is scripted and whether the onstage murder is real (230). Like Grady, he therefore retreats to a cowboy script, replacing the wolf (a silent but symbolically essential prop) with his brother, Boyd. He is, as his name suggests, a boyish version of Billy whose performance of cowboy ritual verges in parody. Together they reinforce each other's playacting: their greeting after years of absence and the murder of their parents offers their own version of scripted self-reliance: 'Are you ready to go? he said / Yeah said Boyd. Just waitin on you' (171). Throughout their Mexican quest we are continually reminded that they are engaged in a performance without a 'referent in the world'. When a dusty rider emerges from a shallow lake like a character from *Blood Meridian* to ask them who they are and where they are going, he claims that they are like a mirage before conceding 'you aint who I thought you was' (174). They aren't; they are childish runaways not Shane: simulations of fictionalities. Significantly, when the rider invites Billy to observe his party as they ride off, they appear as a mirage – laying bear the self-reflexive nature of their shared performance (174). Throughout Billy and Boyd's Mexican venture we are continually made aware that we are watching a Western (it is a visual experience that reads like a Hollywood B Movie) and its performance by two unsophisticated boys. When they stop at a waterhole which, we are told, presents a history of use stretching from Tarahumara Indians through 'armored Spaniards and hunters and trappers', the ironic third person voice observes that 'two pale and wasted orphans from the north in outsized hats were easily accommodated' (193). There are times when Billy seems to recognize that he is play-acting; the mirrors that in *All the Pretty Horses* had symbolized Grady's imprisonment, now become a means of deconstructing his identity. At one stage as they ride into town, we are told that 'Billy was watching the reflections of the two riders passing in the glass of the building's window across the street where the gaunted horses slouched by segments through the wonky panes ... and realized that the rider of the head of the unprepossessing parade was he himself' (195–6). The 'pale riders' of their romantic imagination are splintered into disjointed parts and Billy, Lear-like, finds himself head of an 'unprepossessing parade' of ghostly horses and malnourished kids. Such revelatory moments are rare – inserted into the narrative to challenge our reading, like the truck full of itinerant Mexican workers who drive through the middle of the carefully choreographed standoff between the boys and the men sent to retrieve their horses. The truck is a reminder of modernity; the workers are the reality of ranching, not the glamour represented by the boys, and they dismiss Billy as a 'boy sitting with the shotgun' (244). Not only does Billy fail to read such signs, but he is also, like Shane, the victim of a childish adulation that prevents his self development. The same truck later picks up the injured Boyd whilst Billy makes his escape on horseback from chasing riders. Now it is Boyd who understands the bloody reality of Western violence; the bullets that seem to have little effect on Shane really hurt!

Signs and symbols – old photographs, rising suns, bones and wrecked airplanes – dominate the last part of narrative, interrogating how we construct a Western identity. The living room of Billy's elderly Texan neighbour, Mr. Sanders, is lined with sepia-tinted pictures of men with rifles 'sitting among cardboard cactus in a photographer's studio'. He also treasures an ashtray from the 'Chicago World's Fair which reads 1833–1933, A Century of Progress' (344–5). Ironically, there has been no progress in this room, which both memorializes and recreates the West as an emotional lifebelt. However, the warnings are here. The 'historical photographs' are posed using archetypal cowboy signifiers that blur the distinction between 'artifice' and 'authenticity'. Is the rifle as fake as the cactus? Gerald Vizenor's study of the highly stylized pictures of Native Americans taken by the photographer Edward Curtis leads him to ask why contemporaries should treasure pictures of their ancestors posing in 'authentic' but borrowed attire in order to represent themselves as 'real' subjects for the photographer. He offers no answer.[57] McCarthy's answer is playful: he notes the 'haunted eyes' of the subjects 'like people photographed at gunpoint' to suggest that the subjects haven't bought into their Western identity as much as surrendered to it (344). These pictures mix with others that further challenge our notions of the West: there is a picture of John Slaughter, an historical Texas lawman who slaughtered an Indian camp and brought back an infant Indian wrapped in an 'election poster'. McCarthy's inclusion suggests a parable of Western exploitation at odds with that presented by Turner at the 'Chicago World's Fair': first slaughter the Indians, then rape the land and its women, all of which is sanctioned by democratic values. Another of the pictures is of James Autry, not the 'singing cowboy' Gene, but a petty criminal with the soubriquet the 'cowboy' who was executed in 1984 for murdering a convenience store clerk. The pictures 'bleed into one another' to suggest the cowboy's gradual degradation in a century of violence without the concomitant Turnerian promise of progress.

Billy's return home coincides with the Second World War and the emergence of a new set of masculine codes. Because of a weak heart, he is unable to sign up: symbolically, having been heartbroken by missing the Wild West, he now faces missing the next milestone in the shaping of the American male. McCarthy illustrates Billy's alienation through two tense barroom confrontations. Both deploy similar narrative architecture – verbal goading, expectant silences, dangerous drunkenness, wreaths of cigarette smoke, shadowed expressions – but Billy's sense of himself differs in each. The first takes place in a dingy Texas bar where Billy is accused of being a coward for failing to enlist by a barman and drunken soldier. Billy's cowboy repertoire of terse, wisecracking one-liners and performance signifiers – 'he pushed back his hat with his thumb and ordered a beer' – remain the same, but everything else has changed (347). 'Uniform dont mean nothin to him' the soldier complains, the barman adding 'it'd mean something if it had that risin sun on the collar' (349). Costume has always been significant to Billy's masculine identity (we are told that he entered the town like a 'ruined dandy'), but it has always been aligned with the redness of the setting sun, not the rising sun of this new Frontier. Behaving as a coward goes against everything Billy stands for, but he does not have the script to deal with such provocation. He therefore manufactures a suitably Western confrontation upon his final return to Mexico, during which the narrator's overwrought participation transforms pastiche to parody. The bar is dingy and full of drunken card players who 'looked to be posed for some album of outlawry' (363). As Billy enters the music stops, the musicians leave and Billy, having 'pushed his hat back slightly on his head', proceeds to goad the players through a tense drinking game. The card playing, the dusty mescal bottle, the sullen and sunken eyes are all props with which he is familiar, but even he recognizes that they are playing out a ritual. At one stage he even checks with one of the sober drinkers whether his drunk companion will adhere to the script or 'will he shoot me in the back?' (362). As in Texas, however, Billy finds his cowboy code overshadowed. Lost in his own performance, he is unable to read the broader context in which his actions resonate, that the drunk he is goading is a disgruntled revolutionary for whom Billy is a northern colonizer rather than Western cowboy. When, in the tense denouement, Billy walks to the door and, against all advice, turns, he expects to be faced with a Colt and a challenge to draw. Instead, he finds himself confronted with a chest bared to show the wounds received in the battles of the Mexican revolution: the iconography of a different script. And yet even here there is an air of camp; the shirt snaps are worn as if from previous theatrical displays, reinforcing our sense of a more generalized crisis of masculinity. When Billy removes his hat (a suitably cowboy demonstration of emotion), he is acknowledging both the patriot's suffering and also the quality of his performance: both are trapped in genre rituals that inhibit real connection.[58]

Billy's narrative bind is illustrated clearly by his return to Mexico to reclaim his missing brother. He discovers that he is dead and his story is being celebrated in a 'corrido' that mythologizes him as the pale cowboy who fights for justice and dies in the arms of his lover (381). It is all Billy has ever wanted, but he is troubled by his knowledge of the less than heroic 'truth' of Boyd's earlier gunfight, and the lies underpinning his Western apotheosis. The problematic relationship between 'truth' and 'narrative' and the 'artefacts' transformed into cultural signifiers which underpin them both is elevated to an epistemological level by McCarthy's inclusion of the curious scene in which Billy meets a group of gypsies transporting the wreckage of a plane out of the mountains. It is one of two identical planes that have been requested by a cowboy who is grieving the death of his pilot son (415). The symbolism asks us to consider the relationship between the 'authenticity' of the 'artefact' (does it matter if it is the correct plane?) and the 'truth' of the 'narrative' we weave around it. As one of the gypsies explains, because we can never know the past, we are forced to make our own history from 'bits of wreckage. Some bones. The words of the dead' (411). It is an apt description of the scavenging activities undertaken by McCarthy's protagonists in their construction of a fantasy West, and a warning against Billy's own act of reclamation.

Boyd's bones lie buried in a small graveyard, but as artefacts they are incidental to the mythology that has accrued around them. Billy is told that the song that celebrates Boyd's exploits 'does not owe its allegiance to the truths of history but to the truths of men' so that 'even if the guerito in the song is your brother he is no longer your brother. He cannot be reclaimed' (386). But reclamation, whether of wolves, horses or brothers, is part of Billy's reclaiming of the West in general – hence his determination to dig up Boyd's bones and return them to Texas for burial. It is a magnificent gesture that recalls Woodrow Call's return of Gus McCrea's body in McMurtry's *Lonesome Dove*. But it is absurd outside the context of the Western, a local sheriff making it clear to a shocked Billy that 'You caint just travel around the country buryin people' before harrying him to apply to a judge for 'a death certificate' (422). What is really being judged here is how we reclaim the vanishing West: we have Judge Holden's careful cataloguing of Western artefacts (plants, animals and people) before they are erased and reanimated in his Darwinian narrative of blood and destruction; we have the judge who is desperate to believe Grady's cowboy story in order to bolster his own Western romance; but upon Billy's return, Western romance hits the buffers of health and safety, reclamation is detached from artefact, and Billy is revealed for the poseur he is.

The fate of McCarthy's cowboys is a shared restlessness and alienation which is made clear through their participation in distorted versions of the long lonely ride into the sunset. Where Grady, like Will Andrews before him, has been chastened by his Mexican exploits and rides 'West' with determination tempered by deeper self-knowledge, Billy's experiences have left him shattered. He began his quest with the wolf; by the end of the novel his only companion is a mongrel whose signs of misuse and distress are an analogue for the similarly troubled state of the cowboy. The final image of him weeping in the spectral glare of the Trinity nuclear test is one of the few passages when Billy is unobserved and he allows his cowboy mask to slip. What is revealed is his grief for the death of everything that he has loved and that has given his life meaning – the wolf, his parents, his brother and ultimately the West.

IV

The third part of McCarthy's *Trilogy* is unusual in that it preceded the other two instalments and began life as an unsuccessful film script. Thus, as Philip Snyder notes, there is a cinematic element baked into its construction: dialogue rather than an authoritative narrative voice propels the action forward and there is a focus on interiors [brothels, dark corridors, morgues] as opposed to wide open spaces.[59] However, though written first, our reading is shaped by a knowledge of the preceding volumes, the repetitious nature of which (Grady gets into another nasty knife fight; he falls in love with another Mexican beauty; his failure to save Blevins foreshadows Billy's failure to save him) presents the two central character as still locked in their cowboy fantasy and moving towards an inescapable conclusion. *Cities of the Plains* offers closure, but the characters of Billy and Grady that appear in its pages (and have remained separate in the preceding volumes) differ so wildly from their former selves that some critics have complained of narrative inconsistency.[60] However, Billy's bitterness (he is only 28 but we are told he looks 48) derives from his increasing suspicion of the cowboy fantasy: 'I used to think rawhidin a bunch of bony cattle in some outland country would be just as close to heaven as a man was likely to get. I wouldn't give you much for it now' (77). As such he becomes McCarthy's means of critiquing Grady's continuing self-destructive romanticism. For Grady, now aged nineteen, appears in comparison a walking anachronism. Where formerly his behaviour was romantically misguided, its repetition in this novel highlights his fatal stubbornness.[61] He lacks the postmodern sensibility acquired by Billy, which allows him to mimic a role from which he is ironically detached whilst aware of its absurdity.[62] Thus, the resonance of Billy's demand at the outset: 'Where's the all-American cowboy at?'

The simple answer is that he's in the brothel eying up the girls; a mythical degradation reinforced through the transformation of the sunset that once illuminated their ride West into the neon bar lights. The free range has been replaced by the brothels in El Paso and Juarez – contemporary versions of the Biblical Sodom and Gomorrah (the 'Cities of the Plain'), mythical cities whose cultural resonance, much like the West itself, outweighs their historical presence. They are notorious for their destruction; Lot's wife was turned into a pillar of salt for looking back on the event, which once again alerts us to the fatal consequences of nostalgia.[63] Unfortunately, looking backwards is what the cowboys do in this novel – if only to the manufactured identities that made up the first two parts of the *Trilogy*. On our first sight of Grady he is observing a prostitute – Magdalena (herself a degradation of Christ's Magdalen) in a mirror trying to conjure up Alejandra. We have travelled a long way from the pier glass and dreams of Grandad's West.

Grady is one of a group of cowboys (McCarthy uses pronouns so the men remain interchangeable performers in a cowboy narrative) living out a *Bonanza* fantasy on the 'sorriest land' that the army could find to carry out nuclear tests. They are presided over by a patriarchy that has been emasculated on a mythological and domestic level. The only woman is the idealized dead Margaret, wife of the owner, Mac, and niece of its spiritual head, the totemic veteran cowboy, Old Mr Johnson. She hangs over the ranch as a symbol of a particular feminine ideal, and is conjoined with another lost Margaret – Billy's younger sister – whose grave becomes the object of an unsuccessful quest at the end of both *The Crossing* and this novel (*C* 419, *COP*, 289). Women, and this includes Magdalena, become symbols of loss and longing, which through their elision with ranches (Billy's place, the Hacienda and Mac's ranch) become representative of nostalgia for the Old West. Old Mr Johnson is a living connection: he has witnessed the change of the West 'from the oil lamp and horse and buggy to jet planes and the atomic bomb' and his experiences with his niece (and wolves) have taught him 'that when things are gone they're gone. They aint coming back' (106, 9). The story plays out this judgement. He revisits the past through what the narrator describes as 'stories of the old west that once was' – a curious syntactical arrangement that draws attention to the fact that despite the authenticity guaranteed by Johnson's age and experience, the West is first and foremost a narrative creation (91). His relationship with the present, by contrast, is spectral, his sleepwalking in long johns and Stetson symbolizing the degradation of the cowboy in general. To Billy, already entertaining doubts about the myth, Johnson's Lear-like performances are a 'pitiful' sight; to Grady, however, he evokes a combination of pity and reverence, largely because this ghostly, lost figure seems to say something about his own position (104).

The land, which in the previous instalments had occasionally offered a dramatic backdrop to their fantasies, is depicted in this volume as littered with evidence of human activity – litter, roads, constructions sites – which problematizes, rather than reinforces, their cowboy identity. The cowboys now drive trucks, the 'blood red sun' reflected in the astonished eyes of the jack rabbits caught in their headlights, which in turn reflects the cowboys' own paralysis before the glare of modernity. Indeed, when Troy (his name suggestive of the archetypal cowboy) tells the story of how during an all-night drive he hit so many rabbits that their decapitated heads formed a grotesque gallery in the truck grille, we sense that another trophy to be added is the all-American cowboy (21). Billy, whose three trips to Mexico have taught him the futility of romantic reclamation, is aware that 'this country aint the same. Nor anything in it' but continues to go through the motions of what he acknowledges is childish and increasingly unsustainable role play because he is incapable of finding an alternative (78). McCarthy dramatizes this self-deception through the cowboys's ritualistic hunt for an animal that has attacked their cattle, which they romanticize into a 'lion hunt'. Once in the mountains, the landscape does its mythical work, and Johnson's notion 'of the old west that once was' is reborn through the narrative detailing of a romantically complicit narrator: 'They sat against a rock bluff high in the Franklins with a fire before them that heeled in the wind and their figures cast up upon the rocks behind them enshadowed the petroglyphs carved there by other hunters a thousand years before' (87).

Momentarily his audience of lost young men see themselves, like the hunting dogs that have been bred for generations by their sides, as part of a Western legacy. Dogs are symbolic in this scene but not in the way the boys think. Two years before the publication of the novel, the *Denver Post* ran a headline that drew attention to the invention of the 'Prairie-Dog Vacuum' which literally sucked these 'hated and hunted' vermin out of their burrows and into a tank on the back of a truck. It is heralded as a 'Dream solution' that stands in opposition to the dream of McCarthy's young cowboys.[64] When one of their dogs returns blood spattered, they can only conceive of its condition in relation to a confrontation with a lion; like Billy's wolf, they confer upon it the status of 'witness to things they could only imagine' (91). As the dog snuggles up to Grady – who is at the time whimsically preoccupied with his view of Mexico (and by extension Magdalena) – it becomes clear that it is his dream in particular that is under threat. For the lacerations have been caused by a pack of wild dogs, another debasement of their Western dream and a graphic foreshadowing of the wounds caused to Grady by Eduardo's knife. We have moved a long way from the imaginary West secured by Billy's return of the wolf to the wild, which is made ironically apparent through McCarthy's choice of the same linguistic palette to depict their mounted dog hunting as that used to describe Billy's pastoral interlude in *The Crossing*. Only Billy is aware of the irony – 'Dogropers ... I knew it'd come to this' (164). Grady remains blind, figuratively suggested by his decision to blindfold his horse with his jacket in an act of protection, and by his decision to take one of the cubs for a pet (166). The expert horse breaker has become dog trainer; like the mongrel that befriends Billy at the close of *The Crossing*, it suggests the ignominious position to which the cowboy has descended in cultural consciousness.

Throughout the *Trilogy* Grady's cowboy credentials have rested on his skill with horses, in the pursuit of which his normal performance of cowboy taciturnity gives rise to a string of aphoristic speeches punctuated with notions of 'truth' and 'justice'. However, in this volume the utterances that previously suggested wisdom come to sound trite and representative of a limited moral outlook. Troy notes that horses are crazy because they 'got two brains, He don't see the same thing out of both eyes at once', which becomes a pertinent metaphor for Grady's increasingly blinkered attitudes (150). This is illustrated most clearly by his obsession with re-breaking a horse from which he is thrown four times and eventually lamed: the revered horse breaker is reduced to the spectacle of circus clown (20). It is presented more obliquely in his transformation from excellent chess player – for which his knight is dominant – to serial loser, and finally in his obsessive pursuit Magdalena. Juraz, Billy claims, 'ain't no place for a cowboy' because both his intuition and moral code do not work in the city at night (59). It is cowboy folklore amplified intra-textually through discussions about riding at night – a quality that Johnson conceives of as the true mark of a cowboy. Grady's youthful night ride along the Comanche trail was formative in the construction of his Western identity, but for Billy night riding is irresponsible bravado because the rider is likely to get his horse 'snakebit' – which is what happens, metaphorically, in the brothels of Juraz (181).[65] Although in the brothel Grady tries to exercise the skills that have made him essential at horse auctions – looking hard into the faces of the women on display in an attempt to interpret 'who they might be behind the caked sizing and the rouge' – they remain a mystery (55). He is trapped in a world of interiors within a narrative over which he has diminishing control. In this world, he is conscious of appearing fraudulent (his insistence that the shoeshine blackens the edges of his boots aligns him with coverup practised on the lame filly that he refused to train) because it is Eduardo (the calm, confident brothel keeper) who dominates the role play.

Eduardo's role in this novel is that of anti-cowboy: he wears silk not denim; he is loquacious rather than taciturn; he pimps not quests; his 'pardner' is not a cowboy but an 'incubus of uncertain proclivity' (183). He is constantly located in blue interiors in contrast to the cowboys' green exteriors, striking poses 'he had perhaps admired or read of' amidst furniture that 'looked as if had been brought in and set in place solely for the purpose of this scene' (79, 134). He situates himself in the world by embracing the 'new protocols' and disparages Grady's escapist fantasies, observing that 'your kind cannot bear that the world be ordinary. That it contain nothing save what stands before one' (253). It echoes Judge Holden's warning that 'your heart's desire is to be told some mystery. The mystery is that there is no mystery' (*BM* 252) and MacDonald's condemnation of Andrews's naivety in *Butcher's Crossing*: 'You always think there's something to find out … Well, there's nothing' (*BC* 250). These generalized existential pronouncements are given more specific resonance in this novel through Eduardo's role as pimp and lover, in which capacity he offers a dark commentary on Grady's shared love of Magdalena and the shadowy world of cowboy sexuality in general. As such he makes explicit the sexual dysfunction that has thus far remained implicit within the Trilogy.

V

Women and Sex have remained largely absent from this account of Grady and Billy's Western Odyssey, but, as was seen in *Butcher's Crossing*, sexual relationships provide both a measure of maturation and a searing indictment of the cowboy code. For all their macho swagger, the cowboy heroes around whom McCarthy's protagonists construct their identity provide suspect role models when it comes to relationships with women. The mentors who embody the legacy of the West and dispense gnomic advice on free will and destiny are silent on relationships. When Billy confides to one elderly rancher 'I've got to say that I don't understand the first thing about [women]' he knows that he is in good company (*C* 352). His relationship with the she-wolf makes this discomfort metaphorically apparent. The descriptions of them staring into each other's firelit eyes read like an embryonic love affair, but the way she is gagged, tied up in an elaborate series of constricting knots and then ritually slaughtered symbolizes much of his, and by extension the cowboys, discomfort around women (*C* 79). They are the silent objects of male apprehension, which McCarthy emphasizes through the wolf's transformation into Magdalena, who is, as Nell Sullivan observes, gagged and strapped to hospital tables for her own good by men who venerate her as a beautiful and vulnerable object of attention (*COP* 183, 229).[66] Billy remains furtive around women. When, during his pastoral interlude, he is introduced to a woman we surmise is being offered for sex, his horrified response, like Andrews before him, is to mount his horse and ride off (*C* 132). When he glimpses the Prima Donna bathing, we are told that 'his heart labouring under his shirt' caused him to remove his hat (his Stetson being incompatible with such emotions) and that as 'the sun rose and the river ran as before but nothing was the same nor did he think it ever would be' (*C* 220). Except that for Billy nothing changes; the deliberately sententious description of his momentary arousal reflects his preference for narrative over emotions, particularly when lensed through the masculine prism of the rising sun.

Grady's pursuit of women is reducible to a quest; they are exotic, young, unattainable ideals rather than real women, which is why Alejandro can be replaced seamlessly with Magdalena. The violent restraint that echoes Billy's treatment of the wolf also reminds us of the uncomfortable parallels between Grady's horse breaking and his attitude to women. His speciality is 'spoiled horses' – those badly broken by others – and he is therefore drawn to Magdalena, in whose reclamation he seeks to put right the cowboy story that refused to develop according to script with Alejandra. And yet it is clear that Grady offers not freedom, but a different form of captivity, signalled symbolically by the blue paint (a colour associated with Eduardo) with which he decorates his honeymoon cottage. It is a dolls house in which Magdalena will battle dust and cook hearty meals like a traditional white settler, whilst Grady and Billy play cowboy. It is a childish dream; even Billy, who is forced to act as a reluctant go-between, remains incredulous but is trapped in a cowboy narrative in which Eduardo is the bad guy, women are suspect, and a cowboy's only real duty is to his partner.

Throughout *the Trilogy*, McCarthy allows his protagonists' confusion around women to mount a more critical appraisal of Western mythology. When, for example, Billy and Boyd stop to question a young girl who appears to have been taken hostage by a group of Mexican riders it is clear that neither really knows what they are doing. It is left to the narrative description of the eyes to do the psychological work. Not only do Billy and the girl's furtive glances recall his romance with the wolf, but the meeting is reflected in the eye of his horse: '[Billy] could see curved like a dark triptych in a glass paperweight the figures of the two men and the girl burning in the fugitive light of the fire at the black center of the animal's eye' (C 207). It's enough that the light is 'fugitive' for the initial emotional confusion caused by the girls' presence to be transformed into a 'captive narrative' when refracted through the lens of the horse. The boys know the script, their heroics are gently mocked by a narrator who describes how Boyd pulled the girl onto the back of his horse like 'a circus rider' before they break for the country where 'they had the look of storybook riders conveying again to her homeland' (210, 213). But having rescued her, Boyd's question 'what do you aim to do with her?' receives a nonplussed: 'Hell. How would I know?' (213). That last bit – what happens after the cowboy gets the girl and they ride off into the sunset – is never revealed.

Her anonymity and her habit of silently watching Billy implies that she is simply a replacement for his wolf. For Boyd, however, she becomes a love interest, a relationship that in the classic Western drives a wedge between saddle partners whilst undermining the cowboy's rugged independence. His announcement that they are going off together is deliberately worded to protect his brother's feelings and the vestiges of his cowboy identity: 'She wants me to go with her / What for? / I don't know. Because she's afraid' (236). To admit that he may be in love is a betrayal, so they are happier operating in the world of external threat. Playing chaperone is an act of validation, the irony of which is exposed in Billy's observation 'I sure would hate to be a woman in this country' (237). As a statement it critiques a Western mythology that reduces unaccompanied women to fair game whilst simultaneously drawing attention to the inadequacy of her would-be protectors. Boyd rides into a new mythology in which he trades his Stetson for a straw hat and she, in the tradition of the Mexican revolutionaries, gets to ride the horse as an equal partner. Billy, by contrast, remains the lonesome rider who is both a threat to and is threatened by domesticity. McCarthy dramatizes this liminal state though a scene in which Billy rides into a small Mexican town in which a wedding and a funeral are taking place simultaneously. The attendees are attired for both events, the bride sitting in a cart that will be later used to transport a coffin. We are told that she sees 'him sitting the horse by the roadside like some pale witness of ill omen and she blessed herself and turned away' (371). He is ill-omened: he represents the masculine restlessness that is a threat to the security that femininity and domesticity affords; she, by contrast, signals the death of the cowboy.

The ultimate cowboy death is Grady's, which McCarthy presents in an ostentatious scene in which he is carried Pieta-like through the streets of Juraz, whilst a hysterical Billy rails against the 'Goddamn whores' he claims are responsible (*COP* 261). It's a curious deflection from the real cause – Eduardo – but makes clear the violent misogyny that is the obverse of a cowboy code that categorises women as 'virgins' or 'whores' without letting them come into view as women. We have glimpsed it in throwaway comments such as the old rancher's advice to Billy – 'Don't get married. Women are crazy' (*C* 37), Lacey Rawlins's denouncement of Grady's girlfriend – 'She aint worth it, none of them are' (*APH* 10), and Troy's account of the fate of his brother, Jonny, the all-American hero undone by his affair with a local girl. Eyes are once again central, but here they articulate a shared condemnation: 'Satan hath power to assume a pleasing form. Them big blue eyes. Knew more ways to turn a man's head than the devil's grandmother' (*COP* 25). The tired Temptress trope combines with the fairy tale big eyes of the wolf in *Red Riding Hood* in what is a further degradation of Billy's she-wolf to a symbol of the predatory woman. Women are tricksters, their youthful appeal proving the instinctive evil of their fallen status rather than their vulnerability.

This is the violent misogyny to which Billy appeals in the denouement, demanding of a group of watching school children and their school mistress – 'Do you see? Do you see?' (*COP* 261). It is *Shane* and *The Virginian* rolled into one: we, along with the embryonic Joe Starretts, observe Billy's manly grief over the death of his partner. However, perhaps we are being invited to look more closely at this highly theatrical display in which Billy, albeit briefly, is confident enough to embrace his partner and damn all women: Do we see? Shouldn't it be the school mistress in Billy's arms rather than Grady; furthermore, the eyes of Grady are open but unseeing – an apt symbol of his wide-eyed blindness throughout the novel (261). Have we ever really looked closely at the Western narrative? Both *Shane* and *The Virginian* appear very camp to twentieth-century eyes, revealing a deep well of homoerotic desire between the male protagonists. Our first sight of *The Virginian* is mediated through an enthralled narrator who describes him as a 'slim young giant, more beautiful than pictures' before claiming, 'had I been the bride, I should have taken the giant, dust and all'.[67] In the only outburst of male emotion in the novel, when the Virginian is out of his mind in agony, it is Steve (the only person to call him by his name), not his intended, Molly, who he calls for, leaving the tending women to observe, 'it was a name unknown'. It is the love that dare not speak its name and, as Tompkins observes, we get 'the feeling that if times had been different this could have been a story about "Jeff and Steve" '.[68] Similarly, the most important relationship in *Shane* is that between Shane and Joe Starrett, which is safely enacted through their shared love of Marion, with occasional hints at something deeper.[69] An important scene is when they dig up the roots of a tree in the ranch yard (an act suggestively symbolic of overturning deep-rooted conventions) their rhythmical chopping punctuated by moments when Joe looks across at Shane's shirtless body as if there was 'some unspoken thought between them that bothered him' (24). When they have finished, 'their eyes met and held' before Schaefer intervenes to tell us that it was all 'clean and wholesome'.[70]

To some extent, the *Trilogy* could have been a story about Grady and Billy, for despite the crushing conformity of the masculine code by which they order their lives, gender identity and same-sex desire are further borders to be crossed. Through their relationship McCarthy interrogates the paradox of a genre rooted in the erasure of women but fearful of homoeroticism; that reduces complex emotions to wise-cracks and plaintive cowboy ballads; that invites us to gaze at the cowboy whilst discouraging the lingering look. No other genre is as invested in the spectacle of male display, the choreography of which (poker games, barroom brawls, cattle drives and shootouts) allows us to observe men being constructed before our eyes.[71] And yet, ironically the homoerotic is seldom far from the traditional Western, which shows men's fascination in other men's guns (which are inherently phallic), which are fondled, measured, pressed into each other's faces and slotted into low-slung, leather gun belts. Cowboys can't keep their appreciative gaze off one another: the lingering glances that pass between Victor Mature and Glenn Ford during their first meeting in John Ford's *My Darling Clementine* (1946); the spectacle of a youthful Montgomery Clift gazing at John Wayne's crotch while sucking on a piece of straw that opens Howard Hawks' *Red River* (1948).[72] These men are brought together by an attraction exemplified later in the exclusionary homosocial relationship between *Butch Cassidy and the Sundance Kid* (1969): as Vito Russo quipped – 'Who remembers

Katherine Ross?'[73] And who, we might ask, remembers the slightly drawn Alejandro and Magdalena, who, as a number of critics have argued, are simply place holders for the real relationships that develop between the men in *the Trilogy* in a closed circuit of male desire.[74]

Everybody loves Grady: he evokes a love that combines both nostalgia for lost ideals and pity. However, McCarthy also makes clear that he inspires a love that proves more troubling to the Western myth; a love that he presents as a consequence of a genre that removes women and allows the 'feminine' to be 'performed' by male characters. Lacy Rawlins is his first admirer and 'pardner', a dynamically submissive role with clear psycho-sexual implications. His relationships with Grady is compromised by the presence of Blevins. When the latter puts a hole through Rawlins's billfold, it is an act of cowboy prowess that figuratively emasculates him, a degradation amplified by the detail of one of the bullets passing between the eyes of a picture of Rawlins's sweetheart. The symbolic murder of this heterosexual ideal confirms Rawlins's feminine presence in the struggle over Grady's affection (a role brutally confirmed by his implied rape in the Saltillo jail[75]). At various stages he serenades Grady like a lover – 'Will you miss me, Will you miss me when I'm gone' – and takes on the role of pragmatic mother to Grady's idealistic father in relation to their parental duties towards the young Blevins (*APH* 37). When he understands the true threat posed by Blevins, he presents Grady with a 'me or him' ultimatum dressed up in cowboy cliché that makes clear the love triangle. Grady is bound to Blevins as repository of an absurdly hyperbolized version of his cowboy identity, an identity that the feminized and cynical Rawlins is in the process of challenging.

Billy also loves Grady and, like Rawlins, he follows a process of feminization antithetical to the cowboy code. His rescue, repatriation and ritual slaughter of the she-wolf symbolizes the death of his cowboy idealism and also the rejection of a certain kind of rugged masculinity symbolized by his trading of his father's phallic rifle for the dead corpse. In the ultra-masculine arena of the dog-fighting pit he sides with the only feminine presence, his own feminization, Nell Sullivan argues, symbolized by the vicarious form of menstruation he experiences when he feels 'the blood of the wolf against his thigh where it had soaked' (*C* 125).[76] The Billy of *The Crossing* is also an extraordinarily lachrymose character, his regular shedding of tears (shooting the wolf (122), discovery of his parents' murder (165), dreaming of Boyd (400), the final page (426)) contrasting with the spitting of his companions. This is significant, because the Billy we meet at the beginning of *Cities of the Plain* performs such a foul-mouthed version of cowboy masculinity that it appears to be a mask. And what it masks is his attraction to Grady. This emerges in humorous songs – 'John Grady Cole was a rugged old soul … With a buckskin belly and a rubber asshole' and occasional slips when drunk (*COP* 76). In one particular exchange he responds to Grady's announcement that his affair with Magdalena 'don't have nothin to do with you' (the aptly placed double negative signalling Grady's own mixed emotions) with the highly emotional: 'The hell it don't' (*COP* 121). It does, but to admit it would be an admission of intimacy that violates their shared understanding of the cowboy code. Elsewhere in the text, it is through horses that their wordless attraction is conveyed. When Billy is worried that Grady is going to leave the ranch, he is reassured by the latter's statement – 'I aint going nowheres' – which is augmented by the narrator's observation that 'John Grady ran the brush down the horse's loins. The horse shuddered' (150).[77] In a code in which touching among men is an anathema, such euphemism shares the power of those cinematic clichés of sexual congress – erupting volcanoes, firework displays – which are both erotically suggestive and parodic in drawing attention to the expressive limitations of the medium. Here, it highlights the presence of the horse in another triangulation of male desire found in the Classic Western – the Lone Ranger, Trigger, Tonto; the Virginian, Joe D, Steve – their wordless but milling presence suggesting both cowboy virility and, more importantly, control.

Billy's love is also on display when seeking to avenge the murder of Magdalena, an act that confirms her centrality to another triangular relationship. Billy first beats up Eduardo's sidekick, Tiburcio – 'an incubus of uncertain proclivity' – who performs the role of the archetypal sinister and feminized Mexican in contrast to the upright, heterosexual Anglo-cowboy. Peter Boag observes that part of the process of transforming the Frontier into a cradle of virile white masculinity was the simultaneous identification of non-Anglos with elements of womanliness (the Chinese queue with voluminous clothing, for example) and sexual deviance. The emasculation of Mexican men was accelerated by the US Mexican war, in which men were projected as cowardly (particularly in comparison with the archetype of his fearless female counterpart), and also the common depiction of cross-dressing Mexican bandits in both late century Newspaper articles and Dime novels.[78] To an audience acculturated on such stereotypes, which includes Billy, Tiburcio is simply a more exaggerated version of the silk-shirted Eduardo (a dark other to the dark other) and is clearly coded gay. Billy's symbolic castration of this figure by snapping his knife in half announces the arrival of the cowboy in Billy's very own Dime Western narrative; on a broader level it also suggests that he has symbolically beaten back his feminine side and is ready to face Eduardo (237). Their encounter, however, when Billy bursts into his office, reveals a psychosexual sub-plot that disrupts Western conventions. Eduardo is calmly looking for a cigar – an obvious masculine signifier – and is amused rather than frightened by Billy's challenge – 'You better have a shoebox full of pistols in there' (239).

It is pastiche B movie that comically alerts us to Billy's more feminine dislike of clutter. No wonder Eduardo and by extension the reader cannot take his bravado seriously.

Grady is clearly coded heterosexual in the *Trilogy*, but his tendency to fall for idealized women suggests a process of arrested development in which he is never quite ready to throw off the emotional demands of his saddle partner. As 'the all-American cowboy' his feelings for other men remain entirely sublimated, but they find expression through Eduardo who seems to know more about Grady's story than Grady himself. As anti-cowboy he holds the mirror up to the dark side of cowboy mythology, which extends to its misogyny and homoeroticism; this latter element is central to the highly eroticized presentation of the climatic knife fight that kills them both. It is important that their relationship ends in violence, for, as has been noted, within the genre the fist fights, shoot-outs and barroom brawls are the way that the male is deconstructed and remade as the 'true man'.[79] Grady's fight with Eduardo turns this model on its head, allowing disfigurement that borders on the surgical to question exactly what we might mean by a 'true man'. Its symbolic import begins with the act of self-castration suggested by Grady' pawning of his father's Colt: an act that severs his connection to the weapon with which he manfully cauterized his bullet wounds at the end of *All the Pretty Horses*. Once again, McCarthy is retooling Hollywood cliché to expose darker possibilities. When Zane Grey's Lassiter hangs up his guns it is presented as a form of ritual emasculation, which he himself acknowledges when he puts them back on again: 'Where would any man be on this border without guns? ... It's the difference between a man and somethin' not a man.'[80]

It is this 'unmanned cowboy' who faces Eduardo in an erotic ballet that reads, as Sullivan has noted, like a description of intercourse.[81] It begins with Eduardo's announcement that their coming together 'is like a first kiss' and is followed by highly suggestive movements (Eduardo at one moment 'almost kneeling' before Grady 'like a supplicant'(249)) whilst through a constant monologue he promises to lay claim to Grady – 'I name you completely to myself' (248). The penetrative act of stabbing becomes erotically illustrative, as Eduardo explains that he is performing 'a medical transplant. To put the suitor's mind inside this thigh', and that having read Grady's mind, he carves an E not an M (250). Such insights are, however, lost on Grady whose own act of penetration (stabbing Eduardo through the mouth) effectively stops the commentary that is as damaging to his sense of cowboy identity as the blade. Once silenced, however, the delirious Grady wraps himself in Eduardo's shirt and in a suggestively Freudian outpouring of grief announces three times to Billy 'I just wanted him' (259). Such context invites us to reassess the Pieta scene and question what Billy wants us to see in the form of the dead Grady: is it the death of the clean-cut but sexually repressed all American cowboy in acknowledgment of his sexually rapacious but ambiguous nemesis? Billy, though it may come as a surprise to him, mourns both – so it should come as no surprise to the reader that he never marries and ends up a 78-year-old down and out.

McCarthy's daring epilogue, in which we enter the existential landscape of *Waiting for Godot*, presents the last of McCarthy's gnomic mentors. He lectures a down-and-out Billy under an interstate flyover on how we assemble and order disparate human experience into a meaningful life. His dream within a dream about walking amidst the ruins of a deserted Native American village encourages the individual to author his existence whilst resisting the temptation to appropriate the artefacts, codes, tropes and values that have already been woven into the histories of vanished peoples. It is the warning implied the moment Billy released the wolf and Grady set off along the ghostlike Comanche road. They have continually ignored such mentors, which has led to early death (Grady, Boyd, Blevins) or, in Billy's case, the caricature performance of himself in Hollywood movies. We are guided to pity him, not simply because of the debasement of his dreams, but because he remains trapped into a role that prevents a more mature understanding of his life. At the end of the novel it is Betty who cares for this relic of a bygone age and who rejects his confession – 'I'm not what you think I am' – with motherly reassurance:

> She patted his hand. Gnarled, ropescarred, speckled from the sun and the years of it. The ropy veins that bound them to his heart. There was map enough for men to read. There's God's plenty of signs and wonders to make a landscape. To make a world.
>
> (291)

His hands provide a map rather than a history; they place him in a landscape about which we care because we are guided by a cultural mythology constructed on an archetype of masculinity. However, where the previous volumes close with the image of the lone horseman riding into the sunset, here the rider seems to be returning to the childhood lullaby that began the *Trilogy*. The prevailing childish sensibility is reinforced by the lullaby encoded in the dedication, which, in its echo of Wordsworth, is reminiscent of the opening pages of *Blood Meridian*. We have 'seen the child' whose cowboy dreams have splintered, but he still rides on. The lessons of the *Border Trilogy*, like those of *Butchers Crossing*, are that the dreams of youth – all the pretty horses, the draw of the wild, the quick draw Blevins, exotic beauties – are all reflections that fragment in the harsh light of reality. Yet, though these dreams are doomed, they are also ennobling; we both pity and admire McCarthy's 'cowboys'. They are young boys with a simplified view of the world playing a part, but we respect their romanticism and the dedication of their pursuit. Thus, where Judge Holden initiated the Kid to a brutal West, Betty's judgement offers a more comforting vision that conjoins Billy to the world that is passing.

Notes

1. Campbell, 'Liberty beyond Its Proper Bounds: Cormac McCarthy's History of the West in Blood Meridian', in Rick Wallach (ed.), *Myth, Legend, Dust: Critical Responses to Cormac McCarthy* (Manchester: Manchester University Press, 2000), 217–26 (p. 218); Spurgeon, *Exploding the Western: Myths of Empire on the Postmodern Frontier* (Texas: Texas A&M University Press, 2005), p. 39. Quoted in David H. Evans, 'True West and Lying Marks: The Englishman's Boy, Blood Meridian and the Paradox of the Revisionist Western', *Texas Studies in Literature and Language* 55: 4 (Winter 2013), 406–33 (p. 419).
2. See Jonathan Pitts's excellent discussion of the connection between 'vision' and 'revision' in '*Blood Meridian* as Revisionary Western', *Western American Literature* 33: 1 (Spring 1998), 6–25 (p. 8) https://www.jstor.org/stable/43021783 [accessed 15 January 2020].
3. See Barcley Owens' perceptive reading of the opening in *Cormac McCarthy's Western Novels* (Tuscon: The University of Arizona Press, 2000), p. 3.
4. Michael Lynn Crews, 'Cormac McCarthy's *Blood Meridian* Was Almost a Plain Old Western', *Literary Hub* (16 January 2020) https://lithub.com/cormac-mccarthys-blood-meridian-was-almost-a-plain-old-western/ [accessed 4 July 2020].
5. See Harold Bloom in Harold Bloom (ed.), *Cormac McCarthy: Modern Critical Views* (Philadelphia: Chelsea House Publishers, 2009), p. 1; Noah Gallagher Shannon, 'Cormac McCarthy Cuts to the Bone *Blood Meridian*', *Slate* (October 2012) https://slate.com/culture/2012/10/cormac-mccarthys-blood-meridian-early-drafts-and-history.html [accessed 4 July 2020].
6. Quoted in Woodward, 'Cormac McCarthy's Venomous Fiction', *New York Times* (19 April 1992).
7. Ibid., Crews, 'Cormac McCarthy's *Blood Meridian*'.
8. Steven Shaviro, 'The Very Life of Darkness: A Reading of Blood Meridian', in Edwin Arnold and Dianne Luce (eds.), *Perspective on Cormac McCarthy* (Jackson: University Press of Mississippi, 1999), 145–58 (p. 145); see also Robert Jarrell, 'Revisioning the Western?: Three Cases', *Canon: The Journal of the Rocky Mountains* ASA 2: 2 (1995), 24–51 (p. 32). See also Gregg Lambert's observations about McCarthy's use of the baroque in *The Return of the Baroque in Modern Culture* (London and New York: Bloomsbury, 2004).
9. Mark Eaton makes this argument in 'Dis (RE)membered Bodies: Cormac McCarthy's Border Fiction', *Modern Fiction Studies* 49: 1 (Spring 2003), 155–80.
10. See Pitts for excellent discussion, p. 17.
11. For excellent reading of this scene see Thomas Pughe, 'Revision and Vision: Cormac McCarthy's *Blood Meridian*', *Revue Française d'études Américaines* 62 (November 1994), 371–82 (p. 373) https://www.jstor.org/stable/20872451 [accessed 15 January 2020].
12. See Kate Montague, 'Between Myth and Actuality on the American Frontier', in Louise Jillett (ed.), *Cormac McCarthy's Borders and Landscapes* (London and New York: Bloomsbury, 2016), 95–105 (p. 103).

13   See Wade Hall, 'The Human Comedy of Cormac McCarthy', in Wade Hall and Rick Wallach (eds.), *Sacred Violence: A Reader's Companion to Cormac McCarthy* (El Paso: Texas Western Press, 1995), 49–60 (p. 50).
14   Quoted in McGilchrist, *The Western Landscape in Cormac McCarthy and Wallace Stegner: Myths of the Frontier* (New York and London: Routledge, 2010), p. 122.
15   Petra Mundik makes a similar observation and uses such scenes of carnival to emphasize the Gnostic belief that the manifest world is both fraudulent and impermanent. In 'Terra Damnata: The Anticosmic Mysticism of *Blood Meridian*', in Jillett (ed.) *Cormac McCarthy's Borders and Landscapes*, 29–43 (p. 41).
16   Dudley, 'McCarthy's Heroes: Revisiting Masculinity', in Steven Frye (ed.), *The Cambridge Companion to Cormac McCarthy* (Cambridge: Cambridge University Press, 2013) 175–87 (p. 179).
17   Bell, *The Achievement of Cormac McCarthy* (Baton Rouge: Louisiana State University Press, 1988), p. 119.
18   McMurtry, *Lonesome Dove* (1985) (Simon and Schuster Pocket Books, 1986), p. 83. He noted in interview that 'by 1884 the plains were already overgrazed. We killed the right animal, the buffalo, and brought in the wrong animal, wetland cattle'. John Spong, 'True West', *Texas Monthly* (January 2013), p. 130.
19   Spurgeon, *Exploding the Western*, p. 32.
20   Mundik makes a perceptive connection with the sea in *Moby Dick*, of which Melville has stated: 'Consider, once more, the universal cannibalism of the sea; all those creatures prey upon each other, carrying on eternal war since the world began.' In 'Terra Damnata', in Jillett (ed.), *Cormac McCarthy*, 29–43 (p. 36.).
21   The invention of barb wire in 1874 brought to an end the cowboy's way of life, as made clear in the lyrics of this lament: 'They say that Heaven/Is the free range land/Good-by, good-by, O fare you well;/But it's barb wire fence ' for the Devil's hat band/And barbed wire blankets down in hell.' Robert Clifton, *Barbs, Prongs, Points, Prickers, and Stickers: A Complete and Illustrated Catalogue of Antique Barbed Wire* (Norman: University of Oklahoma, 1970), p. 2.
22   Moore Morrison, '*All the Pretty Horses:* John Grady's Expulsion from Paradise' in Edwin Arnold and Dianne Luce (eds.), *Perspectives on Cormac McCarthy* (Jackson: University of Mississippi, 1993), 173–93.
23   Bailey, 'The Last Stage of the Hero's Evolution: Cormac McCarthy's *Cities of The Plains*', in Harold Bloom (ed.), *Cormac McCarthy: Modern Critical Views* (New York: Chelsea House Publishers, 2009) 131–40 (p. 136).
24   Alarcon, 'All the Pretty Mexicos' in James D. Lilley (ed.), *Cormac McCarthy: New Directions* (Albuquerque: University of New Mexico Press, 2002), 141–52 (p. 147); Spurgeon, *All the Pretty Horses, No Country for Old Men, The Road* (London: Continuum, 2011), p. 42; McGilchrist, *The Western Landscape*, p. 149.
25   Philip Snyder has observed that 'Grady does not have a choice between naivete and maturity, or between romance and reality… rather, his choice is between enacting his idealistic cowboy codes or not' and 'those codes have meaning only as they enacted within the communal context of the real world'. 'Cowboy

Codes in Cormac McCarthy's Border Trilogy', in Edwin T. Arnold, Dianne C. Luce (eds.), *A Cormac McCarthy Companion: The Border Trilogy* (Jackson: University of Mississippi Press, 2001), 198–227 (p. 205).

26 Vizenor, *Manifest Manners: Postindian Warriors of Survivance* (Hanover: University Press of New England, 1994), p. 11.

27 Fiedler, *Love and Death in the American Novel* (New York: Criterion Books, 1960), p. 27.

28 King, '"Where is Your Country?": Locating White Masculinity in *All the Pretty Horses*', *The Cormac McCarthy Journal* 12 (2014), 69–89 (p. 73).

29 Limerick, *Legacy*, p. 158; see Robbins, *Last Refuge*, p. 262; Dan Burkhart, 'Home on the Range', *Atlanta Constitution* 12 (November 1991), p. 1.

30 Robinson, *Marked Men: White Masculinity in Crisis* (New York: Columbia University Press, 2000), p. 21 (Quoted King, p. 74).

31 Deloria, *Playing Indian* (New Haven: Yale University Press, 1998), pp. 161, 173.

32 McMurtry, *Lonesome Dove* (1985) (New York: Pocket Books, 1986), pp. 349, 357.

33 McMurtry, *In Narrow Grave*, p. 56.

34 McMurtry, 'The Southwest as the Cradle of the Novelist', in Robert Walts (ed.), *The American Southwest: Cradle of Literary Art* (San Marcos: Southwest Texas University, 1979), p. 34; for critical approval see Andrew Nelson's essay, 'Larry McMurtry', in J. Golden Taylor (ed.), *A Literary History of the American West* (Fort Worth, Texas: Texas Christian University Press, 1987), 612–19 (pp. 618–9); Billie Phillips, 'McMurtry's Women: 'Eros [Libido, Caritas, and Philia] in [and out of] Archer County', in Clay Reynolds (ed.), *Taking Stock: A Larry McMurtry Casebook* (Dallas: Southern Methodist University Press, 1989), 86–93.

35 Michael L. Johnson, *New Westers: The West in Contemporary American Culture* (Kansas: University of Kansas Press, 1996), p. 147; Kollin, 'Genre and Geographies of Violence: Cormac McCarthy and the Contemporary Western', *Contemporary Literature* 42: 3 (Autumn, 2001), p. 569.

36 Mitchell, *Westerns: Making the Man in Fiction and Film* (Chicago: University of Chicago Press, 1996), p. 7.

37 For an excellent discussion, see Daniel Weiss, 'Cormac McCarthy, Violence and Borders: The Map as Code for What is Not Contained', *The Cormac McCarthy Journal* 8: 1 (Fall 2010), 73–89 (p. 77).

38 Valerie J. Matsumoto and Blake Allmendinger, *Over the Edge: Remapping the American West* (Berkeley, London: University of California Press: 1998), p. 1. Dianne Luce argues this point convincingly in 'When You Wake: John Grady Cole's Heroism in *All the Pretty Horses*' in Hall and Wallach, *Sacred Violence*, 155–67 (p. 159); see also Robert Jarrett, *Cormac McCarthy* (University of Houston: Twayne Publishers, 1997), p. 99.

39 Alarcon, 'All the Pretty Mexicos', p. 145. For Mark Busby the border represents the line between opposing forces: 'civilization/wilderness, individual/community, fate/free will, past/present, aggression/passivity. 'Into the Darkening Land, the World to Come: Cormac McCarthy's Border Crossings', in Harold Bloom (ed.) *Cormac McCarthy: Modern Critical Views* (Philadelphia: Chelsea House Publishers, 2002), 141–67 (p. 146).

40 Judith Butler, 'Merely Cultural', *New Left Review* 227 (1998), 33–44 (pp. 34–5).
41 Spurgeon, 'Pledged in Blood: Truth and Redemption in Cormac McCarthy's All the Pretty Horses', *Western American Literature* 34: 1 (Spring 1999), 25–44 (p. 30).
42 Tompkins, *West of Everything*, pp. 94–5.
43 See Lydia Cooper for a perceptive reading of these scenes. *No More Heroes: Narrative Perspective and Morality in Cormac McCarthy* (Baton Rouge: Louisiana State University Press, 2011), p. 17.
44 Mitchell, *Westerns: Making the Man*, p. 179.
45 Steinbeck, *East of Eden* (1952) (London: Penguin Classics, 2017), p. 11.
46 Ibid., pp. 12, 11.
47 Stegner, 'A Sense of Place', *Where the Bluebird Sings*, pp. 201–2.
48 Elizabeth Cook-Lynn, 'Why I Can't Read Wallace Stegner', in *Why I Can't Read Wallace Stegner and other Essays: A Tribal Voice* (Madison, Wisconsin: University of Wisconsin Press, 1996) 29–40 (p. 40).
49 Arthur, *The Default Country: A Lexical Cartography of Twentieth Century Australia* (Sydney, Australia: University of New South Wales Press, 2003), p. 26.
50 Lynch, 'Strange Lands', *Interdisciplinary Studies in Literature and Environment* 22: 4 (Autumn 2015), 697–716 (p. 712).
51 Kollin, 'Genre and the Geographies of Violence', p. 578.
52 Vizenor, *Manifest Manners*, p. 11.
53 Louis Owens, *Other Destinies: Understanding the American Indian Novel* (Norman: University of Oklahoma Press, 1992), p. 4.
54 See Diana Luce, 'The Vanishing World of Cormac McCarthy's Border Trilogy', in Edwin T. Arnold, Dianne C. Luce (eds.), *A Cormac McCarthy Companion: The Border Trilogy* (Jackson: University of Mississippi Press, 2001), 161–98 (p. 168).
55 Excellent summary and analysis made by Barcley Owens, *Cormac McCarthy*, p. 71.
56 Jean Baudrillard, *Simulations* (New York: Semiotext(e), 1983), p. 4.
57 Vizenor, 'Edward Curtis: Pictorialist and Ethnographic Adventurist', in Nathaniel Lewis, William R. Handley (eds.), *True West: Authenticity and the American West* (Lincoln, Nebraska: University of Nebraska Press, 2004), 180–93 (p. 180).
58 The power of the scene, as David Holloway has observed, derives from the interplay of the two stories that we are simultaneously told – the ludicrous pastiche of a real 'Western' character, and that of a resentful revolutionary. David Holloway, *The Late Modernism of Cormac McCarthy* (Westport: Greenwood Press, 2002), p. 75.
59 Ibid., Snyder, 'Cowboy Codes in Cormac McCarthy's Border Trilogy', p. 209.
60 See Edwin T. Arnold, 'The Last of the Trilogy: First Thoughts on Cities of the Plain', in Arnold and Dianne Luce (eds.), *Perspective on Cormac McCarthy* (Jackson: University Press of Mississippi, 1999), 221–47 (p. 232).
61 See Holloway, *Late Modernism*, p. 76.
62 See Jarrett, 'McCarthy's Sense of an Ending', p. 329.
63 See Kollin, 'Genre and the Geographies of Violence:', p. 583.

64 Limerick, 'The Shadows of Heaven Itself', in William Riebsame (ed.), *Atlas of the New West: Portrait of a Changing Region* (Boulder Co: Center for the American West, 1997), 151–178 (p. 152).
65 Barcley Owens offers a perceptive reading of this discussion and a more general discussion of the symbolism in the novel *Cormac McCarthy's Western Novels*, p. 103.
66 Nell Sullivan, 'Boys Will Be Boys and Girls will Be Gone: The Circuit of Male Desire in Cormac McCarthy's Border Trilogy', in Edwin Arnold Diana C. Luce (eds.), *A Cormac McCarthy Companion: The Border Trilogy* (Jackson, Mississippi: University Press of Mississippi, 2001), 228–55 (p. 232).
67 Wister, *The Virginian* (1902) (Oxford: Oxford University Press, 1998), pp. 12, 13. Handley, 'The Past and Futures of a Story and a Film', in William R. Handley (ed.), *The Brokeback Book: From Story of Cultural Phenomenon* (Lincoln and London: University of Nebraska Press, 2011), 1–23 (p. 14). See also Forrest Robinson, 'The Virginian and Molly in Paradise: How Sweet Is It?' *Western American Literature* 21 (1986), 27–38 (p. 31).
68 Tompkins, *West of Everything*, p. 150.
69 Eve Kosofsky Sedgewick has identified it as a 'triangular circuit of desire' in which the shared love for a woman is a means of exploring 'homosocial desire'. *Between Men: English Literature and Male Homosocial Desire* (New York: Columbia University Press, 1985), p. 21. Quoted in Blake Allmendinger, *Ten Most Wanted: The New Western Literature* (New York and London: Routledge, 1998), who provides an excellent analysis for both novels under discussion here, pp. 157–9.
70 Schaefer, *Shane* (New York: Bantam, 1983), p. 11.
71 See Lee Clarke Mitchell for a fascinating discussion of this topic in *Westerns: Making the Man*, pp. 187, 159.
72 See Gary Needham, *Brokeback Mountain* (Edinburgh: Edinburgh University Press, 2010), pp. 60–1.
73 Russo, *The Celluloid Closet: Homosexuality in the Movies* (New York: Harper and Row, 1985), p. 81.
74 Arnold, 'The Last of the Trilogy', pp. 236, 8.
75 See Jay Ellis, 'The Rape of Rawlins: a Note on "All the Pretty Horses"', *The Cormac McCarthy Journal*, 1: 1 (Spring 2001), 66–8 https://www.jstor.org/stable/42909335 [accessed 15 March 2019].
76 Sullivan, 'Boys Will Be Boys', p. 237.
77 McGilchrist offers an excellent reading of this relationship, *Western Landscape*, pp. 182–4.
78 Peter Boag, *Re-Dressing America's Frontier Past* (Berkeley: University of California Press, 2011), particular pp. 145, 154.
79 Ibid., Mitchell, *Westerns: Making the Man*, p. 155.
80 Grey, *Riders of the Purple Sage* (1912) (Lincoln: University of Nebraska press, 1994), p. 272. Quoted from David Fenimore, '"A Bad Boy Grown Up": The Wild Life Behind Zane Grey's Westerns', in David Rio Raigadas, Amaia Ibarraran, José Miguel Santamaria, M.a Felisa López (eds.), *Exploring the American Literary West: International Perspectives* (Bilbao: Universidad del Paris Vasco: 2006), 57–68 (p. 64).
81 See Sullivan, 'Boys will be Boys', p. 249.

3

Lost in the Hyperreal: Proulx's Broken Cowboys

WITH *CLOSE Range,* Annie Proulx deftly appropriates a male literary preserve. Her Wyoming stories owe little to John Ford or Cormac McCarthy. The West's heroic dream is dead, its past more inglorious than its present. Only the landscape, beautiful and cruel, retains its mystique.

Proulx does not share McCarthy's romanticism. Her characters are poor people, struggling in rustic squalor against a harsh environment. They inhabit trailers and failing twice-mortgaged ranches or take to the road, driving hundreds of miles in clapped out cars to try their luck at rodeos. Everything's broken and there's no money to mend it. The gun culture, with physical injuries, unfulfilled desires and chronic loneliness, engender violence, madness and a painful stoicism. 'If you can't fix it, you've got to stand it.'[1]

With this perceptive review of *Close Range*, Mary Flanagan welcomes us to Proulx country: a region in which the landscape and mythology that fuelled McCarthy's bravado conspire to bend her characters out of shape. Everything is broken: her characters are broken by the weight of the mythological West; the economy is wrecked by a president who deploys cowboy rhetoric to undermine Western values; the land itself is ruined by a mythology that condoned and encouraged exploitative attitudes and practices. And yet despite the horror, Proulx's tone remains arch (occasionally screwball), her postmodern approach reminding us of the tenuous distinction between 'fiction' and 'reality' when applied to the West. The tagline to *Close Range* claims 'Reality's never been of much use out here' – but neither has narrative 'realism' as a means of recording it. Proulx's narrative strategies include dirty realism, journalistic reportage, historical notation and flights of magic realism; her characterization combines historical figures with fictional creations, gothic grotesques and laughable caricatures; her settings blend real locations identifiable on a map with descriptions of highly stylized faux Western landscapes to create a hyperreal vision of the West. Thus, her *Wyoming Stories* range widely through history, genre and narrative approach to offer a comprehensive vision of the region. Each story, she claims, opens out like a window upon a different view.[2]

The common denominator in the fictional approaches shared by the writers in this study is the youthful eye, sometimes detached sometimes naively participatory, but always a means of deconstructing Western mythology. This deconstructive sensibility is symbolized most clearly by Proulx through her creation of 'The Sagebrush Kid' (*FJW*), who, like McCarthy's 'Kid', is a witness to bloodiness that turns Turner on his head. Proulx's Kid, however, is a plant whose name combines the archetypal Western hero with a species perfectly adapted to the desert harshness. She takes Erben's Czech fairy tale, *Otesanek,* in which a desperate childless couple raise a tree root as a baby which starts consuming the neighbours, and relocates it to a telegraph station in the Red Desert in the 1860s.[3] Here, a couple of childless Anderson-like grotesques raise a sagebrush on a diet of blood that transforms it into a man-eating monster. The Kid is used initially to explain the historical case of a number of 'inexplicable vanishings' that took place around the Deer Creek region of Ben Holladay's overland stagecoach route in the 1860s; then, as it continues to work its way through a menu of careless settlers, deserting Civil War soldiers and methane gas rednecks, he offers a warning to contemporary Westerners as to how we consume the land. As such, The Kid bestrides Proulx's postmodern Wyoming as a Cowboy Colossus, drawing attention to its surreal geography, bloody regional history and the inadequacies of historical, discursive and genre methods of presenting it. This process is highlighted by Proulx's inclusion of a genuine historical source – *The Life of Oscar Collister, Wyoming Pioneer, as told by himself to Mrs Chas. Ellis of Difficult* – which, like Chamberlain's scalp-hunting account in *Blood Meridian,* is a 'difficult' document. It advertises its authenticity through its complex framing structure, yet seems to owe more to the author's consumption of Dime novels than authentic observation. Collister blames the 'inexplicable vanishings' on the activity of the Sioux. Proulx's own historical research, however – published in the scholarly collection *Red Desert: History of a Place* (2009) – suggests that Holladay exaggerated their threat so he could move to a more lucrative route. She blames the disappearances on a surreally inhospitable land where cattle disappear down sink holes, were blown away or eaten by marauding lions.[4] If, Proulx appears to be suggesting, the explanations for events provided by 'eyewitness accounts' and 'historical scholarship' can range from Native Americans to cyclones and lions, why not the fairy-tale presence of a man-eating sagebrush?

In Proulx's narrative it is not just the characters and events that are absurd, it's the means of recording and explaining them. From the outset her narrator self-consciously adopts a register of historical analysis, contextualizing past events against modern equivalents, and dispensing with landscape description and character development in favour of reportage. It is a style that both resurrects and simultaneously critiques Cody's historical methodology: the detailing of historical artefacts (Holladay ran Red Rupert coaches) is replicated in the mock-historical detailing of the notebook used by the Kid's last victim (the same as those 'used by Ernest Hemingway and Bruce Chatwin' (91)). The absurdity of such incongruity serves as an indictment of the West's uneasy relationship with the notion of 'authenticity'. Cody is no fraud but the exemplary historian of a region in which notions of 'reality' are fluid – a region symbolized by the seemingly passive, but all-consuming, Kid. For as the years pass and the landscape changes and the stagecoach gives way to the Union Pacific railroad, the Lincoln Highway and methane gas prospectors, the one constant remains the giant sagebrush. Thus, it becomes emblematic of a West built on the fiction of 'savage Indians', the blood of settlers and countless brutal cowboy sagas. To sophisticated consumers of the New West, the 'Sagebrush Kid' now offers a picture-postcard picnic spot; the wilderness that awed and destroyed the first emigrant parties can now be crossed in hours rather than days, its sublimity transformed to a tourist destination, its dangers consigned to a romanticized past. This, however, is to misread both the landscape and the mythology upon which it is constructed, which remains dangerous to the unwary. For, although the Old West may appear to have surrendered to modernity (the Kid in some lights appears to be holding his 'arms up against the red sky' in an attitude of surrender) it will eat up everything that the modern world has to throw at it – literally! This is certainly true of one of the Kid's last victims, a delivery driver who is so engrossed in the Western novel *Ambush on the Pecos Trail* that he fails to see the real danger of the Western landscape around him (88).[5]

II

Proulx's West remains dangerous because it is surreal; it is a potent mixture of mythology and exoticism that is both easy to idealize and fatal to underestimate. Its dangers are central to a group of stories that dismantle the mythology of the 'lone pioneer' through the disastrous experiences of idealistic young men and their reluctant families. Settler colonial theorists are concerned with the stories that we (individuals, communities, and nations) tell in order to validate the dispossession and erasure of indigenous peoples and the settlement of land. The 'pioneer myth' with its easily identifiable cultural signifiers – the prairie schooner, the log cabin, the plough, the Madonna of the trail (canonized in statues all over the West) – is a theatrically foundational part of the Turnerian West.[6] At its heart is the notion of struggle against a hostile environment, which includes redefining indigenous people as shadowy and nomadic savages, underpinned by 'Manifest Destiny' (honed through the Mexican American war of 1846–8) and the foundational story of Eden and *Exodus*. For Lorenzo Veracini, Turner is simply a Western manifestation of the spiritually endorsed tropes of promise, struggle, liberation and eventual success shared by all settler colonial projects in the narratives they tell about the establishment of a new homeland.[7] American exceptionalism, therefore, is simply stylistic, the product of an exceptional understanding of the power of symbols (log cabins and cowboys), rather than spiritually and morally exceptional. Proulx's revisionism focuses on how this symbolism was manipulated by unscrupulous railway companies and property developers to construct a seductive Settler narrative. Her intention is made clear through the prologue to the first of her stories – 'Them Old Cowboy Songs' (*FJW*) – which is typographically separate from the narrative: 'There is a belief that pioneers came into the country, homesteaded, lived tough, raised a shoeless brood and founded ranch dynasties. Some did. But many more had short runs and were quickly forgotten' (47). It's a curiously offhand addition that through its phrasing draws attention to the lazy assumptions concerning the settler experience that the subsequent narrative will seek to dispel.

In the tradition of the New Historians, Proulx sets out to give voice to the silent victims of a false mythology; Rose and Archie McLaverty are homesteading emigrants brought West by the promise of cheap land made by railroad companies. Proulx's most fervent attack on such practices is ventriloquized through a character in *That Old Ace in the Hole* who implores the central protagonist to 'forget that pioneer and first-settler stuff' because 'it was all the rayroads. The rayroad corporations said where the towns was goin a go and that's where they went. Nothin a do with pioneers. It was all corporate goals and money and business. Then they sold lots and hoped it would all work out' (*TOA*, 91–2). Unfortunately, for many it didn't. As Proulx makes clear in her Memoir *Bird Cloud* (2012), the lots were too small, the settlers untrained in arid farming methods, the results entirely foreseeable.[8] Novelist, Ivan Doig, recalls that for his ancestors, the dream of freedom connoted by the grid system of lot allocation quickly transformed into a net of captivity;[9] Kittredge is excoriating in his aptly titled essay 'White People in Paradise' – they came, 'they built shacks, they tried to farm, most failed, most left having wasted years in dirt-eating poverty'.[10] Proulx's sympathies are directed towards the young men (whose idealism is presented as reckless rather than heroic) and more specifically the reluctant wives whose suffering is inversely aligned to that of their husband's childishness and remains unalleviated by mythological glamour. In this Proulx is intervening on the re-evaluation of the female 'Frontier experience' inspired by the work of the New Historians of the eighties, such as Sandra Myres's *Westering Women and the Frontier Experience* (1982), Susan Armitage's and Elizabeth Jameson's edited collection *The Women's West* (1987), and Glenda Riley's *The Female Frontier* (1988). Limerick is clear in her dismissal of the myth of the feisty prairie Madonna – at home with a hoe, shotgun or broom – in favour of a more damaged victim:

> Of all the possible candidates, the long-suffering white female pioneer seemed to be the closest thing to an authentic innocent victim. Torn from family and civilisation, overworked and lonely, disoriented by an unfamiliar landscape, frontierswomen could seem to be tragic martyrs to their husbands' wilful ambitions.[11]

Rose McLaverty is one such victim. It is just that we have not heard her story in what Susan Armitage has dubbed the 'Hisland' of the American West; a space that echoes to the heroic exploits of men recorded admiringly by male historians.[12] In this story, it also echoes to 'them old cowboy songs' which celebrate a spirit of hardy self-reliance combined with fierce masculine loyalty in which women only appear as sweethearts, prostitutes or the prairie Madonna.

Archie, 'face as smooth as a skinned aspen', believes these songs, his performance acting as an ironic soundtrack to the actual experience of his family. If only Rose had listened carefully when during their courtship he had warned her 'Never marry no good-for-nothing-boy', or, more menacingly, 'Little girl, for safety you better get branded ... ' – which makes clear that in cowboy-country the only safe women are married (50). His laconic version of 'The Old North Trail' is greeted by the listeners at the 'all-male roundup nights' as 'the true history they all knew' but woefully out of context when sung to his wife (49). As is his ritual of singing the 'metes and bounds' of their joint homestead, which he does alone since Rose does not know the words to any of the songs. Their neighbour, Tom Ackler, would be a better singing partner for Archie. An old sailor, he is no stranger to nostalgic sea shanties that sentimentalize a world that he is only too ready to reject. There is a further irony here, for Archie and the reader assume that he has been singing songs passed through generations of cowboys – an assumption reinforced through the title. In fact, David Fenimore notes that many 'traditional' cowboy songs were learned from books and re-oralized. Thus, Archie is merely the first of many young Proulxian protagonists whose search for authenticity actually leads him to buy into a pre-packaged Western dream.[13]

It is the truth beneath these plaintive lyrics that Proulx's narrative seeks to expose. When, after his catastrophic crop mismanagement, Rose suggests that Archie takes a job in a mine, he refuses because mining does not conform to his vision of the West, and sings: 'I'm just a lonesome cowboy who loves a gal named Rose, I don't care if my hat gets wet or if I freeze my toes' (57).

His song not only announces his selfishness, but also predicts the manner of his death: a cowboy's end. Rose doesn't know the words; rather, she is their object. Her lyrical isolation becomes literal when she becomes pregnant, a condition which, as Elizabeth Jameson's research has made clear, 'formed an important difference between male and female experience'.[14] Proulx signals this dislocation typographically by the narrative splitting into two and psychologically through Rose's sudden realization that 'they were not two cleaving halves of one person but two separate people' and where 'he could leave any time he wanted', she was trapped (61). Archie does leave to work for a rancher whose restriction on married men – 'No MaRRIED MeN' – is a crude formalization of the all-male bunk house world to which Archie has subscribed (59). It is here that his cowboy songs – which tell of the warm hearth and a girl named Rose – make sense, because they describe a dream rather than reality. As Archie's ear becomes attuned to an open range we enter the romantic West of *All the Pretty Horses* and *The Crossing*, where the only form of boundary is imaginative and auditory: 'On the clear, dry nights coyote voices seemed to emanate from single points in straight lines, the calls crisscrossing like taut wires' (63). In such a landscape he is able to conceive teaching a young boy (a girl isn't even considered) cowboy skills. In a world without women, Rose's emotional place is taken by Sink, a cowboy bachelor who takes on a fatherly role. He teaches him how to fall properly (63); he tells him 'the facts of life' concerning bunkhouse homosexuality (62); and, despite avowing that he is no 'wet nurse', he loyally takes care of Archie when he freezes (73).

Rose has no such friends; not only is she abandoned by her husband, but her suffering is exacerbated by damaging codes of behaviour that prevent her turning to other women in her loneliness. The 'Cult of True Womanhood' (a nineteenth-century equivalent to Betty Friedan's 'Feminine Mystique') was imported into newly urbanized Western towns and comprises of an unlikely alliance of fashionable ladies' magazines, the church (which extolled virtues of temperance, chastity and loyalty) and medical practitioners (whose discourse constantly evoked a 'feminine nature') which presented the new woman as modest, accomplished and submissive – 'virtues' at odds with the hardships of the settler experience.[15] The 'cult' offered a view of femininity just as dangerous as the model of masculinity presented in 'them old cowboy songs' – harshly illustrated by the real-life experience of Beulah Pryor, who suffered a hysterectomy after carrying out heavy manual labour in a corset.[16] In Proulx's story, Rose is presented as trapped between her desire to support her husband's settler dreams and the censure of her nearest female companions, the town-dwelling Flora and her stepdaughter, Queeda. Out of abandonment and snobbery Proulx fashions her domestic tragedy, as Rose dies alone in childbirth; a form of female agony unrecorded on those old cowboy songs. Indeed, so far from the male experience is it, that when their neighbour, Tom Ackler, discovers her bloody body, he immediately explains events through a typically Western narrative – that she had been 'raped and murdered and mutilated by Utes' (75). His rounding off the story with a rendition of 'when the green grass comes, and the wild rose blooms' offers an ironic contrast to the fate of Rose in the narrative that we have just read (77). The true monument to their deaths is the doorstep (a symbol of their failed family life) hauled upright as a tombstone, which significantly, like the female voice in Western history, remains blank.

Fast forward sixty years to the late 1920s and in 'The Great Divide' (*FJW*) Proulx presents another settler couple undone by unscrupulous outside interests. They are representative of the first generation of automotive settlers, Proulx noting that 'by 1927 26 million cars stank and jarred around the country, each driver a pioneer'.[17] 'Pioneer' is the important word here, suggesting that once freed from the linear prescription of the railway, the newly enfranchised driver could once again imagine himself (it was always men at the wheel) doing battle with the wilderness whilst participating in a national creation myth. Hi Alcorn, his name suggestive of pastoral abundance and a spiritual attachment to the Hiawatha of Longfellow's eponymous epic poem, has recently returned from the war carrying an injury and, like a Hemingway hero, wishes to embrace the ultimate 'great divide' – the Frontier. But quite where and how he is to live a life of rugged self-reliance when 'it seemed to him that the frontiers had all disappeared in his grandfather's time' becomes the quintessentially Turnerian problem. His belief that he and his recent bride 'would make their own frontier' is quaintly inclusive, but proves naive in the context of a Frontier mythology that is insistently masculine and predicated on division (104). Division is central to the story: Hi's settler dream (the male dream of '*his*land') is neatly divided from reality by real estate agents (real historical figures) who encourage him to join 'The Great Divide Homestead Colony Number One', a 'real' real estate project set up in 1915.[18] The term 'colony' is an admission that the settlement is on foreign ground, the enumeration contrasting with the mythical symbol of the 'homestead' to suggest a broader colonial project. It is the first of many such divisions between rhetoric and reality. Veracini draws our attention to 'Carter Goodrich and Sol Davison's pioneering 1930s work on working-class participation in "Westward movement" [which] described a multitude of associations, societies, cooperative endeavours, schemes, and subscriptions, all constituted for the purpose of settler migration'.[19] Proulx's is one such 'scheme' (a term redolent with negative connotations), and she makes clear in her research in *Red Desert* that there was always an air of corruption over this one, whose founders were publicly horsewhipped and shot at various stages of their careers.

Within the story, the homestead is presented as a site of division from the outset. We join the couple as they shiver on their first visit: Helen swaddled in 'an old-fashioned buffalo robe' that reminds us of the displaced Native Americans; Hi in 'Oxfords' that signal his unpreparedness. His repeated appeal to '*our* own place' is undercut by Helen's unspoken thoughts that inform us that this is '*my*' land since her father's money bankrolled the venture (101, Proulx's italics). There are fence posts, but there is no wire between them and no neighbour to help him to string out to make a division. The only division is with his wife.

Hi, like Archie before him, remains incurably romantic; he envisions a life of breaking horses not sitting on a tractor. Thus, when the farm fails due to his economic mismanagement, he is reluctant to resort to coal mining – the narrator observing by way of exoneration that 'the coal mines were hard for a man who'd once owned his place and worked all his life outdoors' (114). However, the mining town, with its electricity, running water and a social life offers an oasis for Helen, thus proving David Potter's assertion that for most settler women, emancipation began where the frontier ended, in the urban rather than the wilderness.[20] For Hi, the opposite is true, symbolized by the fate of their son, who is so full of the fresh air of the plains that he cannot breathe in the town without an iron lung (114). Hi instead crosses the divide into criminality by making whiskey in a Native American burial site – an ironic location that reminds us of the role of whiskey in destroying the indigenous population, and also the disregard for those living beyond the 'great divide' of Manifest Destiny. Ironically, Hi, or Hiawatha, has more in common with the displaced corpse than he realizes: he too is invested with the spirit of the wild and shows himself spectacularly unsuccessful in adapting to modernity (105).

This is made particularly apparent through his next Western venture as a horse catcher; a role that sees him progressively aligned with the horses he is tasked to trap. Initially, it seems that he has found work commensurate with his dream. As in *Cities of the Plains*, Proulx deploys a series of signifiers – 'the keen wind, the Badlands and outlaw cliffs, the smell of horses' – to enable the remoulding of a Western identity (117). This rebirth is problematized, however, by the characterization of his partner, Fenk Fipps, whose 'womanish voice' and brutal treatment of horses are a corruption of the cowboy ideal. Furthermore, the horses that they catch are not, as Hi naively assumes, destined for rodeo stock, but pet food – thus signalling a further degradation of cowboy dreams. There is a desperation about Hi's range-riding that he shares with McCarthy's 'dog ropin' cowboys, which is brought to an abrupt end by Proulx's deployment of the fence post that had initially made his dream possible. The cowboy undone by fences is an eloquent visual signifier for a closed range and a narrowing of imaginative possibilities. David Miller signals the alienation of his brave cowboy, Jack Burns, in his *Lonely Are the Brave* (1962), by presenting him trapped by fences and interstates; McCarthy takes up the imagery to suggest the frustration of Grady and Billy and to justify their escape to Mexico. Proulx is more nuanced, making clear that the fence post that had signalled the liberty of ownership has become a symbol of corporate exclusion, and drawing out the irony that Hi should be killed trying to avoid one (117).[21] He dies trying to lasso a horse that has escaped his trap; his rope, like his conception of the West, is out of date, and only serves to trip him up; Fenk would never have attempted such a romantic manoeuvre: he would simply have shot the horse. The fact that cruelty flourishes while romanticism is sacrificed highlights the ultimate 'great divide' in this story. For Proulx demonstrates her suspicion of settler mythology, positing instead a 'great divide' between romance and reality and notions of justice on what remains a gendered Frontier.

Fast forward another sixty years to 'The Wamsutter Wolf' (*BD*) and we meet Buddy Millar – a Grady or Billy of the Reagan era. In an ironic reworking of McCarthy's wolf/Comanche imagery, Buddy (a name that advertises his everyman role) is an idealist who believes himself a 'lone wolf'. He rejects his parents' comfortable home and Republican values and hits the 'dirt tracks' following the 'ghostly ruts' of the old Overland Trail in search of 'authentic' West (164). When he hits the Wamsutter trailer park, dismissed by the narrator as a 'desperate place', he believes that he has found it. For Kittredge, trailer parks foster easy money 'gambling, prostitution, sewage problems, and all the macho you could hope for', observing of the Wamsutter site, that it 'lasted three years. They're still getting over it'.[22] Proulx is no apologist for trailer communities; at the end of *Postcards*, she deploys the symbolic opportunities afforded by its vulgar stereotypes – the 'Saturday afternoon target practice. Assorted trucks, cars, motorcycles, snowmobiles, three-wheelers, ATVs' to provide an apt and conclusive symbol of the failure of the American Dream (*P* 337). In 'The Wamsutter Wolf', by contrast, Proulx is interested in how the trailer park questions the reader's notions of what constitutes the authentic West.

She poses a similar question in her story 'Florida Rental' (*BD*) in which she updates Wyoming's notorious Johnson County War 1892 (which pits nesters against the original cattle barons) to the struggle between local ranch owner, Otis Wainwright, and his trailer neighbour, Amanda Gribb. Nightly, his cowboys cut the fences to allow his cattle to take advantage of her carefully tended garden, until she hits upon the deterrent of introducing alligators into the stream that borders their territory. Her victory doesn't simply celebrate female ingenuity overcoming bullying chauvinism, it also invites us to look more closely at how we view the West. For all is not as it seems: Rench is not the independent rancher suggested by his name, but fronts a conglomerate that talks up the 'free range' whilst demonizing Amanda as 'trailer trash'. His vision is dominant, because, as Proulx points out through various subplots, his economic power means that he can rewrite the past to satisfy his own agenda (It is a lesson that Bill Cody taught the West a hundred years ago). Gribb is isolated, but demonstrates a more nuanced understanding of the interconnectedness of the contemporary West, both geographically (she imports the alligators by truck) and notionally with its various pasts. She loves the 'authentic' feel of the Western theme bar where she works, but her landlord's decision to install a television so that his patrons can watch remastered DVDs of 1950s football games demonstrates his power of control: he who controls the present controls the past. In another subplot, one of the cowboys employed to repair the cut fences is invited to Hollywood to star in an update of the Johnson County War, in which it is not the ranchers that force the homesteaders from the land, but a tornado (211). It is another historical reworking that emphasizes the role of money and imagination in the creation of 'history'. Gribb's alligator solution asks us to consider who owns the cultural capital of the New West, reminding us that our view is more often constructed by TV Westerns than 'natural' ecosystems. If cattle, relative newcomers to the West, are to be considered a 'natural' part of the Western landscape, why not alligators and, by extension, trailer parks?

The narrative effect of 'The Wamsutter Wolf' derives from Buddy's naivete. He thinks that his trailer neighbours, the Wham family, are authentic 'poor, hard-working transients, tough as nails and restless, going where the dollars grew', but to the reader, acculturated by daytime TV shows in which trailer families are paraded in a form of Victorian freak show – drunken, violent men with a penchant for monster trucks with their large, sweat-panted wives – the Whams seem authentic 'trailer trash'.[23] The tension between these two perspectives provides the narrative dynamism through which Proulx constantly interrogates our own prejudices. The shattering of Buddy's idealism is foreshadowed by his discovery of a deserted trailer in which he finds an old newspaper cutting that proudly boasts: 'This is our dream come true, to own our own ranch. We're the new pioneers' (150). It is another of Proulx's documents that blurs the distinction between fiction and reality. In her essay 'Inhabitants of the Margins' she records the activities of 'The Triad Land Company' which encouraged families to take up 'forty-acre ranches' in this area in the mid-1970s, despite the objections of locals who scoffed at the idea of farming on such *bad dirt*.[24] The settlement failed, the 'settlers' were left stranded and it is their descendants that Proulx fictionalizes in her story. A cynical crayon addition to the clipping – 'Dad says' – reminds us that for Proulx the real victims were the women and children dragged in the wake of male optimism. Ironically, 'Dad' has adapted and now owns the trailer park, while the cynical daughter is 'the fat woman in grimy sweatpants' who is happy to introduce customers to their modest homes because she never shared her father's delusions (148). Buddy never achieves such accommodation because he only works in cliché. When he is invited into the Wham's trailer for drinks, he expects woodworking tools and maybe a shotgun; he records instead 'wads of trodden gum appeared as archipelagos in a mud-coloured sea while bits of popcorn, string ends, torn paper, a crushed McDonald's cup, and candy wrappers made up the flotsam' (153–4). There is no need for the narrator to broach the subject of broken dreams: Buddy was looking for 'bad dirt', not 'bad housekeeping'. His disillusion, rushing back to his own trailer where he 'quickly made his bed and washed the dishes lest he become like them' transforms him into a figure worthy of ridicule.

Proulx's mockery of Buddy's behaviour also extends to the reader, who she leads into similar misreadings. There is, as *Vogue* columnist Margo Jefferson has noted, a form of 'trailer chic' clearly exhibited in a taste for chunky costume jewellery and the kind of black and white photography that fills art galleries.[25] Proulx explores the thin dividing line between cultural curation and poverty porn in an early story 'Negatives' (*HS*), in which wealthy photographer, Walter Welter, goes West in search of the 'down and dirty'. He identifies it in the character Albina Muth: He 'saw her at the mall supermarket standing in line with children clustered on the cart like flies, or carrying bags of beer and potato chips out to a pickup truck in the parking lot' (172). She is less a person than an agglomeration of clichés (in his dinner party accounts he indulges the fiction that she is a welfare fraudster married to a wife-beater) which he exploits in a photo-shoot in which she poses nude in a series of increasingly degrading positions. This is the 'negative' aspect of Walter's art. He is exercising through her the sadistic fantasies suggested by his name and her social class transformed into art for middle class titillation. By contrast, Proulx has written positively on Carl Mydans' photographic record of the Great Depression; Richard Avedon's no-nonsense portraits of working people collected in *In the American West* (1985); and Andrea Modica's photographs of the trailer community of *Treadwell* (1996), work which carefully navigates between controlling agent and voyeuristic detachment.[26] Avedon's photographs openly challenge the image the West has of itself, replacing handsome cowboys and noble ranchers with blood-splattered slaughterhouse workers, women truckers, drifters and roughnecks. Their scratched, scraped and mangled bodies, Proulx writes in her review of the collection, are a testament to 'tough lives lived in tough places'. The reaction of Westerners was one of fury: they saw the dirt but not the stern beauty.[27]

Proulx's story is about misreadings, in which Buddy and the reader struggle with culturally endorsed models of authenticity. Having dismissed the Whams as hardworking transients they emerge as tattooed trailer rednecks, without ever coming properly into view. The key to the story, however, is their bow-hunting friend, Craig Deshler, who is only concerned with how others see him. He projects himself as latter-day Claude Dallas: 'Everybody tells me I was born a hundred years too late … I should a been a mountain man, they tell me. I'm a throwback and proud of it' (156, 157).[28] Billy dismisses him as a lone crank and a phoney who is not immune to the confusion between authenticity and cultural cliché and has made plenty of concessions to the modern age – Power Wagon, rifle, watch. Deshler's theatrical performance, however, allows Proulx to unpack both the thematic and symbolic centre of the story. When he narrates the story of how Wyoming's indigenous lone wolf was wiped out by the more ubiquitous pack wolf, it seems that he is expressing Darwinian sensibilities that Buddy's Republican parents are happy to ascribe to those trailer families who are losers in Reagan's free market jungle. However, the point of Deshler's story is that this is a misreading: the supposed predator and victim are, in fact, the 'same animal' (159). Thus, Proulx's central metaphor invites us to make a much more considered distinction between evolutionary winners and losers, between predators and victims, and whether we can be one while seeming the other. When Deshler claims 'I look at a wolf, I look at myself' – he does not mean the big, bad wolf – that's Rase – but he is announcing the presence of Wyoming's most adaptable predator, which has survived precisely because everybody thinks that it has disappeared. The same extends to Cheri Wham, the sweat-panted wife whose survival (which means her successful seduction of Buddy) is dependent on his contempt for her. The spirit of the Wild West lives on but it emerges in surprising places and, in The Sagebrush Kid, Craig Deshler and Cheri Wham, in surprising forms that remain dangerous to the unwary.

Proulx's settler stories demolish a powerful founding myth by exposing its victims – the idealistic young men and the families they drag behind them. They are stories in which notions of 'authenticity' and 'heritage' are bent out of shape by both exploiters and exploited and in which victims are those characters whose search for the values and customs of an imaginary Old West leaves them prey to the unscrupulous business practices of the New West. In such stories Proulx's protagonists are the victims; the land provides either the hostile environment for a Turnerian struggle or a prop to cowboy fantasies. This is the role it plays in *Butcher's Crossing*, the desert-ride and snow-entrapment providing the necessary conditions for identity change. In McCarthy's *Blood Meridian* the land is nothing more than a baroque stage upon which theatrical acts of depravity are committed, whilst in the *Border Trilogy* it is presented as tired and unequal to the romantic demands of his young protagonists: a test site for nuclear rather than cowboy dreams. In Proulx's 2002 novel *That Old Ace in the Hole,* however, geography takes centre stage, the ace in question being both the land and the characters with whom it forges a symbiotic relationship.

III

It is also Proulx's protagonist, Bob Dollar, an abandoned orphan whose search for identity and a sense of belonging becomes an analogue for the struggle faced by all the Westerners he meets. Bob is another naive outsider. He takes a job as a site scout for a corporate hog farm enterprise and travels to the Texas Panhandle to work incognito. He becomes the passive ear to which an array of quirky Western archetypes tell stories, the most important being that which characterizes their relationship with the land. It is a relationship gone awry; a century of telling the wrong story (Eden, Manifest Destiny, plucky pioneers, cattle trails) has led to environmental catastrophe. In what is Proulx's most environmentally conscious novel, she joins a formidable array of Western commentators – Kittredge, Edward Abbey, Sharman Apt Russell and Rick Bass – to critique both contemporary farming practice and the rhetoric that has made it possible. For Abbey the West is a giant feedlot in which overstocking is rampant and, because 'you can't eat scenery', diversity unwelcome. The rancher is the bad guy – a welfare parasite who has clogged up the West with ill-adapted cattle whilst telling us 'how much he loves the American West'.[29] Proulx is more ambivalent; her Abbey-like ecoterrorist Wade Walls in *The Governors of Wyoming* (CR) is as stodgy and blinkered as his name suggests, and throughout her *Wyoming Trilogy* she reserves an imaginative sympathy for her curmudgeonly ranchers.

Her target in *That Old Ace* is the controversial activities of *Seaboard Corporation*, which was secretly purchasing tracts of land to site hog farms to feed a new 16,500-hog-per-day slaughterhouse sited near Dumas. To its critics, hog farming is an environmentally damaging business: it is water intensive, cruel to animals and poisons the air for miles around.[30] Proulx's tone is neither polemical (this is not Abbey), nor regretfully wistful (Proulx avoids Kittredge's nostalgia). Her combination of satire (screwball at times) combined with social realism is closer to Jane Smiley's *Moo* (1995) (which humorously exposes the link between corporate enterprise and academic research), Ruth Ozeki's *My Year with Meats* (1999) (in which US beef conglomerates encourage the public to use more of their hormone enhanced product through a cooking programme) and also her *All over Creation* (2003) (which follows a group of contemporary ecoterrorists). By making her young protagonist the advocate for an enterprise of which she clearly disapproves, Proulx provides the narrative tension in the novel, as various parties – ecologists, oilmen and ranchers – struggle over his soul.

Bob's first view of the West is through his car windscreen, a familiar trope that reminds us that even in modern times the landscape can still perform its traditional function as agent of change. When, in Robert Penn Warren's *All the King's Men* (1946), Jack Burden (a name that deliberately recalls Willa Cather's Jim Burden in *My Antonia*) enters the West for the first time he notes, 'I pulled the sun screen down and squinted and put the throttle to the floor. And kept on moving west. For West is where we all plan to go someday … It is where you go to grow up with the country. It is where you go to spend your old age. Or it is just where you go.'[31] The West is 'just where you go' – the process of Westering so deeply engrained in a shared cultural consciousness that the rationale – to grow up or grow old with the country – seems immaterial. Resonant in such examples, as Krista Comer notes, 'are the links between masculinist visual ideologies' that structure the observer as active and, of course, male, and the 'landscape' as passive, virginal and coded female: a postcard image of a 'pristine' landscape that becomes the authentic American West.[32] Ten years later and Jack Kerouac's Sal Paradise, a Grady for the Beat generation, goes *On the Road* obsessed with the notion of the West as revealing national myth: 'All winter I'd been reading of the great wagon parties that held council there before hitting the Oregon and Santa Fe trails' where he is electrified by his sight of his first cowboy.[33] Bob, like Jack and Sal, is entering the West for the first time, and we are immediately made aware of his sense that this is a special landscape intimately tied up with history and mythology:

> In late March Bob Dollar, a young, curly-headed man of twenty-five with the broad face of a cat, pale innocent eyes fringed with sooty lashes, drove east along Texas State Highway 15 in the panhandle, down from Denver the day before, over the Raton Pass and through the dead volcano country of northeast New Mexico to the Oklahoma pistol barrel, then a wrong turn north and wasted hours before he regained the way. It was a roaring spring morning with green in the sky, the air spiced with sand sagebrush and aromatic sumac ... It was all flat expanse and wide sky. Two coyotes looking for afterbirths trotted to a pasture to the east, moving through fluid grass, the sun backlighting their fur.
>
> Bob Dollar had no idea he was driving into a region of immeasurable natural complexity that some believed abused beyond saving. He saw only what others had seen – the bigness, pump jacks nodding pterodactyl heads, road alligators cast off from the big semi tires. Every few miles a red-tailed hawk marked its hunting boundary. The edges of the road were misty with purple-flowered wild mustard whose rank scent embittered the air. He said to the rearview mirror 'Some flat-ass place.' Though it seemed he was not so much in a place as confronting the raw material of human use.
>
> (1, 3)

Bob is presented as our naïf for whom the long-sight lines of the West provide the background to fantasy. His 'innocent eyes' see the land seen by both Jim and Jack Burden – the curiously archaic 'the raw material of human use' deliberately echoing the former's description of the Nebraska plains as 'not a country at all, but the material out of which countries are made'.[34] However, this is a landscape prompted as much by his imagination and decades of Western acculturation as the geography in front of him. The bucolic beauty of scented purple flowers and wild mustard combine with the iconic symbol of the 'red-tailed hawk' and a more ancient past reimagined in the 'pterodactyl' pump jacks and the 'alligator tire treads'. Meanwhile the Wild West of Hollywood imagination lives on in names like 'Pistol Barrel' and the ubiquitous coyotes, the detailing of their backlit fur suggesting that they are trotting out of a movie set. Essentially, Proulx is conjuring a scene that says less about a specific landscape than the reader's cultural expectations – a fantasy shattered when we engage with the pump-jacks and shredded tyres unmetaphorically. For despite seeming 'some flat-ass place' Proulx makes clear that 'beneath the fields and pastures lay an invisible world of pipes, cables, boreholes, pumps and extraction devices, forming with the surface fences and roads, a monstrous three-dimensional grid' (2). The empty landscape has been 'caged' by modern technology and 'abused beyond saving' – it's just that Bob is not aware of it yet.

In this novel, finding yourself implies seeing beyond the idealized surface to acknowledge a more complex relationship between the land and the people it sustains. Thus, as in *The Border Trilogy*, maps become a way of measuring the protagonist's engagement with his environment. Indeed, in many ways the novel can be read as a parable in which Bob comes to understand that knowing the West, its people and therefore himself, involves more than being able to read a map. His tendency to idealism is prefigured in his misunderstanding of the map that stands in the hallway of his childhood home, which 'showed fifty great rivers of the earth arranged as dangling strings and graded as to length' (18). Bob takes it to be some fabulous distant land, until his uncle points out that 'It's not a real place … you dunce. It's only for the sake of comparison'. This, as Alex Hunt observes, sets the tone for Bob's engagement with the West, which exist in a state of comparison between representation and reality.[35] Maps appear in all shapes and sizes, from the pictorially imaginative through the cartographically precise to those internalized in memory. Sheriff Hugh Dough, for example, has mapped most of the state through the average roadkill.

The most important are those contained in Lieutenant William Albert's journal, *Expedition to the Southwest, An 1845 Reconnaissance of Colorado, New Mexico, Texas and Oklahoma*, which is presented to Bob on the eve of his departure. It is another one of those historical artefacts that Proulx introduces into her text, blurring the distinction between fiction and historical documentation. Albert's mission was to produce accurate military maps on the eve of the Texas Mexico conflict, but a faulty chronometer meant that his maps were militarily useless, leaving his diary and illustrations to provide a more articulate engagement with the land he was sent to measure. He proved a scientifically enlightened and artistically gifted draftsman who demonstrates a keen eye for both geology and flora (for which he knew Latin classifications), and whose prose, according to the Introduction to the original edition, 'swings between the discourse of science and the language of art and romantic imperialism'.[36] The oxymoronic notion of 'romantic imperialism' is a rhetorical sleight of hand that applies to both the maps (which are beautifully drawn but cartographically inaccurate), Albert's description of Native Americans (Noble Savages soon to be removed) and, ironically, the character of Albert himself. His relationship with Bob is both personal (both are outsiders bullied at school) and ironic; it is no accident that the first thing Bob does on entering the West is take a wrong turn and get lost: neither man knows where they are or the implications of what they are doing. Initially, Bob is determined to follow in Albert's footsteps, but in his edition 'the only map was execrable – extremely small and devoid of any detail', which forces him to use his 'Western States road map'. This proves equally problematic because 'its maker had dispensed with the smaller rivers and tributaries' (92–3). In both cases we are reminded that maps, like the narrative of La Von's *Rural Compendium*, construct rather than reflect a reality through careful selection and curation.[37] Eventually, Albert's Journal performs the function of palimpsest, as Bob reads through the land attempting to retrieve the innocence of the earlier narrative. An afternoon spent scouting for hog farm sites is recorded in a linguistic palette redolent of the journal: 'One late afternoon he was under the brow of the caprock hiking along a trail of orange dust so fine it seemed a kind of defiant liquid, climbing a slight incline through shrubs and violet-colored cacti like spiny cow tongues' (198). Both men are naive idealists who fall in love with the beauty of the region while unwittingly opening it up to exploitation – a pattern repeated in the activities of all central characters.

Another important map is that internalized by windmill man, Ace Crouch. When he summons his wife to join him, he tells her: 'County Road J and turn north on Wrink Road. Watch the tracks, the wheel tracks ... About half a mile and there's a gate. It's kind of hard to open so I'll git somebody to keep a watch for you and open the gate' (164). It's a map of cowboy country (those tracks could have been made by Ace's truck or settler wagons) for a person who knows the signs but has never been there; significantly when she arrives, she can't open the gate. For Ace, the landscape is not a static surface, but a palimpsest that reveals a site of cultural struggle signified most clearly by the adaptability symbolized by his windmills. Those engaged in this struggle acquire not only the inherited internalized deep maps, but also, more alarmingly, 'historical and psychological rights' over the land (333). There are no Native Americans in Ace's cowboy vision, an omission he justifies to Bob by pointing out that they were nomadic and therefore had no 'rights' to the land they did not farm. His internalized map, therefore, is both an expression of personal engagement and an assertion of interiorized cultural imperialism; as such he ventriloquizes a rhetoric or imperial inversion. As an incomer he projects upon the indigenous population (projection being a defensive mechanism[38]) a state of nomadic rootlessness which contrasts with the fixedness ironically suggested by his windmills. Not only does such discourse ignore the presence of Indigenous peoples who did practise agriculture but it also leads to the irony that even if they were not nomadic when the settlers arrived, they were soon made so.[39] And this in turn leads to what anthropologist Ana Maria Alonso has identified as a form of 'sedentarist metaphysics' through which the displaced native is transformed into the morally suspect character of the wanderer – whether the wandering Jew, or nomadic gypsy or other groups beyond both the cultural and moral pale.[40]

Proulx explores this element of cultural displacement through her presentation of Native American characters as hitchhikers: they wander into her narratives and allow Proulx to explore a number of familiar Native American tropes. Joe Blue Skies (*Postcards*) is Proulx's most postmodern literary figure as he is created from textual fragments (diary entries, his gnomic utterances, the postcards of the title) which present conflicting clichés of Native American identity – from the profoundly taciturn, to the shaman who can conjure a tornado, to the confidence trickster who metaphorically 'scalps' the novel's central protagonist. The process of piecing together the clues guides us to an interpretative strategy which invites the reader to construct their own 'Indian' archetype. In 'The Governors of Wyoming' (*CR*) Proulx uses the presence of another hitchhiking Native American character to expose the sexual exploitation of the indigenous population by the first white settlers and its continued practice in the contemporary West. The recent work of Sarah Deer and Mary Kathryn Nagle, and Taylor Sheridan's neo-Western *Wind River* (2007) have both made clear that a long history of the 'sexual exploitation of Native women and children' has been given a new lease of life in the 'man camps' created to support drilling and mining.[41] In Proulx's story, it is Shy Hemp (a name that suggests his tentative attachment to the land) whose ecoterrorist activities are juxtaposed to his paedophile exploitation of a young Native American girl. Ironically, in attempting to return the land to a 'state of nature' before the arrival of his white ancestors, it is clear that he is attempting to remove all exploitative elements, a process that includes himself.

The 'wandering Indian' hitchhiker picked up by Bob Dollar is Moony Brassleg, whose presence asks us to consider the relationship between heritage, nostalgia and authenticity in the construction of a viable identity. In 'How the West was Spun' Proulx explores the 'Indian' as hyperreal fiction, a copy without a referent, whose identity has changed in accordance with consumer tastes, evolving from the Hollywood 'Savage Indian' to the equally fanciful victim of Kevin Costner's *Dances with Wolves* (1988) to the environmental shaman who promises to show today's harried white population the way to serenity and health.[42] Lisa Aldred picks up this last invention in 'Plastic Shamans and Astroturf Sun Dances' in which she argues that Anglos tend to romanticize an 'authentic' and 'traditional' Native American culture 'whose spirituality can save them from their own sense of malaise'.[43] Unfortunately, as Patricia Limerick has noted, the shift towards 'the Indian side' shows a 'unitary, simple, pristine, and victimized Indian' just as un-illuminating as the old myth.[44] Thus, as Native Americans have been transformed from character to symbol it has proved difficult for both historians and writers to bring them into view. Sherman Alexie's work continually warns us of the dangers of trying to posit an 'authentic' Native American identity existing separately from the complex negotiations that have created the 'Indian'. His *Lone Ranger* stories (1993) offer a mocking meditation on what it might mean to be an Indian ensnared by generic models of behaviour that vary from the loyal Tonto to the self-destructive drunk. As one of his disaffected characters remarks: 'How many times have you seen *Dances with Wolves*? ... Do you think that shit is real? God. Don't you even know how to be a real Indian?'[45]

This question floats over Bob's encounter with Brassleg. His views have been shaped by the romanticism of Albert's Diary (in which the 'Indians' appear as noble) and the settler tales of his landlady ('They got hold of a clock salesman last year, cut open his stomach, pulled out his guts a ways' (76)), so when he cheerily asks, 'Where are you from?' he is clearly hoping for a tribal affiliation that connects the man in front of him with either of these projections. The comically bathetic response – 'Oklahoma' – masks a serious point: it is a white answer to a white question that narrows identity to the name a specific place. Like Ace, Brassleg also has an internalized map, but where Ace's is full of named landmarks that reinforce the sense of ownership, Brassleg's reveals a more imaginative relationship with the land. It is typical of the 'deep maps' theorized by Anglo-Native American writer William Least Heat-Moon, which reveals a symbiotic relationship with the land without the politically motivated impulse towards division that underlies Western cartographic practice.[46] As Bob and Brassleg drive in silence, Proulx records how they enter 'sand sage and dune country' where 'it was impossible not to think of blowing dust gradually covering everything', a landscape that reminds us of the Indigenous culture that has vanished and elicits Brassleg's sardonic: 'Most there, ain't we?' (286).

'There' is a cultural as well as a geographic location. Ostensibly, it is the house of Brassleg's daughter, which, conventional on the outside with a log-cabin interior, reflects her own mixed identity – a nurse who has taken an Anglo name but who continues to identify with her cultural heritage. Part of that Anglicization is that she knows how to draw a map that Bob will understand. Her husband, another Bob, is a recovering alcoholic whose therapy is based on learning the ceremonies and traditions of their ancestors. Vine Deloria Jr calls this process 'retribalisation', a practice which marks not an evasive nostalgia for a vanished past but a confidence amongst Native Americans to resist total assimilation within the white hegemony.[47] In this environment, Brassleg reverses the traveller and guide roles, and like one of McCarthy's mentors, advises the orphaned Bob: 'There are chances for you, a white young man. How you like it on the reservation, forty to eighty-five per cent unemployment, no jobs at all, not money to get out, no school, nothing but get drunk, make babies, use the ADC check for bottle?' (294). There is clear political punch in an apocalyptic vision that would not look out of place in the work of Kittredge, Alexie or Louise Erdrich; but there is also a theatricality about the evening that puts us on our guard. Bob Mason's aphoristic, faux-Indian register narrowly avoids parody, and the traditional Indian paintings produced by Brassleg that seem 'full of meaning' to Bob appear kitsch to the reader (292, 3). Proulx seems to be warning us that her Native American characters, like her cowboys, are just as susceptible to participation in caricatured versions of themselves. Brassleg seems to occupy two worlds, but here they are contrived to deliberately thwart our expectations: his gnomic advice – 'you will have to find your way alone' – is balanced by our sight of him settling down to watch television: he is both Shaman and consumer of pulp culture (294).

Bob's search for identity, like that of Bob Mason, provides an analogue for the West struggling do define a regional identity within an increasingly global market economy. When, for example, he drives into the fictional town of Cowboy Rose (a name suggestive of archetype), he expects to see the roaming cowboys suggested by the town's name, but is greeted with enormous feedlots and Chicano workers emerging from a meat packing plant (43). The imaginative is shattered by the reality. And yet, despite the clear participation of the residents in a market economy, their identity is crafted around a highly stylized version of Western character in which, through a knowingly overwritten version of regional identity, the narrator is complicit. It begins with the evocatively sentimental chapter title – 'No Room in Cowboy Rose' and continues with the town's boast – 'once a cattle town, then a ghost town, now slowly reviving' (44). The term 'reviving' implies 'restoring' its cowboy past and ignoring the suffocating present (44). It may be ringed by feedlots, but ranch fences are 'hung with dead coyotes' and signage that would not look out of place in Hollywood mock-up: 'TRESPASSERS WILL BE SHOT SURVIVORS WILL BE PERSECUTED' (44). This is not, however, a tourist trap; the only concession to tourism is the town's hilariously irrelevant 'TORNADO & BALL POINT PEN MUSEUM'. The locals are not recreating a Western idyll for outsiders, but for themselves; they are living a caricature of Western identity to protect them from the existential threats posed by the globalization they are forced to embrace.

Woolybucket provides a more muted version of this self-reflexive performance as Bob listens to the stories of a gallery of Western caricatures (struggling under an assortment of parodic names) that define their identity with the West. Narratives matter and are fundamental to the creation of community identity, particularly for those communities, according settler colonial theorists, whose careful curation of stories vindicates a history of seizure and settlement. Proulx draws our attention to the dangers of selective curation through La Von Fronk's *Rural Compendium* – a collection of random photographs, newspaper cuttings and diaries dropped into her mailbox which comprises her highly partial regional history. Significantly these items are 'filed by family, not by year' because she believes that a regional identity is not to be traced through a clear line of historical evolution, but is the sum of its family stories (68). The result is as chaotic as the 'thrift museum' run by the uncles who raised Bob, who deliberately conferred meaning and value (placing them on pedestals) on those everyday artefacts usually dismissed – light bulbs, vacuum cleaners and even Bob himself. The West that emerges from the *Rural Compendium* is a deliberate challenge to cultural expectations. An 1884 photograph of cross-dressing farmers (complete with catwalk descriptions – 'C W Pool, a pumpkin coloured blonde, wore overskirt ecru denims, with corsage of lemon color cretonns' (103)) leaves Bob reflecting that it 'was not what he associated with old-time cattlemen' (104); a photograph of the young cowboy, Muddy Fanny – who 'died for love of a little bitty pig-tail seven-year old' – resurrects the West of cowboy ballads whilst simultaneously reminding us of the eccentric relationships that developed on the margins of society. An even more radical challenge to regional identity is contained in 'the light bulb cemetery' that Bob discovers on the margins of the town. Colloquially known as 'a nigger graveyard', it rests beneath a lifeless windmill (a dusty relic symbolizing the death of a certain vision of the West) and contains those elements left out of la Von's predominantly white history (242). The lesson taken from both is that evasion and selective curation combined with the deployment of recognizable cultural signifiers (windmills rather than light bulbs) are central to the creation of a unifying regional mythology.

The stories that most interest Proulx in this novel, however, are more directly related to the characters' and community's relationship with the land. Settler colonial theorists draw the distinction between mapping narratives like those of Albert that are concerned with discovery and exploration, colonial narratives that are circular (the colonizers eventually returning home), and the narratives of settlers who carry their cultural expectations with them and 'transform the land into their image'.[48] Kyle Whyte notes that since such narratives rely on the erasure of Indigenous economies, cultures and rights to the land, they are evasive and constructed around moral justification (such as cultural or agricultural inferiority) combined with both legal and religious exoneration.[49] We have already noted Ace Crouch's troubling espousal of the myth of the indigenous nomad as a justification for land seizure: for Ace, who is Proulx's disconcerting Ace in the hole, it is a relationship with a specific landscape that forges a community, just so long as you happen to be white – and male. Within the body of the novel, Proulx sets out to explore further her protagonists' chauvinism by drawing attention to the dangers of telling the wrong story. She reconfigures the rhetorical tropes and mythical symbolism of the Old Testament to construct a frame narrative of Eden discovered, nurtured and destroyed. There is nothing new here. As early as the mid-sixties, historian Lynn White Jr was challenging the ethical and environmental implications of Manifest Destiny, arguing that Adam's duty of naming in the Garden fostered the exploitative attitudes and practices that created the ecological crisis facing the West.[50] Wallace Stegner argues that a childish sense of entitlement meant that settlers entered the West not as the promised land 'but as Egyptian grave robbers might approach the tomb of pharaoh'.[51] Kittredge is similar, as suggested by his provocative titles 'Owning it All' and 'White People in Paradise' which record the disastrous experiences of his own family in the Warner Valley:

> We were doing God's labour and creating a good place on earth, living the pastoral yeoman dream – that's how mythology defined it ... And then it all went dead ... We had reinvented our valley according to the most pervasive ideal given to us by our culture, and we ended with a landscape organized like a machine ... a dreamland gone wrong.[52]

A dreamland gone wrong because his family listened to the myth rather than the land. McCarthy hints at the damage of spiritually endorsed narratives, whether Billy's naming of the features around his Cloverdale home or Grady's 'Fall' from the Paradise of his Texas ranch. But, having fallen they simply relocate Paradise to Mexico which becomes the unspoilt wilderness for their ill-conceived cowboy fantasy.

Proulx's Panhandlers are in trouble because the stories they have told and continue to tell about their relationship with the land don't work anymore on an environmental, economic or trans-cultural level. Such stories are ironic; her training as an historian in the *annales* tradition makes clear that a regional identity is not forged by grand narratives but the interactions of ordinary people with a specific land, climate and set of economic conditions over the longue durée.[53] In the case of Woolybucket, however, the foundational mythology is imported and upholstered in biblical tropes that condone exploitation through evasion and euphemism. Proulx offers a critique of such an approach through the inclusion La Von's story of her grandfather, Moises Harshberger. He is a caricature 'harsh' prophet of Manifest Destiny who promises to lead his cowboys to a promised land but finds instead a harsh desert. The biblical underpinning vindicates a Stegnerian sense of entitlement as we are told that 'in fencing the land a certain balance shifted. Now Harshberger felt that the land was servant to him and it owed him a living, owed him everything he could get from it' (86). It is a psychological shift towards what Proulx terms elsewhere 'the elixir of ownership' – a drunken belief in possession as an end in itself detached from economic and social context.[54] With possession comes rights, and having failed to discover Paradise, Proulx notes that he seeks to create it through the importation of 'shady trees' and cattle that transform a 'strange land' into home. In this, he is following the behaviour of colonial settlers who do not arrive empty handed, but bring their plants and animals with them. And since, Tom Lynch notes, many who made the journey west did so from a culture for whom green is a synecdoche for environmental health, it should come as little surprise that they should seek to green the healthy desert, much as Adam Trask does in Steinbeck's *East of Eden*, through the planting of shrubs and trees.⁵⁵ Proulx's critique of such domestication is full of wry irony: not only, despite the constant watering by disgruntled cowboys (who do not see themselves as gardeners), do most of Hashberger's trees die, but his cattle that are wiped out in blizzards of biblical severity. He is applauded for his tenacity, but this particular Promised Land proves a dry, arid plain that rejects his changes, leaving him to sell the dry bones under his feet to enrich the land of others (89). In this last gesture, as with McCarthy's buffalo bone-pickers, we are reminded that he is not a biblical prophet, but part of an inter-connected farming community whose advanced practices will grind bones into fertilizers that will transform the land into a giant feedlot.

Harshberger fails because he does not adapt, which is not the case with Abner Skieret, who, like his biblical forebear (Abner was commander of Saul's army who when faced with defeat changed sides), adapts to changing circumstance. Skieret resists fencing the free range until he loses a bet with a travelling barb wire salesman – Blowy Cluck (a name that suggests that he knows which way the wind is blowing) – who promises that his wire 'is making Texas a farmer's paradise' (193). Like his forebear, and also Albert and Bob, he becomes the reluctant advocate of a new vision of the panhandle parcelled up into neat packages: old notions of freedom are overwhelmed by a stronger instinct towards possession. These are the sentiments that guide the contemporary residents of Woolybucket, who exercise their veneration of the concept of enclosure in their annual 'Barb Wire Festival'.

Another ambiguous model of adaptation is presented through the activities of the novel's Dutch windmill engineer, Van Meerbeek Habakuk (Habakuk is the Old Testament prophet who sought divine justice on earth). The rise of the eccentric, clean-living Dutchman to petro-billionaire through a combination of hard work and ingenuity seems the very stuff of the American dream: because he is just he is blessed. His windmills are similarly symbolic: not only are they adaptive in a Darwinian sense to the way the wind is blowing, but the penetration of the Virgin land by phallic drills to make the plains fertile fits in with an insistently male Turnerian narrative. And yet, as Ace later concedes, the windmill may have 'made the panhandle a *Garden of Eden*. But that same technology has kept us from adjustin to the bedrock true nature a this place and that's somethin will catch up to us one of these days' (my italics, 111). Thus, a symbol of adaptation and progress is reintegrated into a narrative of exploitation and stasis, represented most clearly by the rusty windmill on Jim Skein's desiccated ranch. Furthermore, Proulx allows Bob late in the novel to offer a socially grounded attack on the windmill as an 'anti-community technology' because it replaced old water-co-ops with an 'every man for himself' attitude (335).

The descendants of these men make up The Ladies Baptist sewing circle, whose quilting offers a conservative, small-town interpretation of the community's relationship with both the land and its past. It is, as Alex Hunt argues, a symbiotic process, as our tendency to domesticate landscapes by projecting our cultural stories on to them is mirrored by the way in which those landscapes tend to reshape our narratives.[56] The quilt that the ladies are working on when Bob visits is the biblical story of Cain and Abel. The story exemplifies the time-honoured struggle between herdsman and farmer and is a master narrative woven into the cultural fabric of the West through Steinbeck's *East of Eden* and Hammerstein's playful call to all the Oklahoma Cain's and Abel's to forget their differences for the good of the Territory.[57] Proulx exemplifies this process of regional appropriation through the ladies eschewing 'those stripy robes and sandals ... to make it more real-like' – 'reality' in this context being a copy of a copy, since Bob notes a resemblance to James Dean rather than a biblical figure. The less dramatic brotherly struggle is played out by the way in which Ace's windmills have domesticated the landscape and opened it up to the modern agricultural practices that are now suffocating his brother, Tater. Figuratively, he is a contemporary Laocoön (the Trojan priest strangled by snakes) symbolized by the narrative description of the reins of his cherished freight wagon (a Trojan horse that, like Albert and Bob, opened up the region to exploitation) being 'twined like Laocoön's snake' (246). Another of the ladies' tapestries shows the Fall:

> In the center of the Garden stood a magnificent apple tree loaded with shining satin apples, and twined in its branches was an oversize diamond back rattler ... Adam was naked except for two cowboy boots and a hat, which he held in front of his crotch ... Eve, chatting gaily with the snake, her back to the viewer, showed long pink buttocks. She was wearing a charm bracelet, each charm sharply detailed, and Bob could make out a dangling state of Texas. An apple core lay on the ground.
>
> (173)

It is perhaps not surprising that in the eyes of such a conservative body Adam should be an embarrassed cowboy and Eve an unashamed post-Fall flirt. More broadly, Proulx reminds us through Eve's Texas 'charm' anklet of the tendency for the land to be coded female – both an 'Earth Mother' and 'Virgin Wilderness' waiting to be 'penetrated' (or 'deflowered') 'husbanded' and seeded with the components of masculine culture.[58] We have already noted Habakuk's drills, but through a subplot involving Evelyn Chine – who is Bob's competition as a site scout – Proulx explores fully the metaphorical implications of this tired trope. This particular 'Eve' fulfils the role of sexual temptress by using an affair with a local rancher to prepare the way for hog farming operations. However, in this particular Paradise, 'Adam' has already eaten of the tree of knowledge and used science to enable him to take over the role of god. Though he bathes himself in the rhetoric of Texas past, he is 'a scientific rancher' who uses antibiotics and artificial insemination from 'champion bulls' – a procedure that underlines the masculine virility underpinning his engagement with the land (198, 56). He is a rancher who has clearly lost contact with the land his forebears struggled to make fruitful, his scientific approach seeming a natural precursor to the intensive hog farming methods represented by Bob.

Proulx's focus in this novel is not simply in Paradise unwittingly lost, however, but also the possibility of its being regained. Within the narrative the re-wilding projects of Ace Crouch and his brother – returning the plains to their 'original state' through the removal of cattle and the reintroduction of buffalo and wild grasses – stands in opposition to corporate hog farming. Such projects were introduced in the mid-eighties through the environmentalists Frank and Deborah Popper (name-checked intratextually as inspiration) and popularized by moguls like Ted Turner. Having made millions selling commercials during old John Wayne movies, he made a number of revisionist series such as *The Native Americans: Behind the Legends, Beyond the Myths* (TNT 1993) and bought the Flying D ranch near Bozeman. Much to the horror of the local cowboys, he tore down the barb wire fences and reintroduced buffalo claiming that they 'are better looking than cows'.[59] Limerick heralded a new environmentally conscious 'Turnerian West' to replace Frederick Jackson's exploitative Old West: 'He wanted to make this change ... because the buffalo were the emblematic animals of the Old West and especially the days before the white American conquest (he was going to turn the clock back at the ranch, he said, nearly two hundred years).'[60] To the Poppers, the extermination of the buffalo signals the corruption of white conquest left out of mythology, thus the notion of 'buffalo commons' (as the term 'commons' implies) is a 'decline-and-redemption story' in which a move towards treating the land as a common source may heal the wounds of history.[61]

Ostensibly, Proulx's novel becomes a Western morality tale in which the white-hatted eco-cowboys struggle against the black-hatted hog farmers for the soul of Bob Dollar. The sanctity of an already one-side struggle is reinforced by the policy's chief advocate, Brother Mesquite (a name that advertises his spiritual unity with the landscape). He challenges the Christian orthodoxy that man was given dominion over the land and animals with a 'moral geography' predicated upon the belief that certain people, things and practices belong in certain spaces, places and landscapes and not in others. As an environmental approach it shares similarities with Aldo Leopold's environmental manifesto 'The Land Ethic' (1970) (which calls for a sustainable form of land use) and Kathleen Norris's *Dakota: A Spiritual Geography* (1993) (in which 'desert wisdom' combines rural discipline with monastic asceticism).[62] Brother Mesquite is concerned with reversing the symbolism of 'cow country' and establishing a spiritual relationship:

Now the buffs, they evolved in the plains with the plants – the two grew up together, they *belong* together in this place, this landscape. The bison and the native plant species have a relationship. Your cow is out of place here … you've got to give them water – those thousands of windmills … the buff rustles for hisself. He'll walk a long way for water … the bison is self-reliant and belongs in this country. The cow, bred to be placid and sluggish and easy to handle, is a interloper.

(274–5)

His message is a moral vision entirely consistent with Proulx's *annales* historiography in which identity is constructed upon a symbiotic relationship with the land. It is also, as his reconfiguration of Genesis suggests, highly adaptable. In Ace Crouch's settler mythology his windmills represent a hardy adaptability that gives rights of possession over interlopers like the ill-adapted Bob and the corporate farmers he represents. It is only recently that he has acknowledged that his windmills 'kept us from adjustin to the bedrock true nature a this place' and they are now paying the price (111). Ace's rolling out of the Buffalo Commons, therefore, is a literal and metaphorical act of decolonization in which the cow – a symbol of imposition and domestication is removed in favour of the buffalo, which is self-reliant, adaptive and therefore biologically and morally superior. It is also indigenous and has a special place in Native American cultural consciousness. Jonathan Lear's ethical and psychoanalytical examination of the relationship between Native peoples and the land is grounded in Chief Plenty Coups' (Crow Nation contemporary of Sitting Bull) chilling observation: 'When the buffalo went away the hearts of my people fell to the ground and they could not lift them up again. After this nothing happened.'[63] For Plenty Coup the buffalo removal brought a 'end of history' more potent than that theorized by Fukuyama; it removed not simply a practical source of food, clothing and homemaking, but a source of ritual and symbolism that left them without a means of constructing a meaningful narrative about their lives.[64] For Sitting Bull, the dreams of the 'Ghost Dance' elided the return of the buffalo with a spectral army of braves to preach a radical message of resistance to the white colonizer; Plenty Coup, by contrast, presents a dream in which he walks in a wood where tribesmen react to the threat of an oncoming tornado, to preach a message of adaptation and accommodation.[65] According to such a reading, the return of the buffalo is not simply, as Nick Estes has observed in *Our History is the Future* (2019), a highly symbolic act for a people whose dependence upon it was literal, metaphorical and spiritual, it also returns the means of creating stories.[66]

Proulx's story withholds a 'happy ending' that envisions Bob finding both friends and saving the land in a manner approved by Moony Brassleg. There is to be no redemption for either character or land. Proulx seems troubled by re-wilding schemes, particularly the paradox of returning the land to an original state without ever being able to conceptualize such a space. She mock's the efforts of moguls like Ted Turner through characters like Frank Fane in 'A Pair of Spurs' (*CR*) who has made his money playing a Jupiterian warlord in a science-fiction television series and has moved West with plans to buy a ranch and return it to a state of nature. He is not, however, interested in regional authenticity, but a notional authenticity, which is a generic Western space (complete with imported Texas cowboys) that conforms to the one of his Hollywood-inspired imagination: a film set every bit as inauthentic and artificial as those that back his science fiction series. Proulx picks up this criticism by foregrounding the contradictions that lie at the heart of Ace's scheme: not only is it funded by money made from oil (an irony which further tarnishes his white hat) but it will be subsidized further by building retirement homes – 'Prairie Restoration Homesteads' – that will provide a view of 'unspoilt nature' (118). Thus, the land, as John Brinckerhoff Jackson has theorized, becomes the property of a cultural elite who transform it into something to be looked at rather than lived in.[67] As William Cronon was to observe in his essay 'The Trouble with Wilderness' (1996), environmentalists seemed to be 'getting back to the wrong kind of nature' structured around a 'bourgeois anti-modernism' redolent of a male-gendered romanticized Frontier mythology.[68] It is the very opposite of Proulx's approach to the land as a dynamic, lived space, in which buffalo herds and wild grasses mingle with the pump jacks and trailer parks to announce the presence of a population going about its business. Essentially, her message appears to be that in the pursuit of blinkered ideology, environmentalists must not be allowed to *Close* the *Range*.

Proulx's denouement centres on two generic symbols of the West – the windmill, which is both symbol of adaptation and progress or exploitation and stasis (there are a lot of defunct specimens in the narrative) – and the barbwire that signals closure. In the end it is the latter that is dominant, as Proulx closes the novel with the annual 'Barbwire Festival' in which the inhabitants of Woolybucket reinforce their shared identity through the worship of the wire that made the closure of the range possible. Within it they perform a synthetic version of their past, which includes stalls selling 'bad cowboy art', recitations of cowboy poetry and even a 'Grand Parade' worthy of Disneyland. Here Bob forgoes the T-shirt and shorts that have proclaimed his outsider status and puts on jeans and cowboy boots and embraces the local community (344). He believes that in the mirror he looks like a real Texan but acknowledges that the change is purely cosmetic, that he is simply appropriating the costumery. Thus, Proulx artfully brings Bob's story of abandonment and self-discovery together with a regional story of identity crisis to create a dominant sentiment of shared desperation. However, his personal story (abandonment by feckless parents) means that he alone understands that problems cannot be dealt with by looking backward, only by adapting to the present: 'He wanted to tell them that nothing worked out for the best, that ruined places could not be restored, that some aquifers could not recharge' (358). Bob has not put his life together, remains suspicious of nostalgia and uncertain of the future, but has found in Woolybucket a community as conflicted in its search for an identity as himself. His participation in the festival simply draws attention to the demeaning reality faced by Westerners forced into performative rituals to reinforce a shared identity based upon a synthetic version of the past.

IV

The 'Barbwire Festival' is a distillation of Proulx's hyperreal; an exaggerated version of the lives of 'real' Westerners in New Western towns like Jackson and Laramie. To take a walk with journalist JoAnn Wypijewski is to enter a cowboy theme park:

> Wild Willie's Cowboy Bar anchors on corner downtown; a few feet away is The Rancher. Father up the same street is the Ranger Lounge and Motel; down another, the legendary Buckhorn Bar, with its mirror scarred by a bullet hole ... Around the corner stands the Cowboy Saloon, with its tableau of locomotives and thundering horses, lightning storms and lassos, portraits of grand old men who'd graced the town in history (Buffalo Bill Cody) and in dreams (Clint Eastwood).[69]

The distinction between fiction and reality seems inadequate. In the geographical Wyoming – the self-styled 'Forever-West' – towns such as Jackson resemble film sets and Cheyenne resident, Carina Evans, explains: 'You're encouraged to dress western during the summer because that's when the tourists come.'[70] These are the already conflicted spaces that Proulx 'fictionalizes' in towns like Woolybucket, Cowboy Rose and Redsled, in which 'the pawnshop, the Safeway, the Broken Arrow bar, Custom Cowboy, the vacuum cleaner shop' jostle with incongruity ('The Mud Below', *CR*, 67). Getting lost is easy, as becomes apparent when we follow the fictional Sutton Muddyman through the streets of a 'real' Signal to be confronted with two visions of the West: a computer store selling 'sun-faded boxes of obsolete software' sits next to Harold Batts' shop selling spurs. As he bends his '4X Cattleman crease' against the wind, we, and indeed he, are unsure to which world he belongs. He is an 'authentic' rancher, but also a 'Dude rancher' (a performance of Western identity for outsiders) and also part of the decorative cowboy background ('A Pair of Spurs', *CR*, 178).

How to make a meaningful life growing up in this Disneyland is the quintessential problem facing the young men (and occasionally young women) that Proulx presents in her *Wyoming Stories*. They are full of young men trapped in dead-end jobs who model themselves on nostalgically puerile codes of behaviour, which, if they ever existed outside *Shane*, are celebrated and reviled in equal measure in the New West. Proulx's women, by contrast, are generally more circumspect. Indeed, characters like Kaylee Felts ('Mud Below', *CR*) and Roany Hemp ('The Governors of Wyoming', *CR*) make a good living selling a commodified version of the West back to itself in kitsch stores specializing in cowboy regalia. Ironically, they share contempt for their customers because they understand the gap between the reality of ranch work and the pre-packaged myth reduced to the rodeo buckles, Stetsons and bumper stickers that they are selling. The young men buying into the myth do not, which makes them both ridiculous and, when it comes to their sexual development, dangerous. The cowboy, we have observed, represents a distorted fantasy of male sexuality every bit as unsubtle and dangerous as Hugh Hefner's pornographic projection of womanhood.[71] In a number of her *Wyoming Stories* Proulx sets out to expose the damaging effects of a mythology that privileges male relations and reduces women to horses to be tamed and ridden. Roany (a name that suggests a horse) is a case in point; her husband dresses like a cowboy but because he cannot tame and ride his wife, he exploits a more pliant Native American teenager in a re-enactment of Anglo sexual exploitation. Kaylee may want her son to go to college, but the sexual emasculation suffered when his father walks out leads him to become a bull rider, a hyper-masculine Western ritual that, as will be seen in due course, offers Proulx a deep well of psychosexual symbolism. Proulx's most darkly symbolic exploration of these themes is the shortest of her short stories – the two-sentence reworking of the legend of *Blue Beard* that is '55 Miles to the Gas Pump' (*CR*) – which clearly and economically announces her suspicion of cowboy sexuality.

The first scene depicts a drunken rancher Croom in full cowboy regalia, rearing above a canyon before throwing himself in. He does not die but rises 'like a cork in a bucket of milk' (279). The second presents his wife's discovery of the dead bodies of a group of female victims in a locked attic, all of which show the 'marks of boot heels' and of being 'used hard' (279–280). Through the symbolism of this compressed narrative Proulx seems to be suggesting that the isolation and much vaunted rugged independence of the cowboy from social norms does not necessarily stimulate the heightened sense of morality suggested by the Virginian. Indeed, a model of masculinity that privileges horses over women, and treats the sexualized woman as a horse to be 'ridden hard', is more likely to bring deviance. This is the conclusion to which we are guided by the narrator's laconic observation: 'When you live a long way out, you make your own fun' (280). The most frightening aspect, however, is that the cowboy's miraculous levitation suggests that whatever his sexual malpractice, the myth will not die.[72]

In 'People in Hell Want a Drink of Water' (*CR*) Proulx updates *Shane* to expose the dark underbelly of the sexual machismo he represents. In her retelling, the cattle baron Fletchers become the Dunmire family, a hardy father and six sons whose femininity stops at their curiously feminine names. Their mother is conceived as livestock for producing cowboys 'as fast as the woman could stand to make them' and when, after years of being 'ridden hard and put away dirty', she runs off with a tinker, they can only conceptualize her behaviour in accordance with the only other women of whom they have knowledge: prostitutes (109). Attention within the narrative settles on the eldest boy, Jaxon, who comes to represent a particularly predatory form of cowboy sexuality. In his youth he had been a bronc-buster, the epitome of vigorous masculinity, but was so badly torn up inside that he was reduced to riding 'easy horses broke by other men' (110). By the time we join the narrative, he is selling the ironically named Morning Glory windmills, whilst bringing cowboy swagger to lonely ranch wives: 'Some a them women can't hardly wait until I get out a the truck' (111). Significantly, in his choice of women he maintains the rhetoric of the broken rodeo cowboy: he refuses the 'bad' women of the brothel and will only 'ride' the women broken by another man.

Within the story, the Starrett family are transformed into the Tinsley's, ill-adapted urban outsiders with no feeling for the land. Their bookish son, Rasmussen, is the opposite of Jaxon and is horribly disfigured in a near fatal car crash. When, during convalescence, he takes to riding the plains and exposing himself to the women ranchers his symbolic function becomes clear. As a horseman – 'a half-wild man with no talk and who knew what thoughts' – it is clear that he has become a grotesque parody of Shane (120). As such he holds up the distorting mirror to Jaxon, the character he most unwittingly resembles. His outward disfigurement is a contrast to Jaxon's inward deformity; his desire to expose himself a parody of the Dunmire's sexual machismo. When faced with this outsider, Jaxon retreats into a protective cowboy mythology that does not accept deviance and deals with it in the only way he knows how, through his knowledge of livestock. His castration of Rasmussen is justified on the grounds that women must be protected, reasoning that reveals his hypocrisy whilst reducing women to damsels in distress. However, Rasmussen's castration is necessary not because he is a threat to women, but because he is a threat to the standing of men, both sexually and mythologically.[73] The narrator's final observation – 'We are in a new millennium and such desperate things no longer happen. If you believe that you'll believe anything' – ridicules our smugness while cajoling us into an acceptance that this is not a period piece, but an exploration of the legacy of cowboy culture (128).

As if to prove the point, Proulx brings us up to date in her story 'The Mud Below', which centres on the character of Diamond Felts, a vulnerable young man as disfigured on the inside by the cowboy myth as Ras is on the outside. Fatherless, short, a 'virgin at eighteen' demeaned by the pejorative names Half-Pint, Shorty, Sawed Off, Diamond is a 'rapping, tapping, nail-biting' ball of unease in search of a masculine role model (47–48). He builds his identity around rodeo, a ritualistic means of affirming and perpetuating Western protocols and, according to some commentators, a symbolic re-enactment of the taming of the West.[74] Proulx's interest is the psychosexual dynamic afforded by the spectacle of men riding wild horses and bulls. Brutal sexuality is never far from the glamour of rodeo, in which horses, like women, are mastered and discarded before they dilute through domestication. A subset within the rodeo community is the bull rider, Diamond's speciality: loners among the lonely – 'a breed apart'.[75] Bull riding has no basis in cowboy skills; there is no ritualistic taming of the West because the bull remains a symbol of the wild. This gives rise to a very different psychosexual symbolism in which the rider's goal is not to tame the bull, but to merge with this symbol of exaggerated masculinity. In effect, bull riding is an exclusively male domain with no vestige of the feminine.[76]

Intra-textually, Proulx strengthens this suspect male exclusivity through a childhood memory in which Diamond's father takes him to visit a funfair merry-go-round. He refuses to mount the vandalized horses because he is appalled by their 'swelled buttocks and the sinister holes', so he is lifted by his father onto a 'glossy little black bull' (53). Symbolically, bull riding becomes a misogynistic closed circuit that reignites his relationship with his father and leaves his mother on the outside. Her exclusion means that she is powerless to prevent her son's career path without the aid of another man. She introduces Diamond to Hondo Gunsch, a now brain-damaged rodeo legend who works in the stables of a male 'friend' – Kerry Moore. Gunsch's glory days are captured in the framed picture of a bronc rider on the cover of *Boots 'N Bronks*; its glamour contrasts vividly with the wreck of a man they meet: an image of where Diamond is heading. However, Diamond is not interested in lessons for the future; he is still living in his sexually traumatic past, memories of which are revived in the secret messages flying between Moore (who even wears a black hat) and his mother; messages that once again leave him on the outside (67). In a moment he is reduced to the figure of Shorty in a closed circuit of masculine control in which Moore becomes the bull and Gunsch a symbol of Diamond's shattered attempts to assert his masculine vision.

In Diamond's own Western narrative 'only the ride gave him the indescribable rush' and the ride, whether on the bull or in the truck, is a particularly personal experience, which translates uneasily into the world beyond (73). He sees himself as a Lone Ranger, his lack of empathy apparent in his aggressive sexual behaviour towards the numerous 'in-and-out girls' who keep him company in motel bedrooms, and especially the parking lot rape of the wife of one of his travelling companions. Narrated from Diamond's perspective, the scene becomes a bronc-busting ride in which a tall woman (who had earlier mocked his size) is tamed ('she was not willing. She bucked and shoved and struggled'). It is not simply Diamond's wayward moral compass that creates the full horror of this incident ('Hush up. I didn't hurt you. I'm too damn small to hurt a big girl like you, right?' (70)), but rather, as he glibly reminds her offended husband, that his behaviour is simply a more forceful extension of that sanctioned by the 'buckle-bunny' stereotypes of rodeo mythology. Diamond is not, as his companion seeks to suggest, an aberration, but a distorting mirror. The rodeo community, however, is not prepared for such blistering honesty, as is evinced by their reaction to Diamond's drunken harangue on the subject of cowboys and families. The carefully staged scene takes place in the 'Saddle Rack Bar', which, like the riders themselves, teeters between authenticity and kitsch (78). The music is Country and Western and the talk of 'babies and wives' – leaving it to Diamond to point out the glaring hypocrisy: 'You all make a big noise about family … but none of you spend much time at home and you never wanted to or you wouldn't be in rodeo. Rodeo's the family. Ones back at the ranch don't count for shit' (80). It is an inflammatory speech that allows Proulx, as she did in 'Them Old Cowboy Songs', to draw attention to the damaging hypocrisy of masculine codes that marginalize women through their sentimental veneration, a process made easier when lensed through the bottom of a pint glass.

Diamond only begins to question the life he has chosen when he is gored by a bull and told by the local Doctor to 'cowboy up' (83). The implication of this phrase is made apparent when Diamond catches sight of himself in the mirror and sees a black-eyed and bloodied parody of the mythical cowboy of his imagination. Now his inner and outer deformity coincide, and it appears that the narrative is preparing us for a moment of self-revelation. Proulx, however, resists a happy ending: on a psychosexual level his goring is an act of emasculation similar to that received when his father walked out on the family with the damning announcement: 'Not your father and never was. Now get the fuck out of the way, you little bastard' (72). It is no coincidence that at this time he chooses to phone his mother to claim reassurance of his paternity, only to find that she is in bed with another man; a man who Diamond can only conceive of as wearing the 'black hat' of the cowboy's antagonist, which further reinforces his sense of emasculation. As the story moves towards its conclusion, Proulx reinforces this sense through Diamond's childhood memory of visiting a ranch and watching the castration of the cattle by 'slitting the scrotal sac'. It is a an image that leads to a rare moment of reflection and the conclusion that 'life's events seemed slower than the knife but not less thorough' (87). In effect, growing up in the contemporary West and continually measuring oneself against symbols of masculinity that can never be equalled is a form of slow emasculation (88).

Despite such misgivings, the mythology refuses to die. 'Cowboying up' ultimately means hitting the road in search of the excitement of the next rodeo. For despite the solidity of its signifiers (its costumery, rituals and dialogue) it is a mythology constructed on transience– the generic ride into the sunset symbolizing a constant evasion of reality. This is why, as the histories of Andrews and Grady have already suggested, the myth, whatever the personal experience, remains peculiarly resistant to deconstruction. Thus, at the story's close, Proulx leaves Diamond, like Andrews, Grady and Billy, on the road. Our last glimpse of him is stopped at a level crossing watching a coal train passing. Where for McCarthy, such imagery would suggest entrapment, for Proulx, the parade of uniform squares symbolizes the dullness against which the cowboy life rebels. Thus, Diamond makes an unlikely bedfellow with Andrews, who, despite the brutal shattering of his dreams, rejects his grey Bostonian heritage, to continue his ride West. Proulx also captures something of Williams's comic pathos (articulated through MacDonald) in her elevation of the rodeo clown, rather than the lone rider, as the surest symbol of the West: the clown makes us laugh whilst he protects cowboys lying injured in the mud below.

V

Like 'People in Hell' and 'The Mud Below', Proulx's most famous story, 'Brokeback Mountain', is also concerned with the disastrous effects of cowboy mythology on the sexual evolution of vulnerable young men. More specifically Proulx sets out to explore the paradox of a macho but sexless mythology that erases women and celebrates male friendship whilst forbidding intimacy. Larry McMurtry, reading the story prior to turning it into a screenplay with Diana Ossana, observed: 'I was more stunned when I read "Brokeback Mountain" because I realized that it was a story that had been sitting there all my life.'[77] It may have been sitting there, but quite clearly repressed by a lifetime of presenting a particular vision of the West in such film and television classics as *Hud* (1963), *The Last Picture Show* (1971) and the *Lonesome Dove* series (1989). Furthermore, McMurtry clearly wasn't looking too hard: the archetypal Shane and the Virginian, as was noted last chapter, look extremely camp to contemporary eyes, as do the leathers, pistol waving and lingering stares of a number of classic Westerns. McCarthy's Grady and Billy revel in homosocial appreciation, but, as with all these examples, intimacy is masked. Repressed desire is channelled through horse talk; the horse itself is woven into a narrative symbolism that expresses men's attitudes towards nature, women, a variety of supposed masculine qualities – loyalty, determination – and eventually each other.

Two novels that also slipped under McMurtry's radar and which were influential in the development of Proulx's story are Thomas Savage's *The Power of the Dog* (1967) (for which she wrote an appreciative afterword when it was republished in 2001) and William Haywood Henderson's Wyoming novel – *Native* (1993). Set in the early 1920s, Savage's protagonist is Phil Burbank, an intelligent and cultivated rancher who presents himself as a hard-bitten cowboy: he eats in the bunkhouse with his cowboys; he is violently misogynistic to his brother's wife, Rose; and hates what he terms 'sissies' (typified by Rose's sensitive son – Peter). Yet beneath this tough exterior lies an emotional turmoil revealed by fleeting references to his boyhood adoration for the now deceased character of Bronco Henry, an idealized cowboy and object of Phil's adolescent, erotic affection. This relationship exists for Phil on the symbolic level (which allows him to repress his own homosexuality and Savage to avoid presenting contact between men), signalled by their ability to read the form of the running dog in the shape of a distant rocky outcrop. Thus, the 'power of the dog' is an exclusionary bond that conjoins Bronco Henry with Phil and also the only other person who can see it, his 'sissy' step-nephew, Peter, to a 'manly' sensitivity to the Western landscape. However, it also references Psalms – 'Deliver my soul … from the power of the dog' – reminding us that they are prey to a Christian cowboy culture that would, if they ever caught them, tear them to pieces.[78] Published twenty-four years later, the more explicit *Native*, focuses on the affection of young Wyoming ranch foreman, Blue Parker, for his young ranch hand, Sam. Their repressed desire (both are beaten up in homophobic attacks by their ranching 'friends') only finds release when they are isolated in a mountain camp, which is transformed through long passages of landscape description, into a verdant 'Mount Parnassus' – a Classical realm in which same sex love is celebrated.[79]

In fairness to McMurtry, both novels remained marginal even within the Western genre (neither were reviewed by mainstream publications) and as Proulx's afterword makes clear, so deft is Savage's handling of the relationships that most critics failed to recognize it.[80] 'Brokeback Mountain' effectively outed the cowboy for a wider audience, and yet even then its initial publication in the highbrow liberal arts magazine the *New Yorker* (the text positioned just a few pages after a picture of a topless Truman Capote) suggests that this is a story with which the West is still not comfortable. Its subsequent publication as a novella and in *Close Range* brought the story further mainstream, but, as Proulx herself recalls, she was surprised that her original text did not cause more of a stir, particularly in the gay community.[81] What gave Proulx's story national and international prominence was Ang Lee's film version. Proulx was justifiably incredulous at the choice of Taiwanese born Lee, whose directorial repertoire includes the martial arts extravaganza *Crouching Tiger Hidden Dragon*, the English satire of manners *Sense and Sensibility*, and the comic strip action, adventure, *Hulk*. However, his sensitive handling transformed the story into an international phenomenon.[82] 'Brokeback Mountain' is no longer simply a short story: it has become an interpretative collaboration involving scriptwriters, director, actors, critics and consumers, spawned numerous websites and even entered common speech as a noun (it's a bit 'Brokeback'), adjective (I'm a Brockoholic) and even verb to describe various emotional states.[83] It has forced the West to look closely at its sexual politics and for us all to scrutinize the models of masculinity in Westerns. And yet at its heart it is the story of two vulnerable young men, Ennis del Mar and Jack Twist, who are torn apart by their attempts to reconcile their desire to be cowboys with their desire for each other.

Both Jack and Ennis are acculturated into a deeply homophobic Western culture: Ennis recalls aged nine being taken to see the mutilated body of a suspected homosexual; Jack remembers being urinated upon by his father and noticing that he hadn't been circumcised: 'I seen they'd cut me different like you'd crop a ear or scorch a brand. No way to get it right with him after that' (315). Fearing 'difference' is important in this story; but where Jack is prepared to acknowledge and adapt, Ennis remains terrified of disclosure (his father's lesson has been all too successful). To accentuate this complexity, Proulx sets the story in the early sixties, meaning her protagonists grew up in the repressive 1950s. Furthermore, it enables her to contextualize their struggle against a period of liberation (Vietnam protests, the civil rights movement, second- and third-wave feminism, and the rise of Stonewall), in which the machismo represented by the cowboy was under attack. Thus, as cowboys – either gay or straight – Jack and Ennis are struggling against forces that condemn their way of life.

It was noted in the Introduction that Proulx believes that 'if you get the landscape right, the characters will step out of it, and they'll be in the right place' – which is clearly illustrated by the power of the titular Brokeback Mountain. The Western wilderness, as Krista Comer reminds us, 'is a "final frontier" of white male privilege, a cornerstone of masculinist western and national discourse', which, ironically for Proulx, becomes the idealized site of male transgression.[84] Proulx notes that 'In such isolated high country, away from the opprobrious comment and watchful eyes, I thought it would be plausible for the characters to get into a sexual situation'.[85] It is a fictional location within the context of a very real Wyoming, the cartographical geography of which is described during Jack and Ennis's fishing trips whilst the imaginative geography does its transformational work. The very name is suggestive of both back-breaking labour and an individual crushed under the weight of oppressive social norms. As such it acts as both a catalyst for, and later a symbol of, their relationship, which, by mutual consent, both men refuse to revisit after their initial summer herding sheep. Proulx is aided in this task by her reconciliation of narrative tropes that signal the changing codes of masculine behaviour in the great outdoors. Hemmingway's buddy narratives, particularly during his 'men without women' phase, are often concerned with such crises; we need only think of Bill Gorton's protestation of love to Jake Barnes during one of their fishing trips: 'Listen. You're a hell of a good guy, and I'm fonder of you than anybody on earth. I couldn't tell you that in New York. It'd mean I was a faggot.'[86] The denial of homosexuality is implicit in the conditional, yet there is also a startling realignment of masculine mores brought about by outdoor companionship.

Proulx's imagery of the 'great flowery meadows' and 'glassy orange' dawns also suggests that she is following Henderson in her evocation of an Arcadia. The untamed American landscape becomes, as it does in Whitman's *Calamus* poems, a region in which shepherds drink and make merry amidst pastoral beauty and in which male love, through a form of pathetic fallacy, is both naturalized and sanctioned.[87] Encoded in the Arcadian allusion, however, is the tradition that defiance entails retribution: the mountain air is both 'euphoric' and 'bitter' (291). Thus, the mountain is both sanctuary but also rich in allegorical warning signs: Jack wears an eagle feather in his hat, which aligns him with both the Ancient Mariner (punished for shooting an albatross) and Hercules, whose act of shooting an eagle is punished when his male lover, Hylas, disappears leaving him with only a *shirt* for remembrance (shirts will become significant at the story's denouement).[88] The relationship between pastoral pleasure and retribution is also played out in the mythical expulsion from Eden, which the narrator invokes through the description of Ennis's descent from the mountain as a 'headlong, irreversible fall' (292).

Despite the richness of Proulx's allegorical references, we have no doubt that we are reading or watching a contemporary Western; the landscape may conflate Eden with Arcadia, but it also serves as a suitable backdrop to *Ride the High Country*. All the usual Western signifiers are present, largely because Ennis and Jack, like Grady and Billy before them, have bought into the myth with their ten-gallon hats and pearl-buttoned yoked shirts. From the minute they park their trucks at the bottom, both men disappear into a cowboy fantasy. It is 1963, yet there is no mention of the Vietnam War or the assassination of Kennedy; instead, their days are spent on horseback, their nights round the camp fire discussing horses and dogs and even playing the harmonica. Their theatricality is accentuated in the film through their deployment of studied movements, gestures and poses that they consider appropriately cowboy. Ennis is first pictured, like Grady, leaning against a wall, one leg hooked behind the other the brim of his Stetson masking his face; Jack is presented affecting a stiff cowboy swagger whilst continually glancing in mirrors to check the authenticity of his performance. Their role playing is underscored by background music that both diegetically (Country and Western songs heard on truck radios and jukeboxes) and non-diegetically (Gustavo Santaolalla's guitar soundtrack) provides a Western accompaniment to their lives whilst simultaneously offering an ironic commentary for the viewer. In one scene, Ennis is depicted riding through an idyllic John Ford landscape whilst humming 'The Cowboy's Lament'. For Ennis the song augments his authenticity, but the knowledgeable viewer may recognize the performative irony encoded in the lyrical refrain – 'I'm a young cowboy and I know I've done wrong.' Ennis will do wrong and spend his days in lamentation. In another example, Jack performs a brief riff of 'He was a Friend of Mine' on the harmonica whilst separating the sheep flocks that have become mixed on the mountain. The mingling suggests their confused emotions, the lyrics, in which the singer laments the death of a friend, signpost where these emotions tend. The next time we hear the song, it is following Ennis's emotional pledge to the dead Jack in front of his makeshift shrine, when the question of tense is moot.

Beneath all the cowboy posturing that we have seen already enacted in the appreciative homosocial relationships enjoyed between Rawlins, Grady and Billy, Proulx sets out to manoeuvre her characters into a transgressive sexual relationship. It is prepared by the narrative emphasis on those aspects of the cowboys's job – cooking, midwifery, nurturing – that are traditionally coded feminine and which have led Gretel Ehrlich to coin the term 'androgynous cowboy'.[89] Lee's film version, to the consternation of some critics, spends a great deal of time establishing the 'camp' routine, adding a scene which comes perilously close to drifting from the domestic to the intimate. When Ennis's horse is spooked by a black bear (itself a metaphor for male sexuality) he returns to a Jack impatient for his food. It leads to a familiar heterosexual domestic encounter, until Jack notices the injury and unthinkingly takes off his bandana and raises it to Ennis's forehead. Ossana's direction reads: 'Jack hesitates … awkward … hands the bandana to Ennis.' It is a moment of instinctive tenderness brought under control at the last minute.[90] In the very next scene, also additional, they are shooting a deer together – bonding in a safely masculine manner.

The same sanitization of emotions becomes even more apparent when they become lovers and sex is absorbed into a rhetorical web that is personalized, steeped in Western signifiers and in which the narrator actively participates. Of central importance is horse symbolism, a rich vein of sexual euphemism in the Classic Western, which, as we have seen, became an object of scrutiny in McCarthy's *Border Trilogy*. A man astride a horse is rarely just riding a horse in the *Trilogy*; horses are objects of quest and admiration, they are broken and ridden hard, and they provide ears into which McCarthy's young cowboys can pour their unshaped feelings within a safely Western context. Occasionally, such feelings, when augmented by quivering horse flesh, can lurch towards the erotic. In 'Brokeback Mountain' horses can provide similar ironic commentary; Ennis's campfire rendition of 'The Strawberry Roan' is a traditional tale of a cowboy's failure to master a wild horse, which evokes the Wild West virility that brings the protagonists together, whilst simultaneously foreshadowing the trouble that Jack will have mastering Ennis (290).[91] At other times, however, horses become a screen between character and event rather than a wink between author and reader. Proulx's characters aren't worried about repression, it's too late for that, but sanitizing their acts through references to 'a one-shot thing' in which the orgasm becomes the almost parodic 'gun's goin *off*' (291, Proulx's italics). The nearest Ennis comes to self-reflection is his assertion – 'there's no reins on this one' – the 'one' euphemistically replacing their desire with the more satisfactory image of the unbroken horse, which enhances rather than compromises their shared sense of masculinity (299). Horses are also woven into Jack's most important memory of his time on Brokeback Mountain, when Ennis stole up behind him as he stood in front of the fire and held him in a silent embrace:

> They had stood that way for a long time in front of the fire, its burning tossing ruddy chunks of light, the shadow of their bodies a single column against the rock. The minutes ticked by from the round watch in Ennis's pocket ... Ennis's breath came slow and quiet, he hummed, rocked a little in the sparklight and Jack leaned against the steady heartbeat ... until Ennis, dredging up a rusty but still useable phrase from the childhood time before his mother died, said, "Time to hit the hay, cowboy. I got a go. Come on, you're sleepin on your feet like a horse," and gave Jack a shake, a push, and went off in the darkness. Jack heard his spurs tremble as he mounted, the words "see you tomorrow," and the horse's shuddering snort, grind of hoof on stone.
>
> (310–11)

Henderson employs a similar pose in *Native*, the lack of eye contact implicit in the wrap around hug allowing Blue to question 'What would it take to turn round and hold him?'[92] Like Sam, Jack never turns round, for to do so would be to acknowledge the presence of another man and shatter the illusion. In Proulx's version, the illusion is not simply sexual, but an exploration of their boyhood dreams. Passion is replaced by a 'shared sexless hunger', with an anonymous Ennis fulfilling the role of mother and lover allowing Jack to return to a childhood dream of being a cowboy. It is a dream forged in the glimmering of the campfire, the nickering of horses and the tremble of spurs. Through Ennis's observation, 'you're sleepin on your feet like a horse', the narrator artfully extends the myth that a cowboy's best friend is his horse. It is a moment of perfect reciprocity symbolized by their merging together into a single shadow. However, the shadows also present dark foreshadowing, the symbolism reinforced by the presence of the pocket watch given to Jack by Joe Aguirre; a reminder of the world where time is work-time. On Brokeback Mountain, time is measured by their humming, gentle rocking, and the steady heartbeat that counts off their time of happiness together.

Elsewhere in the story Proulx offers a less personal account of her protagonists' behaviour in favour of a more historically significant explanation. Her description of the hotel room following one of their assignations pivots from the horse to the description of the stable: 'The room stank of semen and smoke and sweat and whiskey, of old carpet and sour hay, saddle leather, shit and cheap soap' (297). It's grim – some critics recoiling at its sordidness – but Proulx is breaking the link between homosexuality and effeminacy, allowing for relationships which do not fall into the camp stereotypes portrayed in contemporary media, which will give some validity to Ennis's confused claim 'I'm not no queer'. Robert Kinsey identified 'a type of homosexuality which was probably common among pioneers and outdoor men in general' in which 'sex is sex, irrespective of the nature of the partner'. Such 'hard-riding, hard-hitting assertive males', he argues, would be intolerant of the 'affectation' of urban homosexuals, 'but this, as far as they can see, has little to do with the question of having sexual relations with other men'.[93]

These surprisingly liberal views are articulated in Proulx's writing by the tough cowboy poet Rope Butt (Proulx seems never without archness even when deadly serious), who 'didn't much care for the two nancy boys who had lately come up from Dallas, but he was willing to live and let live, for certain bunkhouse friendships were not unknown, though little talked about'.[94] They were, however, written about. Proulx notes in 'How the West was Spun' that the evidence gleaned from letters and poetic fragments amassed by historians John D'Emilio and Estelle Freedman in their comprehensive study of American sexuality – *Intimate Matters* (1988) – suggests that cowboys 'were not the pure heterosexual tough guys we might think'. Instead their 'Poetic fragments' illuminate not only the tenderness of men who love 'in the way men do', but also the dangers of the bunkhouse: 'Young cowboys had a great fear / That old studs once filled with beer / Completely addle / They'd throw on a saddle, And ride them on the rear.'[95] This is the 'unspoken' cowboy-lore passed down from Sink Gartrell to the wide-eyed Archie McLaverty – to avoid 'the leathery old foreman [who] was well known for bareback riding the new hires' – advice that, ironically, does not make it into the sanitized 'Old Cowboy Songs' that make up his Western repertoire (*FJW*, 62). The relationship that Proulx presents between Ennis and Jack also represents an ironic 'outing' of bunkhouse behaviour: an 'intimate matter' that grows out of their isolation and the smells of 'sour hay, saddle leather, sweat, semen and shit' that characterize the fecundity of their ranching world.

Ironically, the same ranch backdrop enables Ennis to transition seamlessly to a heterosexual life following their descent from Brokeback Mountain. His marriage to Alma is compressed into a couple of paragraphs suggesting that marriage is simply time away from Jack in which he attempts to conform to safer sexual stereotypes. But this is not how the text reads. Ennis shows no inclination for other men and he is initially content with family life as he is able to conceive of it as an extension of ranch work. His horse, daughters and Jack – the things he cares for most – all receive the same endearment 'little darlin', and Hi-Top Ranch is 'full of the smell of old blood and milk and baby shit, and the sounds were of squalling and sucking and Alma's sleepy groans, all reassuring of fecundity and life's continuance to one who worked with livestock' (293). As Proulx notes in 'A Lonely Coast', men who 'spend so much time handling livestock' are left emotionally stunted; they are 'hot-blooded and quick, and physically yearning' incapable of operating beyond an instinctual level in which the caress is just as likely to end in a 'backhand slap' (CR, 216). The evidence for this is all over the *Wyoming Stories:* thrice married Mero Corn can never quite escape the image of his father's girlfriend on all fours whinnying like a horse ('The Half-Skinned Steer', CR, 22); Diamond Felts rides women like he rides bulls; and the character of Riley takes time out of an all-night calving to have sex with the young helper from the neighbouring ranch, explaining to his wife by way of exoneration – 'I seen my chance and I taken it' ('A Lonely Coast', CR, 213). The same is true of Ennis with Alma; he just takes it – 'working at it until she shuddered and bucked against his hand and he rolled her over, did quickly what she hated' – an act that transforms Alma into the reluctant replacement for the 'bucking horse' that is Jack (294).

Gender, sex and violence seem to blur into one another when you take your cue from ranch life. But things get worse, Proulx makes clear, when the family move above a laundry and the sound of tumbleweed gives way to tumble driers. The screenwriters acknowledge the influence of Richard Avedon's *In the American West* for their visualization of the interiors, whilst Judy Becker, the film's production designer, claims she utilized a more muted palette in order to make the urban scenes 'feel a little greyer, a little harsher than the mountain scenes', whilst the low lighting of Ennis's apartment helps to give the impression that he is too big for the room, around which he paces like a caged animal.[96] It is this animal rage that explodes in scenes of inarticulate fist-pounding directed at those he cares for, such as Alma when he believes she 'overstepped his line' (303). At other times Proulx presents a variation on the classic barroom brawl: a brief reference to a short, grubby fight at the 'Black and Blue Eagle bar' reminds us that we have travelled a long way from the Classical imagery of Brokeback Mountain whilst simultaneously indicating the pounding Ennis will receive if anyone discovers his Herculean secret. Lee added a more dramatic fight in which, much to the delight of the cinema audience, Ennis dispatches two foul-mouthed bikers during a fourth of July picnic.[97] As he stands silhouetted against the celebratory fireworks, he appears to embody all the masculine virtues of cowboy mythology: a brooding presence prepared to leap to the defence of insulted women and his family with actions rather than words. However, in the very act of defending his family, Ennis demonstrates the characteristics that will undermine it. He is not applauded by Alma, she is terrified. Furthermore, cowboy violence is always a prelude to riding off into the sunset, far away from the femininity and domesticity that threatens his mythical status. Ennis, we know, is not riding anywhere, and if he was, it would be with Jack in a relationship that offers the most overt challenge to the family unit.

Through Jack's experiences after Brokeback, Proulx explores the dangers faced by the more 'feminine' male in cowboy culture. Wyoming, Proulx notes, is notoriously homophobic; the murder of the student Matthew Shepard just outside Laramie in the year after the story was published horrified the nation because it seemed to crystalize a mindset of intolerance.[98] Matthew, a sensitive blonde-haired college boy, was strung up on a buck fence (the ultimate symbol of Western settlement and division) and was bludgeoned to death by two local boys marinated in a distorted cowboy mythology. Wallace Stegner argues that 'the hoodlums who come to San Francisco to beat up gays' are simply the contemporary equivalent of 'the ranchers who rode out to exterminate the nesters in Wyoming's Johnson County War': the assailants may not don spurs and chaps, but at some level, they are enforcing a Western code.[99] Jack, we are guided to believe, turns to bull-riding as a hyper-masculine cover for his behaviour, which since it excludes the feminine in favour of mastering the masculine, is open to various psychosexual interpretations. We see nothing of him in action, his exploits are related to Ennis during their reunion in the Motel Siesta, a narrative ploy that deliberately contrasts Jack's macho discourse with his sexual activity with Ennis (298). In Proulx's story, his career is a catalogue of personal injury, but for Lee it is a means of amplifying the dangers facing both men. An offer to buy a drink for a rodeo clown who had earlier saved Jack from a mauling is given the screen direction: 'There is something, a frisson, a vibe, that gives the CLOWN an uneasy feeling' – a feeling amplified by the detail of 'Trust in Lies' by *The Raven Shadows* playing on the juke box. When the clown joins a group of drinkers, he shares something that makes them all stare over at Jack, who realizes he had better leave.[100]

People seem to know about Jack. Marriage to Lureen (a barrel racer, the only rodeo event designed for women) finds him taking up the 'feminine' role that he occupied on Brokeback – worrying about his son's schooling while 'Lureen ha[s] the money and call[s] the shots' (307). As the sound of the rodeo gives way to the image of Lureen behind a desk with a calculator, we are reminded of the domestic imprisonment of both men. This sense is amplified by the presence of Lureen's father – L.D. (whose farming machinery business represents everything that the cowboy dream refutes), who clearly senses something 'different' in the behaviour of Jack. In the film this marginal figure becomes the full-fledged character; a replacement 'stud duck' for Jack's father who continually undermines Jack's own attempts to be a father. When Bobby is born, it is L.D. who is pictured with the radiant mother, dismissing Jack from the reproductive process with his cooing, 'he's the spittin' image of his grandpa'.[101] Later, L.D.'s contempt for Jack's effeminate behaviour is made clear in his insistence that Bobby watches the football during the Thanksgiving supper: 'You want your son to grow up to be a man don't you, daughter? (direct look at Jack) Boys should watch football.'[102]

Escape from domesticity comes through hunting and fishing trips that are presented as a compressed travelogue – 'the Big Horns, Medicine Bows ... Owl Creeks, the Bridger-Teton Range' through which they ride 'like Randolph Scott and Joel McCrea in *Ride the High Country*' (304).[103] In both story and film these times present a picture of a loving relationship that contrasts with the dysfunctional couplings that surround them. Lureen ages gracelessly, her big hair and heavy make-up failing to hide the hard, chain-smoking businesswoman. Both L.D. and Jack's father are presented as bullies who have successfully terrorized their wives into submission. Alma's second husband, Monroe, offers a glimpse of the new man, but the way he primly slices the thanksgiving turkey with his electric carver almost makes us nostalgic for L.D.'s insistence that 'the stud duck does the carving'.[104] Ennis's relationship with Cassie, which develops out of an aside in Proulx's story, is half-hearted. Their drunken daytime dancing in seedy bars is a symbolic degradation of the idealized moment that symbolizes his love for Jack, which in turn leads to a dramatic queering of the jukebox Country and Western to which they dance. Steve Earle's 'The Devil's Right Hand' is ironically suggestive of Jack (the devil in question is a pistol, which reminds us of Jack's climatic 'gun's goin off') and also the masturbatory means of alleviation, emphasized by Ennis's escape to the 'men's room'. Linda Ronstadt's 'It's So Easy ... to fall in love' is the very opposite of Ennis's traumatic experiences because he fails to adhere to the heteronormative trajectory set out in such sentimental ballads. More fitting is Merle Haggard's 'I'm Always on a Mountain When I Fall', which reminds us where his heart lies and the biblical consequences of his choice. Perhaps most damning of all are Jack and Lureen's friends the Malones, other Proulxian characters fleshed out by Lee. Lashawn is presented as a vacuous chatterbox, to escape from whom her husband proposes to Jack that they find a cabin where they can 'drink a little whiskey, fish some. Get away, you know?'[105] Jack does *know*, and the film's message is disturbingly clear: domesticity and dominant women drive men to rediscover their masculinity in the woods with sometimes surprising consequences.

Proulx recollects that when writing the end of the story she 'was occasionally close to tears. I felt guilty ... [yet] It couldn't end any other way'.[106] To some critics this acknowledgement simply panders to the cliché that homosexual love must end badly, but her meaning is psychologically consistent in its vindication of Ennis's homophobia.[107] We never learn what happens to Jack, but Ennis has provided the gravitational pull of Proulx's narrative, which means that we privilege his version of events. Proulx makes clear that Ennis remains homophobic to the end; during their climatic final parting he is ferocious in his assault upon Jack for his euphemistic visits to Mexico, not because of his infidelity, but because an acknowledgement of Jack's sexual orientation would entail his own. In the screenplay, his bitter accusation 'I hear what they got in Mexico for boys like you' expels Jack's homosexuality to a region outside the idea of Brokeback and the notional virility of the Anglo West, to the Dime Mexico of sexual deviance.[108] In an additional scene, Jack is observed trawling the streets of Juarez at night; a border town in which, as Peter Boag has noted, men picking up men is presented not as an aberration, but as a part of people getting on with their lives.[109] Hence, Jack's exasperation is made clear through his assertion – 'We could a had a good life together, a fuckin real good life. You wouldn't do it Ennis, so what we got now is Brokeback Mountain' – which is true; they could have had a better life together if they had moved to the city, Mexico, anywhere where there were no cowboys (309).

Ennis's tragedy is that he can only countenance his relationship with Jack when lensed through the prism of a cowboy culture that actively seeks to destroy it. His father's violent lesson has been spectacularly successful and Ennis remains paranoid: 'You ever get the feelin', I don't know, when you're in town, and someone looks at you, suspicious ... like he *knows*.'[110] The film is full of moments that dramatize this fear: the car that slows down to prevent Jack and Ennis embracing outside their 'little place'; the cowboy who stops to help the retching Ennis who is challenged – 'What the fuck are you looking at!'; the scene of the boys cavorting on the mountain observed through Aguirre's binoculars. Hence, when he takes the telephone call from Lureen informing him of the circumstances of Jack's death, we are aware that his response is filtered through a life of fear. Significantly, we do not hear her account directly, it is reported through the narrator from Ennis's perspective. The detail that 'she was polite but the little voice was cold as snow' suggests that she is parroting the account of somebody else – the police, her father – which she may or may not believe (312). Ennis dismisses her account in favour of his belief in a violent attack (symbolized by the tire iron), which is, through its recreation on screen, the account privileged in the film. The threat of violence was always present for Ennis; even in dreams that take him back to Brokeback, the spoon handle sticking out of their cowboy beans 'was the kind that could be used as a tire iron' (318).

If the tire iron symbolizes the threat of homophobic violence, the shirts that Ennis keeps in his makeshift shrine symbolize their repressed love. They first appear in the prologue – 'The shirts hanging on a nail shudder slightly' – when the intransitive 'shudder' implies both sexual excitement and fear – an apt foreshadowing of their relationship (283). They are referenced obliquely through Jack's eagle feather – which intertextually references the shirt left for Hercules by his lost lover, Hylas – an act of homosexual remembrance which they perform in Proulx's story. They are the shirts worn on their last day on Brokeback, when an emotionally charged fight leads to the drawing of blood. Ennis discovers them – 'like two skins, one inside the other, two in one' – in the closet within a closet (an obvious symbol of repression) within Jack's childishly furnished bedroom (316). Noticeably, Jack's shirt enfolds Ennis's, a reversal of their position in the symbolic flashback scene on Brokeback, suggesting that Jack considers himself the protector of the emotionally vulnerable Ennis. Furthermore, it is only through the substitute of the shirts that Ennis is prepared to embrace Jack face to face as he presses his face into their fabric. By the end of both story and film, however, they are safely back in the closet in Ennis's trailer. And yet beyond this, the endings diverge significantly.

Proulx's story ends with the elliptical 'Jack, I swear', which, in mimicking the wedding service, suggests that, given another chance, Ennis would be ready to step out of the closet and embrace his sexuality with Jack (317). However, it is a conclusion undercut by the narrator's observation that 'Jack had never asked him to swear anything and was himself not the swearing kind'. This pragmatic assertion leads us to Proulx's prologue and the older, sadder Ennis shuffling around his trailer surviving on his memories. Lee's more upbeat ending is signalled by the introduction of Ennis's daughter, Alma Jr, who stops by to invite him to her wedding. He offers his stock response to evade emotional commitment – 'supposed to be on a roundup over near the Tetons'. However, where previously he proved inflexible with Jack, he is moved to a new resolution: 'I reckon they can find themselves another cowboy ... my little girl ... is getting' married.'[111] Familial duty and affection at last conquer the spirit of the cowboy, celebrated with cheap white wine left by Cassie; a reminder of his own failed heterosexual relationship. When Alma Jr leaves, therefore, his emotional 'Jack, I swear' is clearly to be understood in the context of his daughter's wedding and becomes an affirmation of his own secret marriage.[112] As the camera pans, Lee constructs a final shot of multiple frames: the closet door frames his secret shrine, the trailer window frames the straight road outside. The symbolism is clear: he remains wedded to Jack in secret but is determined to travel the straight road, starting with the ultimate symbol of familial and heterosexual love, his daughter's wedding. Ennis understands from the death of those he has loved – his parents and Jack – the dangers of deviation from the straight road.

Proulx's young men are lost on a frontier – geographical, economic and sexual – in which their idealism and models of masculinity are no longer understood and valued, if, as her historical stories show, they ever were. For what becomes clear from her settler stories is the disparity between the Turnerian vision of redemption through struggle and the crushing reality of blinkered idealism that divided men from the land, their wives, each other and reality itself. The evolution from the 'threatening' to the 'threatened' West is aptly symbolized by the 'true history' of 'The Sagebrush Kid' repeated in the story of Bob Dollar (doubled through the shadowy presence of Albert), whose search for identity and a sense of belonging becomes an analogue for the region as a whole. The 'forever West' in which the Kid is rooted and into which Bob stumbles is, like them, orphaned from its mythological past, its inhabitants reduced to performing a kitsch version of Western identity. Notions of reality seem inappropriate in this Proulxian hyperreal, but the environmental damage is real as is the psychological harm suffered by those young men growing up in the shadow of the Kid. Finding oneself – a self – is problematic in a West in which the free range has given way to the driving range and in which Shane is celebrated and derided in equal measure. It is an identity crisis from which Proulx's characters cannot escape and to which those of Thomas McGuane return.

Notes

1. Mary Flanagan, 'Rough and rednecks', *The Independent* (19 June 1999). https://www.independent.co.uk/arts-entertainment/books-rough-and-redneck-1100964.html [accessed 14 June 2020].
2. Ibid., Interview, *Missouri Review*.
3. Turned into the surrealist film *Little Otik* by Jan Svankmajer in 2000.
4. Proulx, 'Forts Halleck and Fred Steele', in *Red Desert: History of a Place* (Texas: University of Texas Press, 2009), 283–92 (p. 284).
5. A fictional invention that is a conflation of two Bradfield Scott cowboy novels.
6. Grossman, *The Frontier in American Culture*, p. 9.
7. Veracini, *Settler Colonialism: A Theoretical Overview* (New York: Palgrave Macmillan, 2010), p. 102.
8. Proulx, *Bird Cloud*, p. 139.
9. See Elizabeth Simpson, *Earthlight, Wordfire: The Work of Ivan Doig* (Moscow, Idaho: University of Idaho Press, 1992), p. 147.
10. Kittredge, *The Next Rodeo: New and Selected Essays* (Saint Paul, Minnesota: Graywolf Press, 2007), p. 168.
11. Limerick, *Legacy*, p. 48.
12. Armitage, 'Through Women's Eyes: A New View of the West', in Armitage and Elizabeth Jameson (eds.), *The Women's West* (Norman and London: University of Oklahoma Press, 1987), 9–18 (p. 9).
13. Fenimore, 'Folksinging in the West, 1880–1930', in Nicolas Witschi (ed.), *A Companion to the Literature and Culture of the American West* (Oxford: Blackwell Publishing, 2011), 316–35 (pp. 326–7).
14. Jameson, 'Women as Workers, Women as Civilisers: True Womanhood in the American West', in Armitage and Jameson (eds.), *The Women's West*, 145–64 (pp. 151–2).
15. See Sandra L. Myres, *Westering Women and the Frontier Experience, 1800–1915* (Albuquerque: University of New Mexico Press, 1982). See in particular, pp. 6–7, 11, 269–70.

16 Jameson, 'Women as Workers', p. 154.
17 Proulx, 'Dangerous Ground', in Timothy R. Mahoney and Wendy J. Katz (eds.), *Regionalism and the Humanities* (Nebraska: University of Nebraska Press, 2008), 6–25 (p. 17).
18 Proulx discovered a photograph of the inaugural picnic in John Rolfe Burroughs, *Where the Old West Stayed Young* (New York: Morrow, 1962), pp. 332–3.
19 Ibid., Verancini, p. 60.
20 Potter, 'American Women and American Character', in Barbara Welter (ed.), *The Woman Question in American History* (Hinsdale, Illinois: The Dryden Press, 1973), 117–32 (p. 120).
21 His death, like that of Archie McLaverty, is drawn from a historical account that Proulx unearthed during her research for 'Horse Bands of the Red Desert', *Red Desert*, p. 331.
22 See Kittredge, 'Overthrust Dreams', *Owning it All*, pp. 114–15; 'White People in Paradise', *The Next Rodeo*, p. 177.
23 See Jim Goad, *The Redneck Manifesto: How Hillbillies, Hicks, and White Trash became America's Scapegoats* (New York, London: Simon and Schuster, 1997), p. 23.
24 Proulx, *Red Desert*, p. 308.
25 Quoted in Diana Kendall, *Framing Class: Media Representations of Wealth and Poverty in America* (Lanham: Roman and Littlefield, 2005), p. 325.
26 Proulx, Introduction to *Fields of Vision: The photographs of Carl Mydans* (The Library of Congress in association with D. Gilles, London, 2011); Proulx, 'Reliquary', in *Treadwell: Photographs by Andrea Modica* (San Francisco: Chronicle Books, 1996), 9–12 (p. 10).
27 Proulx, 'After the Gold Rush', *The Guardian* (23 November 2005).
28 Dallas became a Western hero in 1986 when, following his murder of two game wardens, he managed to evade the police for a year in the sagebrush of Idaho.
29 Abbey, 'Even the Bad Guys Wear White Hats: Cowboys, Ranchers and the Ruin of the West', *Harpers* (January 1986), 51–5. Quoted Limerick, *Legacy*, p. 157.
30 See Ken Midkiff, *The Eat you Eat: How Corporate Farming has Endangered America's Food Supply* (New York: St Martins Griffin, 2004), p. 48.
31 Penn Warren, *All the King's Men* (Harcourt: Brace and Company, 1946).
32 Krista Comer, *Landscapes of the New West: Gender and Geography in Contemporary Women's Writing* (Chapel Hill and London: The University of North Carolina Press, 1999), p. 57.
33 Kerouac, *On the Road* (1955) (Harmondsworth: Penguin Modern Classics, 2000), p. 51.
34 Cather, *My Antonia* (1914) (London: Virago Classics, 1983), p. 7.
35 Hunt, 'The Ecology of Narrative: Annie Proulx's *That Old Ace in the Hole* as Critical Regionalist Fiction', in Hunt (ed.), *The Geographical Imagination of Annie Proulx: Rethinking Regionalism* (Lanham: Lexington Books, 2009), 183–95 (pp. 183–4).
36 Albert, Lieutenant James William, *Expedition to the Southwest: An 1845 Reconnaissance of Colorado, New Mexico, Texas, and Oklahoma,*

Introduction and edited by John Miller Morris (Lincoln and London: University of Nebraska Press, 1999) v, vii.

37 See B Harley 'Maps, Knowledge, Power', in Cosgrove and Stephen Daniels (eds.), *The Iconography of Landscape* (Cambridge: Cambridge University Press, 1988), pp. 296–8.

38 Patrick Wolfe, 'Settler Colonialism and the Elimination of the Native', *Journal of Genocide Research* 8: 4 (2006), 387–409 (p. 393).

39 Veracini, *Settler Colonialism*, p. 79.

40 Quoted in Ibid., p. 78.

41 Sarah Deer and Mary Kathryn Nagle, 'The Rapidly Increasing Extraction of Oil, and Native Women, in North Dakota', *The Federal Lawyer* (April 2017), 35–7 (p. 36); Sheridan makes explicit this exploitation in the film's epilogue. See Anna Klassen, *Bustle Entertainment* (August 2017) https://www.bustle.com/p/the-true-story-behind-wind-river-is-this-hidden-injustice-against-native-american-women-75304.

42 Proulx, 'How the West was Spun'.

43 Lisa Aldred, 'Plastic Shamans and Astroturf Sun Dances: New Age Commercialization of Native American Spirituality', *American Indian Quarterly: Journal of American Indian Studies* 24: 3 (2000), p. 329.

44 Limerick, *Legacy*, p. 215.

45 See John Warren Gilroy, 'Another Fine Example of the Oral Tradition? Identification and Subversion in Sherman Alexie's Smoke Signals', *Studies in American Indian Literatures (SAIL)* 13: 1 (spring 2001) 23–39 (pp. 23–25). Also, Suzanne Lundquist, *Native American Literatures: An Introduction* (New York, London: Continuum, 2004), pp. 156–7.

46 The text chronicles his perambulations through Chase County, Kansas, during which he exposes the limitations of Western mapping in favour of just wandering. Heat-Moon, *PrairyErth* (A Deep Map) (Boston: Houghton Mifflin, 1991), p. 273.

47 Deloria Jr, *Custer Died for Your Sins: An Indian Manifesto* (1969) (Norman: University of Oklahoma Press, 1988), pp. 230–2.

48 Veracini, *Settler Colonialism*, p. 98.

49 Kyle Whyte, 'Settler Colonialism, Ecology, and Environmental Injustice', *Environment and Society* 9 (2018), 125–44.

50 Lynn White Jr, 'The Historical Roots of Our Ecological Crisis', *American Association for the Advancement of Science* 155: 3767 (March 1967).

51 Quoted in G. Holthaus, Patricia Limerick et al. (eds.), *A Society to Match the Scenery: Personal Visions of the Future of the American West* (Boulder: University of Colorado Press, 1991), p. 227.

52 Kittredge, 'Owning it All', p. 56; *The Next Rodeo*, 51–66 (p. 59).

53 For more on Proulx and *Annales* school see 'An Interview with Annie Proulx', *Missouri Review* 22: 2 (Spring 1999), pp. 84–5. http://www.missourireview.com/content/dynamic/view_text.php?text_id=877 [accessed 4 September 2013].

54 Proulx explores its consequences through the aged rancher Gilbert Wolfscale in 'What Kind of Furniture would Jesus Pick?' (*Bad Dirt*), p. 72.

55 Lynch, 'Strange Lands', *Interdisciplinary Studies in Literature and Environment* (Autumn 2015), 22: 4, 697–716 (p. 702).

56 Hunt gives an excellent analysis of this scene in 'The Ecology of Narrative: Annie Proulx's *That Old Ace in the Hole* as Critical Regionalist', in Hunt (ed.), *The Geographical Imagination*, 183–95 (pp. 188–90).
57 See Matthew Cella, *Bad Land Pastoralism in Great Plains Fiction* (Iowa City: University of Iowa Press, 2010), p. 56.
58 Louise Westling, *The Green Breast of the New World: Landscape, Gender, And American Fiction* (Athens: University of Georgia Press, 1996), pp. 5–6.
59 Robbins, *Last Refuge*, p. 95.
60 Limerick, 'The Shadows of Heaven Itself', in Riebsame, *Atlas of the New West*, 151–89 (p. 165).
61 Deborah Epstein Popper and Frank J. Popper 'The Great Plains: From Dust to Dust', *Planning Magazine* (December 1987) http://www.lacusveris.com/The%20Hi-Line%20and%20the%20Yellowstone%20Trail/The%20Buffalo%20Commons/From%20Dust%20to%20Dust.shtml [accessed 14 August 2020]. See Cella, pp. 174, 182–3.
62 Leopold's essay is published in his collection *A Sand County Almanac: With Essays on Conservation from Round River* (New York: Ballantine, 1970). See Matthew Cella for brief discussion of Norris, p. 212.
63 Lear, *Radical Hope: Ethics in the Face of Cultural Devastation* (Cambridge, MA: Harvard University Press, 2006), p. 3.
64 Ibid., p. 37.
65 Ibid., p. 151.
66 Estes, *Our History is the Future: Standing Rock Versus the Dakota Access Pipeline, and the Long Tradition of Indigenous Resistance* (London: Verso Press, 2019), p. 78.
67 Jackson, *Discovering the Vernacular Landscape* (New Haven: Yale University Press, 1984), p. 89.
68 Cronon, 'The Trouble with Wilderness, Or Getting Back to the Wrong Kind of Nature', in William Cronon (ed.) *Uncommon Ground: Towards Reinventing Nature* (New York: Norton, 1995), 69–90 (p. 78).
69 Wypijewski, 'A Boy's Life: For Matthew Shepard's Killers, What does it take to Pass as a Man?' *Harper's Magazine* (September 1999), p. 7. https://abrahamson.medill.northwestern.edu/WWW/READINGS/10-05_Toolbox/Wypijewski_Boys_Harpers_Sept1999.pdf [accessed 12 August 2020].
70 Beth Loffreda, *Losing Matt Shepard: Life and Politics in the Aftermath of Anti-Gay Murder* (New York: Columbia University Press, 2000), p. 60.
71 See William Savage Jr., *The Cowboy Hero: His image in American History and Culture* (Norman and London: University of Oklahoma Press, 1979), p. 101.
72 See Milane Duncan Frantz, 'My Heroes have Always been Cowboys: the De-romanticizing of the Cowboy Mythology in Annie Proulx's *Close Range*', MA dissertation (University of Houston: 2007), pp. 31–2, for an excellent analysis of this story.
73 See Frantz, 'My Heroes', pp. 11, 26–7, 45.
74 Elizabeth Atwood Lawrence, *Rodeo: An Anthropologist Looks at the Wild and the Tame Rodeo* (Knoxville: University of Tennessee Press, 1982), pp. 48–9.
75 Ibid., p. 28.
76 Ibid., p. 193.

77 McMurtry, 'Adapting Brokeback Mountain', in Larry McMurtry, Diana Ossana, *Brokeback Mountain: Story to Screenplay* (New York, London: Scribner, 2005), p. 140.
78 Proulx Afterword, Savage, *The Power of the Dog* (1967) (Boston: Little Brown, 2011), p. 286.
79 Henderson, *Native* (New York: Plume, 1993), p. 192.
80 Proulx, *Afterword*, p. 278.
81 Interview with Sandy Cohen: 'Annie Proulx Tells the Story behind *Brokeback Mountain*' http://ww.advocate.com/arts-entertainment/entertainment-news/2005/12/17/annie-proulx-tells-story-behind-brokeback [accessed 3 September 2020].
82 Proulx, 'Getting Movied', in *Story to Screenplay*, 129–38 (p. 135).
83 Ibid., p. 137.
84 Comer, *Landscapes of the New West*, p. 193.
85 Ibid., p. 131.
86 Hemmingway, *The Sun Also Rises* (New York: Scribner, 1926), p. 116.
87 See Eric Patterson for an excellent discussion of this aspect of the story, *On Brokeback Mountain: Meditations about Masculinity, Fear, and Love in the Story and the Film* (Lanham: Lexington Books, 2008), pp. 78–83.
88 See Ginger Jones, 'Proulx's Pastoral as Sacred Space', in Jim Stacy (ed.), *Reading Brokeback Mountain: Essays on the Stories and the Film* (Jefferson, North Carolina: McFarland and Company, 2007), 19–28 (p. 26).
89 Ehrlich, *The Solace of Open Spaces* (Harmondsworth: Penguin, 1985), p. 51.
90 Ossana/McMurtry, *Screenplay*, p. 11.
91 Patterson, *On Brokeback*, pp. 28–9.
92 Henderson, *Native*, p. 186.
93 Alfred Kinsey, Wardell Pomeroy, Clyde Martin, *Sexual Behaviour in the Human Male* (Philadelphia and London: W. B. Saunders, 1949), pp. 457, 459.
94 Proulx, *That Old Ace*, p. 138.
95 D'Emilio and Estelle Freedman, *Intimate Matters: A History of Sexuality in America* (Chicago: University of Chicago Press, 1988). Proulx, 'How the West was Spun', *The Guardian: Saturday Review* (25 June 2005), pp. 4–6.
96 John Calhoun, 'Peaks and Valleys', *American Cinematographer* 87: 1 (2006), 58–67 (p. 62); http://www.ennisjack.com/forum/index.php?topic=16905.0 [accessed 3 September 2020]; Ossana, 'Climbing Brokeback Mountain', *Story to Screenplay*, 143–51 (p. 150); Proulx, 'After the Gold Rush', *Guardian* (23 November, 2005) http://www.guardian.co.uk/world/2005/nov/23/usa. [accessed 4 August 2020].
97 Ossana/McMurtry, *Screenplay*, p. 37.
98 Proulx, 'Getting Movied', *Story to Screenplay,* pp. 130–1.
99 Stegner, *Where the Bluebird Sings to the Lemonade Springs* (Harmondsworth: Penguin Books, 1992), p. 107.
100 Ossana/McMurtry, *Screenplay,* p. 35.
101 Ibid., p. 43.
102 Ibid., p. 66.
103 Ibid., p. 70.
104 Ibid., p. 65.
105 Ibid., p. 76.

106 Quoted in W. C. Harris, 'Broke(n)back Faggots: Hollywood gives Queers a Hobson's Choice', in Stacy (ed.), *Reading Brokeback,* 118–34 (p. 127).
107 Harris cites as counter-examples Tom Outland and Roddy Blake in Willa Cather's *The Professor's House* (1925), and the gay relationships in rural environments in the work of Tennessee Williams and Alice Walker (p. 129).
108 McMurtry/Ossana, *Screenplay*, p. 82.
109 Ibid., Boag, p. 237-8.
110 McMurtry/Ossana, *Screenplay*, p. 71.
111 Ibid., pp. 95–6.
112 See Roy Grundmann's review, 'Brokeback Mountain', *Cineaste* 31: 2 (Spring 2006), 50–2 (p. 52). www.jstor.org/stable/41689972 [accessed 14 April 2020].

4

Lost in the Shadow of the Crazies: McGuane's Dislocated Cowboys

'The West, whatever that is, is still there, believe it or not, in its entirety,' McGuane writes. It is signalled by 'the stove-up cowboy at the unemployment office, the interstate that plunges through the homesteads' but 'what is lost is the connection' between the Old and New.[1] Stegner makes much the same point in 'History, Myth, and the Western Writer' (1967) when he notes that millions of Westerners have 'no sense of any continuity between the real Western past which has been mythicized almost out of recognizability and a real Western present that seems as cut-off and pointless as a ride on a merry-go-round that can't be stopped'.[2] If Stegner can be accused of a tendency to validate an Anglo rhetoric constructed around 'a sense of place' he also urges contemporary Westerners to recognize both their connection to the historical past and the falsity of the mythology. The madness of the fairground ride seems particularly apt, suggesting the circularity of a continuous and evasive present tense. It is an apt symbol of McGuane's Deadrock, the cliché of a Western town to which his protagonists return. They are not idealists entering the West for the first time (Andrews, Bob Dollar), nor disenfranchised cowboys in search of an imaginary West (Grady, Billy), nor dreamers trapped in dead end jobs (Diamond Felts, Ennis del Mar). They are lost men (culturally sophisticated but psychologically empty) returning to the West of their youth to put themselves back together again only to find a New West as fragmented as themselves. They are, as Gregory Morris has it, 'dislocated cowboys'.[3]

The irreverent approach of the *Deadrock Novels* is foreshadowed in McGuane's early film work, particularly his screenplay for *Rancho Deluxe* (1975). The *New Yorker* described it as full of the 'romantic absurdism and disconnectedness' that characterizes McGuane's West.[4] Jack McKee and his Native American sidekick, Cecil Colson, try their hardest, aided by a buddy narrative construction that mirrors and mocks the Anglo/Native American model of the traditional Western, to find a connection. They are anti-heroes on the run from middleclass respectability (Jack is married to a rich woman in the East), and their cattle rustling is a joke against the establishment, which allows them to indulge their 'last of the plainsmen' fantasy. They are, like all the young men in this study, heroic in their childish adherence to a nostalgically fanciful code of wilderness freedom, and also symbols of a degraded myth. We can say the same of Nicolas Payne, the 'counter-culture cowboy' at the centre of McGuane's 1971 novel *The Bushwhacked Piano*. He is another young man who lights out to escape the 'Waring blender' of his parents' homogenized lives hoping that the West will do its job and 'his life could be reconstituted like frozen orange juice' (*BP* 56). 'Lighting out' continues to be an existential act, but where Andrews, Grady and even Buddy Miller demand that we take their youthful exploits seriously, Payne, in common with all McGuane's protagonists, is fully engaged in his own self-parody. Waking up in a roadside motel and thinking of Ann, the girlfriend spirited away to their hobby ranch by suspicious parents, the narrator notes:

> He woke up thinking of how he had camped one night on the Continental Divide and pissed with care into the Atlantic watershed. Now he wasn't sure he should have. He tried to imagine he was saying toodleloo to a declining snivelization; and howdy to a warhoop intelligentsia of redskin possibility with Ann as a vague Cheyenne succubus – the complete buckskin treatment. But under his window, attendants drifted into a Stonehenge of gas pumps. Fill er up! America seemed to say ... Poised against the distant, visible mountains, the attendants stood by a rainbow undulance of Marfak.
>
> (50)

There are no transparent eyeballs or wolves, and the only border crossed is by a carefully directed arc of piss. Ancient Native American monuments are replaced by a 'Stonehenge of gas pumps' and the solitary rainbow offering hope is that puddled in the Marfak grease. And though, like McCarthy's cowboys, Payne associates Western authenticity with Cheyenne Indians, he is also aware that they are merely a Hollywood-inspired prop – 'the complete buckskin treatment' – to resurrect a faltering romantic relationship. It is not simply the corrupting influence of modernity that is at stake here, it is the way in which Payne's desire for a spiritual transformation is undermined by his inability to take it seriously. 'Filling up' is transformed into both commodification and performance; we learn that 'he felt if he could hit on the right boots, things would be better' but is horrified by the 'all-American' varieties on offer 'finished in buff-ruff, natural kangaroo or antique gold' (49). The same is true when he considers trading in his motorcycle: 'One day I'm going to have me a Ford Stepside station with the 390 engine and a four-speed box. I want a stereo tapedeck too with Tammy Wynette and Roy Acuff and Merle Haggard' (100). In such cases, Payne seems aware that this New West may not be able to perform a suitable backdrop to his voyage of self-discovery, that crooning sentimentality has replaced 'authenticity' and his own role, reinforced by his studied local vernacular, has become painfully self-parodic. And yet he still cannot quite divest himself of the hope such lyrics inspire. In this context, the 'Bushwhacked Piano' of the title becomes an apt symbol for his confusion: as a boy he used a neighbour's piano for target practice in an act of rebellion against an overly domesticated world. Since then it has grown to symbolize a man and a West dangerously out of tune.

II

The protagonists of the *Deadrock Novels* are out of tune with the New West because they are culturally attuned to the values of an imagined Old West. Patrick Fitzpatrick is their dislocated archetype, and *Nobody's Angel*, according to Dexter Westrum, 'announces the arrival of Thomas McGuane's fictional sensibility in the contemporary West' for which 'his film scripts seem to have been light rehearsals'.[5] Patrick is 'a fourth-generation cowboy outsider, an educated man, a whiskey addict and until recently a professional soldier' who is returning to Deadrock ostensibly to save both the family and the ranch, but really to cure himself of his 'sadness-for-no-reason' (61). It is, McGuane observes, 'the modern situation: the adhesion of people to place has been lost' leading to the 'malaise of alienation' that afflicts characters like Binx Bolling in Walker Percy's *The Moviegoer* (1961).[6] Patrick's malaise is captured in an opening paragraph:

> You would have to care about the country. Nobody had been here long enough and the Indians had been very thoroughly kicked out. It would take a shovel to find they'd ever been here. In the grasslands that looked so whorled, so cowlicked from overhead, were the ranches. And some of these ranches were run by men who thought like farmers ... the others were run by men who thought like cowboys ... The farmer-operators were good mechanics and packed protein off the land ... The cowboys might have gotten here last week or just after the Civil War, and they seemed to believe in what they were doing; though they were often very lazy white men.
>
> (1)

That 'very thoroughly' combined with the 'shovel' immediately calls into question the search for salvation upon which McGuane's central protagonists are engaged in the *Deadrock novels*. Having, like the Indians he so appreciates, been kicked off the land, Patrick followed the family tradition and joined the cavalry (ironically, his great grandfather had fought in the cavalry against the Indians) becoming a tank commander in Germany (ironically helping to save the West from the East (104)). In returning West, he is hoping that the ranch and surrounding countryside will provide meaning: from a distance it looks like a Hollywood backdrop and he desperately wants 'his heart to seize the ancient hills, the old windmills and stock springs'. However, he is also aware that his idealized vision is out of place in a New West in which ranchers have been replaced by 'farmer-operators' and cowboys, who might dress as if they had arrived 'just after the Civil War', but were 'usually lazy white men' (86). The ranch's own history provides a salutary lesson: his great-grandfather's dining room contains a collection of paintings 'depicting smallpox epidemics among the Assiniboine from the point of view of a Swiss academic painter' (67). Patrick, we are told, feels like the Englishman who commissioned the paintings – trapped in the vision of a world that is dying.

Finding a place and identity in a region undergoing an identity crisis is the conundrum unpicked by the symbolism of 'Nobody's Angel'. Angels abound in their absence – sisters, the landscape, cowboys and Native Americans – the most obvious being the West itself, which refuses to be Patrick's 'guardian Angel'. In a typically Proulxian manoeuvre, Patrick's domestic arrangements become a means of critiquing his relationship with a wider regional family and also the Western tropes that define such relationships. His mother, for example, is presented as cold and disloyal, sending him to boarding school and escaping the ranch to a new life in Santa Barbara. Her desire to be 'nobody's angel' has no corollary in the Western architecture to which Patrick aspires and so, like Grady's mother, she is vilified. His father, by contrast, was a bullying alcoholic who goes through a process apotheosis when he is killed during a test flight for Boeing; a cowboy hero on the new aerial frontier whose death transforms him into 'an archangelic semaphore more dignified than death itself' (6). Ursula Le Guin identifies this type of literary veneration as the 'Lost Pa' syndrome, a phenomenon which, as we have seen, possesses added significance within the Oedipal codes of the Western genre, in which father's pass on models of masculinity through rugged rituals.[7] It is, as will be seen, a cultural transference from Old to New under scrutiny throughout the Deadrock series and dramatized clearly in this novel through Patrick's discovery of a crashed plane that he takes as a symbolic reminder of his father's accident.[8] Despite his sister's warning that 'Daddy's not in the plane' Patrick believes that by looking 'into the pilot's eyes' he can construct a displaced confrontation with his father and resolve his own 'sadness for no reason' (5). In what is a richly illustrative moment, Patrick is brought face to face with the stinking corpse beyond veneration and whose literal fusion with the landscape foreshadows Patrick's disappointed engagement with the West as a whole. As he concedes later, the search for a sense of place within the family or the wider regional family is fraught – 'the connection had not been in the airplane on the mountain; it had not even been a sign' (86). It was: it's just that Patrick is too blinkered to read it.

The most obvious means of connection is his grandfather, Francis Fitzpatrick, an old-time cowboy who had 'seen gunfighters in their dotage' and whose ranch had been a childhood sanctuary from warring parents (61). Grandad, however, will be 'nobody's angel'. He is 'too cowboy' to be woven into Patrick's web of nostalgia and is looking for a way out himself – something he identifies in the vast emptiness of Australia: 'This country used to be just nothing and that's when it was good. And they say the Australia is one big nothing. I'm telling you, Patrick, I bet we'd do good out there. You can run a spread with just your saddle horses' (122–3). McGuane's insistence on 'Nothing' is a variation on the 'Nobody' that is the novel's dominant symbolic trope, and weaves grandad into a nostalgic rhetoric of absence that is a shared component of settler colonial discourse. Tom Lynch notes the pervasiveness of the 'nothing but' phrase throughout literary works that describe the wilderness of both the Australian Outback and US West – typified by Jim Burden's seminal description of the Nebraska plains at the beginning of Cather's *My Antonia* (1914): 'There was nothing to see … There was nothing but land: not a country at all, but the material out of which countries are made. No, there was nothing but land.'[9] Such rhetorical clichés, Jay Arthur argues in in *The Default Country* (2003), create an '*un*land' of deficiency, awaiting the fences, drainage and clearing (of both geographical and human impedimenta) in order for it to become 'actual land' – the ill-defined 'spread' (suggestive of increasingly fluid borders) that grandad encourages for Patrick.[10] Ironically, for grandad, as for Patrick, the contemporary West does not function as he remembers – 'it's not like it used to be. They've interfered with the moon and changed our weather' – which offers an evasion of his culpability in the decline, combined with a desire to return to the figurative Ur-landscape represented by Australia.

The complexities of their shared engagement with the West are symbolized by their discovery of an ancient burial site and the 'skeleton of a Cheyenne girl dressed in an Army coat, disinterred when the railroad bed was widened' (23). She is 'nobody's angel', representative of a lost West that can only be excavated by means of a shovel. She, like Patrick's father, has become part of the landscape: the army coat reminds us of the brutal Indian wars; the railroad, the march of progress that made her elimination inevitable. Francis refuses to disturb or reveal her presence to anyone, saying, 'you do not disturb the Old Ones' – thereby cloaking the past in dignity and nostalgia (23). And this is the beauty of the buried Indian, according to Drucilla Mims Wall, 'the magic resides in imagining the long-gone Indian' whose bones, hidden by earth, time and cultural distance, can be resurrected and made to perform a version of 'Indianness' for American white males.[11] William Carlos Williams mocks this Anglo tendency towards apotheosis in his observation

– 'The land! Don't you feel it? Doesn't it make you want to go out and lift dead Indians tenderly from their graves, to steal from them as if it must be clinging even to their corpses some authenticity?'[12] Patrick's more muted version comes through the search for arrowheads, symbols, as Lisa Knopp has argued, that only take on significance in the West (there were plenty of arrows fired in Europe) in which the colonizer has the luxury of transforming them into a symbol of a romanticized past.[13] As the impotent weapons of a defeated enemy, it could be argued that they symbolize a fruitless yearning for a romanticized past – which is their function in McGuane's novels. Certainly, Patrick hopes through them to establish 'that he was part of something in the course of what was to come' – a trait shared with a number of McGuane protagonists (63). Joe Starling records 'a ticklish feeling that he was searching for part of his own earlier life' – an authentic bond with the past which, ironically, stands in contrast to the commodification of the New West (*KC* 189). However, in McGuane's West the past does not just sit there awaiting excavation. A backhoe operator in the short story 'Weight Watchers' marvels at the fact that an obsidian arrowhead cuts through 'Six plies of Jap snow tire and it never broke' – the past ripping through to the present (*CF* 7). In a similar manner, the girl is disinterred and displayed in a rancher's cocktail bar and a potentially spiritual connection between Old and New West is transformed into kitsch.

A more muted disinterment befalls grandad, who responds positively to an audition invitation for a Western movie, *Hondo's Last Move*: 'In order to reflect the hardships endured in the West in the 1880s, we would especially welcome the physically eccentric, those with permanent physical injuries, such as scars, missing teeth, broken limbs, broken noses, missing limbs etc.' (14). Exploration of the past through its contemporary recreation is a bridging manoeuvre deployed by both McCarthy and Proulx. For Proulx, films – whether the remake of 'The Johnson County War' in 'Florida Rental' (*BD*) or the discovery of Cody's lost epic 'The Indian Wars Refought' (*BD*) – demonstrate the lesson that Cody taught the West some time ago, that those who control the present can recreate the past. McCarthy's usage, by contrast, is more personal. When his aging Billy, like Francis Fitzpatrick, signs up as a Hollywood extra, it is both a debasement of his dreams and a trap that prevents his more mature understanding of his life. McGuane bridges the two by drawing attention to the pathos of the Frontier struggle with a characteristic tone of mockery. The film's casting co-ordinator, Arnold Duxbury, reflects the artificiality of the New West, whose idea of authenticity is purely superficial (he dresses entirely in denim (15)). The irony of his vision is suggested by an Old West that comprises of a catalogue of those things that are missing. This includes the movie itself since Duxbury believes that Westerns were beginning to show signs of 'metal fatigue' and he has moved onto Science Fiction instead (15).

The choice of genre, like Proulx's introduction of the Jupiterian warlord-turned-re-wilding rancher in 'A Pair of Spurs' (*CR*), draws attention to the artificiality of our vision of the West. 'Grandad's last move' is off the ranch and into a small apartment, convenient for the cinema and the Hawk bar, in which Patrick has mounted the head of the last elk his grandfather had ever shot (226). This is what the Old West has been reduced to: a stuffed head glimpsed through the window of a tiny apartment and a retirement spent watching films about himself so that he 'won't have to watch [Patrick] do things worse than I did them' (163).

If grandfather represents a version of the West content to revel in its own nostalgia, Patrick's sister, Mary (a thinly veiled portrait of McGuane's sister who died of a drug overdose in the mid-seventies), reflects a more damaged victim of Western history. She is 'nobody's angel' – her prostitution and addiction to animal tranquilizers presenting the true legacy of the settler days: not stoical resistance but damaged people. The stories told by grandad that so enthral Patrick, appal her. His tale of a Virginian – a 'big old violent cracker with protruding ears' – who is shot for ruining the town's dances – is received by Patrick as an illustration of Frontier justice; but it's Mary's 'Kill, shoot, whack, stab, chop' that proves the more eloquent summation of the romanticized violence celebrated in Wister's eponymous hero (55). Patrick may wallow in cowboy glamour, but Mary represents those women left behind on isolated ranches whose loneliness is not appeased by mythological scaffolding. Patrick intuits as much in a letter to their mother: 'As this high lonesome plays out right after its use in calendar photos ... it was quite hard to find anybody to talk to around here' (181). Her isolation is compounded by her revulsion of what the West has become, the kitsch horror Americana – TERRI'S BEAUTY SHOP, YUMMEE FREEZE, HEREFORDS: MONTANA'S GREATEST TREASURE, U-NAME IT WE'LL FIND IT – that greets her upon release form the state asylum (27). Whilst Patrick's West was safely locked in his German tank, she has been forced to confront a land of what she calls 'Despos' – not the romantic Desperados of folklore, but the *despo-riche* and *despo-chic* buying up America (107). They are represented in *The Bushwhacked Piano* by the FitzGerald family. Their hobby-ranching is brutally exposed through the absurd juxtaposition of contemporary vanity and triviality in the shadow of the magnitude of past crimes. In one scene, after his wife reminds him of his offensive nasal hairs, Mr Fitzgerald is depicted going:

> Back up the stairs of a house built on the ancestral hunting grounds of the Absoroka Indians, with a gloomy certainty that the rotary nose clipper had been left at home. And even though he knew it was irrational, he began to lose interest in the West.

(*BP* 147)

In *Nobody's Angel* such absurdity is represented by Anna Adams of the Z6 ranch, whose lawn, New York clothes, Missouri fox-trotter horse are a caricature of the vulgar wealthy Western woman (32). They are also mocked through Tio Burnett, a caricature oilman who idealizes the New West and performs the role of 'good-old-boy' by tucking his trousers into his cowboy boots to show his connection with the land that rarely he is rarely seen upon. Patrick dismisses him as a South Westerner, not even a proper cowboy but a yearling boy, and representative of 'the first part of the West with gangrene' (38). For Patrick he is a personification of the wrecked West. However, McGuane makes clear through their shared love of horses, good cooking and the same woman – Tio's wife Claire – that Tio is simply an exaggerated version of Patrick, whose Western identity has slipped into grotesque parody.

For Patrick, saving Mary becomes a means of scripting himself into a heroic narrative, which proves difficult in a West with diminishing scope for cowboy theatricals. Throughout the novel, McGuane draws attention to the tragicomedy of Patrick's attempts through his pastiching of a number of cowboy tropes layered with references to *Hamlet* – the archetypal brooding prodigal who is trapped in genre. Hamlet's problem is one of justice and genre; he is unable to revenge his father's murder in accordance with either his filial duty or to satisfy the generic conventions of the 'Revenge Tragedy'.[14] The same is true of Patrick, the original 'Hamlet in mule ear boots' who is so absorbed in his own brooding alienation that there is no room for Mary. When, just before her suicide, he meets her by a pool at a Crow burial site, he notes offhandedly that 'Ophelia would have sunk in it like a stone', suggesting that he is alive to the dramatic but not the personal resonances of the situation (103). The same blindness is filtered through a Western revenge script in his struggle to stop Deke Patwell (editor of Deadrock's local newspaper) reporting Mary's condition. He reconfigures the role of *Shane*, which neither he nor the narrator can take seriously. The tension of the cowboy shootout is re-enacted in the buying of cleaning products in a supermarket – 'I'd use rubber gloves with those hands of yours, Deke. Dish pads are full of irritating metal stuff' (97). Hands, those barometers of cowboy ruggedness, become ironic measures of stifled masculinity. When, following publication of an exposé, Patrick thrashes Deke with a cane, he claims to the police by way of explanation: 'Deke wanted me to act out the Ronald Colman part from *The Prisoner of Zenda*.' Once again, it is a knowing reference, augmented by the free indirect narrative observation that 'It was turning into a western' – a comment that embraces the views of characters, narrator and reader in Patrick's own confused role play (140).

McGuane employs similar referencing in Patrick's dealings with Mary's lover, the Cheyenne cowboy and pool hustler, David Catches. According to his grandfather, Catches was a good worker, but he got tired of him trying to 'tell you how it was' so 'I told him how it was' (123). This is his function with Patrick: he is the one person who tells him how it is. They meet in a whiskey-fuelled encounter following Mary's funeral in which each tries to establish a more valid connection with the dead woman. Catches shares a self-reflexive bemusement at his own cultural performance that foreshadows Sherman Alexie's *Lone Ranger* stories. For just as Alexie's characters find themselves bumping up against the scripts assigned to them by popular culture – the heroic brave, taciturn shaman or self-destructive drunk – Catches finds himself trapped and goaded by a man who recognizes his entrapment as a version of his own. Indeed, Patrick's mocking interrogation of his behaviour seems to be posing the question that Alexie will ask ten years later: 'Don't you even know how to be a real Indian?' McGuane explored elements of this question through his presentation of Cecil Colson's relationship with his father in *Rancho Deluxe*. Where his partner, Jack McKee, is in rebellion against his wealthy family and white heritage, Cecil is in awe of his: he loves to hear his father's stories, an opportunity that McGuane creates during a rare pastoral interlude when father and son go fishing. The cinematography offers a moment of stillness amidst the chaos of the film, but McGuane's detailing constantly reminds us that both father and son are trapped by generic expectations. When Cecil picks him up, he is watching cowboys and Indians on the TV, a sad incongruity highlighted further through the story he tells of the death of his own father. Unable to cremate him, his body is stored on top of the propane tank of a neighbour – Bob Not a Small Crow – who later appears on a TV quiz show having anglicized his name to Bob Small. What is missing in the absurdly disconnected narrative is the connection between the stories and the teller, between the idealized Indian and the man in front of us. Thus, McGuane teasingly unhitches the symbolic 'Indian' from any expected referents, allowing Cecil's attempts at heritage reclamation to be derailed by the descent into triviality.

Patrick's encounter with Catches offers a more threatening, but no less ridiculous, variation.[15] It begins in grandad's kitchen before they remove to the mountains in search of the flickering firelight, the snickering horses and scent of balsam that will provide what they believe to be the suitable Western scaffolding for their exploration of complex masculine emotions. In Patrick's fantasy, it is a struggle between cowboy and Indian, but Catches recognizes his provocation for what it is: his guilt and fear of cliché masking itself through objectification. Catches, like Patrick, is well aware of his own performance, which makes him a difficult opponent, and both recognize themselves as degraded versions of their idealized role models and therefore cannot take their roles seriously. Even the potentially violent denouement is botched through self-awareness:

> Catches: 'We are now to the place where one of us is inclined to kill the other ... on the basis of two men revenging themselves upon each

other for what they haven't done themselves. Boy, I don't know what that means.'
You came close.
'I know ... but I fell on my ass.'

(127)

Ironically, nothing happens because they are protected by self-irony; they are more evolved versions of McCarthy's protagonists who recognize their entrapment within the rhetorical tropes and masculine rituals of the outmoded Western genre upon which they construct their identity. Grandad is appalled by their behaviour because he recognizes that they are all just talk and have no place in his vision of taciturn Western gunfighters. And yet, ironically, acknowledging their own performance actually allows for greater revelation.[16] Patrick is able to admit that his venerated father was a drunkard and that, because he abandoned Mary whilst in Germany, if Mary was anybody's Angel, she was Catches'. Thus, Mary is conjoined with the novel's other absent buried angel, the Cheyenne princes.

The only time that time Patrick seems to achieve the equanimity he seeks is when he is on his horse – Leafy – in a John Ford landscape. McGuane's sporting essays emphasize how the importance of the customs and rituals that surround its various practices – cutting, breaking, rodeo – (what McCarthy would sanctify as ceremonies), provide riders with a link to a Western heritage that enables them to make sense of their lives.[17] To be mounted in orderly attire on a friendly horse in the 'wilderness' is to be in harmony with the West free from self-irony. The cowboy and his horse encodes a narrative of mutual loyalty, which both McCarthy and Proulx deconstruct to reveal a surrogate for the female presence that maintains their protagonists in a state of arrested development. Horses provide ears to be whispered into and, more troublingly, models and metaphors of sexual dominance. McGuane explores similar territory with familiar comic irony. The backstory informs us that Patrick saved Leafy from freezing to death when she was a foal and he identifies a 'sadness-for-no-reason in her eyes' that enables her to become a way to talk about emotions: 'Leafy, am I not thoughtless? I am. Left you in the cold corral with no kisses. Here is kiss' (161). There is linguistic juvenility here that is absent from Grady's horse whispering and undercuts his emotional investment. Leafy, as Evgeniya Butenin notes, becomes just another means for Patrick to talk about Patrick; he may perceive 'sadness' in her eyes but cannot prevent himself from speculating that her manure 'would be so useful to a determined gardener with a nice ass' (161).[18] McGuane's comic irony is even more pronounced in his deconstruction of the horse as surrogate and metaphor for sex. The love-triangle between Patrick, Claire Burnett and her husband, Tio, is constructed around their passion for horses. Tio is the outsider who plays cowboy through breeding horses; he values Patrick for his fabled horse-breaking skills and believes that his friendship validates his own cowboy persona. Their shared affinity is a complete misreading, as is his belief that he can trust Patrick with his wife because he is 'cowboy enough to keep it in [his] pants' (59). Patrick certainly isn't. Both Tio's horse and Claire arrive on Patrick's ranch at the same time: the former is described as broken to ride, which is how Patrick views Claire, compliant to his cowboy fantasy. But both remain dangerous: the 'new stud' immediately tramples him – a clear warning that he should be wary of Tio but also of Claire.

Claire is dangerous because she refuses to conform to a culture in which 'pretty little horses' are conflated with 'pretty little senoritas'. McGuane's women, despite his reputation for 'bad boy' misogyny, tend to be subversive.[19] In *The Bushwhacked Piano* Ann Fitzgerald is the spoilt rich girl who finds herself trapped in a cowboy fantasy, both Payne's Gary Cooper narrative and, more menacingly, the ranch manager's sexual fantasies. Wayne Clodd is a cowboy voyeur who regularly watches her undressing during which times we are told: 'He banished a rather piddling inclination to self-abuse ... [and] felt the virile prominence of the cowboy in the mythological ecosystem of America ... He shinnied down ready for ranching. He hadn't cried since he was a child' (*BP* 88). The image is both hilarious and pathetic; the punning 'virile prominence' is offset by the 'childish tears' of a man who knows that he cannot delude himself by scripting his lewd behaviour into a glorious history of the West. Clodd, as his name suggests, is a screwball version of Payne's interpretation of cowboy machismo. Ann is happy to join him in his fantasy, but on her own terms. As a photographer, she seeks 'authenticity'. she rejects the picture postcard landscape that he finds essential to his identity construction in favour of 'trash, gas stations and Dairy Queens'. Similarly, she rejects picturing Payne on either his motorbike or on horseback in favour of him padding around their motel in his sagging underwear (145, 177). The 'sagging underwear' guides us to the absurdity of her search as she replaces one cliché of representation with another. This tendency extends to her own performance: 'She wanted to be along for the ride just like those cowboy's floozies she saw at all hours sitting under rear-view mirrors of pickups ... she broke out the peroxide, pouted at herself in the mirror and squeaked, "Call me Sherri"' (*BP* 145–6). Payne recognizes her 'hillbilly act' and condemns it as more Country and Western than trailer park, but the difference is that she knows it (160). In the extravagance of her self-conscious performance she throws into sharp relief the absurdity of his own act and their shared confusion when it comes to forging authentic Western identities.

Powerful women are also presented as problematizing the masculine hegemony presented in *Rancho Deluxe* and McGuane's most traditional Western script – *The Missouri Breaks* (1976). In the former, Laura Beige (Charlene Dallas) plays a cameo role as the virginal daughter of the seemingly bumbling 'regulator' sent to catch Jack and Cecil. Her deployment of a combination of wide-eyed innocence ('she's a regular bambi' exclaims a ranch hand) and sexual promiscuity is presented as screwball, but by taking control of her own performance she is exposing the simplicity of the classic Western 'virgin/whore binary'. The *Missouri Breaks* places a similar plot in the Montana of the 1880s. Jane Braxton (Kathleen Lloyd) is the strong-willed daughter of a local cattle baron who falls in love with the rustler responsible for stealing his cattle, Jack Logan (Jack Nicholson).[20] Reviewing the film when it was released, Betsy Erkkila claims that Jane is a more emancipated character than the feted Mrs Miller in Altman's *McCabe and Mrs Miller* (1971), who, for all her feistiness, is 'the same old whore, except now she smokes opium instead of cigarettes'.[21] Jane is a free spirit who challenges the genre: we never see her by the hearth but on horseback, and when Logan comes courting, she is sharp in her rejoinder: 'What've you got in mind? ... Sexual intercourse? Well, all right! Get down from that horse.' It is a throwaway challenge, but it also symbolically deconstructs the cowboy's troublesome relationship with women by making clear that the only way to get down to sex with a real woman is to stop being a cowboy. It signals a more general role reversal in which she is the one who holds the reins when they go riding together. Defending McGuane from accusations of anachronism, the director, Arthur Penn, notes: 'I think Tom was making an educated guess that there was a more forthright version of a genteel lady available than has been represented in classic Westerns. She's not the schoolmarm. She's a woman of appetites, and she articulates those appetites – something which was absolutely not permitted in all of the other Westerns that I've ever seen.'[22]

McGuane presents a similar challenge to Western archetypes in the screenplay for the biopic of *Tom Horn* (1980). Horn's (Steve McQueen) love interest is the school teacher, Glendolene Kimmel (Linda Evans), whose radicalism is presented by her depicted bathing in a horse trough – an act that literally and symbolically breaks the hallowed link between a cowboy and his horse. McGuane allows Horn to pose the question that Westerns never feel the need to ask: 'Why you hangin' around with me?' Her response – 'Because you are a link to the Old West' – is more sentimental than erotic, reminding us that though the Western has been colonized by symbols and rituals that answer to male needs, the spirit of freedom at its core is gender neutral.

The women who populate the *Deadrock Novels* are proudly 'individualistic' and not afraid to 'articulate their appetites'. As such, they provide a check on the protagonists' tendency to fantasize, which in Patrick's case is so pronounced that he has made up his own girlfriend in the shape of Marion Easterly. Marion, who was invented by the teenage Patrick to excuse his staying in town late, is the archetypal cowboy girlfriend (Marion suggests John Wayne seen from an Easterly perspective) against whom all others have fallen short. When he is forced to kill her off, he visits her imaginary 'grave' in search of solace, transforming her into Leafy – a silent partner whose function is to listen and perpetuate a general Western nostalgia

(181). When she does speak to Patrick it is in a dream in which she merges with Mary to become a voice that promises to put right the offences of his bullying father whilst simultaneously challenging his adolescent tendency to male fantasy (119). She offers a more subversive psychoanalytic solution to Patrick's malaise that contrasts with his Old West tendency to make Marion flesh in his affair with Claire Burnett. At one stage Mary asks Patrick why he had never got married, to which he answers – 'I didn't have a picture of a good home life' (145). He does, but it's a mythological one in which his relationship with Claire becomes 'a big simp love story' in which he gets to play Gary Cooper (147)). Patrick wants a 'Calamity Claire', but when seated before a portrait of her illustrious Deadrock forebear in a tacky themed bar his thoughts drift to the juke box tune – 'Mamas, don't let your babies grow up to be cowboys ... Lost souls on the big sky.' Patrick and Claire are the 'lost souls' amidst a West in which women are eroticized as feminized cowboys and complex emotions are reduced to warbling sentimentality (75). Claire, however, refuses to be part of Patrick's Westernized scenario; she will, ironically, 'stand by her man' and remain loyal to her husband. It is a position made easier by a growing appreciation that the Western myth has become an ugly warn out cliché. A visit late in the novel to the same themed bar describes Patrick's awareness of 'the impossibly ugly Calamity Jane in the clothing of a scout' and how now 'they danced from cheating to trucks to lost love to faded love again, which seemed sadder than lost love' (208, 9). McGuane's desperate adumbration draws attention to their shared suspicion that they are trapped in a world in which romance has given way to mawkish cliché.

In this particular Western, the usual genre conventions do not apply; the cowboy doesn't save the ranch and neither does he get the girl: instead, he remains lost.[23] As such, at the novel's close it is the application of genre conventions that enables McGuane, as it has done throughout the novel, to unpick his protagonist's childishness in the face of serious emotions. In order to carry out his affair with Claire, it has been necessary to script her husband into the role of gunslinger nemesis manoeuvring him into a 'major showdown' to see who is 'the stand-up gunslinger of the two' (154). As with Catches and Deke Patwell, however, both men are paralysed by a narrative that they find unconvincing and comical. When, at one stage, Tio draws a gun on an unimpressed Patrick, he is forced to admit 'I thought it would have a different effect' – an effect learned from the Hollywood Westerns that he has always doubted (220). In a fitting denouement, Patrick and Claire are depicted making love in the living room of their house whilst Tio sits in the plexiglass capsule of his helicopter (a version of Patrick's tank) listening to the weather forecast prior to committing suicide. Patrick is aware of the sordid irony of the situation and his diminished experience of the West, McGuane undercutting his bravado with the bawdy acknowledgement that 'the West's last stands were less and less appropriate to epic poetry and murals' (223). The long-awaited shoot out with Tio has failed to materialize, Tio turning the proclivity for Western bloodshed upon himself, therefore denying Patrick the possibility of regeneration through violence. The West, as Evgeniya Butenin notes, has broken Patrick: he now acknowledges that 'he wasn't a captain or a cowboy ... he was superfluous', an acknowledgement that takes him out of the West to his Spanish retreat accompanied by the imaginary Marion Easterly (223). His last act is to present Claire with Leafy – a symbol of the West that he has broken with one he has not. What has been broken is Tio, a man attempting to live a hyper-stylized version of a Western dream.[24] The last sentence – 'In any case, he never came home again' – is the antithesis of the first: he cares about 'the country' but has been unable to find it in the contemporary West. The West is best viewed at a distance, like the bird's-eye view of the opening description, for the distance between the imaginary and real leaves the individual lost.

III

In his next two novels, *Something to Be Desired* (1985) and *Keep the Change* (1989), McGuane turns his attention to a theme that he had wilfully avoided in *Nobody's Angel*: how the West, particularly its landscape, becomes part of the bond that ties fathers to sons. Troubled filial relations are what drive many of the young men in the work of Williams, McCarthy and Proulx to escape West. Fathers are too austere (Will Andrews's thinly drawn Calvinist preacher; Buddy Millar's Mid-West Republicans) or violent (the parents of McCarthy's Kid, Jack Twist and Ennis del Mar) or emasculated (Grady's mother owns the ranch) or absent (the fathers of Diamond Studs and Bob Dollar) or dead (Billy and Patrick's father). Their presence is fleeting (mothers barely figure at all), buried in a backstory designed to explain the development of their son's character (Ennis Del Mar's homophobia; Grady's mistrust of women; Diamond's misogyny; Bob's misplaced loyalty; Andrews's love of Emerson) before the real action begins. It is in the cultural practices and rituals associated with the geography of the West and the iconic figure of the cowboy that these lost sons seek a surrogate model of masculinity: a model made grotesque in the fatherly figure of Judge Holden, who transforms orphans into killers of men. McGuane offers a variation: his fathers are a negative influence, but they linger – literally in the case of Tom Skelton's father who has retreated into a giant bed sited on the front porch from which he continues to control his son's life (*Ninety-Two in the Shade* (1973)). This is the ghostly presence that hovers over *Nobody's Angel* and is made flesh in both *Something to Be Desired* and *Keep the Change*, novels that from the outset seem troubled by the hyper-masculine 'Western' legacy handed down from fathers to sons. It is apparent in the opening scene of *Something to Be Desired*, which depicts two men lost in an archetypal cowboy landscape:

> The moon lofted off the horizon to drift low over the prairie, white and imperious as a commodore ... Now they were lost. They had been lost for two days. Not seriously lost, because they could see the lights of Deadrock: but they had lost their own camp on the rocky escarpment of the Crazy Mountains.
>
> (3, 4)

These are not saddle-pardners, but the young Lucien Taylor and his estranged father, who has returned from South America to abduct his son in order to enjoy a few days bonding in a suitably Western environment. The latter is our focalizing agent, the over-wrought simile drawing attention to a landscape constructed from cliché rather than an actual geographical location. Symbolically, the mountains should act as a site of spiritual regeneration, but the aptly named Crazies are emblematic of Deadrock men struggling for self-definition in the shadow of a hyper-masculine mythology. For where the young Lucien is acculturated into this tradition through his reading of Ernest Thompson Seton and Theodore Roosevelt, his father has exploited their rhetoric of self-reliance to excuse his irresponsibility. He presents himself as searching for the 'wide open spaces ... where they don't hamstring a man for standing a little tall' – thereby justifying his flight to South America (the preferred escape of other emblematic westerners in the novel) (17). His return and abduction of Lucien for a weekend of hiking underlines both his recklessness and superficiality, for though he sentimentalizes the 'big sky' he quickly abandons it to book into Deadrock's ersatz 'Big Sky' motel. Here, despite railing against cultural homogeneity, he enjoys a commodified version of the West that satisfies his inclination for cliché over authenticity.

Keep the Change opens with a similar scene of filial bonding as the 10-year-old Joe Starling joins his banker father, Sonny, at the foreclosure of a ranch house. They are both captivated by a picture of a range of white hills, which age has transformed into a mysterious representation of shadows. The picture stays with Joe and inspires his artistic career, but when he returns to take another look late in the novel he discovers that there is nothing there: 'There was no picture. There was a frame hanging there and it outlined the spoiled plaster behind it. It could have been anything' (214). It is a symbolic moment in which McGuane, as he does through the titles *Nobody's Angel*, *Something to be Desired* and later *Nothing but Blue Skies*, draws attention to the emptiness at the centre of his protagonists' lives; a feature that is clearly apparent in both their relationship with their fathers and, by extension, their relationship with the West. In this particular example, Joe is drawn to the beauty of Western romance and therefore he fails to see that there is nothing there; whereas his father is attentive to the beauty of the emptiness, but interprets it as a business opportunity. He is 'a cold-blooded westerner at heart' whose bank has just taken back this ranch, a pattern repeated in the novel (154). He brings the same 'cold blooded' manipulation of Western tropes to other aspects of his parenting. When thirteen-year-old Joe gets into an argument with his much stronger friend, Billy Kelton, his father's insistence that they settle it 'like men' reads like a Hollywood script, as does the life-lesson drawn from the humiliation: 'You'll think about this for a long time' (96). Sonny is right, but not in the way intended. Joe dreams of joining a band of Native Americans who attack a settler couple who look like his parents and raise their homestead to the ground so that 'everything was gone. Even the stony white of foundations and bones was gone' (97). The dream signals the death of the filial bond that existed as they contemplated the picture by inverting it – the white hills becoming the deathly white bones. It also reminds us that even on the level of Western violence, Joe remains romantic whilst Sonny is more practical.

Lucien and Joe leave the West to become painters, their vocation confirming their outsider status and tendency towards idealism. Joe's artistic pretensions quickly founder when removed from the Western landscape and he finds work as an illustrator in an advertising company depicting everything from hair-driers to toilet cleaners. In the world of contemporary art and Nouvelle Cuisine all is superficial and under-nourishing. Where his father 'had the Westerner's ability to look into pure space and see possibilities', Joe now sees Western cliché as a way of selling junk back to Americans: his memory of the light of the White Hills is degraded into the light reflecting off a toaster in an advertising poster (31, 36). He also falls in love with two women – Ellen, daughter of the neighbouring rancher he dated as a boy, and Astrid, an exotic Cuban whose cosmopolitan superficiality is signalled by her first appearance dressed as a hood ornament on a Rolls Royce. Despite their binary opposition, they are fully fleshed out characters whose presence draws attention to Joe's naivete. This character configuration is replicated in Lucien's two lovers: under his childhood sweetheart, Emily, 'he was going to be a rancher and a painter of sporting subjects on the order of Thomas Eakins', whilst under Suzanne he is offered a high-powered job in the US Information Agency in Latin America. He opts for sophistication over wilderness; a cacophony of languages over the monosyllabic; the bustle of humanity over the static painted scene (22). Both men, however, fall into existential crises for which they seek the antidote in the West. For Lucien, this crisis is hastened whilst on holiday in the replica slave colony of Nevis when, during a visit to the chapel in which Admiral Horatio Nelson had married, he compares his own life with this heroic vanishing event:

> He wanted to be in the country he loved once more. He wanted to paint, though he set only a modest store by that; he just wanted to get a few things down, like the Indians who traced the red ocher elk on the walls of

the old hobo caves outside of town. He felt that his life had transformed him into a functionary. He felt lost.

(29)

Lucien wants to escape from a world of geographical and linguistic fragmentation represented by the US Information Agency to the solidity he associates with the West (24). He also wants the straight-talking glamour: his visit coincides with news that his childhood sweetheart, Emily has dispatched her abusive husband 'Calamity Jane style'. However, McGuane has made clear that the warning signs are there, most palpably in Lucien's belief that the West is caught in aspic, captured by the Native Americans whose style he is seeking to imitate. The *Something to be Desired* is clearly locked in the past, symbolized by an artistic primitivism that he equates with authenticity and a glamorous straightforward Frontier justice that contrast with his 'rumpled seersucker' existence. Furthermore, it is significant that the revelation takes place in the 'remodelled ruins' of an old slave colony, an act of historical renovation and replication that alerts us to Deadrock's own troubled relationship with its mythical past, whilst simultaneously foreshadowing the creation of his own Western themed spa.

In *Keep the Change*, Joe's return home is precipitated by a similar crisis, but once again the warning signs are clear. The long journey West (ten pages in McGuane's narrative) is a mockery of the trail rides:

There was a perfect Texan urban river bottom at Grand Prairie with scrub willows whose roots gathered trash in the flash floods that shot through the neighbourhoods. Joe was maddened by joy at being in the country of the West. He felt that he would find a restored coordination for his life here. This was the West's job. Gustav Mahler of all people was on the radio. Great Southwest Parkway! Lone Star Homes! Texas Toyota! A subdivision of multifarious grandeur, half-timbered Tudor homes baking in the dry air and clinging to the hillsides.

(53–4)

Joe maintains the sensibility of a painter, an 'outsider' or 'ghost' – the latter motif running throughout the novel. His shadowy ambivalence is illustrated in this journey during which he takes his cues from the landscape to measure whether 'the West had begun' in order to monitor his feeling of gradual restoration. Unfortunately, the West of his imagination has already been trashed (the real trash produced by his advertising campaigns catching in tree roots), its symbolic heritage living on in strangely distorted manifestations ('Great Southwest Parkway!' 'half-timbered Tudor homes'). Like Lucien, Joe is haunted by the dichotomy between childhood ideal and the depressing reality of the 'fetishistic paved driveways', the 'portraits of Elvis on black velvet', and the 'sentimental Spanish haciendas' of the New West (54, 51). A similar conflict marks his relationship with his Western sweetheart Ellen: he wants to play the Virginian opposite his schoolteacher, but when they meet again it is not amidst the free range in which they forged their relationship, but on a golf driving range:

> Ellen stood up on a kind of rubber mat and began firing the balls out through the bug-filled flood of light, almost to the darkness beyond. At first Joe just watched her. There were gophers speeding around, running, stopping, looking, whistling, trying to fathom life on a driving range.
>
> (103)

It is a dramatic illustration of the challenges faced by all those lost in the New West as both golfers and gophers struggle with the contours of their new environment. Ellen, like most of the women in the *Deadrock Novels*, proves much better adapted; Joe, by contrast, maintains a romantic distance. Like Patrick, he hunts for arrowheads and is enraptured by characters like Bill Smethwick, the archetypal Western horse-breaker who wears suspenders and a shabby Stetson. Accordingly, there is an elegiac quality to much of his engagement with his surroundings: he bursts into tears when he catches sight of a man standing in an attitude of helplessness 'next to a horse whose head hung close to the ground' – a tableau suggestive of a fagged-out West beyond the help of all those who care (155). Essentially, he believes that you can 'keep the change' to the West; it is, as Proulx makes clear in the last part of her *Wyoming Trilogy, Fine Just the Way It Is*.

Joe's sloppy romanticism is brought into sharp relief when faced with the inheritance of the family ranch. The ranch, as with McCarthy and Proulx, offers McGuane a metonymic connection between Old and New West which enables him to explore the dangers of romantic attachment. Grady's idealism is charted through his relationship with ranches: he is disinherited from the family ranch by his mother; he seeks and finds an idealized equivalent in Mexico from which he is ejected due to his illicit love affair; finally, he becomes a sad figure on a desolate ranch in the shadow of a nuclear test site. At the end he is locked into the performance of an increasingly desperate cowboy role, which we are invited to admire and pity in equal measure. For Proulx the ranch is a trap. Ranchers like Gilbert Wolfscale ('What Kind of Furniture Would Jesus Pick' (*BD*)), Verl Lister ('Tits-Up-In-a-Ditch' (*FJW*)), and Buckskin Bill (*TOA*) are curmudgeons possessed by the need for possession as an end in itself, lost in a world of agribusiness, oil speculators, real estate developers and environmentalists. They are unable to reconcile the timeless beauty of the ranch of their imagination with the desiccated reality that they hope to pass onto their reluctant children; a myopia that makes them figures deserving of our sympathy. Like Proulx's reluctant inheritors

(Gilbert's son prefers working in a video store, Verl's daughter joins the army), McGuane's protagonists are torn between a romantic attachment to what the ranch represents and a recognition that it is unviable. Joe Starling is typical; inheritance is part of his Western DNA, but the reality is daunting – a state of affairs that allows McGuane to draw unfavourable comparisons with the South's maintenance of its cultural legacy:

> Joe had come to believe from reading books that in many landholding families, there existed perfect communication between the generations about the land itself. He noticed how Southerners believed this. Even if they were in New York there was always a warm-hearted old daddy holding out for their possession and occupancy an ancient farm – viewed as sacred tenure on earth rather than agriculture – whenever they should choose to take it up. Price of admission? Take a few minutes, after the soul-stirring train ride down yonder, to make friends with the resident darkies. Where had the people gone wrong in the West? In the latest joke, leaving a ranch to one's children was called child abuse.
>
> (63)

If the 'South' has been successful in forging a powerful if superficial sense of 'Southernness' where has the West gone wrong? McGuane's answer, like Proulx, is to show how Western mythology and rhetoric participates in its own economic destruction. Ranch ownership for Joe's father was part nostalgic dream and part business strategy: he was less concerned about the landscape than the sense of identity it conferred. He is a caricature ruthless banker and absentee landlord who is happy to play at being the cowboy (even changing out of his suit into his cowboy 'costume' prior to his ranch inspections), but is more used to 'pounding the ball around the fairways with hostile force' than herding cattle in a hostile blizzard (6). The neighbouring rancher, Mr Overstreet, appears more authentic but the narrator warns us that 'like many old-time ranchers, there was nothing "Western" about him. A topographical map on the wall illustrated the boundaries of the ranch' which describes a perfect square, but for the bite taken out by the Starling place (20). In a novel concerned with the painterly eye, Overstreet's map is the perfect symbol of dislocation; it says nothing about the quality of the land but rather, like Larry Cook – the aging rancher at the centre of Jane Smiley's *A Thousand Acres* (1991), Overstreet is only concerned with acreage and aesthetics. By the time that Joe returns, Overstreet's focus has shifted from inheritance to solidifying his Western posterity. He is trailed by a reporter from a German travel magazine, to whom he quips Western clichés – 'That's how the West was won … Prendergast, write that down!' – in a knowing Western performance (87). Significantly, as with Proulx's ranchers, his retreat into nostalgia is prompted by the troubling assault on the mythological cowboy caused by his having to hire jailbirds, coke addicts and any 'alky who wants to be in the hills to dry out' – the only people desperate enough for cowboy work in the New West (101).

For Joe, the ranch exists at a symbolic level best nurtured when riding in the hills above it: 'It was a vanity to think about owning this sort of thing ... looking out at the pastures that ran to threadlike rivers at eye level, Joe could feel his bones blowing in the wind of the future, and it was a cheerful feeling' (94). It's Joe's 'feeling' augmented by his performance of a familiar repertoire of cowboy roles – checking fence lines, stock pond water levels, distributing salt blocks – that sustains his romanticism. His banker warns him that he is too nineteenth century in his hopes for the ranch and observes that 'Nationally, we're looking at a foreclosure every seven minutes' – a practice that enabled his father to get ahead but leaves a trail of destruction in his wake (80). It is a depressing picture articulated by Sonny's brother, Smitty and his wife Lureen, who have been looking after the ranch in Joe's absence and who complain of 'the collapse of the cattle industry, the ill effects of the Texas and Midwestern feedlots, the evils of hedging and the betrayal of the agricultural family unit by the Secretary of Agriculture Earl Butz' (70). Smitty is a distorted version of Sonny: they are both war veterans and ranchers, but only Smitty has been damaged by the experience. He dresses up in his old army uniform to re-enact nocturnal military manoeuvres and develops an outrageous plan to import shellfish in refrigerated lorries in order to facilitate his escape to Hawaii. He is a figure deserving of our pity, but through his eccentric behaviour McGuane is also interrogating the reader's sense of the West. Is his dressing up, for example, any more ridiculous than his brother's habit of donning cowboy regalia? And though his crabmeat plan may appear outlandish, it asks us to consider the distinction between those elements native to the Western rather than the West. Proulx, as we have seen, covers similar territory through her introduction of alligators into a contemporary 'Johnson County war' in 'Florida Rental' (*BD*) and the 'emus' bred on the themed ranch 'Down-Under Wyoming' in 'The Half-Skinned Steer' (*CR*). Such examples draw attention to the fact that cattle, like alligators, emus and shellfish, are not indigenous to the West, but custom has made us blind to the fact. All are ill-adapted, which is also true of Joe who, like the shellfish, is out of his depth on the ranch. Instead of providing him a sense of identity, he complains that 'I feel like I've been living in a graveyard' – a legatee of a Western heritage and overbearing father who reduces him to a ghost (224). At such moments, the emptiness represented by the picture of the White Hills and his chimeric presence coincide.

The character of Lucien explores a less sentimental and more ironic relationship with the West; Gregory Morris argues that he understands the disparity between the legacy and its contemporary performance, hence the more insistent tone of mockery and self-mockery that permeates the novel.[25] It is apparent in his relationship with W. T Austinberry, the cowboy hand who looks after Emily's ranch. He is a living reproduction of the cowboys that father and son read about in cowboy books, and when he rides it is:

> With one elbow held out from his body like the old-timers one saw when Lucien was a boy. He had jinglebobs on his spurs, which tinkled merrily as he went. How Lucien loved this vaguely ersatz air of the old days! ... They rode on and crossed a creek where W. T Austinberry said that he had poured Clorox to kill a couple of hundred pounds of trout for his freezer.
>
> (37–8)

In each other's company, Lucien and Austinberry reinforce their shared need for nostalgia: they play chequers, drink a 'Hundred-proof whiskey' and fight in the bunkhouse. And yet the warning encoded in the Clorox poisoning is that we should guard against nostalgia. Lucien would love to take Austinberry seriously but 'in W. T. he thought he saw a ridiculous version of himself' and therefore embraces his 'vaguely ersatz air' for what it is (57). Emily's defence lawyer, Wick Tompkins, cultivates a more aggressively knowing performance that Lucien admires. He dresses like an old-time cowboy in a 'herringbone topcoat with a velvet collar and a John B. Stetson hat' but carries out business in a Chinese restaurant under a ceiling fresco of hawks and prairie falcons (he is the bird of prey in this environment). He is clear that Emily is guilty of murder, but argues that in a land of 'Japanese horseshoes, Taiwanese cowboy shirts and Korean bits' anything can happen (51). What does happen is that Lucien gives up his pursuit of a unifying Western dream in order to create his themed spa: the ersatz Western hell implied by his sulphurous name.

Part of the legacy of working for the US Information Agency is Lucien's awareness that he is living 'in an epoch when it seemed to him there actually were *signs*, an era in which you could join the rest of the populace in the wonderful ongoing melodrama of inanimate objects' (149–50 McGuane's italics). Lucien's themed spa is an exercise in cultural semiotics through which he takes control of a degraded version of his Western vison which simultaneously parodies the region's fabled function of putting people back together again. Everything is corrupted. It is located on a secret source 'as full of goodness as amniotic fluid is to a developing infant' suggesting the possibility of rebirth (88). All the most important relationships in Lucien's life take place here: he discovers it with his father; he first makes love to Emily here after which it becomes the venue of several atavistic couplings amidst the mud and slime, the sordidness of which suggest its corruption (47). The debasement of this symbol of birth and baptism mirrors the corruption of another watery aspect of Lucien's personal Odyssey in this novel – his penchant for rowing. Where for Patrick and Joe personal reflection takes place on a horse in the hills, Lucien takes to the water, floating Rousseau-like whilst meditating on the dark depths below. Hence, his decision to stop up the source and turn it into a spa signals his rejection of 'self-discovery' in favour of 'self-transformation' based upon the commodification of the West he venerates (148). His buildings are all 'authentic' – 'evocative bentwood dude-ranch furniture from the twenties', a kitchen taken from an 'ancient way station found at Silver Star, Montana', and line shacks from the pastures of 'Froze to Death' – and yet the way this eclectic mix has been yanked out of its original surroundings and given new context exposes the curating eye of Lucien, whose vision of Westernness is revealed as shallow and corrupted (89). Representation becomes inseparable from history, the authentic from imitation. Umberto Eco's search for the 'Absolute Fake' in his *Travels in Hyperreality* led to the conclusion that 'because everything looks real, it is real, even if, like Alice in Wonderland, it never existed'.[26]

Throughout, McGuane engages in a gentle mockery of the divergence between the West Lucien cherishes and projects to his customers and the ersatz version in which he participates. A knowing aside 'a cowboys work is never done' introduces his evening routine: 'He had Shane paint out the graffiti in the bar men's room and he checked the liquor inventory against the bartenders sheet ... He filled the bird feeders and did up the wire ties on the garbage bags behind the kitchen' before checking on his son: 'He could see James sound asleep on the daybed with true stories of the American West piled by his side' (104,156–7). His son is already being acculturated into a particular vision of the Old West, but in the version outside his door the bartender fills birdfeeders rather than poker chips and Shane combats graffiti artists rather than gunslingers. Finding himself alienated from the New West, Lucien has created his own highly stylized version of the Old West: it has made him rich and popular, but it has not given him a sense of belonging, merely exacerbated his sense of cultural schizophrenia.

His alienation is reinforced by the visit of a delegation of sarong-clad Pacific Islanders to the spa. They are greeted by a band playing Western classics like 'Red River Valley' and Lucien's promise that 'we'll sure try to make them feel at home. If we only knew what home was' (145). It is a poignant reminder of the difficulty Lucien has experienced during his return 'home' – a journey that has left him more lost than ever. The fugitive Emily faces a similar feeling of displacement in the South American hideaway to which she has eloped with her cowboy manqué, W. T. Austinberry. She claims that the country is full of Nazis 'who couldn't go back to *their* little countries' but who nevertheless 'knew how to dress fashionably in the tropics' (169). Austinberry, by contrast, believes that he is playing opposite his fantasy version of 'Calamity Jane' and wears cowboy boots on the beach. The implication for all McGuane's Westerners seems to be that 'belonging' implies adapting to the present, not transforming the present into the past.

In the end, both novels are about fathers and sons, and how a sense of belonging is intimately bound up with the filial bond. The non-existent picture of the 'White Hills' seen by Joe and his father reminds us that there is something missing at the centre of their relationship. Similarly, Lucien's quest for the 'something to be desired' has proved elusive; his absent father has left a hole for his own parental desire to which the West has proved unequal. Lucien is haunted by this betrayal but is nevertheless drawn to a ritualistic means of bonding with his own son – not riding or fishing (the ultimate Hemingway masculine ritual), but the more esoteric ritual of 'hawk ringing' (in which a hawk is captured through the use of live bait and ringed). McGuane's scene shares similarities with Richard Ford's much anthologized story *Communist* (a work that McGuane encouraged him to write) in that an afternoon of filial bonding whilst hunting is problematized by the combination of beauty and brutality that are part of the sport.[27] McGuane appears to choose hawk ringing because it allows him to combine Lucien's idealization of his family in relation to the heritage and traditions of the regional family represented by the Native Americans. Thus, he is able to valorize his idealized personal geography, the place where he shot his first pronghorn (which an old cowboy rather than an absent father helped him pack out) by contextualizing it within the framework of an idealized Indian heritage. In so doing, he wants to be this cowboy figure in his own son's life:

> 'I'm ninety-nine percent certain that this is where the Indians caught their birds.' Lucien like so many had always felt the great echoes from the terminated history of the Indians – foot, dog and horse Indians. How could a country produce orators for thousands of years, then a hundred years of yep and nope? It didn't make sense. It didn't make sense that the glory days of the Old South were forever mourned while this went unmentioned. Maybe the yeps and nopes represented shell shock, a land forever strange, strange as it was today to a man and a boy with a caged bird and makeshift camouflage. Well, thought Lucien, it's not a bad spot for coyotes, schemers and venture capitalists.
>
> (122–3)

McGuane returns to the notion of 'Southerness' to suggest that the West has allowed its history to be reduced to rhetorical muteness. The landscape, which should offer a palimpsest of cultural awareness, has been exploited by hawkish venture capitalists like Tompkins (a reminder of the frescoed hawks in the Chinese restaurant) and Lucien, who espouse an attachment to the ancient landscape whilst simultaneously selling a corrupt version of it back to Westerners. Thus, when Lucien rings the hawk with the announcement 'we're married at last' he figuratively announces his intention to perform the role of husband and father whilst simultaneously embracing his hypocritical 'marriage' to both Old and New West (125). As always, however, the solipsism of McGuane's protagonist proves misguided. James refuses to celebrate Lucien's vision, expressing an affinity with the pigeon that they are using as bait and establishing a softer set of values and alliances. Similarly, his estranged wife, Suzanne, also refuses to be scripted into his narrative of forgiveness in which the 'lonesome cowboy' eventually 'gets the girl'. She is determined to introduce James to the actual vestiges of the Old West – 'the Wind River Range and the Red Desert' – in order to demonstrate the superficiality of Lucien's spa and the misguided romanticism that attends his vision of fatherhood (173). At the conclusion, a father is once again divided from his son, though here it is the father who remains in the West – or his fantasy version – whilst the son is whisked to South America, from where, like his grandfather, he can dream Western dreams.

Like Lucien, Joe also struggles to find a home in the New West. His sense of alienation is amplified by the presence of Astrid – a 'goddess of the Florida night' – who finds herself stuck on the 'sagebrush prairie' (180). Her mediating presence allows for McGuane's gentle mockery of Joe as a 'man in translation' and 'dime store Hamlet' who, like Patrick before him, is so absorbed in his introspection that he is blind to the reality of his surroundings (147, 128). It is a West 'where you could shoot buffalo and put it on your credit card', where gunfighters play golf, and a beer-bellied backhoe operator offers the perfect synergy of man and machine that traditionally marks the cowboy and his horse (105, 100, 80).[28] But Joe refuses to see it – his myopia dramatized throughout by McGuane's characteristic irony. At one point Joe is pictured sitting on his porch reflecting that 'it seemed unbearable that Astrid didn't enjoy this. A car surged past far across the fields on the highway, a big American flag streaming from its antenna' (167). Where Lucien is attentive to both the charm and vulgarity of the West, Joe prefers a blinkered self-delusion which 'keeps the change' to a minimum.

His belief in the Old West, however, does enable him to recognize that he is not the one to look after either Ellen or the ranch. In presenting the ranch to Billy Kelton, his one-time tormentor and Ellen's partner, he is acknowledging his possession of qualities that tie together the domestic and regional family. He now recognizes that Billy's anger is that shared by all McGuane's cowboys and is caused by a lack of land that indentured him 'to people smaller than himself' with no understanding of the connection between land and people (225). The novel closes as it opens, with the White Hills, not the imaginary version, but the snow-covered peaks that prompt memories of his father cleaning grouse at the sink. The memory is gently ironic, a warning to take in the view rather than the associated memories. It is warning reinforced in Astrid's parting 'they would pretty much have to see' – which, as the final line of the book, gives her the last word (230). Significantly, she invites Joe to 'see' what is in front of him before they can recalibrate their relationship on an equal rather than idealized footing.[29]

IV

The capitalist excess of *Something to Be Desired* is at the root of *Nothing but Blue Skies* (1992) in which the tone of mockery transforms into something noticeably harsher. McGuane has claimed of the novel that 'I was interested in the discrepancy between the official West and the West we were all living in. Instead of cowboys and ranchers, a lot of the people I knew had car lots and drove Toyotas'.[30] This is, as noted, his most political novel, Nathaniel Lewis claiming that McGuane is offering a 'sweeping vision of the post-Reagan West, a landscape blighted by environmental, economic, and spiritual frailties'.[31] Proulx covers similar territory in her short stories – her collection *Bad Dirt* focussing on the residue left in the wake of Reagan's economic revolution. 'The Trickle-Down Effect' (*BD*) critiques the distributive economic policies celebrated by the title and the cowboy rhetoric of one-time screen cowboy Ronald Reagan through the screwball activities of Deb Sipple. He exploits his ownership of his town's only flatbed truck at a time of a cattle-feed crisis to drive a hard bargain with his neighbour, behaviour that contrasts unfavourably with the cardinal Western rule of helping a friend in need. Sipple is a caricature buffoon lost in a world of powerful women and economic turbulence, which is not the case for Leeland Lee in the short story 'Job History' (*CR*). He, as his name suggests, is attempting to shelter from the economic storms that swirl about him. In a present tense reportage (none of the characters speak) all his entrepreneurial schemes (hog farm, garage owner, lorry driver) fail, providing a catalogue of the suffering of a contemporary Western Job.[32]

McGuane's economic victims sit somewhere between the screwball Sipple and the despairing Job, their spiral of economic decline, like Proulx's, announced through radio broadcasts that suggest a West both isolated and absurdly out of kilter. McGuane's anti-Reaganism is apparent from a scathing essay published in the same year as the novel – 'Some Notes on Montana.' In it he accuses the 'entrepreneurial capitalism' encouraged by Reagan as creating the febrile Darwinian culture responsible for much of the social and environmental degradation afflicting the region.[33] Frank is its personification. A man suffering, as McGuane has claimed in interview, from a 'plateau of spiritual bankruptcy' following the 'Greed is great' years.[34] Like Lucien and Joe Starling's father, he is torn between a romance for the West and a determination to make it pay, a dilemma summarized in the epigraph – 'If you come to a fork in the road, take it.' Once again, McGuane conflates the domestic with the wider regional family; when the former breaks down, Frank finds himself turning to a notional West that his cynical exploitation has left diminished and inadequate to his spiritual needs. It makes him a conflicted character worthy of our sympathy.

Frank's dilemma is dramatized in the novel's opening scene in which he is depicted asking Gracie, who is leaving him for another man, whether she would like to be driven to the airport via the 'scenic route'. What constitutes the 'scenic route' resonates throughout the novel. The drive takes in various agribusiness concerns and the jewel in the crown of his property portfolio, The Kid Royale Hotel. It is 'one of the monuments of the Montana frontier' – which Frank wants to restore it to its original glory, thereby finding acceptance within the community by forging an authentic link with the past. It is a regenerative plan that he hopes to exercise on himself, inhibited only by his inability to reconcile his romanticism and cynicism. Throughout the novel, McGuane artfully keeps them in balance: Frank's collection of ancient maps – 'the shrinking terra in-cognitae of the old world; flat or round, what was the difference?' – would suggest that it is the poetry of people's attempts to make sense of their surroundings that appeals to Frank, rather than either their success or usefulness. But Frank can never shake his father's utilitarian approach, reflecting that next to the 'unstinting forward movement' of his 'free market capitalism' he 'felt like a pudding' (7). This tension is brought to life by a humorous backstory in which as a young man Frank held a Wild West fancy dress party in one of his father's vacant offices to which guests came as characters from the Old West. His father's furious intervention, including Frank's expulsion from the family home, is a Proulxian reminder of the power of capital and ownership and the dangers of nostalgia (7). Frank's wishy-washy romanticism comes under further scrutiny when he takes on a job salvaging old fixtures and fittings from demolished houses to provide instant 'authentic' ambience in cafes and hotels 'without tediously waiting for human life to create it' (11). As with Lucien's Western spa, Proulx's themed bars and even McCarthy's Mexican cantinas, notions of 'authenticity' and 'nostalgia' are suspect in a postmodern hyperreal created by symbols and ritual. McGuane offers twist on this familiar theme through his presentation of the McDonalds where Frank meets his brother for their business meetings. Frank finds it appalling, not because it is brash and new but because it is quaint and charming; the faux nostalgia of 'its fiberglass animals and carousel horses [that] looked like they'd come up the trail with the longhorns' means that it is becoming part of a very real nostalgia (111). It is no-longer a symbol of corporate greed, rather it has become part of 'the scenic route', its folksy 'McThis and McThat' indicative of the standardization and stagnation which comprises 'the escalating boredom of life in the monoculture' (115, 97).

Life in the monoculture comes with its own soundtrack: a number of Country and Western ballads echo throughout the narrative bonding characters together in an incongruous and saccharine celebration of the Old West: two laughing cowboys sit in a truck in a McDonald's parking lot listening to the Neville Brothers' 'Yellow Moon' (118); two old cowboys in a themed restaurant listen to Neil Young as they sit 'staring past each other in silence, waiting for their litchi nut' (47); the lyrics of a Stetsoned cowboy warbling 'Put a futon on your wish list/I'm kicking you tonight' leave Frank nonplussed (51). Elsewhere, such tunes offer an ironic commentary on Frank's engagement with his surroundings. His wild party takes place against an ironic seemingly endless loop of Neil Young's 'Are you ready for the country, 'cause it's time to go!' (6). The novel's title is taken from the upbeat chorus of a Willie Nelson song – the 'Blue Skies' in question drawing attention to the existential 'Nothing' that becomes a narrative marker which charts Frank's decline. 'Blue Skies' serve to mark his financial ruin ('up in the blue'(115)), Gracie's sexual betrayal ('with a big blue sky overhead' (343)), his own descent into criminality (scanning the 'the dome of blue sky' for cops (175)) or his general malaise ('his head was full of clouds'(98)). Frank's debasement means that when he looks for the sanctity he associates with the Big Skies, generally on buddy fishing trips, he can't find it. Throughout the novel, such lyrics do the introspective work of which Frank, burdened by a richly developed strain of self-irony, proves incapable. He admits that 'the messages of my formative years all came from Little Richard, who has never soiled himself with an inner journey', which leaves him incapable of dealing with his breakdown with Gracie other than by reducing it to plaintive song lyrics (324): 'Gracie was there, then she went forth, then returned. She was following her star! He was stuck in the mud. She was on a high wire. He was sucking wind. Other times, it was his star and her mud' (213–14).

How to make sense of life in the New West is the quintessential problem that Frank shares with Proulx's and McCarthy's protagonists. He is symbolized by the lone silver wolf (Billy's symbol of a particular Western nostalgia) whose progress is tracked by a radio collar throughout the novel: the lonely rather than lonesome cowboy, whose spirit of wildness is mapped by modernity (19). We know where he is, but everybody, the reader included, can see that Frank is lost. In this novel, however, McGuane turns an eye to the victims of Frank's behaviour – the region's 'cowboys and Indians'. Proulx, it will be remembered, explores the issue of indigenous dispossession by means of the ideological construction of Manifest Destiny through the character of Ace Crouch, who articulates the myth of the indigenous nomad as a pretext for land-seizure and settlement. Proulx's Native Americans are the descendants of a process of population removal, their dispossession symbolized by their reduction to wandering hitchhikers. Ace's justification is unsettling but suggests a sense of guilt; this is not the case for McGuane's protagonists for whom the West's Native Americans are buried under a nostalgia that replaces justification with respect. In doing so, McGuane opens up Vine Deloria's distinction between the spiritual owners of the land – the Native Americans – and the political ownership exercised by whites. Deadrock does not concern itself with land rights, but in this novel, which is concerned with the unworthiness of those who possess it, the issue erupts into the narrative:

> The Fourth of July ... This year, what no one expected was that the hundreds of Indians who lived away from their reservations, on small plots or in tenements or in streets and alleys, would march on this quiet city with its sturdy buildings, broad central avenue and flowery neighbourhoods, and ask for their land back. It ruined the Fourth of July. Indian ragamuffins, crones, wolfish men, pregnant women, fancy dancers and boys dressed as prairie chickens carried hand-lettered signs or simply chanted 'you know it's not yours, give it back!' Finally, the police frightened them off with flashing lights and uniformed appearances. The Indians dispersed. Some were seen at their jobs in town the next day. Like a dream without an obvious explanation, the event went unmentioned. It was pushed out of the newspapers by perestroika.
>
> (61)

The effect of this curious stand-alone passage derives from its length: the subject is as politically marginalized as the narrative space it occupies; a brief digression before we return to the business activities of Frank. It's an anti–Independence Day celebration in which the old wounds of dispossession are opened and McGuane intervenes on contentious contemporary discussion concerning reparations and restoration both within and outside the Native American community. The militancy of 'Wounded Knee Two' (when in 1973 followers of the American Indian Movement seized the iconic site for seventy-one days in a demand that the US government re-open treaty negotiations) has given way to posturing, according to some Native American academics, signified by the apologies of a number of state Governors (Gavin Newsom in California for one). Acknowledgment must come with action, they argue, which means fulfilling ancient treaties.[35] Eve Tuck and K. Wayne Yang have put the case strongly, arguing that decolonization must not be seen as a 'metaphor' but rather 'in the settler colonial context must involve the repatriation of the land, that is, *all* of the land, and not just symbolically'.[36] McGuane's passage stands chronologically between Wounded Knee II and Newsom, and combines irony and humour to stimulate guilt. His ironic critique is built on contrasts – the small plots and alleys of the Indians versus the broad central avenues of the town; threatening 'wolfish men' versus 'boys dressed as prairie chickens'. These are not the militants of Wounded Knee II but a more desperate group who are childishly frightened by flashing lights and uniformed appearances. Crucially, they are not protesting but going through the motions of protest and prompting guilt rather than seeking change, which they fatalistically recognize cannot happen. They are all at work next day, their activities, like those of their forebears, consigned to the realm of 'the vanishing Indian'. McGuane's final irony is that Gorbachev's perestroika is taking the headlines, which offered precisely the political reconfiguration that the Native Americans are seeking.

McGuane returns to the theme of alienation in his description of Frank's 'Eskimo holiday' and the subplot developed around Gracie's lover, Edward Ballantine, an insurance salesman and dealer in Indian artefacts. Frank's visit to the Eskimos (McGuane's deployment of this contentious term highlights a shared colonial experience) is easily read within a settler colonial context because it allows McGuane to talk about Native Americans free from presenting cliched modes of behaviour. This is particularly important for Frank who, in common with all McGuane's protagonists, continues to idealize Native Americans. From the windows of his prefabricated hotel he can see the 'endless granite landscape' which we are told looks 'more of a plan for country than country itself' – a pastiche of Jim Burden's observation of the Nebraska plains at the beginning of Cather's *My Antonia* (1914). However, it is a vision that, like the West itself, looks more real in the brochures than in reality, because his immediate surroundings have all 'the appearance of a military supply dump' (43). The inhabitants are similarly disappointing for Frank: they are broken, violent alcoholics who drive hot rod four wheelers and spend their days drinking, fighting and playing video games. As such, they are surrogates for the Indians who populate the work of Momaday, the *Dakotah* novels of Erdrich, and Chris Eyre's 2002 film *Skins* for whom life, as Sherman Alexie has observed, is a bleak, self-destructive cycle of drinking, frustrated sexual relationships, fighting and early, often violent deaths.[37] Frank's neighbours are acutely aware of 'the injustices Frank's race had committed against them' but otherwise there is no human connection: they spend their days in existential despair 'watching the river melt, go by, freeze, melt and go by' (43–4). McGuane adds nuance to this simple transference by detailing Frank's reading of old newspapers which contain reports of idealistic communities such as 'Seaside Florida' (location for *The Truman Show*), and Richard Reese's 'urban lifescape village' – 'Rancho Santa Margarita'.[38] Frank is horrified by the deadening uniformity implied by such postmodern Disneyfication and is relieved that the Inuit and by extension Deadrock's cowboys and Indians, are not being forced into performing idealized versions of themselves. However, he is mistaking despair for authenticity, for as Louis Owens has observed, the self-destructive drunk is as much a stereotype as the primitive savage – a romantic victim undone by firewater still in the process of vanishing.[39] The 'waring blender' of late twentieth-century commodification and conformity stretches from the Artic to the Florida desert embracing all in performative cliché. Ironically, Frank buys souvenir slides 'hoping they would trigger reminiscences when he got home' but they bear no relation to his experiences and only reinforce his solipsistic sense of loneliness and dislocation (49).

A similar tale of exploitation is introduced through the character of Ballantine who is constructing a mock-up of a Native American village for a 'Trail of Tears Exhibit'. Such an exhibit to the approximately 100,000 Native Americans forcibly removed by Andrew Jackson's government between 1830 and 1850 exists at the Cherokee Heritage Center at Tahlequah, Oklahoma. Edward's is different – his 'gold-plated consciousness raiser', as the hyperbolic advertising rhetoric suggests, is kitsch, thus drawing attention to the ways in which we remember and memorialize the past. His living exhibit is reminiscent of the colonial pavilions that made up the Paris Exposition Universalle of 1900 (in which living exhibits performed stereotypical activities in mock ups of villages), a project that combined anthropology with entertainment under the guise of education, whilst confirming a firmly Imperial (or patrician) view of otherness. The superficiality of Edward's project is suggested by his advert for 'a well-preserved fortyish woman with dark complexion and hair' to play the part of a living exhibit; it recalls film producer Arnold Duxbury's appeal to old men with missing limbs to represent the 'Frontier spirit' thereby reducing people, like other cultural signifiers (tomahawks and six-shooters), to stage props in another Anglo-centric recreation of history. Through the positive reply of Frank's wife, Gracie, McGuane is able, as he has done throughout the *Deadrock novels*, to make the 'connection' (that allusive quality identified by Stegner) between the Old and the New – this time around the sentiment of betrayal.

A number of recent revisionist works – Daniel Blake Smith's *American Betrayal: Cherokee Patriots and the Trail of Tears* (2001), and Dean Arnold's *Cherokee Betrayal: From the Constitution to the Trail of Tears* (2013) – remind us that the feeling is synonymous with the event. Edward's betrayal begins with kitsch and continues with his first making love to Gracie in a fake tepee, an act which she betrays to Frank by her guilty tears (344). On one level, Edward's behaviour is simply an echo of Frank's exploitation of heritage reclamation and Western nostalgia for his own benefit. On a deeper level, Edward is re-enacting the sexual exploitation of female Native Americans by Anglo settlers, which, as Deer and Nagle note, 'dates back to the times of the Spanish Conquistadors, [and] often times accompanies the colonial conquest of tribal lands'[40] As Kittredge observes, 'in the fur-trapper days, it is said, Indian women were so incessantly raped by white men that they resorted to a strategy called "going for sand". When trappers showed up those women would go to the creeks and pack their vaginas with sand.'[41] Edward is no rapist, but having set out in his advert the characteristics of his fantasy 'squaw' and manoeuvred Gracie into the role, his behaviour follows a pattern of sexual exploitation endorsed by the insistent othering of the victim. A deeper interpretative layer is added by Edwards's role as an insurance salesman. He has carved out a clientele comprising largely of AIDS patients because he believes that insurance companies fail to understand some people's strong sense of being doomed. This is the sentiment he has sought to capture in his exhibition by fostering the mythology of the 'doomed Indian' and which he exploits in his seduction of Gracie (288–9). Deception runs through this novel: Frank's life is built on it – from his business to his romantic interests, but the biggest delusion is reserved for himself.

Another victim of Frank's economic practice in this novel is the 'cowboy'. According to McGuane, cowboys are 'part of the deliquescence of the ranch culture, which is falling apart' a tension that he explores in the short story 'Cowboy' (*GC* (2006)).[42] It is a rare first-person narrative that reconfigures *Shane* to reveal the unspoken exploitation and entrapment beneath the cultural icon. The archetypal status of the anonymous cowboy protagonist is immediately established in the opening scene when, fresh out of jail, he is caught in a pen trying to steal a horse. This elicits the opening exchange between captor and his sister: 'What's he supposed to be?' / 'Supposed to be a cowboy' (22). What a cowboy is supposed to be and do is under examination in this story. The pen is full of horses destined for the cannery in France, suggesting that they like him have served their mythological purpose. When he starts working for the 'old feller' and his sister he is advised to 'tell people around here your name is Shane, and they'll always believe you' (30). All are trapped: the sister was once a Hells Angel, but is now a grotesque parody of Marian Starrett attempting to seduce the cowboy through apple pie; the 'old feller' is broken and spends his time dreaming of the 'good time' fighting in Korea; the cowboy has simply exchanged his role on the prison ranch for another form of entrapment (32). And yet McGuane makes clear that the cowboy's role of nurturing cows in a hostile environment extends to the ranchers themselves who are regenerated through the archetypal ritual of putting 'the ranch back together again' (24). When, following years of procrastination, the 'old feller' moves his cattle corral so the calves don't 'shit themselves into the next world' it is clear that figuratively it is himself he is releasing from the 'shit' of inertia (29). When the cowboy breaks a frisky colt so that the 'old feller' can once again ride the plains, his regeneration is complete; a transformation marked by his decision to shoot his unwanted horses rather than allowing them to suffer the mythological indignity of the cannery. As the relationship becomes more paternal, McGuane seems to be preparing us for a happy ending in which the ranch passes to the one man who really understands it. But possession is not part of the cowboy's story. He is removed by neighbours who complain that he has allowed the weeds to grow; he is the 'weed' who must not be allowed to contaminate either the land or their mythological grasp upon it. He is last pictured riding off into the sunset on a horse originally bound for the cannery – not the romantic figure of Shane, but a desperate 'old feller' deserving of our sympathy.

Through 'The Cowboy' and the depiction of Billy Kelton (*KC*), McGuane allows the degradation of the cowboy to become symptomatic of the West as a whole; their anger is the manifestation of a region as lost in its own cultural mythology as themselves. Frank and his fishing buddy, Phil, revere the cowboy but find that those of their acquaintance are 'drunken, wife-beating, snooze-chewing geeks with big belt buckles and catfish mustaches' who 'spend all their time reading magazines about themselves [whilst] college professors drive out and tell them that they're a dying breed' (59–60).

McGuane's depiction of Frank's hired hand, Boyd Jarrell, is less comic and more brutal. He is presented as an alcoholic wife beater with a chip on his shoulder. However, when Frank considers Boyd's work detached from the mythology, he is buoyed by a respect that connects a person to the land with a sense of vocation:

> Boyd was a perfect cowboy. All he cared about was cows ... He was as kind to cows as he was unreasonable to people ... Frank thought about the cows being by themselves, without Boyd tending to them ... There had to be someone who tried to close the gap between the cows and an environment not always friendly to them. He had to admit to himself that there was real satisfaction in seeing Boyd ride through a herd of cattle, knowing that when he got out the other side he'd have learned as much about them as the graduating class of the average veterinary school.
> (163)

Boyd is the perfect midwife for animals lost in a hostile landscape; it is his bad luck that the 'cowboy' responsible for his welfare is Frank. Frank is not up to the job; he is an economic 'cowboy' rather than knight of the plains, who, though he admires Boyd's craft, is prepared to sack him as part of his portfolio divestment. When, during a nocturnal ramble he sneaks round to Boyd's house to see how he is taking his sacking, Frank is faced with the usually cantankerous figure slumped under a print of Charlie Russell's *Last of the Ten Thousand* moaning 'I have nothing, I have nothing' (70–1). The sentimental vision represented by the picture and the 'snap-button shirts' and 'cowboy boots with curled up toes' that Frank glimpses in a wardrobe is reduced to the reality of the indentured labourer before him. It is a moment of revelation which, with less sophisticated handling, would lead to understanding and rapprochement. However, even in such circumstances, Frank remains unable to detach himself from an awareness of his mawkish sentimentality; it is therefore fitting that a scene of such potential pathos should be exploded by a slapstick gunfight with bubble bath and shower attachments.

The ultimate victim of Frank's predatory economic practice is the land that is essential to his Western identity. In this novel, fishing takes the place of horse riding as the ritualized means by which his protagonists participate in a culturally endorsed performance of 'Westerness'.[43] And through its foregrounding McGuane opens up for wry scrutiny a number of hyper-masculine shibboleths. Fishing holds a special place in the Western ecosystem: a number of critics have noted the importance of Redford's hugely successful film adaptation *A River Runs through It* (1992) in establishing a rugged cowboy aesthetic combined with the reinforcement of fishing as an Oedipal ritual. Kittredge complained in a 1993 issue of *Time* that the Rockies were a 'bumper-to-bumper raceway' of Jeeps and

Winnebagos of 'fly fishing nuts who saw *A River Runs through It*' and have sold their house in the suburbs to move to Montana'.[44] Published in the same year, Liza Nicholas's (et al) *Imagining the Big Open: Nature, Identity, and Play in the New West* (1992) offers an academic analysis of the remaking of the Western landscape as a playground – its subtitle seemingly offering a roadmap of the strands that make up Frank's character.[45] McGuane is a keen fisherman (he confesses that it was the primary motive for moving to Montana[46]) and has written widely on the subject. The essays that make up his collection *The Longest Silence: A Life in Fishing* (1999) emphasize the ceremonial aspect of the sport: the equipment that takes on the significance of religious artefact (the bamboo rods passed from father to son; the uniquely tied flies bearing the names of their originators); the water courses that become the sites of spiritual pilgrimage; the existential and metaphorical possibilities suggested by the image of a contemplative man (buddies or father and son) on the river bank. As he claims in his introduction, 'I decided that fishing would be my way of looking at the world. First it taught me to look at rivers. Lately it has been teaching me how to look at people, myself included.'[47] In this he joins his fishing and drinking buddy in the Montana circle, Jim Harrison, for whom 'a life properly lived' is analogous to being in a river: 'You touch things lightly or deeply; you move along because life herself moves.'[48] His spiritual perspective is echoed by Richard Brautigan, whose *Trout Fishing in America* (1967) – described by McGuane as 'an original, wonderful book' – updates Emerson's critique of materialism for the age of psychedelia.[49] The fishing excursions by the unnamed narrator are constantly corrupted – the wilderness is shrinking, the rivers are polluted and by the end of the book a used trout steam is being sold by foot, along with associated items like waterfalls, trees, birds and animals. Insects are given away free.[50]

Brautigan is McGuane's kind of author because, as he makes clear in a review in the *New York Times*, he takes fishing seriously but is not without self-irony.[51] McGuane's similar approach is illustrated in short story 'The Bonefish in the Other Room' in which the narrator's attempts to focus 'on all the proper things' through the 'ceremony of angling' are undermined by his getting his cast caught in his back pocket.[52] Frank is McGuane's surrogate; he would like fishing to offer spiritual redemption but he is unable to distance himself from his part in its literal and mythical pollution. An act of attempted purification following a night of debauchery transforms him into a figure of mockery:

> This seemed to him to be a grand and wholly acceptable arcade where his various sins were simply booths to be revisited with amusement. He wondered how Dante had failed to perfect one of his circles for the philandering sportsman: ravaged by his own hounds, flogged with his own fishing poles, dancing over his own buckshot. He joyously felt

himself idling, an unreflective mood in which water was water, sky was sky, breeze was breeze. He knew it couldn't last.

(234)

The river does not offer redemption through contemplation but brings 'an unreflective mood' in which moral responsibility is transformed into circus booths with Dante playing the ringmaster. As David Ingram has noted, it cannot last because this is an exercise in evasion rather than introspection; Frank is happier outsourcing self-analysis to an increasingly dramatic and lurid series of punishments that transform him into an unconvincing tragic hero.[53]

A similar sense of self-irony makes Frank unable to commit fully to the Hemingway 'fishing buddy' narrative in which men discover self-affirmation and companionship through a form of semiotic psychodrama in which the rod is inherently phallic and talking about fish a vicarious therapy. McGuane (who admits that the critical comparison with Hemingway is an albatross) claims to admire the short stories but is ambivalent about *The Old Man and the Sea* whilst actively 'despising' *Across the River into the Trees*, and *Islands in the Stream*.[54] It is a suspicion shared by Harrison (also celebrated as a 'student of the école de Hemingway') who claimed that Hemingway is like a 'woodstove that didn't give off much heat'.[55] McGuane claims bluntly that 'the kind of hunting and fishing [Hemingway] liked to do is not the kind we (he and Harrison) like to do. A lot of it was that writer bullshit I find so tedious, just utter posturing – kind of grabbing your crotch Joe Piscopo style and saying, "I'm going out and fuck a big fish"'.[56] In McGuane's narratives, the fisherman are inexpert, the conversation desultory rather than profound, the idyllic landscape close to the urban, the fish 'un-fucked' and returned. When Frank goes fishing with his friend, Phil, they are both suffering troubled relationships, but their attempts to recalibrate their sense of themselves is roundly mocked:

Two men on a riverbank, didn't used to be here and someday would be gone. Just now their lives seemed so important. Frank had made a killing in real estate; Phil would never be out of debt. Both of them loners, by choice or not. Brief stories of local life. Frank felt it made sense of think of it this way ...

'I guess that if we didn't have trout fishing, there'd be nothing you could really call pure in our lives at all.'

Frank stared at the road ahead, filling with joy at this inane but life-restoring thought. 'I do like to feel one pull,' he said.

(80, 82–3)

Despite the elegiac tone, in these 'Brief stories of local Life' Frank remains unable to free himself from the recognition that the values he espouses on the riverbank are in tension with commercial practices that keep his buddy in debt. Frank is happy to agree with Phil's insistence on the purity of fishing – 'I do like to feel one pull' – because he recognizes that it is nonsense. There is to be no purification of the soul or emotional reciprocity because fishing represents another Western ritual that has ceased to function for both men. Instead, it is the synthetic alternative provided by the Country and Western ballads they listen to on the truck radio that offers the space for introspection and confession that each man craves and which McGuane dramatizes through the image of 'Dolly Parton from Dollywood' singing about 'country' and 'family' as though 'each man were assigned one of Dolly's big breasts' (303).

The ultimate fishing shibboleth challenged in this novel is the Oedipal ritual by which young boys are acculturated into Western practices. In the essay 'Small Streams in Michigan' McGuane reflects on his youth fishing trout streams and learning the importance of the transference of fishing lore from father to son.[57] The difficulties of such a task are presented in the account of a fishing trip taken with his own son, Thomas, in the story 'Father, Son, And Holy Permit' (*Esquire*, 1993).[58] The pursuit of the permit becomes a troubled metaphor: the father's obsession is analogous to the pursuit of the 'self' through writing; Thomas's carefree, slack-lined approach signals his preference for lived experience rather than plunging into the 'interior dark'. In *Nothing But Blue Skies* McGuane problematizes this already troubled Oedipal relationship through the simple expedient of replacing a son with a daughter: Holly. She is a college-aged woman, whose ability to out-fish her father demonstrates her successful acculturation to the Western values he espouses. Her function within the novel is to offer a new relationship with both the family and the West, a bridging manoeuvre that McGuane dramatizes through her decision to reject the wilder water courses (redolent of Hemingway masculinity) in favour of a private family landmark named the 'otter pool'. In her youth, Holly had followed a family of otters to the pool, to which she had given the names Frank, Gracie and Holly; she had then gasped as they tore apart a trout swimming in the depths (154). Returning to the pool they find a similarly big trout, which they catch and release. Symbolically, their family life has been torn apart, leaving Frank, like this lost, solitary fish, trapped; it is only through his daughter and their joint efforts that he can be released. Unlike his relationship with Phil, they have reconfigured their bonds through the strength of their family but free from sentimentality and cliché.

Holly's relationship with Lane Lawlor, a caricature right-wing populist, also enables McGuane to scrutinize the environmental threat posed by the alliance of corporate interests and nativist movements energized by the environmental de-regulation of the Reagan years. In doing so, McGuane is intervening on the contemporary environmental debates taking place in the early Nineties, signalled by the growth of the *Sagebrush Rebels* (who claimed that federal land-management was unconstitutional) and the secession of a number of the Montana chapters of the *Sierra Club* from the national organization due to disagreements over the Northern Rockies Ecosystem Protection Act (1993). The most important standoff between local, county and federal concerns identified in Riebsame's *Atlas of the New West* concerns irrigation and water shortages.[59] In McGuane's novel, Lawlor fronts a group called 'We Montana' which uses the environment, and in particular the State's rivers, to push forward an anti-progressive agenda based on a retooled rhetoric of Old West community values. His regional family archetype comprises of the 'John Wayne male and his bellicose, gun-toting woman, their cold-eyed, towheaded children' who reveal that the advancement of 'White Water Issues' is clearly 'water for white people' (206). We may be appalled by Lawlor, and yet McGuane is clear that Lawlor's manipulation of the mythological West is simply a more exaggerated version of his commercial nostalgia. For Frank, at his most cynical, 'the tone of the West' is not captured by Lawlor's gun-toting violence nor the great cattle drives but by 'the failure of the homesteads' – in which, as Proulx's writing has made clear, settler dreams were brutally exploited by companies for commercial profit (245). For Frank, Western nostalgia has always been up for sale which is why it is useless when he needs it. This failure is made explicit by his second visit to the and 'otter pool' with Holly. He equips himself with his 'thirty-year-old bamboo rod' and a 'battered aluminium fly box that had been a gift from Gracie' in a clear attempt to bond through shared nostalgia (279). However, the source has been dammed, meaning that Frank's sentimental attachment to his family has been exposed by the literal changes to the land created by Lawlor's appeal to a mythological Western family.[60]

It is the women, Holly and Gracie, who take control and offer direction at the close of this novel. They join other powerful female characters – June Cooper, the foul-mouthed Buick dealer, and Frank's temporary lover, the pugnacious Lucy Dyer. Holly has succeeded in bringing her parents back together through a relationship that demonstrates the terrible dangers of romanticising the past. This experience is shared by Gracie. Like Frank, her early years were spent trying to capture the nostalgia of her parents' Louisiana plantation through authentic kitchenware (16); later, her experiences as part of Edward's 'Veil of Tears' exhibition showed the impossibility of capturing 'vanished glory' and that 'there's nothing crazier than picking up exactly where you left off' (349). This, McGuane makes clear, is Frank's malaise, the belief that it is possible to 'pick up' a Western birthright by going fishing. It is the women's challenge to this cosy nostalgia, whether through Holly's disruption of Oedipal rituals, or Gracie's use of fabricated fishing expeditions in order to carry out her affair with Edward, that eventually brings Frank to his senses (345). Thus, although the novel may close with the traditional ride into the sunset, it is free from the patriarchal baggage of the Old West: it is forward looking and shaped by the subversive feminine presence that is Gracie the wheel.

V

Such is the ideological power of the female characters in *Nothing but Blue Skies* that it should come as little surprise that the lost cowboy protagonist of McGuane's next novel is a woman. His project has always been the interrogation of masculine identity within the context of the mythological West; in his conception of *The Cadence of Grass* he claims that 'without pretending to be a feminist, I really started getting the idea that one of the things that was kind of septic about our lives was there were always these alpha males camped in the middle of our lives'.[61] Toxic masculinity endorsed by a combination of capitalist economics and Western mythology sits in the middle of this novel, its effects explored through the attempts of the central protagonist, Evelyn Whitelaw, to carve out an identity for herself. In McGuane's elegantly constructed Dickensian plot she is torn between competing identities. The ironically named Sunny Jim Whitelaw, owner of a successful bottling plant and 'Oligarch of moisture hoarding' has recently died and in an exercise of patriarchal control beyond the grave has made the inheritance dependent on Evelyn halting divorce proceedings against her deeply unpleasant husband, Paul Crusoe (10). She, however, prefers spending her time riding and working on the ranch of fatherly cowboy, Bill Champion. It's another McGuane triangle: Paul and Bill personify the struggle between the New and Old West for the soul of Evelyn (an Eve in this new Eden), with the former playing the part of the Devil: 'There was really something infernal about Paul' (19).

This titanic struggle is played out in reverse through the relationship between Evelyn's sister, the viperish Natalie, and her husband, the patiently suffering Stuart Cross. Natalie is a Vassar graduate who enjoys expensive clothes, exotic cuisine and loathes the vulgarity of the West; Stuart, by contrast, is an outsider whose nostalgic attachment to things Western (he has furnished their modest house in reclaimed ranch items) is a diluted version of Bill's Westernness. Offstage, Evelyn's mother, Alice, is the shell-shocked victim of life lived with a bullying patriarch; however, towards the end of the novel we learn that in her youth she also had faced a choice between money and the Old West and had chosen the former. In contrast, Paul's mother, Dr Edith Crusoe, is a caricature Western academic (a female Lane Lawlor) who raised Paul according to the principles of 'nativism, appropriate settlement and the dizzying romance of low rainfall', which are ironically bent out of shape when he inherits his father-in-law's bottling plant (131).

The black hat / white hat binary is clearly set out in Paul and Bill. Paul's heroes are not cowboys but men like Ray M. Kroc, the founder of McDonald's, whose motto is 'Life is dog eat dog and rat eat rat' (49). Evelyn had hoped to interest him in the family ranch, but he is immediately cast as an outsider – 'Paul's were the first blue jeans Bill had ever seen with a crease' – who sees running cattle on such beautiful land as like 'sitting on an egg that never hatches' (196–7). When he takes over the family bottling plant, he demonstrates a ruthlessness unhindered by social scruple by bottling water – a contentious issue in the West. Thus, as with Lucien's spa or Lawlor's river damming, attitudes towards water become a barometer of fidelity to Western values. Paul's brief tenure also allows McGuane to satirize both the practice and idiom of Reaganomics: Paul continually deploys a business-speak that he doesn't really understand for purposes of humiliation rather than illumination. In his Darwinian vision the 'mom-and-pop enterprises' that stand in his way are contemptuously put out of business and it is ironic that he himself is taken over by a company equally contemptuous of Western family values, encouraging this particular family to 'crawl back under their log' (194).

Bill Champion, by contrast, is a cowboy cliché, 'old, but straight and lean and ... the owner of the bluest ice blue eyes', who is dismissive of Paul, believing he 'would do well to butter his own toast' (70, 197). However, it is he who is lost in a New West that seems 'wired together with telephone and electrical lines, railroad lines and highways, as if it might otherwise drift apart' (225). It is a world of connectivity in which the only form of communication he enjoys is with his past. It is a familiar McGuane trope, but here it resolves itself into ghostly figures who hover in his memory. John Red Wolf is a semi-mythical brave Cheyenne friend who saved Bill's life during the war and has now become the repository of Western traditions and a self-sacrificial model of rugged masculinity: when Bill talks about treating a bull's hoof before it infects the whole herd (a metaphor for the gangrene afflicting older Western values), it is under the watchful eyes of Red Wolf (70). These values live on in another of Bill's heroes, Robert Wood, an expert horseman whose belief that 'the Old West could be brought back if they'd just quit dammin' up water to make alfalfa' is presented as a direct challenge to Paul (33). When Bill tells the story of how as an old man Robert made a magnificent leap over a cavernous hole, he is really (like the adventure of rancher Croom in Proulx's short story '55 Miles to the Gas Pump' (*CR*)) providing a fitting epitaph to the Old West: it's glamour, personified in the image of the leaping cowboy, refuses to die (37). McGuane reworks the story as 'A Long View West' in the collection *Crow Fair*, when the account is peppered by the bored rejoinders and cynical asides of the delinquent listeners, Karen and Clay. However, 'the long view' that Clay articulates at the end is a realization that 'soon he would be gone and the stories with him. Maybe he'd be able to remember them during hard times or, really, whenever he needed them. Maybe he needed them now' (*CF*, 89).

In this novel, Evelyn shares Clay's speculative need; she is torn between her desire for Paul ('she never doubted that her craving for him was a vice' (176)) and her need for Bill's Western heritage ('Getting out to this unprofitable little ranch had been the most important part of Evelyn's life'

(29)). Throughout the novel Old and New are continually contrasted to the general, but not unreserved, advantage of the former: the bracing air of the 'big lonesome' is contrasted with the 'trotting horse wind vanes' of the suburbs (176); Bill's loving care for his cattle is compared to the behaviour of the dysfunctional families that surround him; Bill's Coyote breakfast of 'a piss and a look around' is contrasted to the shoulder high luggage Alice takes on her trip to Alaska (69); Evelyn's skilled control of her bronc is compared to Natalie's careless driving of her Mustang. It is on horseback that Evelyn, like other *Deadrock* protagonists, identifies the 'vital piece of continuity' linking past and present. Bill is the perfect cowboy, but a suspect father: his care of Evelyn comes purely through advice on her horsemanship, which is both caring and stifling (164). Evelyn wants nurture, but also excitement – a paradox that McGuane dramatizes in a scene in which she rides out searching for pregnant heifers in a winter blizzard. All the important scenes in this novel take place in blizzards, which is suggestive of the violent contradictions at play. Evelyn deliberately chooses a wild horse – a gelding that '*thinks* he's a bronc' (another part of the West's fluid identity) because 'they make beautiful music together' (which is the 'cadence of grass' suggested by the novel's title, 160). Once mounted she tells herself that she is 'heading even farther away from convenience stores and dealerships, fraud protection, exclusive passwords and travel coupons. She felt free' (162). And yet, despite her skill, freedom means giving into a potentially dangerous horse because 'he knew exactly where the cattle were' and knows where to put his feet beneath the snow: it is an analogy that helps to explain her love of Bill and what drew her to Paul. They are both sides of the cowboy: where Bill is the nurturer, Paul is the more dangerous figure celebrated in Country and Western lyrics: 'Good looking, quick witted, a soul rented to darkness, Paul had everything' (129).

How to reconcile these contrasting needs and in the process forge a strong independent feminine identity within a Western context becomes the quintessential problem facing Evelyn in this novel. It's a problem we hear articulated through the first-person narrators in the work of Jayne Phillips, Ellen Gilchrist, Pam Houston and Annie Proulx, who have escaped the oppression of an overbearing patriarchy to find themselves caught in the trap of unfulfilling work and short-term relationships with emotionally stunted men. As the narrator of Houston's short story *Cowboys Are My Weakness* (1992) complains, the men she meets may 'look like a cowboy' but they turn out to be 'just a capitalist with a Texas accent who owned a horse'. It's all there in Country and Western lyrics, she acknowledges, which describe men as 'either brutal or inexpressive and always sorry later. The women were victims, every one'.[62] Proulx's female protagonists aren't simply destroyed by the wrong kind of men ('If it's got four wheels or a dick you're goin a have trouble with it, guaranteed'[63]) but by their own interpretation of the cowboy code. The barmaids of the 'Golden Buckle' in 'A Lonely Coast' exonerate their self-destructive drug abuse, violence and unfulfilling sexual encounters through appeal to a misshapen and dissipated cowboy mythology.

The women in McGuane's novels who have a 'weakness for cowboys' are not in dead-end jobs, but rich girls like Claire Burnett, Ellen Overberry and Ann Fitzgerald, who are determined to embrace the West on their own terms. Evelyn is a more conflicted female presence. She is naturally oriented to the values of the Old West, but as a woman finds herself on the outside. Linguistically, she is alienated by a masculine discourse, which in terms of content and vocabulary leads her to acknowledge – 'Men were always talking like this: You couldn't understand a thing they were saying' (63). Her own locution is schizophrenically split between her monosyllabic ranch discourse (rich in idiom and natural metaphor – 'that colt made you ride pretty good' (71)), the irony she deploys with Paul and the more expansive and sophisticated vocabulary she uses with her sister. Culturally, she wants to be respected as a cowboy and desired as a woman, a dangerous combination in what McGuane reminds us is a dangerous environment for women. Throughout, McGuane details a landscape of predatory masculinity through episodes of clumsy flirtation (being forced to leave her favourite café because a young man is trying to catch her eye (73)), minor sexual harassment (the attempts of her father's Doctor, the aptly named Dr Randy, to seduce her (127)), and, more troublingly, Paul's domestic violence.

McGuane, always more comfortable with the dramatically symbolic than lengthy exposition, crystallizes Evelyn's dilemma through a snapshot. Before going dancing to celebrate the completion of roundup, she visits a local dress shop, *Just the Two of Us* (ironic since the only happy pairings in this novel are horse and rider) which is run by former ranch girls – Violet and Claire – but owned by a cowboy saddler (men are still in the saddle and in control). The women are Western insiders devoted to making ranch women feel sophisticated, a synthesis of Old/New values that Evelyn's sister, Natalie dismisses as 'showing the wives of yokels how to accessorize' (116). They project an image of modernity but are not averse to exploiting Western nostalgia: a disused antique cash register sits next to the card-reading machine. The same duality characterizes their advice to customers: they are happy to discuss cattle stock prices whilst laying out handbags; they advise Evelyn to grow her nails long whilst simultaneously acknowledging the impracticality of such behaviour. Evelyn's choice of a little black dress is transformative:

> Evelyn stood in manure-covered boots, the dress hand-pinned to the shoulders of her ripped, blue-plaid, snap-button cowboy shirt ... Admiring herself in the mirror, she drew the dress up high on her thighs and said to the mirror, and its imaginary occupant, "Will that do?" Tonight she would dance in feral vigilance. She'd find some guy and forget the poor calves, went the plan.

(74–5)

The scene is full of irony. Her 'other' self remains speculative, an 'imaginary occupant' of whose existence she remains sceptical. Tonight, she will play the cowboy – appraising the men as 'uncomplicated units' fed out of 'Kansas feedlots' and selecting and 'cutting out' a victim; but in order to succeed she needs to change out of her actual working clothes and put on a little black dress that she later acknowledges made her look 'like a calf herself' (84). The plan goes awry; she narrowly escapes the attentions of a psychopath and afterwards a group of camouflage wearing men who seek to assist her broken-down car. Her flight into the snow deliberately references her cowboying after lost heifers, but where previously she was the skilled horsewoman and protector, now she takes the part of the calf. McGuane makes this symbolically clear when she collapses beneath a juniper tree (biblical symbol of a protective angel) and is kept alive by the heat from a circle of cows. She had been seeking 'true love' to give her 'an inoculation that could last the entire winter' but she finds instead a dangerous predatory masculinity and the comfort of cows (79).

McGuane's most courageous decision in this novel is to synthesize the masculine/feminine, Old West/New West binaries into a single character: the cross-dressing mountain man Donald Aadfield. We have already met him: he was the 'bearded man in a stadium coat' who was rifling through the accessories whilst Evelyn was trying on her dress in *Just the Two of Us* (75). He is a less visible member of the pairing also negotiating his own complex relationship between gender and the values of the Old West. Donald's cross-dressing is not, like Bob Dollar's discovery of pictures of cross-dressing cowboys, designed to draw attention to an unfamiliar aspect of Frontier life. Nor does it reflect the treatment in novels like Tom Spanbauer's *The Man Who Fell in Love with the Moon* (1991), which reappraises the mythology of the West through the narration of a half Native American, bisexual cross-dressing prostitute. Nor does it perform the same transgressive function as that deployed by Sebastian Barry in *Days without End* (2017), whose story of bounty hunters who spend their days butchering Native Americans and their nights performing as women for their comrades is a blurring of borders. Donald's cross-dressing is not primarily about gender; it is a humorous means of bridging the gender, familial and legacy battles that dominate this novel. Where in the Whitelaw family the divisions are made by character – Paul vs Bill/Natalie vs Evelyn /Sonny vs Bill/Paul vs Stuart/Alice vs Edith – Donald is a cross-dressing old-fashioned rancher who approves of new methods. The living room of the Aadfield ranch is a monument to this complicated identity: a 'bulging elk against an overwrought tangerine sunrise', 'Granddad in the uniform of a Norwegian Navy Captain', 'Donald as a rodeo star in pre-cross-dresser days', a 'colored portrait of Diana, Princess of Wales' – Donald's new hero. The elk head and the Princess of Wales are both Kitsch; the pre-cross-dressing rodeo photograph we suspect is camp; the Norwegian navy captain absurd: there is nothing in this living room that does not challenge our notions of a ranching patriarchy and further our sense of dislocation (101). Ironically, Donald feels trapped by the traditionalism of the ranch and simultaneously liberated by the isolation that allows him his secret life. However, unlike all the other characters in the novel who possess a secret (Bill's secret paternity, Stuart's secret lover, Paul's lie that sees him imprisoned, Edith's closeted secret child) he regrets the secrecy:

> *Secret* lives are incredibly tiring and sort of *unreal* in the long term, and I just have this feeling I'm going to end up some lonely old bachelor rancher leaning on a number-two Ames irrigating shovel, and *not one* tourist driving past admiring me as a traditional part of the landscape on the northern route to Yellowstone will ever realize that once upon a time I was an honest-to-god California faggot!
>
> (McGuane's italics 209)

Donald fears nostalgia whilst embracing it for his own protection; his 'Ames irrigating shovel' is as much a part of his performance as his rodeo outfit and the 'gorgeous outfits so full of meaning' that made up his California chorus line days (94). Donald's presence reminds us that in the shadow of the Crazies, rather like in Proulx's Wyoming, nothing is as it seems.

The Aadfields are the Whitelaws seen through a distorting lens: they are both dysfunctional families coming to terms with the recent death of a patriarch who has left them traumatized. Through this mirrored narrative structure, McGuane probes why the West seems to specialize in such curmudgeonly archetypes and why they always seem to get their way, even beyond the grave. Proulx asks the same question, allowing Jewel Blood, the central protagonist in her first novel, *Postcards* (1992), to exonerate her husband's rage as the energy necessary to 'pull him through difficult work, through a difficult life'.[64] McGuane's Western historian, Edith Crusoe, articulates similar sentiments when she censures Evelyn's criticism of Sunny Jim: 'I despise it when your age group extracts some poor old male from the culture that made him, all the things he survived, only to conclude he was a brute. It's banal' (134). However, Crusoe is a ridiculous figure with a misplaced cultural relativism; the patriarchs in this novel are not hard, they are brutes. They deploy a corrupted Western mythology to condone their misogyny, freewheeling sexuality and sharp business practices. For them the free-range symbolizes lack of constraint – whether sexual, alcoholic or market – and an empty space over which their appetites can range. Meanwhile, Crusoe's West comprises the academic decoding of signs and symbols rather than people and places, which is, like so many of the actions in this novel, motivated by guilt. As a junior academic she had been part of a counselling programme responsible for helping ranching families displaced by the expansion of the campus. Her sexual molestation of a number of young sons in her broom cupboard, including Paul's father, is presented as slapstick, but reminds us once again that the rape of the land that came with Anglo settlement was often a precursor to the rape of its people. Thus, her support for things Western – such as the men who built the West – is actually a means of atoning for the skeleton in her cupboard (147).

The other reason that patriarchs flourish is that the cowboy virtues of nurturing and stoicism prove unviable in the contemporary business world represented by Sunny Jim and Paul. Bill lives in the past: his stories are ways of maintaining continuity, but they are also ways of evading the present. A life governed by the Anglo settler belief that 'on a ranch you don't budge or the ranch and the land will beat you' has led to stultification (165). The land has beaten Bill, it's just that he can't see the reality because it is obscured by the Western ideal. His first job as a teenage cowboy was on a 'twenty-thousand-acre pasture without a division fence' and later we are told that when he returns to his own ranch after the war 'there was nothing there, cows gone, machinery rusted into the ground, saddle horses stolen or eaten' (225, 237). In both cases his memories of a ranch are built on 'nothing': an empty space to be filled with a folkloric notion of what a ranch should be. His grandfather first put the ranch together after being punished for horse stealing by being lowered down a well for three days. Now Bill feels like he is dangling in the well 'and living in a country all too happy to watch him drown in a job that probably didn't exist anymore' (165). He is in no condition to face the handsome and brash young businessman, Sunny Jim, who, it is revealed late in the narrative, turned up one day to take away his family (the darkest skeleton in the cupboard). From the moment of his wife's departure, the ranch is transformed from a means of connecting with the ghosts of a shared Western heritage, to a means of burying the ghosts of a degraded present. Sunny Jim's guilt forces him to keep the ranch alive so that he can bury his secret family, whilst Bill is happy to comply so that he can carry on playing cowboy. The final twist is that the ranch is really owned by an Ohio Bengali businessman who is desperate to hide his drug-running enterprise behind assumed Western credentials. It is another manoeuvre by means of which McGuane deliberately questions the connection between 'ownership' and 'heritage'.

In the end, it is Majub's vision of the West that prevails as both Bill and Paul (who symbolize competing Western visions) die whilst drug running. It is a curiously ambivalent end to the novel that both mocks and celebrates the delusional mythology of the West. The Frontier myth is reduced to two men struggling for supremacy in a small boat as it crosses the Canadian-US border. Significantly, it is Bill who is cast ashore in his long johns and is forced to walk alone into a snowstorm. However, the effect on Paul, left struggling into Bill's ill-fitting cowboy regalia, is, like Evelyn's black dress, transformative:

> He was not happy with these clothes. It was like being in a costume. He hated that everything had gotten so serious ... Paul would deliver this load and take his reward down to Evelyn and save the ranch, just as Whitelaw delivered all the bottles for half a million square miles and saved the ranch. Old Bill was walking into his last snowstorm to save the ranch. It's as if, Paul thought, we're all in some Gary Cooper movie and can't get out!
>
> (230)

Paul's redeeming feature is a cynicism that prevents him taking himself seriously; where Bill and Sunny-Jim filter their activity through a Western lens (drug running transformed into cattle rustling), Paul cannot escape his awareness of cliché. However, in the end it is through Bill's imagined dialogue with John Red Wolf as he walks to his death (a fitting cowboy end) that McGuane is able to interrogate the value of a mythical model of masculinity that has troubled all the works in this study. Red Wolf has been the guiding light in Bill's West, but the war is over, and their battleship has been scrapped, becoming another buried skeleton (238). Bill's death is both comic and full of pathos: his exclamation 'the world has changed, John, and guys like you and me don't really exist' ironically contextualizes their contemporary invisibility through appeal to a heroic past that never existed (237). And yet, as McGuane makes clear, this delusion is infinitely preferable to the insipid masculinity embodied in a character like Paul, whose bawling execution at the hands of Majub's henchmen contrasts so clearly with Red Wolf's exploits. It is also preferable to Natalie's husband, Stuart, whose sensitivity makes him honourable but anaemic. Where Paul reads Nietzsche, Stuart quotes Emerson, which Natalie dismisses as the cod psychology of a 'cigar-store Indian' (an insipid version of Red Wolf) (42). If, McGuane seems to be demanding, this is the new man – Evelyn can imagine Stuart 'coming along before the age of anatomically correct dolls' – then let's get back to Gary Cooper! (59, 141).

Notes

1. Ibid., Allard, *Vanishing Breed*, pp. 6–7.
2. Stegner, *The Sound of Mountain Water*, p. 199 (Stegner's italics).

3   Morris, 'How Ambivalence Won the West: Thomas McGuane and the Fiction of the New West', *Critique* 22: 3 (Spring 1991), 180–9 (pp. 181–2).
4   Pauline Kael, 'Poses', *The New Yorker* 51 (8 December 1975), 163–5 (p. 163).
5   Westrum, *Thomas McGuane* (Boston: Twayne, 1991), p. 88.
6   Ibid., *Paris Review*.
7   Ursula LeGuin, 'The Fabric of Grace', *Washington Post* (2 September 1990).
8   McGuane's acknowledged 'adversarial relationship' with his own father, but notes in relation to this book: 'I was so tired of the pain of the father-and-son issue that I didn't want it to infuse yet another book, so I canonized him and got him the hell out of the book.' Ibid., *Paris Review*.
9   Lynch, 'Nothing but Land', 374–99 (p. 376). Cather, *My Antonia*, p. 7.
10 Arthur, *The Default Country*, p. 85.
11 Drucilla Mims Wall, 'Simulations of Authenticity: Imagined Indians and Sacred Landscape from New Age to Nature Writing', in Handley and Lewis (eds.), *True West*, 97–116 (p. 101).
12 Williams, *In the American Grain* (Norfolk: New Directions, 1940), p. 57.
13 Knopp, *Field of Vision* (Iowa City: University of Iowa Publishing, 1996), p. 37. See Mims Wall, *Identity and Authenticity: Exploration in Native and Irish Literature and Culture*. Unpublished PhD dissertation (University of Nebraska: 2006), pp. 27–8.
14 The conventions of the 'Revenge Tragedy' were laid out clearly to Shakespeare's audiences some years before by Thomas Kyd's blockbuster *The Spanish Tragedy* (1582–92).
15 Jon Wallace provides a detailed a perceptive reading of this exchange, 'Speaking Against the Dark Side: Style as Theme in Thomas McGuane's *Nobody's Angel*', *Modern Fiction Studies* 33: 2 (Summer 1987), 289–98.
16 See Wallace, 'Speaking Against the Dark Side', p. 294.
17 See McGuane, *Some Horses* (New York: Vintage, 1999), p. 3.
18 See Evgeniya M Butenin, 'The Intext of "Superfluous Man",' *Procedia: Social and Behavioral Sciences*, 200 (2015), 403–7 (405).
19 McGuane defends himself saying that his former 'bad boy' image has led to unfair criticism: 'It's like having a German accent in 1919.' Interview with Mark Harris, Torrey *Conversations*, 120–4 (p. 122).
20 Judson Klinger claims that McGuane felt so alienated from the final film that he swapped his shares for a saddle. 'In Pursuit of Crazy Language', *American Film* XIV: 6 (April 1989), 42–4 and 63–4 (p. 42).
21 Erkkila, '*The Missouri Breaks*', *Cineaste* 8: 1 (Summer 1977), pp. 48, 50.
22 Charles Michener interviews Arthur Penn, *Film Comment* 12: 4 (July–August 1976), 40–3 (p. 40).
23 See James McClintock, '"Unextended Selves" and "Unformed Visions": Roman Catholicism in Thomas McGuane's Novels', *Renascence* IL: 2 (Winter 1997), pp. 139–52 (p. 145).
24 See Butenin for excellent reading of Patrick's 'superfluity', 'Superfluous Man', p. 405.
25 Morris, 'Ambivalence Won the West', p. 185.
26 Umberto Eco's, *Travels in Hyperreality*, trans. William Weaver (Orlando: Harcourt Brace, 1986), p. 16.

27 McGuane told him that *Antaeus Magazine* was looking for a hunting story. Bruce Weber, 'Richard Ford's Uncommon Characters', *New York Times* (10 April 1988), p. 299.
28 Dexter Westrum offers these examples, p. 121.
29 See Carlton Smith for an excellent reading of this scene. 'In the Shadow of the Crazies: The Omnipresent Father and Thomas McGuane's Deadrock Novels', in *Coyote Kills John Wayne: Postmodernism and Cotemporary Fictions of the Transcultural Frontier* (Hanover and London: Dartmouth College, 2000), p. 135.
30 J. Fritz Lanham, 'Coming Apart in Montana', *Houston Chronicle* 6 (December 1992).
31 Ibid., Lewis, 'Review', *Western American Literature*.
32 See John Noel Moore for a perceptive analysis of the narrative style of this story. 'The Landscape of Fiction', *English Journal* 90: 1 (September 2000), 146–8 (p. 146). There is also a good analysis of the style of the story available at E-notes. http://www.enotes.com/topics/close-range/in-depth#in-depth-the-stories [accessed 1 November 2013].
33 Thomas McGuane, 'Some Notes on Montana', *Agricultural Digest* (June 1992), 45.
34 'Thomas McGuane Speaks', interview with Deborah Houy, *Buzzworm: The Environmental Journal* (January/February 1993), 32–4 (p. 32).
35 See Kaitlin Reed, 'We are Part of the Land and the Land is Us', *Humboldt Journal of Social Relations* 42 (2020) 27–49 (p. 29).
36 Eve Tuck and K. Wayne Yang, 'Decolonization if not a Metaphor', *Decolonization: Indigeneity, Education and Society* 1: 40 (2012), p. 7.
37 Interview with John Purdy, 'Crossroads: A Conversation with Sherman Alexie', *SAIL* 9:4 (Winter, 1997), 1–18 (p. 12). https://facultystaff.richmond.edu/~rnelson/asail/SAIL2/94.html#1. [accessed 7 Aug 2013]. Quoted Lundquist, *Native American Literatures,* p. 154.
38 See Alex Wilson, Jenifer L Uncapher (and members of the Rocky Mountain Institute), *Green Development: Integrating Ecology and Real Estate* (New York: Wiley and Sons, 1998), p. 154.
39 Owens, *Mixed Blood Messages* (Norman: University of Oklahoma Press, 1998), p. 77. Lundquist makes this argument convincingly, *Native American Literatures,* p. 285.
40 Ibid., Deer and Nagle, 'The Rapidly Increasing Extraction of Oil', p. 36.
41 Kittredge, *The Next Rodeo,* p. 169.
42 McGuane in conversation with Jim Schumock (1999). Repr. Torrey, *Conversations*, 147–56 (p. 153).
43 Carlton Smith provides an excellent discussion of McGuane's presentation of fishing in a subsection 'And a River Runs through It' (Coyote Kills John Wayne, pp. 138–47); see also David Ingram's excellent discussion in 'Thomas McGuane: Nature, Environmentalism, and the American West', *Journal of American Studies* 29: 3 (December 1995), 423–39.
44 Kittredge quoted in Johnson, *New Westers,* p. 343.
45 Liza Nicholas, Elaine Bapis, Thomas Harvey, *Imagining the Big Open: Nature, Identity, and Play in the New West* (Utah: University of Utah Press, 1992).
46 See David Streitfield, 'McGuane Mellows', *Washington Post Book World* XXII: 43 (October 1992), p. 15.

47 McGuane, *The Longest Silence: A Life in Fishing* (1999) (London: Yellow New Jersey Press, 2001), xv.
48 Jim Harrison quoted in Robert J. DeMott (ed.), 'Conversations with Jim Harrison' (Mississippi: University Press of Mississippi, 2002), p. 65.
49 Interview with Beef Torrey, Repr. Torrey, *Conversations*, 186–206 (p. 199).
50 Brautigan, *Trout Fishing in America* (1967) (Houghton Mifflin Harcourt, 2010), p. 101.
51 McGuane, 'An Optimist vis-à-vis the Present', *The New York Times* (15 February 1970), p. 282. https://www.nytimes.com/1970/02/15/archives/an-optimist-visavis-the-present-trout-fishing-in-america-the-pill.html.
52 McGuane, 'The Bonefish in the Other Room', *Esquire* (February 1992), p. 55. https://classic.esquire.com/article/1992/2/1/the-bonefish-in-the-other-room [accessed 23 August 2020].
53 Ibid., Ingram, 'Thomas McGuane', p. 430.
54 Interview Beef Torrey, Repr. Torrey, *Conversations*, p. 195.
55 Tom Bissell, 'The Last Lion', *Outside Magazine* (31 August 2011) https://www.outsideonline.com/1893296/last-lion [accessed 23 August 2020].
56 Interview with Fergus, 1989. Repr. Torrey, *Conversations*, p. 42.
57 Ibid., McGuane, *The Longest Silence*, pp. 3, 11.
58 McGuane, 'Father, Son, And Holy Permit', *Esquire Magazine* (1 March 1993) https://classic.esquire.com/article/1993/3/1/father-son-and-holy-permit [accessed 23 August 2020].
59 Ibid., Riebsame, *Atlas of the New West*, pp. 145–6.
60 Ingram provides an excellent analysis of this scene, p. 427; similarly, Carlton Smith, p. 145.
61 Interview with Robert Birnbaum (2002). Repr. Torrey, *Conversations*, 166–79 (p. 172).
62 Houston, *Cowboys are my Weakness* (1992) (London: Virago Press, 1994), pp. 124–5.
63 Proulx, 'A Lonely Coast', *Close Range*, p. 216.
64 Ibid., Proulx, *Postcards* (1992) (London, New York: Harper Perennial, 2006), p. 242.

Conclusion: Where's the All-American Cowboy Going?

So, where to now the cowboy? Critics are always writing him off because, like the Western he inhabits, he is too violent, racist, misogynist and childish for contemporary sensibilities, sensibilities that continually evolve away from the genre's primary preoccupation with white masculinity.¹ Critical soul-searching tends to be catalysed by dramatic box office flops of Westerns like Michael Cimino's *Heaven's Gate* (1980) and Gore Verbinski's *The Lone Ranger* (2013). Yet, the genre continues to find new audiences by, as Campbell has argued, 'traveling across generic boundaries, poaching and borrowing from many different earlier traditions, whilst contributing to the innovation of the genre'.²

Cowboys have been given steampunk makeovers in Barry Sonnenfeld's comedy *Wild Wild West* (1999) and 'New Weird' treatment in China Mieville's *Iron Council* (2004); they have been blasted into space in Jon Favreau's *Cowboys & Aliens* (2011) and we have seen *Cowboys vs Zombies* (Rene Perez, 2010) and *Cowboys vs Dinosaurs* (Ari Novak, 2015). There have been a number of neo-Westerns such as the Coen Brothers *No Country for Old Men* in 2007,³ David MacKenzie's heist drama *Hell or High Water* (2016)⁴ and Martin McDonagh's black comedy *Three Billboards Outside Ebbing, Missouri* (2017)⁵ that engage in an aesthetic of Stetsons and panned desert shots combined with a soundtrack of contemporary Country and Western. Time-honoured Western tropes and narrative codes have also migrated into long-running made-for-TV series like *24* (2001–10), *Homeland* (2009–12) and Vince Gilligan's *Breaking Bad* (2008–13).⁶ Producer Vince Gilligan, acknowledges a violent aesthetic influenced by 'those great John Ford movies and all those Sergio Leone Westerns' – in which shootouts take place against a Western desert.⁷ There has also been no shortage of 'traditional' Westerns. Ted Turner – an avid Western fan – has used his TNT network to produce 'faithful' adaptations of Louis L'Amour's *Conagher* (1991),

Grey's *Riders of the Purple Sage* (1996) and *The Crossfire Trail* (2001), and Wister's *The Virginian* (2000).[8] On the big screen Ed Harris's *Appaloosa* (2008) was received by *The New Yorker's* David Denby as 'a well-made, satisfying, traditionalist Western',[9] whilst Kevin Costner returned with *Open Range* (2003), which, according to Peter Bradshaw in *The Guardian*, 'is lovingly conceived on traditional lines'.[10] Jacques Audiard's *The Sisters Brothers* (2018) (based on Patrick deWitt's 2011 novel) is a traditional tale of gunfighters alienated from modernity (they are surprised by new-fangled toilets and toothbrushes), from women (their name implies a world without women), from meaning (they ride so far West that they hit the sea and are unsure what to make of it), and the lives they lead (they revel and are haunted by their reputations). Such Westerns seem proudly conventional, uninhibited by the embarrassment that has driven and drives film makers and authors to the protection afforded by irony and critical revision.

In other ways, wide-screen Westerns have also continued to revise and problematize our response to the genre by giving voice to previously marginalized groups. Race is central to Quentin Tarrantino's *Django Unchained* (2012) (an 'unchained' homage to the original ultra-violent spaghetti (*Django* (1968)), in which explosive racial politics are introduced through the ethnic transformation of the central character; Native Americans are given a more historically sensitive treatment in HBO's television film of Dee Brown's classic *Bury My Heart at Wounded Knee* (2007) and Scott Cooper's *Hostiles* (2017): in which a bigoted US Cavalry officer learns to respect the Cheyenne when he is forced to escort a chief back to their Montana home. Aids victims are the focus of Jean-Marc Vallee's *Dallas Buyers Club* (2013) (in which the ultra-masculine cowboy identity is used to explore the stigma of the disease). Women are central to Sami Raimi's *The Quick and the Dead* (1995) (a spaghetti Western in which 'The Man with No Name' is a woman), and also Ron Howard's *The Missing* (2003) (in which women take on Native Americans to free them from slavery), Kelly Reichardt's *Meek's Cutoff* (2010) (in which women settlers ally with a Native American against their Mountain Man guide), and finally Jared Moshe's *Dead Man's Burden* (2012) (where the burdensome woman takes control). Gender is at the forefront in Ang Lee's *Brokeback Mountain* (2005), and also Anna Kerrigan's exploration of cowboy masculinity and transgender in *Cowboys* (2020).

Amongst all this remaking and revision, to which we could add the hugely successful and critically astute HBO series *Deadwood* and *Westworld* (discussed elsewhere), what is of interest is the persistence of the innocent abroad as both a narrative ploy and analytical device. Two interesting examples are James Mangold's *3:10 to Yuma* (2007) (a remake of Delmer Daves's 1957 movie based on Elmore Leonard's 1953 short story) and the Coen Brothers's *True Grit* (2010) (a remake of Henry Hathaway's 1969 film based on Charles Portis's 1968 novel.). Remakes are significant because their balance of nostalgia and revision means that they are speaking to two different audiences and inviting the sophisticated consumer to enjoy the Classic Western whilst simultaneously subverting the genre codes it celebrates. In the former, Dan Evans (Christian Bale) is a one-legged Civil War veteran and impoverished rancher driven by debt to escort the notorious outlaw Ben Wade (Russell Crowe) to the town of Contention to take the 3.10 train to the prison at Yuma. What is really in 'contention' in all versions of the story is the model of masculinity presented by both men to young boys, both intra-textually (through Evans's sons) and for those in suburban living rooms everywhere. It is a variant on *Shane;* indeed in the original film, Evans was played by Van Heflin (who played Tom Starrett in *Shane*) whose two pre-adolescent sons looked up to him much like young Joey Starrett. In Mangold's version, by contrast, it is only the younger son who maintains open admiration for his father, but he is afflicted with a lung disease that suggests a love born of shared weakness which comes out of an inability to adapt to the harshness of the West. The elder son, William (Logan Lerman) has been transformed into a precocious fourteen-year-old who has been brought up on a diet of cowboy heroism and who holds his father's ineffectual uprightness in open contempt. This contempt becomes overt in his father's dealings with the railway company whose henchmen (much like the Fletchers/Rykers in *Shane*) humiliate Evans and burn down his barn. The moral centre remains deliberately difficult to locate at moments like the barn burning that opens the film: we are invited to condemn William's rashness who, disturbed from his reading of a Dime novel *The Deadly Outlaw*, wants to shoot the arsonists. However, as his father explains his behaviour through the platitudinous 'someday William, you [will] walk in my shoes, you might understand', there appears in William's mockingly withering rejoinder – 'I ain't never walking in your shoes' – a suggestion that Evans's passivity signals impotence rather than stoicism.

The shoes William admires are boots and are worn by Wade (*The Deadly Outlaw* made flesh). In the original, Wade is a dangerous criminal brought to justice; in the remake this simple black hat/white hat binary is more 'contentious' as Wade's Old West of intuitive cowboy justice is pitched against a New West of underhand corporate greed. When William first sees him he is robbing a stagecoach owned by the railroads who are robbing his father; his clever deployment of cattle (classic Western fare) and daring pursuit is contrasted with the Pinkerton's less honourable use of a Gatling gun. Thus, when William, against his father's wishes, joins him in taking Wade to Contention, what is really in contention is which masculine role-model will prevail. The film remains ambivalent: Evans is honourable, but helpless; he understands the irony that the two hundred dollars paid to escort Wade amounts to the compensation for his lost leg 'so that the government could walk away from their responsibilities', but nevertheless maintains a belief in an abstract code of justice. Wade, by comparison, is vital and strong, facing down the railroads with an individualist cowboy justice that is glamorous and brutally righteous. And yet, there is a tiredness about him – shared by Henry King's *The Gunfighter* (1950), John Farrow's *Hondo* (1953) and, of course, *Shane* – that leads to the recognition that his days are over and that his example is not to be followed. In these cases the cowboy performs his intra and meta-textual didactic function of acculturating boys into a code in which 'a man's gotta do what a man's gotta do' before riding into the sunset.

3:10 to Yuma offers a playful revision that problematizes this simple morality tale. Wade's first lesson to William is a straightforward denial of his heroism: 'Kid, I wouldn't last five minutes leading an outfit like that if I wasn't rotten as hell.' At the other extreme is his willingness to perform the role of *The Deadly Outlaw* being taken in in order to restore the dignity of Evans in the eyes of his son. Thus, the final gun battle, in which Wade's gang (led by Charlie Prince in Confederate Uniform) attempt to set him free, is a Western cliché performed knowingly by Evans and Wade for the watching William. It is the cowboy codes, as they were in McCarthy's theatrical fight scene in the Saltillo prison (*APH*), that are under examination. Prince conforms to the usual cowboy narrative by shooting the escort, Evans, before presenting, in a ritualistic act of subservience, the newly released Wade with his gun belt. That Wade proceeds to kill both Prince and the rest of the gang would seem to signal his acknowledgement that his days are over and the superiority of Evans's notions of justice and righteous family values. However, this simple happy ending is resisted by Evans's dying message to his son: 'I need a man at the ranch to run things, protect our family, and I know that you can do that because you've become a fine man, William … And you just remember that your old man walked Ben Wade to that station when nobody else would.' There is irony in his demand that William will become a 'fine man' walking in his nester shoes on the benighted ranch whilst reserving for himself the apotheosis that comes from walking with glamorous cowboys. It leaves the question of 'what a man's gotta do' as didactically useless as the tautology suggests. In the end, William's choice is dramatized in the final showdown when, having witnessed his father's murder, he is unable to shoot Wade at point-blank range; it is the ultimate vindication of his father's values, but leaves Wade – *The Deadly Outlaw* – free to ride another day.

True Grit is another remake of a film based on a book in which Western codes are mediated through the observing sensibility of a 14-year-old: this time a girl. Self-possessed Mattie Ross hires washed-up US Marshall, Rooster Cogburn, to track down the man who murdered her father. The bickering duo are accompanied on their quest by a Texas Ranger named LaBoeuf who has been tracking the same man for killing a State Senator. In some sense it is a corrective to both *Shane* and *3:10*, Joey and William's adolescent hero-worship of the lithe, morally incorruptible gunfighter, giving way to Mattie's more critical assessment of the slovenly and morally compromised Cogburn. The 1969 film became a vehicle for John Wayne (who plays John Wayne in broadcast fashion) and a hopelessly miscast Glen Campbell (in his first screen role), with Mattie fading into the background as a feisty girl with a page-boy haircut whose wisecracking is a source of male appreciation. The Coens sidestepped the film, claiming that Wayne is part of a Western landscape that is venerated but has no part in their vision of the novel, the West or the Western.[11] Instead, they sought to reclaim the ambiguity of Portis's original, which left critics unsure whether it was a Classic Western (The *Washington Post* argued that 'Mattie Ross should soon join the pantheon of America's legendary figures such as Kit Carson, Wyatt Earp and Jesse James'[12]), or a parody of a Western (*New York Times*[13]) or a 'pop anti-western in the best tradition of *Cat Ballou*' (*Time* magazine[14]). Western classic, parody or anti-Western, the novel treads the fine line between celebration and mockery, allowing Mattie's presence to disrupt the characters's understanding of the usual revenge narrative and the viewer's expectations of the genre. The Coens tread a similar line, claiming on one hand that the film's aesthetic is typically 'Western' because 'some things you can't mess with', whilst simultaneously confessing 'we weren't thinking: let's shoot widescreen like Sergio Leone' because 'our sensibility has nothing to do with that. If anything, we were more in terms of *Alice in Wonderland*'.[15] This surrealist sensibility is made clear the minute Mattie enters 'Indian Country' and meets a dentist dressed as a bear, a bandit who is half sheep and even falls down a hole. However, such characters and incidents are always hedged with a genre critique that makes the inversions of *Through the Looking Glass* a more viable comparison: It is a Western turned upside down.

Mattie is a disrupter: her unsuitability to her avenging role is made clear when she dresses in her father's oversized coat and hat and puts his gun in a handbag.[16] However, the dominance of her narrative perspective (her prim Presbyterian tones inflect the dialogue throughout the film), means that it is her saddle partners who are brought under scrutiny as both men and Western archetypes. In this capacity they are figures worthy of veneration, mockery and pity in equal measure. Rooster (Jeff Bridges) and LaBoeuf (Matt Damon) are presented as participating in a Western performance that borders on the parodic: LaBoeuf is a poseur whose manner of speech and theatrical costume just miss the ridiculous; Rooster maintains a penchant for personal myth making that will be formalized at the end of the film in his performance of himself as part of Cody's Wild West Show. They don't know how to deal with Mattie who has no part of their Western code. Her decision to ford the river on her horse whilst they take the ferry challenges them on both a manly and mythological level. Where a young boy, like William or Joey, would offer validation through the prospect of initiation into the world of men, Rooster chafes at being labelled a wet nurse, and LaBoeuf is unsure whether to kiss or spank her (both of which are rejected as equally horrible by Mattie). It is therefore she who takes on the adult role reducing them to truculent cowboys: where the wisecracking Rooster is depicted out of his depth amidst the suits and legalese of the film's opening scene, Mattie proves adept in manipulating the law in her horse-trading; when both men decide to test their cowboy credentials through a farcical shooting match (neither man can hit the target), a frustrated Mattie is left to chastise them about the wasted time. Her censure is shared by the viewer, whose reaction is further layered by pity for what they recognize as characters trapped in their own Western fantasy. This is made particularly apparent in Rooster's re-enactment (it is important that he is re-enacting part of his personal mythology) of his death-defying one against four horse charge. Rooster wins, but is trapped under his horse facing summary execution by the mortally wounded leader of the gang, Ned Pepper, he has been chasing. In Pepper's final speech he acknowledges that the glory of the Old West dies with them; a sentiment made explicit when he is killed by LaBoeuf's long-distance shot, which announces the presence of modernity.

The film could end there; the violence of the Old West consigned to storybooks and Mattie and LaBoeuf happily married; but both Portis and the Coens resist such nostalgia. Instead, the traditional warning of the aging gunfighter to his protégé to renounce violence is explored allegorically. When Mattie eventually shoots her father's murderer the pistol kick-back causes her to fall into a hole where she comes face to face with the skeleton of a cowboy with a snake sleeping where his heart should be. The snake bites her gun hand and, despite the desperate attempts of Rooster to extract the poison, she loses her arm. The symbolism is multilayered, but at its heart is the act of killing, which, despite Mattie's Old Testament justification, is the trade of the gunman that sets him apart from both civilization and other men. In killing, Mattie has left behind childish innocence (dramatized by Rooster's riding to death her childishly named horse) and become a killer condemned to a life of isolation. Thus, our final view of Mattie is not the victorious child but the aged one-armed spinster beneath a blasted tree (both have suffered life's vicissitudes) beside the grave of Rooster, which she has moved in a magnificent but futile gesture beside her father's grave. She claims never to have married because she didn't have the time: however, the symbolism makes clear that she is marked by violence, an outcast pining for the past in the shape of LaBoeuf. As she walks into a storm, rather than rides into the sunset, an ironic soundtrack plays 'Leaning on the Everlasting Arms' – those arms belonging to the cowboys who understand a code of lonely vengeance.

I want to finish this study by looking at three Westerns – Guy Vanderhaeghe's novel *The Englishman's Boy* (1996), Sebastian Barry's *Days Without End* (2016), and finally John Maclean's directorial debut *Slow West* (2015) – produced by outsiders (a Canadian, Irishman and Scotsman). They share the conceit of the innocent abroad to deconstruct familiar Western tropes whilst simultaneously introducing transgender themes and questions of cultural appropriation. Guy Vanderhaeghe's novel *The Englishman's Boy* (1996) is like McCarthy's *Blood Meridian* in that it focuses on a 'nameless young man adrift in the West' who joins a gang led by a dangerous older man who leads them into a barbarous world of escalating violence.[17] Like McCarthy's novel, it is also based on a real account, this time of the rape and massacre of a party of Assiniboine by American wolf hunters in 1873, to which our fictional protagonist is witness. One narrative strand follows this event, allowing Vanderhaeghe to critique the racial ideology underpinning Manifest Destiny; a second strand, however, concerns the making of a film of the event in Hollywood in 1923, for which the boy, now grown into an adult, is to provide an eyewitness account. How we re-enact, represent and confer meaning on past events is a familiar revisionist trope, touched on by McCarthy (whose cowboys find themselves performing Hollywood versions of themselves) and McGuane, who mocks the reduction of history to archetype through Edward Ballantyne's call for 'a well-preserved fortyish woman with dark complexion and hair' to become a Native American to be violated anew in his 'Trail of Tears Exhibit'.

Proulx covers similar territory in her 'The Indian Wars Refought' (*BD*), which uses the discovery of Bill Cody's lost film of the massacre of *Wounded Knee* in 1876 by a teenage Native American girl, Linny, as a means of exploring the role of the imagination in historical recreation. Proulx, like Cody, grafts her faux narrative over an authentic prop: the film was made by Essaney in 1914 and was variously called *Wars of Civilization* (extraordinary in cultural insensitivity and also ironic considering the apocalypse in Europe); the more culturally affirmative *The last Great Battle of the Sioux; From the Warpath to the Peace Pipe* (which announces the film's happy ending); and *Buffalo Bill's Indian Wars* (a title that acknowledges its own theatricality). Proulx's title – 'The Indian Wars Refought' – is that under which the film was eventually released, and is entirely consistent with her project of conflating the historical with the domestic struggles of her contemporary characters. It draws attention to the crisis of identity suffered by contemporary Native Americans forced to interpret and adapt their cultural heritage. Her focus throughout is the ethics of re-enactment in relation to the camera. Within the text she has Linny quote the reviewer Chauncey Yellow Robe, who served as a consultant on films sympathetic to Native Americans, the best known been *Silent Enemy* (1929). In this re-creation of the lives of the Ojibwa Indians before the arrival of the white settlers he points out the irony that while white technology removed the Indians it was now bringing them back. He was, however, a lifelong critic of Cody, claiming that his use of authentic props simply created a 'reality' based on appearances.[18] The dangers of such an approach were exposed by the real Edward Owl King who, years after the event, defended his participation in Cody's film, claiming: 'The Indians without thinking went ahead and performed in the ways that were directed by some of the white people, not truthfully but just the way they wanted it presented in the pictures. That tells the wrong story.'[19] What constitutes the 'right' story is under examination in Proulx's story. Linny destroys the film unseen because, having recently read Dee Brown's seminal *Bury My Heart at Wounded Knee* (1970), she believes it will show Native Americans performing a version of 'Indianness' for white audiences: 'An Indian dragging a soldier from a horse, some fake hand-to-hand fighting, Indians poking two white captive women with a stick, the Gatling and Hotchkiss guns spraying, and everywhere Buffalo Bill peering into the distance' (38). And yet Brown's claim to authority is not without critics who point to his selective and un-cited sources as constructing a sentimental account just as suspect as Cody's.[20] The deployment of a critical text to augment the reading of an unseen historical artefact by a fictional character unpicks the complexities of historical re-enactment and personal heritage reclamation that lies at the centre of Proulx's text. For Linny, the battle is not simply an historical event that has become a symbol – potent but static – of white oppression; it is a human catastrophe recreated vividly in her imagination through her present reading of Dee Brown's account.

As with Proulx and McGuane, Vanderhaeghe is focussed on the double violation: the initial murder and rape and its subsequent falsification that transforms the hunters into the victims. The Englishman's Boy has grown up into a gnarled old cowboy, whose name, Shorty McAdoo, announces the hyper-stylized cowboy existence that his buried secret will explode. Vanderhaeghe follows familiar revisionist trends in presenting a Hollywood in the spirit of Cody's Extravaganza. Director Damon Ira Chance (a name that suggests his diabolical opportunism) is determined to produce a Shakespearean epic for the American people which reveals their 'true character'.[21] The irony, of course, is that the horror of the original events and the hypocrisy of their re-telling achieve precisely this aim. For Chance, as for Cody, 'truth' is elided with authenticity, so procuring the right cast ('real' working cowboys) and artefacts ('wampum belts, beaded rifle scabbards' and '*real* Indians instead of Mexicans in wigs') allows him to construct what he terms the 'psychological truth'.[22] For Vanderhaeghe this 'truth' is a product of its time: It is 1923 – Oswald Spengler's *Decline of the West* (1918) was translated in 1926, whilst D. W. Griffith's epic *The Birth of a Nation* (1915) (its original title *The Clansman* making clear its Ku Klux Klan sympathies) echoes throughout the novel reminding us of the thin dividing line between propaganda and reconstruction. Chance's 'psychological truth' rejects what he labels guilty revisionism in favour of a Nietzschean 'celebration of spiritual and physical strength' that resurrects the spirit of Manifest Destiny. The Indians, he argues, like those who rebelled against the Romans, could not see the writing on the wall, and ignored their scripted decline in the face of civilization. They also, however, provide a secondary political function as dangerous outsiders, becoming 'Bolsheviks in loin cloths' who threaten the freedom of the hardy hunters. In the new film – entitled *Besieged* – the cowboys are reinvented as the victims, whilst the Native Americans become savage outsiders.[23] The book's conclusion takes place at the film's premiere where McAdoo is so enraged by the falsification that he guns down Chance and his bodyguard in a cowboy standoff. It is an ironic act that suggests that despite the book's careful deconstruction of the mythical West, sometimes it takes a gunslinger to correct the myth of Western heroism in a clear act of retributive cowboy justice.[24]

Like *The Englishman's Boy* and *Blood Meridian*, Sebastian Barry's *Days Without End* (2016) also revises the mythology of the Indian Wars through the witness of a young male protagonist. The novel is narrated by seventeen-year-old Thomas McNulty, an Irish émigré who flees the famine to escape to America where he befriends John Cole. Together they become cross-dressing dancers in a local bar who nightly entertain miners and soldiers starved of female company until they grow too old to pass for girls and join the army to fight in the Indian Wars and later the Civil War. Reviewing the novel in the *New York Review*, Robert Gottlieb asked: 'How did it come about that an Irishman, Sebastian Barry, has written one of the most illuminating and moving recent novels about America—and nineteenth-century America at that?'[25] It is a question answered by Barry's appeal to a shared settler colonial experience, which is foregrounded by the projection of an 'implied author' – the sensibility behind the narrative that accounts for how the text is constructed and on which the reader bases their interpretations – who is the legatee of a heritage of dispossession. He claims to have found in the indigenous erasure a 'rather Irish story' leading to an experiential rather than a geographical bond: 'What is an Irish person, except a culturally appropriated creature?'[26] Both groups are victims of colonial ambition, the Irish paradoxically participating freely in the destruction of the Native Americans. Barry observes by way of explanation that many men 'quite understandably got off the boats in north America very, very, very angry' – the 'quite understandably' combined with the adverbial repetition inviting us to understand rather than judge.[27] Barry continues this strategy intra-textually by writing what Katy Simpson Smith has described in *The New York Times* as 'a Dreamlike Western With a Different Kind of Hero'.[28] It is 'dreamlike' and McNulty is certainly different; an unreliable narrator whose evasions and suppressions undermine his 'confession' (a form that suggests a unifying consciousness) by suggesting that there is no core identity to be excavated. We are guided to a reading strategy through an opening scene in which, as with *All the Pretty Horses*, a corpse is laid out: where for McCarthy this signals the death of the Old West to which his protagonists aspire, for Barry it presents the subsequent narrative as an autopsy of a young man already dead inside. As McNulty says himself early in the novel by way of explanation:

> We were nothing. No one wanted us ... We were only rats of people ... I only say it because without saying I don't think anything can be properly understood. How we were able to see slaughter without flinching. Because we were nothing ourselves, to begin with.[29]

Like Andrews and the Kid, McNulty becomes the ideal spectral recorder of the atrocities he witnesses; the massacre of an Indian village eliciting the ironic observation: 'There didn't seem to be anything alive, including ourselves. We were dislocated, we were not there, now we were ghosts.'[30] As ghostly outsider, he also becomes the naive ventriloquist of imperial, cultural and economic ideologies he hardly understands, whether democratic jingoism ('we were about the people's business'); exculpatory 'othering' (the Apache are 'just about the worst devils you will ever hear about or see'); or the reminders that they were 'doing God's work'.[31] Throughout the text, Barry, like McCarthy before him, is interested in the development and maintenance of a moral conscience amidst the carnage, its delicacy highlighted by McNulty's internal wrangling during the Civil War – 'It is not like running at Indians who are not your kind but it is running at a mirror of yourself. Those Jonny Rebs are Irish, English and the rest.'[32] Shorn of the rhetorical scaffolding of Manifest Destiny that exonerated his killing of Native Americans, McNulty is brought face to face with himself and left confused. In many ways, McNulty's moral growth depends upon seeing himself as more than the construction of political ideologies and hyper-masculine codes, something that Barry effects through the exploration of gender.

What marks Barry's Western out, of course, is the gender fluidity announced by McNulty's cross-dressing. Alex Clark claims that it is anachronistic and panders to recent cultural trends; it may be fashionable, but, as Peter Boag has made clear in his *Re-Dressing America's Frontier Past* (2011), female impersonators performed popular routines in mining and gold-rush towns throughout the Frontier period.[33] Unlike the cross-dressing Calamity Jane, he argues, male cross-dressing is highly disruptive to the ultra-masculine cowboy codes endorsed by Turnerian myth, which is why, like the cross-dressing pictures discovered by Bob Dollar in *The Regional Compendium*, it has remained buried. For Barry, cross-dressing provides a symbolic means of exploring how violence and love can exist in the same person; it also offers a means of breaking out of the continuous cycle of brutal violence endorsed by the 'masculine virtues' of friendship, loyalty and duty. When McNulty puts on a dress he notes: 'I never felt so contented in my life. All miseries and worries fled away. I was a new man now, a new girl. I was freed, like those slaves in the coming war. I was ready for anything.'[34] Oppression is not simply racial, but gendered, and those that escape the oppressiveness of masculine models of behaviour – like the Native American 'berdache' McNulty admires within the novel (men who dress as women to provide spiritual and ceremonial power to their people) – suggest a more spiritually coherent way of living. This is, however, more than simply a 'Gentle Tamers' narrative. Within the novel, 'femininity' is symbolized by Mrs Neale (the wife of the commander of Fort Laramie) whose 'mixture of beauty and religion' is a 'civilising medicine' that 'could make troopers faint with what can only be reckoned love'.[35] She is a Western cliché: she runs a school and has two daughters – a dark haired Hepzibah (or Jackdaw) and the blonde 'Angel' who make explicit the binary roles ascribed to women in Western texts. And yet she herself dresses like a man, which enables her to become the ideal figurehead for a Fort that turns on its head the Turnerian notion of an outpost of civilization. Outside its walls all is violence vindicated by ideology; inside ideology is violated in the name of community: race blurs as Irish, African Americans and Native Americans all mix in a state of constant degradation; gender becomes fluid, as does class as officers gamble with men and sleep with Native American women. It becomes an ideologically disruptive melting pot of American identity, which is later replicated in the Homestead that Thomas and Cole set up with a couple of freed slaves and their adoptive daughter, Winona, an orphan of one of their massacres. It is a situation worthy of *The Little House on the Prairie*, but Barry resists a happy ending by drawing attention to the problematical white-saviour narrative underlying his protagonists' behaviour; a feature made explicit when Winona is given her own voice in the sequel: *A Thousand Moons* (2020).

Thomas and Cole are now greying father-figures; Winona is a smart girl trying to understand the violence both past and present perpetrated against her (she is brutally raped in the novel) and the development of her own sexuality. She also likes to cross-dress (her identity of an Anglo boy conferring more freedom than that of a Native girl) and falls in love with a member of her own sex, thus maintaining the fluidity that characterized the earlier text. Barry is aware that in ventriloquizing the voice of a young Native American girl he is opening himself up to the charge of cultural appropriation, and meets it head on: 'I am Winona … In early times I was Ojinjintka, which means rose. Thomas McNulty tried very hard to say this name, but he failed, and so he gave me my dead cousin's name because it was easier in his mouth. Winona means first-born. I was not first-born.'[36] Barry accepts the irony that the intra-textual appropriation by Thomas is being reinforced by a middle-aged Irishman giving her a voice, but once again he allows his own history of displacement and silencing (in speaking English he is adopting the language of the colonizer) to do the contextual work. For, though his work is historically and geographically diverse, it is united in its attempts to give voice to the poor and oppressed, often through the McNulty family. *The Secret Scripture* (2008) is the record of aged Roseanne McNulty who has been 'disappeared' into an asylum by the church; *A long, Long Way* (2005) records the alienation of a young

Irishman serving on behalf of the British in the trenches and then against the rebels in the Easter Rising; *The Temporary Gentleman* (2014) of the title is Jack McNulty who records a life of drinking, gambling and absent fatherhood from his African home. They are different voices speaking at different times in different places, but they are conjoined in a feeling of anger and resentment at their marginalized suffering. Winona 'McNulty' is simply another voice attempting to ventriloquize her pain through somebody else's language.

Language is central to the novel because it is central to both the construction and therefore the erasure of identity. There are times, such as after the massacre that kills her family or her rape, when Winona falls into silence – partly because she is unable to find the words to describe what has happened (ravish, ruin, disgrace, attack, murder) and partly to consolidate the marginalization that comes through the actions of others – namely men.[37] In this context, McNulty's parenting is presented as a linguistic performance of motherhood, in which, as Winona observes in an arch critique, he insists on comparing her to things '*he* thought were pretty – roses, robins and the like' whilst simultaneously being aware that 'it was mother's talk he was doing'.[38] The linguistic codes that make homelife safe, which comprises two African American ex-slaves (one of whom is also condemned to silence through a savage beating) is contrasted with the linguistic polyphony of the nearby town of Paris in which Germans, Swedes, Irish and English rub shoulders together to the exclusion of both the African and Native Americans.

It is Winona's grasp of English that enables her survival ('it wasn't a crime to beat an Indian, not at all') and also to flourish as a legal secretary. She works on contracts, transcribing the language that made slavery possible (the contracts of sale) and formalized the removal of Native Americans, on the grounds that 'It had proved impossible to civilise us, the documents said' – the term 'civilization' being another part of the linguistic apparatus used by settlers to disenfranchise indigenous peoples.[39] As such, she becomes the means of ushering in a New West of legislation and written contracts which contrasts with the Old West represented by Thomas: 'In that world if there was a misdeed, you felt like there should be something done to balance it immediately. Justice. Even before the white men came I think it was like that.'[40] Justice and the law are in continual tension in this novel maintaining the problematics of morality common to all Barry's work and his deconstruction of the ethics of the Western in particular. We want McNulty to gun down Winona's rapist, but are reminded that such Frontier Justice led to the removal of her parents. What Barry presents, therefore, is an ambiguous West that dissolves the familiar black hat/white hat binaries: a West in which the sheriff's deputy, Frank Parkman, is a racist bigot, but is kind to Winona when he thinks that she is a boy; a West in which the law and order of Judge Briscoe (who is implicated in the regional slavery industry) is mirrored in the Confederate camp by Aurelius Littlefair; a West in which, as Winona's memories of the 'Lakota boys' make clear, being a girl is a solitary and dangerous existence.

Robert Gottlieb's question as to how Sebastian Barry, an Irishman, managed to breathe new life into the Western could be demanded of Scottish musician, John Maclean (*The Beta Band*), who wrote and directed the film *Slow West* (2015). Set in Colorado in 1870, it tells the story of Jay Cavendish (Kodi Smit-McPhee), a 16-year-old Scotsman who travels West in search of his lost love – Rose Ross. Armed only with a 'West, Ho!' handbook and teapot he enters a world of terrorized Native Americans and brutal bounty hunters and is taken under the wing of Irishman, Silas Selleck (Michael Fassbender). Their journey is episodic, their encounters, which are mostly violent, explore the growth of their relationship whilst simultaneously contextualizing it within a particularly bloody history. It is another story of a European innocent journeying into the heart of American darkness, a familiar trope, observes Rowan Righelato, that runs from Wim Wenders's *Alice in the Cities* (1974), Jim Jarmusch's *Down by Law* (1986) and Emir Kusturica's *Arizona Dream* (1993).[41] Philip Ridley's pastiche of Southern gothic – *The Reflecting Skin* (1990) – is of particular interest in this regard. Beneath the big skies, white-washed homesteads and bobbing wheat he reveals a community of sexual depravity and murder mediated through the uncomprehending gaze of eight-year-old Seth Dove (Jeremy Cooper).

Slow West is a meta-Western in constant dialogue with the genre: viewers at Sundance claimed that it filtered familiar tropes through a European sensibility leaving them slightly off centre. The protagonists may ride through a conventional Western landscape (though the fact that it was filmed in New Zealand reminds us of the portability of generic geographical signifiers), but their progress is underscored by a non-diegetic soundtrack of waltzing two step rather than the customary harmonica. The West through which they ride is full of Europeans (Maclean has described it as a 'Europeans in the West' story[42]), but when we meet them they are not engaged in a Turnerian struggle with a hostile environment, but fighting with each other: a Scandinavian couple that looks as though it stepped out of the pages of Cather or Rolvaag is holding up a store whilst the children wait patiently outside; an Irish Priest brings the blessing of God, but he is really a bounty hunter; a German ethnologist who is 'writing an account of the decline of the aboriginal tribes' is a fraud. The major characters themselves seem to have walked out of Westerns: Ben Mendelsohn's bounty hunter, Payne, wears a fur-coat similar to Hugh Millais's character in *McCabe & Mrs. Miller*; Fassbinder's Silas is a taciturn, cigar-chomping Clint Eastwood.[43] Even Cavendish stumbles into the film coated in ash as he walks ghostlike through a decimated Indian village; a walk that Leonardo DiCaprio's Hugh Glass takes in *The Revenant*, which was also released in 2015. This inter-textuality alerts us to MacLean's central thesis: Cavendish's strange gospel of 'love' is not simply alien to the West but to the Western genre as a whole.

Maclean's film is a love story (he claims to love the melodrama of the old Westerns[44]) in which his protagonists' performance of a number of familiar Western trials and rituals (ambush by Native Americans, liquor store hold up, climatic shootout) explores the fragility of the sentiment within the genre. Selleck has no place for it; when they stop to speak to an incongruous group of Congolese drummers singing love songs they do so in French – a language that Selleck literally doesn't understand. For Selleck, the West is about survival and is filled with the bones of those who ignore its dangers. When they come across the literal bones of a buffalo hunt that is blocking their way, their joint attempts to remove the obstacle is conjoined with Cavendish waxing lyrical about Rose's beauty before Selleck bursts out: 'You haven't bedded her yet.' The implication is clear: whether women (the rambling Rose) or the wilderness West symbolized by the buffalo, there is no room for romance in Selleck's vision. It is a message reinforced when they stumble across the skeleton of an axe-wielding settler who has been crushed by the tree he was felling. It is a moment of humour as they joke about the West as crucible for Natural Selection and the fate of those settlers who did not make it. However, it also makes clear that if adapting to this Darwinian West means becoming Selleck – a cowboy who Cavendish characterizes as 'a lonely man, a silent, lonely drifter' – then what chance love?

This is the question that hangs over the climatic Western shoot-out, when Cavendish and Selleck converge on Rose's cabin which is in the process of being besieged by bounty hunters. The cabin itself is a Turnerian outpost of civilization presented in technicolour: the bobbing wheat, like Philip Ridley's, is a little too sun-saturated; the brilliant white interior with its gingham tablecloth (a symbol of domestication from *Shane* to *The Searchers*) is ostentatiously outsized. Inside, there is fluidity in the patchwork family: the family's Native American helper, Kotori, is dressed in Western clothes and tries to drink coffee; Rose dresses in men's clothes and tries to make butter – both unsuccessfully enacting cultural and gender identities that conflict with their genre participation. When the shooting starts, these performances become more confused. Rose, who proves adept with a rifle, accidentally shoots the ghostly Cavendish when he bursts into the scene with his lovelorn message. As he lies dying, Kotori, who has changed into traditional Indian regalia, smears himself in Cavendish's blood, before going to face the enemy. This is how it must be, Rose claims, 'Until civilisation arrives.' When she is later told by Selleck that Cavendish 'loved you with all his heart', she replies coldly that 'His heart was in the wrong place'. His love is out of place with Rose, who treats him like a brother, but also the West in general – a sentiment expressed forcefully by the silent, slow-motion montage of dead bodies that have littered the film. And yet the closing scene does offer hope: Selleck has clearly taken on the lessons espoused by Cavendish and is playing house with Rose. In the last shot of the film he is nailing up a horseshoe whilst his voiceover points to its signification of 'Hope for the West'.

For young men today dreaming of Western adventure it isn't necessary to take the arduous journeys undertaken by Cavendish, Will Andrews and Thomas McNulty; it isn't even necessary to leave their bedrooms. Rockstar Games's *Red Dead Revolver* (2004) and its critically acclaimed successor, *Red Dead Redemption* (2010) offer strikingly old-fashioned narratives in which players are able to roam the high plains on horseback, play poker in seedy saloons, and participate in multiplayer gunfights. The player even takes on a teenage revenge story, when he gets to track down and kill the sheriff responsible for shooting down his father. The franchise markets its product on its realism, which for so long has been the Holy Grail of games' makers (whether evoking ancient Egypt or Renaissance Italy), and ironically reminds us of the West's problematic relationship with notion of reality. There is something Codyish in its detailed naturalism (*The Guardian's* Keza McDonald called it 'the most realistic video game ever made'[45]) whilst your avatar plays out roles true to genre rather than history.

This is not an issue that affects Gearbox Software's *Borderlands* (2009–14), which removes the Wild West to the distant planet of Gehenna. Creative director, Matt Cox, acknowledges the influence of Classic Westerns for both the aesthetic qualities (players are summoned to their task by a haunting whistle taken from *The Good, the Bad and the Ugly*) and the plotting of redemption and death, but in this West the women are in charge.[46] Our guide is 'Butcher Rose', a steampunk/anime Calamity Jane whose cowboy swagger has been transformed into the more sexualized hip-swinging of an adolescent's fantasy of the eroticized female gunslinger. She's an eroticized school-teacher – 'You're good gunslinger, but I only ride with the best' – with a pared-down Western Darwinism: 'That's the way of the world, gunslinger, useful 'til you're not.' It is a glib pastiche of all those aphorisms and homilies delivered by gunfighters – Hondo, Cogburn and Shane – to their adolescent admirers by way of Western acculturation. But where they abjure violence, she is a celebrant. So, 'Where's the All-American cowboy at?' He's locked in his bedroom, riding the virtual High Country and playing out fantasy Western scenarios, before curling up in bed at night and dreaming of 'all the pretty horses'.

Notes

1 'Somebody is always trying to bury the Western', observes Jim Kitses, 'so that the gravestones would now overflow even Tombstone's cemetery', *Postmodernism,* p. 15.
2 Campbell, 'Post-Western Cinema', in Witschi (ed.), *A Companion to the Literature,* 409–24 (p. 409).

3   McCarthy's *Blood Meridian* is personified in the figure of the serial killer, Anton Chigurh (Javier Bardem) – who emerges from the Texas desert and, like Judge Holden, is guided by his own metaphysics of violence. At the film's end Sheriff Ed Tom Bell (Tommy Lee Jones) visits his uncle Ellis, an ex-lawman, to express his dismay at the violence only to be told that the West has always been violent.
4   *Hell or High Water* (2016) transforms Butch Cassidy and the Sundance Kid into the Howard brothers (Chris Pine and Ben Foster), who carry out a series of small town bank robberies to save their family ranch, whilst being pursued by two Texas Rangers (Jeff Bridges and Gil Birmingham). In both, the action veers between high-octane violence and the reflective presence of the law enforcement officers sent to catch them. Their conversations invite the viewer to contextualize events within a history of oppression and brutality.
5   Xan Brooks is one of many reviewers to label *Three Billboards* as a modern-day Western in which the familiar role of the cowboy vigilante (Wayne's Rooster Cogburn) is taken by a swaggering Mildred Haynes (Frances McDormand) determined to avenge the murder of her daughter. See 'Film Review', *The Guardian* (4 September 2017) https://www.theguardian.com/film/2017/sep/04/three-billboards-outside-ebbing-missouri-review-frances-mcdormand-martin-mcdonagh [accessed 20 September 2020].
6   See Kollin, *Captivating Westerns: The Middle East in the American West* (Lincoln and London: University of Nebraska Press, 2015), pp. 4–5.
7   Paula Brown, 'The American Western Mythology of *Breaking Bad*', *Studies in Popular Culture*, 40: 1 (Fall 2017), 78–101 https://www.jstor.org/stable/44779944; Bill Nevins, 'Contemporary Western: An Interview with Vince Gilligan', *IQ* (27 March 2013) https://web.archive.org/web/20130403091323/http://www.localiq.com/index.php?option=com_content&task=view&id=3019&Itemid=56 [accessed 20 September 2020].
8   David Pierson, 'TNTs Made-for-TV Western Films', in Peter Collins and John O'Connor (eds.), *Hollywood's West: The American Frontier in Film, Television, and History* (Lexington, Kentucky: University Press of Kentucky, 2005), 281–99 (p. 284).
9   Denby, 'Guns and Lovers', *The New Yorker* (22 September 2008). https://www.newyorker.com/magazine/2008/09/29/guns-and-lovers-the-current-cinema-david-denby.
10 Bradshaw, '*Open Range* Review', *The Guardian* (19 March 2004) https://www.theguardian.com/film/News_Story/Critic_Review/Guardian_review/0,4267,1172596,00.html [accessed 20 September 2020].
11 Charlotte Higgins, 'New *True Grit* Owes Nothing to John Wayne, Say Directors', *The Guardian* (February 2011) https://www.theguardian.com/film/2011/feb/10/true-grit-john-wayne-irrelevant. [accessed 20 September 2020].
12 L. Rosenthal, review of *True Grit*, *Washington Post* (11 August 1968);
13 Eliot Fremont-Smith, 'Two Cheers for Mattie Ross', review of *True Grit* by Charles Portis, *New York Times* (12 June 1968), p. 45.
14 'The Ballad of Mattie Ross', *Time* 14 (June 1968), p. 94. For an excellent discussion of the novel and film see Michael Cleary, *Saddlesore: Parody and Satire in the Contemporary Western Novel*, unpublished PhD dissertation (Tennessee State University, 1978).

15 Interview with Max Brantley *Arkansas Times* (22 December 2010) https://arktimes.com/arkansas-blog/2010/12/22/why-true-grit-wasnt-filmed-in-arkansas [accessed 20 September 2020]; Tom Shone, 'The Coen Brothers: the cartographers of cinema', *The Guardian* (27 January 2011) https://www.theguardian.com/film/2011/jan/27/coen-brothers-interview-true-grit [accessed 20 September 2020].
16 See Kollin in Neil Campbell, Susan Kollin, Lee Clark Mitchell and Stephen Tatum, '*Blood Simple* to *True Grit:* A Conversation about the Coen Brothers's Cinematic West', *Western American Literature* 48: 3 (Fall 2013), 312–40 (p. 322).
17 Evans, 'True West and Lying Marks', 406–33 (p. 418).
18 Yellow Robe, 'The Menace of the Wild West Show', *Journal of the Society of American Indians* 2 (July-September 1914), repr. in Frederick E. Hoxie (ed.), *Talking Back to Civilisation: Indian Voices from the Progressive Era* (Boston, MA: Bedford\St Martins, 2001) 117–18 (p. 117).
19 James McGregor, *The Wounded Knee Massacre: From Viewpoint of the Sioux* (1940) (Rapid City, South Dakota: Fenske Printing, Inc., 1987), p. 108.
20 For critical review read Francis Paul Prucha, *The American Historical Review* 77: 2 (April 1972), 589–90.
21 Ibid., p. 180.
22 Vanderhaeghe, *The Englishman's Boy* (Toronto: McClelland and Steward, 1996), pp. 226, 223.
23 Ibid., p. 251.
24 Ibid., Evans, 'True West and Lying Marks', p. 416.
25 Gottlieb, 'An Irishman in America', *The New York Review* (5 April 2018) https://www.nybooks.com/articles/2018/04/05/sebastian-barry-irishman-in-america/ [accessed 8 April 2021].
26 Barry interview with Justine Jordan, *The Guardian* (21 October 2016) https://www.theguardian.com/books/2016/oct/21/sebastian-barry-interview-days-without-end [accessed 20 September 2020].
27 Ibid., Jordan Interview.
28 (3 February 2017) https://www.nytimes.com/2017/02/03/books/review/days-without-end-sebastian-barry.html [accessed 20 September 2020].
29 Barry, *Days Without End* (London: Faber and Faber, 2016), pp. 29–30.
30 Ibid., p. 39.
31 Ibid., pp. 39, 44–5, 53, 173.
32 Ibid., p. 189.
33 Clark, *The Guardian* (28 October 2016) https://www.theguardian.com/books/2016/oct/28/days-without-end-by-sebastian-barry-review [accessed 20 September 2020]; Peter Boag, *Re-Dressing America's Frontier Past* (Berkeley: University of California Press, 2011), particular pp. 59–69.
34 Ibid., Barry, *Days Without End*, p. 11.
35 Ibid., p. 108.
36 Barry, *A Thousand Moons* (London: Viking 2020), p. 1.
37 Ibid., p. 72.
38 Ibid., p. 4.
39 Ibid., pp. 3, 21.
40 Ibid., p. 14.

41 Rowan Righelato, 'Existential Cowboys: Slow West isn't the First European Journey into US Darkness', *The Guardian* (26 June 2015); https://www.theguardian.com/film/filmblog/2015/jun/26/slow-west-european-john-maclean-wim-wenders-philip-ridley-jim-jarmusch [accessed 4 January 2021].
42 Maclean interview with Alex Garofalo IBTimes (22 April 2015) https://www.ibtimes.com/slow-west-director-john-maclean-discusses-his-groundbreaking-western-tribeca-film-1892174 [accessed 4 January 2021].
43 See Jonathan Romney, 'Review of *Slow West*', *Film Comment* (13 May 2015) https://www.filmcomment.com/blog/film-of-the-week-slow-west/ [accessed 4 January 2021].
44 Ibid., Maclean interview.
45 Keza MacDonald, 'Get Real! Behind the Scenes of Red Dead Redemption 2 – the Most Realistic Video Game Ever Made', *The Guardian* (24 October 2018) https://www.theguardian.com/games/2018/oct/24/get-real-behind-the-scenes-of-red-dead-redemption-2-the-most-realistic-video-game-ever-made [accessed 20 October 2020].
46 According to PC Games https://www.pcgamesn.com/borderlands-3/bounty-of-blood-release-date [accessed 20 October 2020].

BIBLIOGRAPHY

Abbey, Edward, *Desert Solitaire: A Season in the Wilderness* (1968) (New York: Touchstone, 1990).
Abbey, Edward, 'Even the Bad Guys Wear White Hats: Cowboys, Ranchers and the Ruin of the West', *Harpers* (January 1986), 51–5.
Abele, Elizabeth, 'Westward Proulx: The Resistant Landscapes of *Close Range: Wyoming Stories* and *That Old Ace in the Hole*', in Hunt (ed.), *Geographical Imagination*, 113–25.
Abell, Stephen, 'Woebegone in Wyoming', *Times Literary Supplement* (12 September 2008).
Abrams, David, interview with Thomas McGuane, *The Montana Pioneer* (December 2010) https://montanapioneer.com/an-interview-with-thomas-mcguane/ [accessed 11 September 2019].
Adams, Noah, Radio interview with Thomas McGuane (25 October 1984).
Adams, Ramon, *The Cowboy and his Philosophy* (Austin: Encino, 1967).
Adams, Robert M., 'Cornering the Market', *New York Review of Books* 39: 20 (3 December 1992), 14–16.
Adler, Warren, 'The State of the Cowboy State in the New Millennium', in M. Shay, D. Romtvedt and L. Rounds (eds.) *Deep West*, 263–70.
Ahearn, Kerry, 'Review of Cormac McCarthy's All the Pretty Horses', *Western American Literature* 28 (1993), 183–4.
Alarcon, Daniel Cooper, 'All the Pretty Mexicos', in Lilley (ed.), *Cormac McCarthy: New Directions* (Albuquerque: University of New Mexico Press, 2002), 141–52.
Albert, Lieutenant James William, *Expedition to the Southwest: An 1845 Reconnaissance of Colorado, New Mexico, Texas, and Oklahoma*, edited by John Miller Morris (Lincoln and London: University of Nebraska Press, 1999).
Aldred, Lisa, 'Plastic Shamans and Astroturf Sun Dances: New Age Commercialization of Native American Spirituality', *American Indian Quarterly: Journal of American Indian Studies* 24: 3 (2000), 329.
Alexie, Sherman, *The Absolutely True Diary of a Part-Time Indian* (London: Little Brown, 2007).
Alexie, Sherman, Interview with John Purdy, 'Crossroads: A Conversation with Sherman Alexie', *SAIL* 9: 4(Winter 1997), 1–18 (p. 12) https://facultystaff.richmond.edu/~rnelson/asail/SAIL2/94.html#1. [accessed 7 August 2013].
Alexie, Sherman, *Reservation Blues* (New York: Time Warner, 1996).
Alexie, Sherman, Speech given as 2008 BGHB 'Fiction and Poetry Award Winner: *The Absolutely True Diary Of A Part-Time Indian*', *Horn Book Magazine* (1 January 2009) https://www.hbook.com/?detailStory=absolutely-true-diary-part-

time-indian-author-sherman-alexies-2008-bghb-fiction-award-speech [accessed 20 September 2020].
Allard, William Albert, *Vanishing Breed, Photographs of the Cowboy and the West* (Boston: Little Brown, 1982).
Allen, Albert C., 'Real Wild and Wooly West', *The Louisville Times* (21 March 1960).
Allmendinger, Blake, *Ten Most Wanted: The New Western Literature* (New York and London: Routledge, 1998).
Ansen, David, 'Saddled Up and Rarin' to Go', *Newsweek* 15 (July 1985), 54.
Anon., 'An Interview with Annie Proulx', *Missouri Review* 22: 2 (Spring 1999) https://www.missourireview.com/article/an-interview-with-annie-proulx/ [accessed 4 July 2020].
Arendt, Hannah, 'French Existentialism', *Nation* 162 (February 1946), 226–8.
Arendt, Hannah, 'What is Existentialism?' *Partisan Review* 13 (1946), 34–56.
Armitage, Susan, 'Through Women's Eyes: A New View of the West', in Armitage and Jameson (eds.), *The Women's West*, 9–18.
Armitage, Susan, with Elizabeth Jameson (eds.), *The Women's West* (Norman and London: University of Oklahoma Press, 1987), 9–18.
Arnold, Edwin, Diana C. Luce (eds.), *A Cormac McCarthy Companion: The Border Trilogy* (Jackson: University Press of Mississippi, 2001).
Arnold, Edwin, Diana C. Luce (eds.), 'The Last of the Trilogy: First Thoughts on *Cities of the Plain*', in Edwin Arnold and Dianne Luce (eds.), *Perspectives on Cormac McCarthy* (Jackson: University Press of Mississippi, 1999), 221–47.
Arnold, Edwin, Diana C. Luce (eds.), with Dianne Luce (eds.), *Perspective on Cormac McCarthy* (Jackson: University Press of Mississippi, 1999).
Arosteguy, Katie, '"It Was All a Hard, Fast Ride that Ended in the Mud": Deconstructing the Myth of the Cowboy in Annie Proulx's *Close Range: Wyoming Stories*', *Western American Literature* 45: 2 (Summer 2010), 116–36.
Arthur, Jay, *The Default Country: A Lexical Cartography of Twentieth-Century Australia* (Sydney, Australia: University of New South Wales Press, 2003).
Arthur, Paul, 'How the West was Spun: McCabe and Mrs Miller and Genre Revisionism', *Cineaste* 28: 3 (Summer 2003), 18–20.
Asquith, Mark, *The Lost Frontier: Reading Annie Proulx's 'Wyoming Stories'* (New York, London: Bloomsbury, 2014).
Asquith, Mark, *Reading the Novels of John Williams: A Flaw of Light* (Lanham: Lexington, 2018).
Athearn, Robert, *The Mythic West in Twentieth Century America* (Lawrence: University Press of Kansas, 1986).
Bailey, Charles, 'The Last Stage of the Hero's Evolution: Cormac McCarthy's *Cities of The Plains*', in Bloom (ed.) *Cormac McCarthy: Modern Critical Views* (New York: Chelsea House Publishers: 2009) 131–40.
Barcott, Bruce, 'Off the Rez', *New York Times* (11 November 2007) https://www.nytimes.com/2007/11/11/books/review/Barcott3-t.html?ex=1352350800e60df68bebea3d68&ei=5124&partner=permalink&exprod=permalink= [accessed 20 September 2020].
Barrett, William, 'Talent and the Career of Jean Paul Sartre', *Partisan Review* 13 (1946), 235–244.
Barry, Sebastian, *A Thousand Moons* (London: Viking, 2020).

Barry, Sebastian, *Days Without End* (London: Faber and Faber, 2016).
Barthes, Roland, 'Discourse of History', trans. Peter Wexler, in Michael Lane (ed.), *Structuralism a Reader* (London: Cape 1970), 145–55.
Bass, Rick, *The Sky, the Stars, the Wilderness* (Boston, New York: Mariner, 1998).
Baudrillard, Jean, *America*, trans. Chris Turner (New York and London: Verso, 1988).
Baudrillard, Jean, *Simulations* (New York: Semiotext(e), 1983).
Baym, Nina, 'Old West, New West, Postwest, Real West', *American Literary History* 18: 4 (Winter 2006), 814–28.
Beauvoir, Simone de, *The Second Sex* (1947), trans. C Borde and S. Malovany-Chevallier (London, Jonathan Cape, 2009).
Bedell, Geraldine, 'Roaming in Wyoming', *The Observer* (12 December 2004); http://www.guardian.co.uk/books/2004/dec/12/fiction.features [accessed 20 September 2020].
Bell, Vereen, *The Achievement of Cormac McCarthy* (Baton Rouge: Louisiana State University Press, 1988).
Bevis, William, 'Native American Novels: Homing In', in Swann and Krupat (eds.), *Recovering the World* (Berkeley: University of California Press, 1987).
Birnbaum, Robert, 'Interview with Thomas McGuane', in Torrey (ed.), *Conversations*, 166–79.
Bissell, Tom, 'The Last Lion', *Outside Magazine* (31 August 2011) https://www.outsideonline.com/1893296/last-lion [accessed 23 August 2020].
Blackburn, Virginia, 'How the West was Slaughtered: Review of *Butcher's Crossing*', *The Express* (5 January 2014) http://www.express.co.uk/entertainment/books/452115/How-the-West-was-slaughtered-Butcher-s-Crossing-review [accessed 5 October 2020].
Bland, Archie, 'Review of *Butcher's Crossing*', *The Independent* (6 December 2013) http://www.independent.co.uk/arts-entertainment/books/reviews/butchers-crossing-by-john-williams-book-review-8985628.html [accessed 5 July 2020].
Bloodworth, William, 'Literary Extensions of the Formula Western', *Western American Literature* 14: 4 (Winter 1980), 287–96.
Bloom, Harold (ed.), *Cormac McCarthy: Modern Critical Views* (Philadelphia: Chelsea House Publishers, 2009).
Boag, Peter, *Re-Dressing America's Frontier Past* (Berkeley: University of California Press, 2011).
Bold, Christine, *The Frontier Club: Popular Westerns and Cultural Power, 1880–1924* (Oxford: Oxford University Press, 2013).
Bold, Christine, *Selling the Wild West: Popular Western Fiction, 1860 to 1960* (Bloomington, IN: Indiana University Press, 1987).
Bowles, Samuel, *Our New West: Records of Travel between the Mississippi River and the Pacific Ocean* (Hartford Connecticut: Hartford Publishing, 1869).
Bradshaw, Peter, '*Open Range* Review', *The Guardian* (19 March 2004) https://www.theguardian.com/film/News_Story/Critic_Review/Guardian_review/0,4267,1172596,00.html [accessed 20 September 2020].
Brantley, Max, 'Interview with Coen Brothers', *Arkansas Times* (22 December 2010) https://arktimes.com/arkansas-blog/2010/12/22/why-true-grit-wasnt-filmed-in-arkansas [accessed 20 September 2020].
Bredahl Jr., A Carl, *New Ground: Western American Narrative and the Literary Canon* (Chapel Hill: University of North Carolina Press, 1989).

Brenner, Jack, '*Butcher's Crossing*: The Husks and Shells of Exploitation', *Western American Literature* 7: 4 (February 1973), 243–59.
Brooks, Xan, '*Three Billboards Outside Ebbing, Missouri*, Film Review', *The Guardian* (4 September 2017) https://www.theguardian.com/film/2017/sep/04/three-billboards-outside-ebbing-missouri-review-frances-mcdormand-martin-mcdonagh [accessed 4 September 2020].
Brown, Bill, 'Reading the West: Cultural and Historical Background', in Brown (ed.), *Reading the West: An Anthology of Dime Westerns* (Boston: Bedford Books, 1997), 1–40.
Brown, Dee, *The American West* (1995) (London: Pocket Books, 2004).
Brown, Dee, *Gentle Tamers* (Nebraska: University of Nebraska Press, 1958).
Brown, Paula, 'The American Western Mythology of *Breaking Bad*', *Studies in Popular Culture* 40: 1 (Fall 2017), 78–101 https://www.jstor.org/stable/44779944 [accessed 4 September 2020].
Burford, Bill, *Granta Magazine* (Summer 1983) http://www.granta.com/Archive/8 [accessed 4 September 2020].
Burkhart, Dan, 'Home on the Range', *Atlanta Constitution* 12 (November 1991).
Burns, R. H., A. S. Gillespie, and W. G. Richardson, *Wyoming's Pioneer Ranches* (Laramie: Top-of-the-World-Press, 1955).
Burroughs, John Rolfe, *Where the Old West Stayed Young* (New York: Morrow, 1962).
Busby, Mark, 'Into the Darkening Land, the World to Come: Cormac McCarthy's Border Crossings', in Bloom (ed.), *Cormac McCarthy: Modern Critical Views*, 141–67.
Busby, Mark, *Larry McMurtry and the West: An Ambivalent Relationship* (Texas: University of North Texas Press, 1995).
Busch, Frederick, 'A Desperate Perceptiveness', *The Chicago Tribune* (12 January 1992).
Butenin, Evgeniya M., 'The Intext of "Superfluous Man"', *Procedia: Social and Behavioral Sciences* 200 (2015), 403–7.
Butler, Anne, 'Selling the Popular Myth', in Milner et al. (eds.), *The Oxford History of the American West*, 771–801.
Butler, Anne, with Ona Siporin, *Uncommon Common Women: Ordinary Lives of the West* (Logan, UT: Utah State University Press, 1996).
Butler, Judith, 'Merely Cultural', *New Left Review* 227 (1998), 33–44.
Butruille, Susan, *Women's Voices from the Western Frontier* (Boise: Tamarack Books, 1995).
Campbell, Neil, '*Brokeback Mountain*'s "In-Between" Spaces', *Canadian Review of American Studies* 39: 2 (2009), 205–20.
Campbell, Neil, *The Cultures of the American New West* (Edinburgh: Edinburgh University Press, 2000).
Campbell, Neil, 'Liberty beyond its Proper Bounds: Cormac McCarthy's History of the West in *Blood Meridian*', in Rick Wallach (ed.), *Myth, Legend, Dust: Critical Responses to Cormac McCarthy* (Manchester: Manchester University Press, 2000), 217–26.
Campbell, Neil, 'Post-Western Cinema', in Witschi (ed.), *A Companion to the West*, 409–24.

Campbell, Neil, *The Rhizomatic West: Representing the American West in a Transnational, Global, Media Age* (Lincoln: University of Nebraska: 2008).

Campbell, Neil, in conversation with Susan Kollin, Lee Clark Mitchell and Stephen Tatum, '*Blood Simple* to *True Grit*: A Conversation about the Coen Brothers' Cinematic West', *Western American Literature* 48: 3 (Fall 2013), 312–40.

Carlson, Ron, 'True Grit: Review of Annie Proulx's *Fine Just the Way It Is*', *New York Times* (7 September 2008) http://www.nytimes.com/2008/09/07/books/review/Carlson-t.html?_r=1 [accessed 5 October, 2020].

Cather, Willa, *My Antonia* (1914) (London: Virago Classics, 1983).

Cather, Willa, *O Pioneers!* (1913) (Nebraska: University of Nebraska Press, 1992).

Caveney, Graham, 'Twisters in the Tale; Tall Stories Meet Big Winds and Dark Secrets in Annie Proulx's Texas: Review of *That Old Ace in the Hole*', *The Independent* (4 January 2003) http://business.highbeam.com/6001/article-1P2-1740879/books-twisters-tale-tall-stories-meet-big-winds-and [accessed 29 November, 2016].

Cawelti, John G., *Six Gun Mystique Sequel* (Madison: University of Wisconsin Press, 1999).

Clark, Alex, 'Review of Sebastian Barry's *Days Without End*', *The Guardian* (28 October 2016) https://www.theguardian.com/books/2016/oct/28/days-without-end-by-sebastian-barry-review [accessed 20 September 2020].

Cleary, Michael, *Saddlesore: Parody and Satire in the Contemporary Western Novel*, unpublished PhD dissertation (Tennessee State University, 1978).

Cella, Matthew, *Bad Land Pastoralism in Great Plains Fiction* (Iowa City: University of Iowa Press, 2010).

Chang, Justin, 'Film Review: *Slow West*', *Variety* (15 February 2015); https://variety.com/2015/film/festivals/film-review-slow-west-1201433922/ [accessed 4 January 2021].

Clifton, Robert, *Barbs, Prongs, Points, Prickers, and Stickers: A Complete and Illustrated Catalogue of Antique Barbed Wire* (Norman: University of Oklahoma, 1970).

Collins, Peter and John O'Connor (eds.), *Hollywood's West: The American Frontier in Film, Television, and History* (Lexington, Kentucky: University Press of Kentucky, 2005).

Combs, Richard, 'Broken Trail Super-Westerns: New Whiskey in Old Bottles', *Film Comment* 45: 1 (January/February 2009), 45–7 https://www.jstor.org/stable/43457626 [accessed 20 September 2020].

Comer, Krista, 'Exceptionalism, Other Wests, Critical Regionalism', *American Literary History* 23: 1 (2011), 159–73.

Comer, Krista, *Landscapes of the New West: Gender and Geography in Contemporary Women's Writing* (Chapel Hill and London: The University of North Carolina Press, 1999), 57.

Conrad, JoAnn, 'Consuming Subjects: Making Sense of Post-World War II Westerns', *Narrative Culture* 2: 1 (Spring 2015), 71–116.

Cooper, Brenda and Edward Pease, 'Framing Brokeback Mountain: How the Popular Press Corralled the "Gay Cowboy Movie"', *Critical Studies in Media Communication* 25: 3 (August 2008), 249–73.

Cooper, Lydia, *No More Heroes: Narrative Perspective and Morality in Cormac McCarthy* (Baton Rouge: Louisiana State University Press, 2011).

Cortes, James, 'Bourgeois Myth and Anti-Myth: The Western Hero of the Fifties', *Substance* 5: 15 (1976), 122–32.
Courtwright, David T., *Violent Land: Single Men and Social Disorder from the Frontier to the Inner City* (Cambridge, MA: Harvard University Press, 1996).
Cowley, Jason, 'Pioneer Poet of the American Wilderness', *The Times* (5 June 1997).
Cox, Christopher, Interview with Annie Proulx, *The Paris Review* 188 (Spring 2009) www.theparisreview.org/interviews/5901/the-art-of-fiction-no-199-annie-proulx. [accessed 11 August 2020].
Crews, Michael Lynn, 'Cormac McCarthy's *Blood Meridian* Was Almost a Plain Old Western', *Literary Hub* (16 January 2020) https://lithub.com/cormac-mccarthys-blood-meridian-was-almost-a-plain-old-western/ [accessed 11 August 2020].
Crimmel, Hal, 'The Apple Doesn't Fall far from the Tree: Western American Literature and Environmental Literary Criticism', in Witschi (ed.), *A Companion to the West*, 367–77.
Cronon, William, 'The Trouble with Wilderness, Or Getting Back to the Wrong Kind of Nature', in William Cronon (ed.) *Uncommon Ground: Towards Reinventing Nature* (New York: Norton, 1995), 69–90.
Cronon, William, and George Miles, and Jay Gitlin (eds.), *Under an Open Sky: Rethinking America's Western Past* (New York: Norton, 1992).
Daly, David, and Joel Persky, 'The West and the Western', *Journal of the West* 29: 2 (April 1990), 133–4.
Deburge, Peter, '*Cowboys*' Review: Unconventional Western Challenges Images of Masculinity', *Variety Magazine* (27 August 2020) https://variety.com/2020/film/reviews/cowboys-review-1234751821/?cx_testId=51&cx_testVariant=cx_2&cx_artPos=1#cxrecs_s [accessed 20 September 2020].
Deer, Sarah and Mary Kathryn Nagle, 'The Rapidly Increasing Extraction of Oil, and Native Women, in North Dakota', *The Federal Lawyer* (April 2017), 35–7.
Deloria, Philip, *Indians in Unexpected Places* (Lawrence: University Press of Kansas, 2004).
Deloria, Philip, *Playing Indian* (New Haven: Yale University Press, 1998).
Deloria, Vine Jr., *Custer Died for Your Sins: An Indian Manifesto* (1969) (Norman: University of Oklahoma Press, 1988).
Deloria, Vine Jr., *God is Red: A Native View of Religion* (Golden, CO: Fulcrum Publishing, 1994).
D'Emilio, John, and Estelle Freedman, *Intimate Matters: A History of Sexuality in America* (Chicago: University of Chicago Press, 1988).
DeMott, Robert J. (ed.) *Conversations with Jim Harrison* (Jackson, Mississippi: University Press of Mississippi, 2002).
Denby, David, 'Guns and Lovers', *The New Yorker* (22 September 2008) https://www.newyorker.com/magazine/2008/09/29/guns-and-lovers-the-current-cinema-david-denby [accessed 20 September 2020].
Deverell, William (ed.), *A Companion to the American West* (Oxford: Blackwell Publishing, 2004).
Dickstein, Morris, 'The Inner Lives of Men', *New York Times Book Review* (June 2007); https://www.nytimes.com/2007/06/17/books/review/Dickstein-t.html [accessed 15 January 2020].

Didion, Joan, 'John Wayne: A Love Song', *Slouching Towards Bethlehem: Essays* (New York: FSG Classics, 2008), 29–42.
Dodge, Richard Irving, *The Plains of the Great West and their Inhabitants* (1876) (New York: Archer House, 1959).
Doig, Ivan, *Ride with Me, Mariah Montana* (New York: Atheneum, 1990).
Doig, Ivan, *This House of Sky: Landscapes of a Western Mind* (1978) (San Diego, New York, London: Harcourt Brace and Company, 1992).
Dowling, Tim, '*Westworld* Review', *The Guardian* (5 October 2016) https://www.theguardian.com/tv-and-radio/2016/oct/04/westworld-review-seamless-marriage-cowboys-dystopians [accessed 20 September 2020].
Dudley, John, 'McCarthy's Heroes: Revisiting Masculinity', in Frye (ed.), *Cambridge Companion to Cormac McCarthy*, 175–87.
Dunlap, Thomas R., *Nature and the English Diaspora: Environment and History in the United States, Canada, Australia, and New Zealand* (Cambridge: Cambridge University Press, 1999).
Eaton, Mark, 'Dis (RE)membered Bodies: Cormac McCarthy's Border Fiction', *Modern Fiction Studies* 49: 1 (Spring 2003), 155–80.
Eco, Umberto, *Travels in Hyperreality*, trans. William Weaver (Orlando: Harcourt Brace, 1986).
Edemariam, Aida, 'Home on the Range', *The Guardian* (11 December, 2004) http://www.guardian.co.uk/books/2004/dec/11/featuresreviews.guardianreview13 [accessed 12 September 2020].
Ehrlich, Gretel, *The Solace of Open Spaces* (Harmondsworth: Penguin, 1985).
Ellis, Brett Easton, 'Review of *Butcher's Crossing*', *The Guardian* (31 October 2014) http://www.theguardian.com/books/2014/oct/31/john-williams-butchers-crossing-great-literary-western-stoner [accessed 11 January 2019].
Ellis, Jay, 'The Rape of Rawlins: A Note on *All the Pretty Horses*', *The Cormac McCarthy Journal* 1: 1 (Spring 2001), 66–8; https://www.jstor.org/stable/42909335 [accessed 15 March 2019].
Emerson, Ralph Waldo, 'Idealism' (1849); 'Self-Reliance' (1847). Repr. in Richard Poirier (ed.), *Ralph Waldo Emerson* (Oxford; New York: Oxford University Press, 1990), 22–9; 131–51.
Erkkila, Betsy, '*The Missouri Breaks*', *Cineaste* 8: 1 (Summer 1977), 48, 50.
Estes, Nick, *Our History is the Future: Standing Rock Versus the Dakota Access Pipeline, and the long Tradition of Indigenous Resistance* (London: Verso Press, 2019).
Etulian, Richard, *Re-imagining the Modern American West: A Century of Fiction* (Arizona: University of Arizona Press, 1996).
Etulain, and Michael T. Marsden, eds., *The Popular Western: Essays toward a Definition* (Bowling Green, OH: Bowling Green University Popular Press, 1974).
Evans, David H., 'True West and Lying Marks: *The Englishman's Boy, Blood Meridian* and the Paradox of the Revisionist Western', *Texas Studies in Literature and Language* 55: 4 (Winter 2013), 406–33.
Faragher, John Mack, '*Deadwood*: Not your typical Western', *Montana: The Magazine of Western History* 57: 3 (Autumn 2007), 60–5.
Featherstone, Mike, 'Localism, Globalism and Cultural Identity', in Wilson and Dissanayake (eds.), *Global/Local: Cultural Production and the Transnational Imaginary* (Durham, North Carolina: Duke University Press, 1996), 46–77.

Fenimore, David, '"A Bad Boy Grown Up": The Wild Life behind Zane Grey's Westerns', in Rio et al. (eds.), *Exploring the American Literary West*, 57–68.
Fenimore, David, 'Folk-singing in the West, 1880–1930', in Witschi (ed.), *A Companion to the West*, 316–35.
Fiedler, Leslie, *Love and Death in the American Novel* (New York: Criterion Books, 1960).
Fiedler, Leslie, *The Return of the Vanishing American* (London: Paladin, 1968).
Fisher, Vardis, *Mountain Man* (Caldwell, Idaho: University Press of Idaho, 1965).
Flanagan, Mary, 'Rough and Rednecks', *The Independent* (19 June 1999) https://www.independent.co.uk/arts-entertainment/books-rough-and-redneck-1100964.html [accessed 14 June 2020].
Fleming, Jr., Mike, 'Quentin Tarantino's Hateful Eight', *Deadline Hollywood* (15 March 2015). https://web.archive.org/web/20150315043043/http:/deadline.com/2014/11/quentin-tarantino-retirement-hateful-eight-international-release-1201280583/ [accessed 20 September 2020].
Forbis, William, *The Cowboys* (New York: Time-Life, 1973).
Ford, Richard, *Rock Springs* (1979) (London, New York: Bloomsbury, 2006).
Fox, William, *The Void, the Grid, and the Sign* (Reno: University of Nevada Press, 2000).
Francaviglia, Richard, *Go East Young Man: Imagining the American West as the Orient* (Logan: Utah State University Press, 2011).
Frantz, Milane Duncan, '"My Heroes have Always been Cowboys: The De-romanticising of the Cowboy Mythology in Annie Proulx's *Close Range*', unpublished MA dissertation (University of Houston, 2007).
Fremont-Smith, Eliot, 'Two Cheers for Mattie Ross', review of *True Grit* by Charles Portis, *New York Times* (12 June 1968).
French, Philip, 'Anthony Mann's Western Masterpiece', *The Guardian* (5 April 2015); https://www.theguardian.com/film/2015/apr/05/man-of-west-review-philip-french-classic-dvd-anthony-mann-western-masterpiece [accessed 3 March 2020].
Frye, Steven (ed.), *The Cambridge Companion to Cormac McCarthy* (Cambridge: Cambridge University Press, 2013).
Gallagher, Tag, 'Shoot-Out at the Genre Corral: Problems in the "Evolution" of the Western', in Grant (ed.), *Film Genre Reader II*, 246–60.
Gard, Wayne, *The Great Buffalo Hunt* (1959) (Lincoln, Nebraska: Bison Books, 1971).
Garofalo, Alex, 'Interview with John Maclean about *Slow West*', *IBTimes* (22 April 2015) https://www.ibtimes.com/slow-west-director-john-maclean-discusses-his-groundbreaking-western-tribeca-film-1892174 [accessed 23 October 2020].
Gilroy, John Warren, 'Another Fine Example of the Oral Tradition? Identification and Subversion in Sherman Alexie's Smoke Signals', *Studies in American Indian Literatures (SAIL)* 13: 1 (Spring 2001), 23–39.
Glotferry, Cheryll, and Harold Fromm (eds.), *The Ecocriticism Reader: Landmarks in Literary Ecology* (Athens, Georgia: University of Georgia Press, 1996).
Goad, Jim, *The Redneck Manifesto: How Hillbillies, Hicks, and White Trash became America's Scapegoats* (New York, London: Simon and Schuster, 1997).
Goodman, Audrey, *Translating Southwestern Landscapes: The Making of an Anglo Literary Region* (Tucson: University of Arizona Press, 2002).

Gottlieb, Robert, 'An Irishman in America', *The New York Review* (5 April 2018) https://www.nybooks.com/articles/2018/04/05/sebastian-barry-irishman-in-america/ [accessed 8 April, 2021].

Grant, Barry Keith (ed.), *Film Genre Reader II* (Austin: University of Texas Press, 1995).

Graulich, Melody, and Stephen Tatum (eds.), *Reading the Virginian in the New West* (Lincoln: University of Nebraska Press, 2003).

Gray, Paul, 'Feckless Disregard', *New York Times* (19 May 2002) http://www.nytimes.com/2002/05/19/books/feckless-disregard.html [accessed 8 June, 2020].

Gregory, Sinda and Larry McCaffery, 'An Interview with Thomas McGuane', *Paris Review* 97 (Fall 1985) https://www.theparisreview.org/interviews/2867/the-art-of-fiction-no-89-thomas-mcguane [accessed 25 April 2020].

Grene, Marjorie, *Dreadful Freedom* (Chicago: University of Chicago Press, 1948).

Grey, Zane, *The Border Legion* (New York: Harper Brothers, 1916).

Grey, Zane, *Riders of the Purple Sage* (1912) (Lincoln: University of Nebraska press, 1994).

Grossman, James (ed.), *The Frontier in American Culture: An Exhibition at the Newberry Library – Essays by Richard White and Patricia Nelson Limerick* (California: University of California Press, 1994).

Grundmann, Roy, 'Brokeback Mountain', *Cineaste* 31: 2 (Spring 2006), 50–52 www.jstor.org/stable/41689972 [accessed 14 April 2020].

Guthrie, A., B., *The Big Sky: A Nov*el (1947) (Boston, New York: Houghton Mifflin, 2002).

Hall, Wade, 'The Human Comedy of Cormac McCarthy', in Hall and Wallach (eds.), *Sacred Violence*, 49–60.

Hall, Wade, with Rick Wallach (eds.), *Sacred Violence: A Reader's Companion to Cormac McCarthy* (El Paso: Texas Western Press, 1995).

Handley, William R. (ed.), *The Brokeback Book: From Story of Cultural Phenomenon* (Lincoln and London: University of Nebraska Press, 2011).

Handley, William R. 'The Past and Futures of a Story and a Film', in Handley (ed.), *The Brokeback Book*, 1–23.

Hanner, John, 'Government Response to the Buffalo Hide Trade 1871–1883', *The Journal of law and Economics* 24: 2 (October 1981), 239–71.

Harris, Katherine, 'Homesteading in Northeastern Colorado, 1873–1920: Sex Roles and Women's Experience', in Armitage and Jameson (eds.), *The Women's West*, 165–78.

Harris, W. C., 'Broke(n)back Faggots: Hollywood gives Queers a Hobson's Choice', in Stacy (ed.), *Reading Brokeback*, 118–34.

Hartigan, John, 'Unpopular Culture: The Case of "White Trash"', *Cultural Studies* 11: 2 (1997), 316–44.

Heat-Moon, William Least, *PrairyErth* (A Deep Map) (Boston: Houghton Mifflin, 1991).

Heilman, Robert, Letter to John Williams (31 August 1965), John Williams Papers MC716: Box 30, folder 3.

Heilman, Robert, 'Review of *Butcher's Crossing*', *Partisan Review* (March–April 1961), 286–297.

Heilman, Robert, 'The Western Theme: Exploiters and Explorer', *Partisan Review* (March–April 1962), 286–97.

Hemmingway, Ernest, *The Sun also Rises* (New York: Scribner, 1926).
Henderson, William Haywood, *Native* (New York: Plume, 1993).
Henderson, William Haywood, Website http://www.williamhaywoodhenderson.com/ [accessed 25 September 2020].
Higgins, Charlotte, 'New True Grit Owes Nothing to John Wayne, Say Directors', *The Guardian* (February 2011) https://www.theguardian.com/film/2011/feb/10/true-grit-john-wayne-irrelevant [accessed 20 September 2020].
Hitt, Jack, 'Where the Deer and the Zillionaires Play', *Outside Magazine* (October 1997), 122–234 www.outsideonline.com/outdoor-adventure/Where-the-Deer-and-the-Zillionaires-Play.html?page=all [accessed 4 September 2020].
Hoberman, John, 'How the West was Lost', in Kitses and Rickman (eds.), *The Western Reader* (New York: Limelight, 1999), 85–92.
Holden, Stephen, 'Riding the High Country, Finding and Losing Love', *New York Times* (9 December, 2005) http://movies.nytimes.com/2005/12/09/movies/09brok.html?_r=0 [accessed 27 December 2020].
Holden, Stephen, 'Wry Twist on Classic Frontier Fable.=', *New York Times* (14 May 2015) m/2015/05/15/movies/review-slow-west-a-wry-twist-on-classic-frontier-fables.html [accessed 4 January, 2021].
Holloway, David, *The Late Modernism of Cormac McCarthy* (Westport: Greenwood Press, 2002).
Holthaus, G., Patricia Limerick et al. (eds.), *A Society to Match the Scenery: Personal Visions of the Future of the American West* (Boulder: University of Colorado Press, 1991).
Horowitz, Mark, 'Larry McMurtry's Dream Job', *New York Times on the Web* http://www.nytimes.com/books/97/12/07/home/article2.html [accessed 9 August 2013].
Houy, Deborah, 'Thomas McGuane Speaks: an Interview with the Writer', *Buzzworm* 5: 1 (January–February 1993), 34–5.
Hoxie, Frederick E. (ed.), *Talking Back to Civilisation: Indian Voices from the Progressive Era* (Boston, MA: Bedford \ St Martins, 2001).
Hubbard, Tasha, 'Buffalo Genocide in Nineteenth Century North America: "Kill, Skin, and Sell"', in A Woodford (ed.), *Colonial Genocide in Indigenous North America* (Durham, NC: Duke University Press, 2014).
Hunt, Alex 'The Ecology of Narrative: Annie Proulx's That Old Ace in the Hole as Critical Regionalist Fiction', in Hunt (ed.), *The Geographical Imagination of Annie Proulx: Rethinking Regionalism* (Lanham: Lexington Books, 2009), 183–95.
Hunt, Alex (ed.), *The Geographical Imagination of Annie Proulx: Rethinking Regionalism* (Lanham: Lexington Books, 2009).
Hutchison, Anthony, 'Young America and the Anti-Emersonian Western: John Williams's Butcher's Crossing', *Western American Literature* 55: 3, 237–60.
Ingram, David, 'Thomas McGuane: Nature, Environmentalism, and the American West', *Journal of American Studies* 29 (December 1995), 423–59.
Jackson, John Brinckerhoff, *Discovering the Vernacular Landscape* (New Haven: Yale University Press, 1984).
Jameson, Elizabeth, 'Women as Workers, Women as Civilisers: True Womanhood in the American West', in Armitage and Jameson (eds.), *Women's West*, 145–64.

Jarrell, Robert, 'Revisioning the Western?: Three Cases', *Canon: The Journal of the Rocky Mountains ASA* 2: 2 (1995), 24–51.

Jarrett, Robert, *Cormac McCarthy* (University of Houston: Twayne Publishers, 1997).

Jeffreys, Julie Roy, *Frontier Women* (New York: Hill and Wang, 1979).

Jennings, William Dale, *The Cowboys* (New York: Bantam Books, 1972).

Jensen, Joan, and Darlis Miller, 'The Gentle Tamers Revisited: New Approaches to the History of Women in the American West', *Pacific Historical Review* 40 (May 1980), 173–213.

Jillett, Louise (ed.), *Cormac McCarthy's Borders and Landscapes* (London and New York: Bloomsbury, 2016).

Johnson, Margaret E., 'Proulx and the Postmodern Hyperreal', in Hunt (ed.), *Geographical Imagination*, 25–38.

Johnson, Michael L., *New Westers: The West in Contemporary American Culture* (Lawrence, Kansas: University Press of Kansas, 1996).

Johnson, Susan Lee, 'Film Review *Brokeback Mountain*', *The Journal of American History* 93: 3 (December 2006), 988–90.

Jones, Ginger, 'Proulx's Pastoral as Sacred Space', in Stacy (ed.), *Reading Brokeback Mountain*, 19–28.

Jones, Karen and John Wills, *The American West: Competing Visions* (Edinburgh: Edinburgh University Press, 2009).

Jones, Nate, 'Antoine Fuqua on Remaking the *Magnificent Seven*', *Vulture.com* (22 August 2016) https://www.vulture.com/2016/08/antoine-fuqua-the-magnificent-seven.html [accessed 20 September 2020].

Jordan, Justine, 'Interview with Sebastian Barry', *The Guardian* (21 October 2016) https://www.theguardian.com/books/2016/oct/21/sebastian-barry-interview-days-without-end [accessed 20 September 2020].

Jordan, Teresa, *Cowgirls: Women of the American West* (Lincoln and London: University of Nebraska Press, 1992).

Joyner, Carol, 'Cultural Mythology and Anxieties of Belonging: Reconstructing the "Bi-cultural" Subject in the Fiction of Toni Morrison, Amy Tan and Annie Proulx', unpublished PhD dissertation (University of London: 2002).

June, Christine, Interview with Thomas McGuane, *Bloomsbury Review* 20: 4 (June/August 2000), 13–14. Repr. In Beef Torrey (ed.), *Conversations with Thomas McGuane*.

Kael, Pauline, 'Poses', *The New Yorker* 51 (8 December 1975), 163–5.

Kakutani, Michiko, 'Books of the Times: Haunted Characters', review of *To Skin a Cat* by Thomas McGuane, *New York Times* (11 October 1986).

Kendall, Diana, *Framing Class: Media Representations of Wealth and Poverty in America* (Lanham: Roman and Littlefield, 2005).

Kerouac, Jack, *On the Road* (1957) (Harmondsworth: Penguin Modern Classics, 2000).

King, Meg, '"Where is your Country?": Locating White Masculinity in All the Pretty Horses', *The Cormac McCarthy Journal* 12 (2014), 69–89.

Kingsolver, Barbara, *Animal Dreams* (New York: Harper Collins, 1990).

Kinsey, Alfred, Wardell Pomeroy, Clyde Martin, *Sexual Behaviour in the Human Male* (Philadelphia and London: W. B. Saunders, 1949).

Kitses, Jim, *Horizons West: The Western from John Ford to Clint Eastwood* (1969) (London: Thames and Hudson and British Film Institute, 2007).
Kitses, Jim, and Greg Rickman (eds.), *The Western Reader* (New York: Limelight, 1999).
Kittredge, William, 'The Last Safe Place', *Time* magazine (6 September 1993), 27.
Kittredge, William, *The Next Rodeo: New and Selected Essays* (Saint Paul, Minnesota: Graywolf Press, 2007).
Kittredge, William, *Owning it All: Essays* (Port Townsend, WA: Graywolf Press, 1987).
Kittredge, William, *Who Owns the West?* (San Francisco: Mercury, 1996).
Klein, Amanda, '"The Horse Doesn't Get a Credit": The Foregrounding of Generic Syntax in Deadwood's Opening Credits', in Lavery (ed.), *Reading Deadwood: A Western to Swear By* (New York: I.B. Tauris, 2006), 93–102.
Klett, Mark, *Revealing Territory* (Albuquerque: University of New Mexico Press, 1992).
Klinger, Judson, 'In Pursuit of Crazy Language', *American Film* XIV: 6 (April 1989), 42–4 and 63–4.
Klinkowitz, Jerome, *The New American Novel of Manners: The Fiction of Richard Yates, Dan Wakefield, Thomas McGuane* (Athens: University of Georgia Press), 1986.
Knopf, Amanda, 'Going West in *Breaking Bad*. Ambiguous Morality, Violent Masculinity, and the Antihero's Role in the Evolution of the American Western', *Center of the American West* (May 2015) https://www.centerwest.org/wp-content/uploads/2015/05/going_west_breaking_bad_knopf.pdf [accessed 20 September 2020].
Knopp, Lisa, *Field of Vision* (Iowa City: University of Iowa Publishing, 1996).
Kohlhasse, Bill, 'Not Really Ranching', *Tributary Magazine* (July 2002), 12–13. Repr. Torrey (ed.), *Conversations* 180–5.
Kollin, Susan, *Captivating Westerns: The Middle East in the American West* (Lincoln and London: University of Nebraska Press, 2015).
Kollin, Susan, 'Genre and the Geographies of Violence: Cormac McCarthy and the Contemporary Western', *Contemporary Literature* 42: 3 (Autumn 2001), 557–88.
Kollin, Susan (ed.), *The History of the Western in American Literature* (Cambridge: Cambridge University Press, 2015).
Kolodny, Annette, *The Lay of the Land: Metaphor as Experience and History in American Life and Letters* (Chapel Hill: University of North Carolina Press, 1984).
Kolodny, Annette, 'Letting Go Our Grand Obsessions: Notes Toward a New Literary History of the American Frontiers', *American Literature* 64: 1 (March 1992), 1–18.
Kosofsky Sedgewick, Eve, *Between Men: English Literature and Male Homosocial Desire* (New York: Columbia University Press, 1985).
Kowalewski, Michael, 'Writing in Place: The New American Regionalism', *American Literary History* 6: 1 (Spring 1994), 171–83.
Lambert, Gregg, *The Return of the Baroque in Modern Culture* (London and New York: Bloomsbury, 2004).
Lamont, Victoria, *Westerns: A Woman's History* (Lincoln: University of Nebraska, 2016).

Lanham, Fritz, 'Coming Apart in Montana', *Houston Chronicle* 6 (December 1992).
Larsen, Eric, 'A Literary Quilt of Faded Colors', *Los Angeles Times Book Review* (17 September 1989), 3.
Lavender, David, *The Penguin Book of the American West* (London: Penguin, 1969).
Lavery, David (ed.), *Reading Deadwood: A Western to Swear By* (New York: I.B. Tauris, 2006).
Lawrence, Elizabeth Atwood, *Rodeo: An Anthropologist Looks at The Wild and the Tame Rodeo* (Knoxville: University of Tennessee Press, 1982).
Lawson, Mike, *Spring Creeks* (Mechanicsburg, Pennsylvania: Stackpole Books, 2003).
Lear, Jonathan, *Radical Hope: Ethics in the Face of Cultural Devastation* (Cambridge, MA: Harvard University Press, 2006).
LeGuin, Ursula, 'The Fabric of Grace'. *Washington Post* (2 September 1990).
Lehmann-Haupt, Christopher, '*Close Range*: Lechery and Loneliness out West', *New York Times* (12 May 1999) http://www.nytimes.com/books/99/05/09/daily/051299proulx-book-review.html [accessed 9 October 2020].
Leith, Sam, 'Review of Proulx's *Fine Just the Way It Is*', *The Telegraph* (12 September 2008).
Leonard, John (ed.), *These United States: Original Essays by Leading American Writers on Their State within the Union* (New York: Nation Books, 2003).
Leopold, Aldo, *A Sand County Almanac: With Essays on Conservation from Round River* (New York: Ballantine, 1970).
Lessinger, Jack, *Penturbia: Where Real Estate will Boom After the crash of Suburbia* (Seattle, Washington: SocioEconomics, Inc., 1991).
Lester, Peter, 'Beyond the Amityville Hogwash, Margot Kidder Rejoices in her Child New Husband and Self', *People* (1 September 1979) https://people.com/archive/cover-story-oh-the-horror-vol-12-no-12/ [accessed 9 October 2020].
Lewis, Nathaniel, 'Review of Thomas McGuane's *Nothing but Blue Skies*', *Western merican Literature* 28: 3 (Fall 1993), 283–4.
Lewis, Nathaniel, *Unsettling the Literary West: Authenticity and Authorship* (Lincoln, Nebraska: University of Nebraska Press, 2003).
Lewis, Nathaniel, with William R. Handley (eds.), *True West: Authenticity and the American West* (Lincoln, Nebraska: University of Nebraska Press, 2004).
Lilley, James D. (ed.), *Cormac McCarthy: New Directions* (Albuquerque: University of New Mexico Press, 2002).
Limerick, Patricia Nelson, *The Legacy of Conquest* (New York, London: Norton, 1987).
Limerick, Patricia Nelson, *The Real West* – Catalog of an Exhibition Sponsored by the Colorado Historical Society and Denver Art Museum (Denver: Civic Center Cultural Complex, 1996), 13–22.
Limerick, Patricia Nelson, 'The Shadows of Heaven Itself', in Riebsame (ed.), *Atlas of the New West*, 151–89.
Limerick, Patricia Nelson, with Clyde A. Milner II, and Charles E. Rankin (eds.), *Trails: Towards a New Western History* (Kansas: University Press of Kansas, 1991).
Loffreda, Beth, *Losing Matt Shepard: Life and Politics in the Aftermath of Anti-Gay Murder* (New York: Columbia University Press, 2000).

Luce, Dianne, 'The Vanishing World of Cormac McCarthy's Border Trilogy', in Arnold and Luce (eds.), *A Cormac McCarthy Companion*, 161–97.
Luce, Dianne, 'When You Wake: John Grady Cole's Heroism in *All the Pretty Horses*', in Hall and Wallach (eds.), *Sacred Violence*, 155–67.
Lundquist, Suzanne, *Native American Literatures: An Introduction* (New York, London: Continuum, 2004).
Lynch, Tom, '"Nothing But Land": Women's Narratives, Gardens, and the Settler-Colonial Imaginary in the US West and Australian Outback', *Western American Literature* 48: 4 (Winter 2014), 374–99.
Lynch, Tom, 'Strange Lands', *Interdisciplinary Studies in Literature and Environment* 22: 4 (Autumn 2015), 697–716.
McCarthy, Cormac, *All the Pretty Horses* (1992) (London: Picador, 1993).
McCarthy, Cormac, *Blood Meridian* (1985) (London: Picador, 1990).
McCarthy, Cormac, *Cities of the Plain* (1998) (London: Picador, 1999).
McCarthy, Cormac, *The Crossing* (1994) (London: Picador, 1995).
McClintock, James, '"Unextended Selves" and "Unformed Visions": Roman Catholicism in Thomas McGuane's Novels', *Renascence* 49 (Winter 1997), 139–51.
MacDonald, Keza, 'Get Real! Behind the Scenes of Red Dead Redemption 2 – the Most Realistic Video Game Ever Made', *The Guardian* (24 October 2018) https://www.theguardian.com/games/2018/oct/24/get-real-behind-the-scenes-of-red-dead-redemption-2-the-most-realistic-video-game-ever-made [accessed 20 October 2020].
McGilchrist, Megan Riley, *The Western Landscape in Cormac McCarthy and Wallace Stegner: Myths of the Frontier* (New York and London: Routledge, 2010).
McGregor, James, *The Wounded Knee Massacre: From Viewpoint of the Sioux* (1940) (Rapid City, South Dakota: Fenske Printing, Inc., 1987).
[Novels] McGuane, Thomas, *The Bushwhacked Piano* (1971) (New York: Vintage, 1984).
McGuane, Thomas, *The Cadence of Grass* (2002) (Vintage, 2003).
McGuane, Thomas, *Crow Fair* (Vintage, 2016).
McGuane, Thomas, *Gallatin Canyon* (London: Harvill Secker, 2006).
McGuane, Thomas, *Keep the Change* (1989) (Vintage Contemporaries, 1994).
McGuane, Thomas, *Ninety-Two in the Sade* (1973) (Vintage Contemporaries, 1995).
McGuane, Thomas, *Nobody's Angel* (1982) (Vintage Contemporaries, 1994).
McGuane, Thomas, *Nothing but Blue Skies* (1992) (Vintage Contemporaries, 1994).
McGuane, Thomas, *Something to be Desired* (1984) (Vintage Contemporaries, 1994).
McGuane, Thomas, *To Skin a Cat* (1986) (Vintage Contemporaries, 1994).
[Essays] McGuane, Thomas, *An Outside Chance: Essays on Sport* (1980) (Harmondsworth: Penguin, 1986).
McGuane, Thomas, *The Longest Silence: A Life in Fishing* (1999) (London: Yellow New Jersey Press, 2001).
McGuane, Thomas, *Some Horses* (1999) (Vintage, 2000).

[Articles/Stories] McGuane, Thomas, 'An Optimist vis-à-vis the Present', *New York Times* (15 February 1970) https://www.nytimes.com/1970/02/15/archives/an-optimist-visavis-the-present-trout-fishing-in-america-the-pill.html [accessed 23 August 2020].

McGuane, Thomas, 'The Bonefish in the Other Room', *Esquire Magazine* (February 1992) https://classic.esquire.com/article/1992/2/1/the-bonefish-in-the-other-room [accessed 23 August 2020].

McGuane, Thomas, 'Father, Son, And Holy Permit', *Esquire Magazine* (March 1993) https://classic.esquire.com/article/1993/3/1/father-son-and-holy-permit [accessed 23 August 2020].

McGuane, Thomas, Foreword to the *Vanishing Breed, Photographs of the Cowboy and the West*, edited by William Albert Allard (Boston: Little Brown, 1982).

McGuane, Thomas, 'Some Notes on Montana', *Agricultural Digest* (June 1992), 45.

McGuane, Thomas, 'The Spell of Wild Rivers', *Audubon* (November-December 1993).

Mackell, Jan, 'Soiled Doves: An Overview of Good Girls Gone Bad in the American West', *True West* (30 September 2013) https://truewestmagazine.com/soiled-doves-good-girls-gone-bad/ [accessed 2 March 2020].

McMurtry, Larry, with Diane Ossana, screenplay to *Brokeback Mountain* and exploratory essay, 'Adapting Brokeback Mountain', in *Brokeback Mountain: Story to Screenplay* (New York, London: Scribner, 2005).

McMurtry, Larry, with Diane Ossana, 'Brokeback's Big Secrets', Interview with Anne Stockwell, *Advocate* (28 February 2006), 42–4.

McMurtry, Larry, *In a Narrow Grave: Essays on Texas* (New York: Simon and Schuster, 1968).

McMurtry, Larry, In Interview with Mervyn Rothstein, 'A Legend who Likes to Deflate The Legends of the Golden West', *New York Times* (1 November 1988) https://www.nytimes.com/1988/11/01/books/a-texan-who-likes-to-deflate-the-legends-of-the-golden-west.html [accessed 2 March 2020]

McMurtry, Larry, *Lonesome Dove* (1985) (New York City: Pocket Books, 1986).

McMurtry, Larry, *Sacagawea's Nickname: Essays on the American West* (New York: New York Review Collections, 2001).

McMurtry, Larry, 'The Southwest as the Cradle of the Novelist', in Walts (ed.), *The American Southwest*.

McMurtry, Larry, 'The Texas Moon and Elsewhere', *Atlantic* 235: 3 (March 1975), 29–36.

Maclean, John, Interview with Alex Garofalo *IBTimes* (22 April 2015) https://www.ibtimes.com/slow-west-director-john-maclean-discusses-his-groundbreaking-western-tribeca-film-1892174 [accessed 4 January 2021].

McPhee, John, *Rising from the Plains* (New York: Farrar, Srauss, Giroux, 1986).

Magagna, Anthony Rudolph, *Placing the West: Landscape, Literature, and Identity in the American West*, unpublished PhD dissertation (University of California, 2008).

Maher, Daniel, *Mythic Frontiers: Remembering, Forgetting, and Profiting with Cultural Heritage Tourism* (Gainesville: University Press of Florida, 2016).

Mahoney, Timothy R. and Wendy J. Katz (eds.), *Regionalism and the Humanities* (Nebraska: University of Nebraska Press, 2008).

Manfred, Frederick, *Lord Grizzly* (1954) (University of Nebraska: Bison Books, 1993).
Martin, Russell, 'Writers of the Purple Sage', *New York Times* (25 December 1981).
Matsumoto, Valerie J., and Blake Allmendinger, *Over the Edge: Remapping the American West* (Berkeley, London: Universtiy of California Press, 1998).
Marx, Leo, *Machine in the Garden* (New York: Oxford University Press, 1964).
Masinton, Charles, '*Nobody's Angel*: Thomas McGuane's Vision of the Contemporary West', *New Mexico Humanities Review* 6 (Fall 1983), 49–55.
Massie, Allan, 'Review of A Thousand Moons', *The Scotsman* (25 March 2020) https://www.scotsman.com/arts-and-culture/books/book-review-thousand-moons-sebastian-barry-2518388 [accessed 20 September 2020].
Mayersberg, Paul, *Hollywood, The Haunted House* (Allen Lane: Penguin, 1967).
Michener, Charlie, 'Interview with Arthur Penn', *Film Comment* 12: 4 (July-August 1976), 40–3.
Midkiff, Ken, *The Eat you Eat: How Corporate Farming has Endangered America's food supply* (New York: St Martins Griffin, 2004).
Miles, George, 'The Gentle Tamers Revisited: New Approaches to the History of Women in the American West', *Pacific Historical Review* 40 (May 1980), 173–213.
Miles, George, 'To Hear an Old Voice: Rediscovering Native Americans in American History', in Cronon et al. (eds.), *Under an Open Sky*, 52–70.
Milner, Clyde A., Carol A. O'Connor, Martha A. Sandweiss, *The Oxford History of the American West* (Oxford: Oxford University Press, 1994).
Milton, John, 'Butcher's Crossing Tells How 4 Men Face Nature', *Minneapolis Sunday Tribune* (3 March 1960).
Mitchell, Lee Clark, Introduction to Zane Grey's *Riders of the Purple Sage* (1912) (Oxford: Oxford University Press, 1995).
Mitchell, Lee Clark, *Westerns: Making the Man in Fiction and Film* (Chicago: University of Chicago Press, 1996).
Mitchell, W. J. T., *Landscape and Power* (Chicago: University of Chicago Press, 1994).
Monfourny, Renaud, 'Go West: Interview with Thomas McGuane' (1990), in Torrey (ed.), *Conversations*, 134–42.
Montague, Kate, 'Between Myth and Actuality on the American Frontier', in Jillett (ed.), *Cormac McCarthy's Borders and Landscapes*, 95–105.
Moore, David, 'The Return of the Buffalo: Cultural Representation and Cultural Property', in Gretchen Bataile (ed.), *Native American Representations: First Encounters, Distorted Images, and Literary Appropriations* (Lincoln: University of Nebraska Press, 2001), 52–79.
Moore, John Noel, 'The Landscape of Fiction', *English Journal* 90: 1 (September 2000), 146–8.
Moore Morrison, Gail, 'All the Pretty Horses: John Grady's Expulsion from Paradise', in Edwin Arnold and Dianne Luce (eds.), *Perspectives on Cormac McCarthy* (Jackson: University of Mississippi, 1993), 173–93.
Moos, Dan, 'Lacking the Article Itself: Representation and History in Cormac McCarthy's *Blood Meridian*', *The Cormac McCarthy Journal* 2: 1 (Spring 2002): 23–39 http://www.jstor.org/stable/42909344 [accessed 15 January 2020].

Morris, Gregory L., 'How Ambivalence Won the West: Thomas McGuane and the Fiction of the New West', *Critique*, 22: 3 (Spring 1991), 180–9.

Morris, Gregory L., *Talking up a Storm: Voices of the New West* (Lincoln: University of Nebraska Press, 1995).

Mottram, Eric, *Blood on the Nash Ambassador: Investigations in American Culture* (London: Hutchinson Radius, 1993).

Moynahan, Jan, *Ladies of Negotiable Virtue: an account of Pioneer prostitutes* (Spokane, Wash: Chickadee Pub., 2010).

Mundik, Petra, 'Terra Damnata: The Anticosmic Mysticism of *Blood Meridian*', in Jillett (ed.), *Cormac McCarthy's Borders and Landscapes*, 29–43.

Mullen, Elizabeth, '"Not Much of a Rind on You": (De)Constructing Genre and Gender in *Westworld*', TV Series 14 (2018) https://journals.openedition.org/tvseries/3304 [accessed 20 September 2020].

Murdoch, David Hamilton, *The American West: The Invention of a Myth* (Cardiff, UK: Welsh Academic Press, 2001).

Myres, Sandra L., *Westering Women and the Frontier Experience, 1800–1915* (Albuquerque: University of New Mexico Press, 1982).

Nash, Gerald D., and Richard Etulain (eds.), *The Twentieth Century West: Historical Interpretations* (Albuquerque: University of New Mexico Press, 1989).

Nash, Henry Smith, *Virgin Land: The American West as Symbol and Myth* (Cambridge, MA: Harvard University Press, 1950).

Needham, Gary, *Brokeback Mountain* (Edinburgh: Edinburgh University Press, 2010).

Nelson, Andrew Patrick, 'Hollywood Westerns 1930s to the Present', in Kollin (ed.), *The History of the Western in American Literature*, 331–44.

Nelson, Andrew Patrick, 'Larry McMurtry', in Taylor (ed.), *A Literary History of the American West*, 612–19.

Nevins, Bill, 'Contemporary Western: An Interview with Vince Gilligan', *IQ* (27 March 2013) https://web.archive.org/web/20130403091323/http://www.localiq.com/index.php?option=com_content&task=view&id=3019&Itemid=56 [accessed 20 September 2020].

Nicholas, Liza, *Becoming West: Stories of Culture and Identity in the Cowboy State* (Lincoln: University of Nebraska Press, 2006).

Nicholas, Liza, with Elaine Bapis, and Thomas Harvey (eds.), *Imagining the Big Open: Nature, Identity, and Play in the New West* (Salt Lake City, Utah: University of Utah Press, 2003).

Oakes, Philip, 'Review of *Butcher's Crossing*', *The Observer* (10 July 1960).

Oates, Joyce Carol, 'In Rough Country', *The New York Review of Books* (23 October 2008) http://www.nybooks.com/articles/archives/2008/oct/23/in-rough-country/?pagination=false [accessed 3 January 2020].

Ossana, Diana, 'Climbing Brokeback Mountain', in McMurtry and Ossana (eds.), *Brokeback Mountain: Story to Screenplay*, 143–51.

Owens, Barclay, *Cormac McCarthy's Western Novels* (Tuscon: The University of Arizona Press, 2000).

Owens, Louis, *Mixed Blood Messages* (Norman: University of Oklahoma Press, 1998).

Owens, Louis, *Other Destinies: Understanding the American Indian Novel* (Norman: University of Oklahoma Press, 1992), 4.
Pace, Robert (ed.), *Buffalo Days: Stories from J. Wright Mooar As told to James Winford Hunt* (Abilene, Texas: State House Press, 2005).
Packard, Chris, *Queer Cowboys and Other Erotic Male Friendships in Nineteenth-Century American Literature* (Basingstoke: Palgrave Macmillan, 2006).
Patterson, Eric, *On Brokeback Mountain: Meditations about Masculinity, Fear, and Love in the Story and the Film* (Lanham, MD; Plymouth, UK: Lexington Books, 2008).
Peavy, Linda, and Ursula Smith, *Pioneer Women: The Lives of Women on the Frontier* (Norman: University of Oklahoma Press, 1998).
Peebles, Stacey, 'Yuman Belief Systems and Cormac McCarthy's Blood Meridian', *Texas Studies in Literature and Language* 45: 2 (2003), 231–44.
Peterson, Levi S, 'The Rocky Mountains', in *A Literary History of the American West* (1987) (Fort Worth: Texas Christian University Press, 1987).
Pitts, Jonathan, '*Blood Meridian* as Revisionary Western', *Western American Literature* 33: 1 (Spring 1998), 6–25 https://www.jstor.org/stable/43021783 [accessed 15 January 2020].
Plotz, John, '*Butcher's Crossing*: An Appreciation of John Williams's Perfect Anti-western', *The Guardian* (3 August 2016) https://www.theguardian.com/books/2016/aug/03/butchers-crossing-an [accessed 6 May, 2017].
Penn Warren, Robert, *All the King's Men* (Harcourt: Brace and Company, 1946).
Phillips, Billie, 'McMurtry's Women: "Eros [Libido, Caritas, and Philia] in [and out of] Archer County"', in Clay Reynolds (ed.), *Taking Stock*, 86–93.
Phillips, Dana, 'History and the Ugly Facts of Cormac McCarthy's *Blood Meridian*', *American Literature* 68: 2 (1996), 433–60.
Pierson, David, 'TNTs Made-for-TV Western Films', in Peter Collins, and John O'Connor (eds.), *Hollywood's West: The American Frontier in Film, Television, and History* (Lexington, Kentucky: University Press of Kentucky, 2005), 281–99.
Pippin, Robert, *Hollywood Westerns and American Myth: The Importance of Howard Hawks and John Ford for Political Philosophy* (New Haven: Yale University Press, 2011).
Popper, Deborah Epstein, and Frank J. Popper, 'The Great Plains: From Dust to Dust', *Planning Magazine* (December 1987) http://www.lacusveris.com/The%20Hi-Line%20and%20the%20Yellowstone%20Trail/The%20Buffalo%20Commons/From%20Dust%20to%20Dust.shtml [accessed 14 August 2020].
Porter, Joy, 'Historical and Cultural Contexts to Native American Literature', in Porter and Roemer (eds.), *The Cambridge Companion to Native American Literature* (Cambridge: Cambridge University Press, 2005).
Potter, David, 'American Women and American Character', in Barbara Welter (ed.), *The Woman Question in American History* (Hinsdale, Illinois: The Dryden Press, 1973), 117–32.
Prendergast, Alan, 'Sixteen Years after his Death, Not-so-famous Novelist John Williams is Finding his Audience', *Westword* (3 November 2010); 2010http://www.westword.com/news/sixteen-years-after-his-death-not-so-famous-novelist-john-williams-is-finding-his-audience-5110462 [accessed 4 September 2020].
Prescott, Cynthia Culver, *Gender and Generation on the Far Western Frontier* (Tuscon: University of Arizona Press, 2007).

Prescott, Orville, 'Books of The Times', *New York Times* (13 October 1954).
Preston, Alex, 'Review of *A Thousand Moons* by Sebastian Barry', *The Observer* (23 March 2020) https://www.theguardian.com/books/2020/mar/23/a-thousand-moons-sebastian-barry-review [accessed 20 September 2020].
[Novels, Stories, Autobiographical Writing, Historical Writing] Proulx, Annie, *Bad Dirt: Wyoming Stories* (2004) (London, New York: Harper Perennial, 2005).
Proulx, Annie, *Bird Cloud: A Memoir* (London: Fourth Estate, 2011).
Proulx, Annie, *Close Range: Wyoming Stories* (1999) (London, New York: Harper Perennial, 2006).
Proulx, Annie, *Fine Just the Way it Is: Wyoming Stories* (London: Fourth Estate, 2008).
Proulx, Annie, *Postcards* (1992) (London, New York: Harper Perennial, 2006).
Proulx, Annie, *Red Desert: History of a Place* (ed.) (Texas: University of Texas Press, 2009).
Proulx, Annie, *That Old Ace in the Hole* (2002) (London, New York: Harper Perennial, 2004).
[Articles] Proulx, Annie, 'After the Gold Rush', *Guardian* (23 November 2005) http://www.guardian.co.uk/world/2005/nov/23/usa [accessed 4 August 2020].
Proulx, Annie, 'Dangerous Ground', in Mahoney and Katz (eds.), *Regionalism and the Humanities* (Nebraska: University of Nebraska Press, 2008), 6–25.
Proulx, Annie, 'Forts Halleck and Fred Steele', in Proulx (ed.) *Red Desert*, 283–92.
Proulx, Annie, 'Getting Movied', in McMurtry/Ossana *Brokeback Mountain: Story to Screenplay*, 129–38.
Proulx, Annie, 'How the West Was Spun', *The Guardian* (25 June 2005), 4–6 http://www.guardian.co.uk/books/2005/jun/25/featuresreviews.guardianreview24 [accessed 3 August 2020].
Proulx, Annie, 'Urban Bumpkins', *The Washington Post* (25 September 1994) http://www.highbeam.com/doc/1P2-911232.html [accessed 29 November 2013].
Proulx, Annie, 'Wyoming: The Cowboy State', in John Leonard (ed.), *These United States*, 495–509.
[Introductions and Afterwords] Proulx, Annie, Afterword to Thomas Savage, *The Power of the Dog* (1967) (Boston: Little Brown, 2011).
Proulx, Annie, Introduction to *Fields of Vision: The photographs of Carl Mydans* (The Library of Congress in association with D. Gilles, London, 2011), viii–xiii.
Proulx, Annie, Introduction to 'Reliquary', in *Treadwell: Photographs by Andrea Modica* (San Francisco: Chronicle Books, 1996), 9–12.
Pughe, Thomas, 'Revision and Vision: Cormac McCarthy's *Blood Meridian*', *Revue Française d'études Américaines*, 62 (Novembre 1994), 371–82; https://www.jstor.org/stable/20872451 [accessed 15 January 2020].
Purdy, John, 'Crossroads: A Conversation with Sherman Alexie', *Studies in American Indian Literatures* 9: 4 (Winter 1997), 1–18 https://www.jstor.org/stable/20739421?seq=1 [accessed 7 August 2020].
Raigadas, David Rio, and Amalia Ibarraran Bigalondo, and José Miguel Santamaria et al. (eds.), *Exploring the American Literary West: International Perspectives* (Universidad del Paris Vasco: 2006).
Rebein, Robert, *Return of the Native: The place of American fiction after Postmodernism*, unpublished PhD dissertation (University of New York, 1995), p. 87.

Reed, Kaitlin, 'We are Part of the Land and the Land is Us', *Humboldt Journal of Social Relations* 42 (2020) 27–49.

Reynolds, Clay (ed.), *Taking Stock: A Larry McMurtry Casebook* (Dallas: Southern Methodist University Press, 1989).

Riebsame, William, James Robb (eds.), *Atlas of the New West: Portrait of a Changing Region* (New York: Norton Publishing, 1997).

Righelato, Rowan, 'Existential Cowboys: Slow West isn't the First European Journey into US darkness' (*The Guardian* 26 June 2015) https://www.theguardian.com/film/filmblog/2015/jun/26/slow-west-european-john-maclean-wim-wenders-philip-ridley-jim-jarmusch [accessed 4 January 2021].

Riley, Patricia, 'The Mixed Blood Writer as Interpreter and Mythmaker', in Joseph Trimmer and Tilly Warnock (eds.), *Understanding Others: Cultural and Cross-Cultural Studies and the Teaching of Literature* (Urbana, IL: National Council of English, 1992).

Risker, Paul, 'Interview with Anne Kerrigan', *PopMatters* (31 July 2020) https://www.popmatters.com/anna-kerrigan-interview-2646805753.html [accessed 20 September 2020].

Robbins, Jim, *Last Refuge: The Environmental Showdown in Yellowstone and the American West* (New York: Morrow and Co., 1993).

Robe, Yellow, 'The Menace of the Wild West Show', *Journal of the Society of American Indians* 2 (July–September 1914), repr. in Frederick E. Hoxie (ed) *Talking Back to Civilisation: Indian Voices from the Progressive Era* (Boston MA: Bedford\St Martins, 2001) 117–18.

Robinson, Forrest, *Having it both Ways: Self-Subversion in Western Popular Classics* (Albuquerque: University of New Mexico, 1993).

Robinson, Forrest (ed.), *The New Western History: The Territory Ahead* (Tuscon: University of Arizona Press, 1998).

Robinson, Forrest, 'The Virginian and Molly in Paradise: How Sweet is it?' *Western American Literature* 21 (1986), 27–38.

Robinson, Sally, *Marked Men: White Masculinity in Crisis* (New York: Columbia University Press, 2000).

Romney, Jonathan, 'Review of *Slow West*', *Film Comment* (13 May 2015) https://www.filmcomment.com/blog/film-of-the-week-slow-west/ [accessed 4 January 2021].

Rood, Karen, *Understanding Annie Proulx* (Columbia, South Carolina: University of South Carolina Press, 2001).

Roosevelt, Theodore, *Ranch Life and the Hunting-Trail* (New York: Century Co., 1899).

Rosenthal, L., 'Review of *True Grit* by Charles Portis', *Washington Post* (11 August 1968).

Rothstein, Mervyn, 'A Legend who likes to Deflate The Legends of the Golden West', *New York Times* (1 November 1988) https://www.nytimes.com/1988/11/01/books/a-texan-who-likes-to-deflate-the-legends-of-the-golden-west.html [accessed 2 March 2020].

Russell, Sharman Apt, *Kill the Cowboy: A Battle of Mythology in the New West* (Lincoln: University of Nebraska Press, 2001).

Russo, Richard, 'McGuane's Montana', *Chicago Tribune* (17 September 1989) https://www.chicagotribune.com/news/ct-xpm-1989-09-17-8901130662-story.html [accessed 14 May 2020].

Russo, Vito, *The Celluloid Closet: Homosexuality in the Movies* (New York: Harper and Row, 1985).

Samuels, Peggy and Harold, *Frederic Remington: A Biography* (New York: Doubleday, 1982).

Sandoz, Mari, *The Buffalo Hunters: The Story of the Hide Men* (1954) (Lincoln, London: University of Nebraska Press, 1978).

Sartre, Jean Paul, *Being and Nothingness* (1943), trans. Hazel Barnes (London: Routledge, 2003).

Savage, Thomas, *The Power of Dog* (1967) (Boston: Little Brown, 2011).

Savage Jr., William, *The Cowboy Hero: His Image in American History and Culture* (Norman and London: University of Oklahoma Press, 1979).

Scharnhorst, Gary, '"All Hat and No Cattle": Romance, Realism, and Late Nineteenth Century Western American Fiction', in Witschi (ed.), *A Companion to the West*, 281–296.

Schlissel, Lilian, *Women's Diaries of the Westward Journey* (1984) (New York: Schoken Books, 2004).

Schumock, Jim, 'Interview with Thomas McGuane' (1999),in Torrey (ed.), *Conversations*, 147–56.

Schweitzer, Daniel, '"Reality's Never been of Much use out," Where? Annie Proulx's *Wyoming Stories* and the Problems of Neoregionalism', unpublished MA dissertation (University of South Dakota: 2011).

Shaffer, Marguerite S., 'Western Tourism', in Deverell (ed.), *Companion to American West*, 373–89.

Shannon, Noah Gallagher, 'Cormac McCarthy Cuts to the Bone *Blood Meridian*', *Slate* (October 2012) https://slate.com/culture/2012/10/cormac-mccarthys-blood-meridian-early-drafts-and-history.html [accessed 16 January 2020].

Shay, Michael, and David Romtvedt, and Linn Rounds (eds.), *Deep West: A Literary Tour of Wyoming* (Wyoming: Pronghorn Press, 2003).

Shaviro, Steven, 'The Very Life of Darkness: A Reading of *Blood Meridian*', in Arnold and Luce (eds.), *Perspective on Cormac McCarthy*, 145–58.

Shields, Charles J., *The Man Who Wrote the Perfect Novel: John Williams, Stoner, and the Writing Life* (Austin: University of Texas Press, 2018).

Shone, Tom, 'The Coen Brothers: The Cartographers of Cinema', *The Guardian* (27 January 2011); https://www.theguardian.com/film/2011/jan/27/coen-brothers-interview-true-grit [accessed 20 September 2020].

Showalter, Elaine, *A Jury of her Peers: American Women Writers from Anne Bradstreet to Annie Proulx* (New York: Alfred A. Knopf, 2009).

Shugart, Helene, 'Consuming Passions: "Educating Desire" in *Brokeback Mountain*', *Critical Studies in Media Communication* 28: 3 (24 May 2011), 173–92.

Simmon, Scott, *The Invention of the Western Film A Cultural History of the Genre's First Half Century* (Cambridge: Cambridge University Press, 2003).

Simpson, Elizabeth, *Earthlight, Wordfire: The Work of Ivan Doig* (Moscow, Idaho: University of Idaho Press, 1992).

Simpson Smith, Katy, 'Review of Sebastian Barry's *Days Without End*', New York Times (3 February 2017) https://www.nytimes.com/2017/02/03/books/review/days-without-end-sebastian-barry.html [accessed 20 September 2020].

Singer, Mark, 'The Misfit', *The New Yorker* (7 February 2005) https://www.newyorker.com/magazine/2005/02/14/the-misfit-2#editorsnote [accessed 20 September 2020].

Skow, John, 'On Strange Ground', *Time* magazine (17 May 1999) http://content.time.com/time/magazine/article/0,9171,990992,00.html [accessed 29 November 2019].

Slotkin, Richard, *The Fatal Environment: The Myth of the Frontier in the Age of Industrialization, 1800–1890* (New York: Atheneum, 1985).

Slotkin, Richard, *Gunfighter Nation: The Myth of the Frontier in Twentieth Century America* (New York: Harper, 1992).

Slotkin, Richard, *Regeneration through Violence: The Mythology of the American Frontier, 1600–1860* (Norman: University of Oklahoma Press, 1973).

Smith, Carlton, *Coyote Kills John Wayne: Postmodernism and Cotemporary Fictions of the Transcultural Frontier* (Hanover and London: Dartmouth College, 2000).

Smith, Henry Nash, *Virgin Land: The American West as Symbol and Myth* (Cambridge: Harvard University Press, 1950).

Smith, Page, *Daughters of the Promised Land: Women in American History* (Boston: Little Brown, 1970).

Smits, David D., 'The Frontier Army and the Destruction of the Buffalo: 1865–1883', *Western Historical Quarterly*, 25: 3 (Autumn 1994), 312–38.

Snyder, Gary, *The Practice of the Wild: Essays by Gary Snyder* (San Francisco: North Point Press, 1990).

Snyder, Phillip, 'Cowboy Codes in Cormac McCarthy's Border Trilogy', in Arnold and Luce (eds.), *A Cormac McCarthy Companion*, 198–227.

Solomon, Jason, 'Interview with Coen Brothers', *Guardian Podcast* (February 2011) https://www.theguardian.com/film/audio/2011/feb/10/film-weekly-podcast-true-grit-coen [accessed 20 September 2020].

Spurgeon, Sara, *All the Pretty Horses, No country for Old Men, The Road* (London: Continuum, 2011).

Spurgeon, Sara, *Exploding the Western: Myths of Empire on the Postmodern Frontier* (Texas: Texas A&M University Press, 2005).

Spurgeon, Sara, 'Pledged in Blood: Truth and Redemption in Cormac McCarthy's All the Pretty Horses', *Western American Literature* 34: 1 (Spring 1999), 25–44.

Spong, John, 'True West', *Texas Monthly* (January 2013).

Stacy, Jim (ed.), 'Buried in the Family Plot: The Cost of Pattern Maintenance to Jack and Ennis', inStacy (ed.), *Reading Brokeback*, 29–44.

Stacy, Jim, *Reading Brokeback Mountain: Essays on the Story and the Film* (Jefferson, North Carolina, and London: McFarland and Company, 2007).

Stamper, Rex, 'John Williams: An Introduction to the Major Novels', *The Mississippi Review* III: 1 (1974), 89–98.

Stark, John, 'The Novels of John Williams', *The Hollins Critic* XVII: 4 (October 1980), 12–13.

Stegner, Wallace, *The American West as Living Space* (Michigan: University of Michigan Press, 1987).

Stegner, Wallace, *The Big Rock Candy Mountain* (1943) (New York: Penguin Books, 1991).
Stegner, Wallace, *The Sound of Mountain Water* (1969) (Harmondsworth: Penguin Books, 1997).
Stegner, Wallace, *Where the Bluebird Sings to the Lemonade Springs* (Harmondsworth: Penguin Books, 1992).
Steinbeck, John, *East of Eden* (1952) (London: Penguin Classics, 2017).
Steinberg, Sybil, 'E. Annie Proulx: An American Odyssey', *Publishers Weekly* 3 (June 1996), 57–8.
Stengel, Richard, 'Hurtin' Cowboy', *Time* magazine (26 April 1982) http://content.time.com/time/magazine/article/0,9171,922926,00.html [accessed 20 August 2020].
Stoltje, Beverly, 'A Helpmate for a Man Indeed: The Image of the Frontier Woman', *Journal of American Folklore*, 88: 347 (Spring 1975).
Stoltje, Beverly, 'Making the Frontier Myth: Folklore Process in a Modern Nation', *Western Folklore* 46: 4 (1987).
Streitfield, David, 'McGuane Mellows', *Washington Post Book World* XXII: 43 (25 October 1992).
Suggs, Katherine, 'Multicultural Masculinities and the Border Romance in John Sayle's *Lone Star* and Cormac McCarthy's Border Trilogy', *The New Centennial Review* 1: 3 (2001), 117–54.
Sullivan, Nell, 'Boys Will be Boys and Girls with be Gone: The Circuit of Male Desire in Cormac McCarthy's Border Trilogy', in Arnold and Luce (eds.), *A Cormac McCarthy Companion*, 228–55.
Swann, Brian, and Arnold Krupat (eds.), *Recovering the World* (Berkeley: University of California Press, 1987).
Tate, Allen, 'My Debt to Alan Swallow', *The Denver Quarterly* 2 (Spring 1967).
Tatum, Stephen, *Inventing Billy the Kid: Visions of the Outlaw in America, 1881–1981* (Albuquerque: University of New Mexico Press, 1982).
Tatum, Stephen, 'The Problem of the "Popular" in the New Western History', in Robinson (ed.), *The New Western History*.
Taylor, Joseph E., 'Many Lives of the New West', *Western Historical Quarterly* 35: 2 (Summer 2004), 141–65.
Taylor, J. Golden, *A Literary History of the American West* (Fort Worth, TX: Texas Christian University Press, 1987).
Taylor, M. Scott, 'Buffalo Hunt: International Trade and the Virtual Extinction of the North American Bison', *The American Economic Review* 101: 7 (December 2011), 3162–95.
Taylor, Sheridan, interview with Anna Klassen, *Bustle Entertainment* (August 2017) https://www.bustle.com/p/the-true-story-behind-wind-river-is-this-hidden-injustice-against-native-american-women-75304.
Thomas, John L., *A Country in the Mind: Wallace Stegner, Bernard DeVoto, History, and the American Land* (New York, London: Routledge, 2002).
Thoreau, Henry, *Cape Cod, Walden and other Writings*, edited by William Howarth (New York: The Modern Library, 1981).
Thoreau, Henry, 'Walking' (1863) in Carl Bode (ed.), *The Portable Thoreau* (New York: Penguin, 1982).
Tompkins, Jane, *West of Everything: The Inner Life of Westerns* (New York, Oxford: Oxford University Press, 1992).

Torrey, Beef (ed.), *Conversations with Thomas McGuane* (Jackson: University of Mississippi Press, 2007).
Tuan, Yi-Fu, *Space and Place: The Perspective of Experience* (Minneapolis: University of Minnesota Press, 1997).
Tuck, Eve and K. Wayne Yang, 'Decolonization if not a Metaphor', *Decolonization: Indigeneity, Education and Society* 1: 40 (2012).
Vanderhaeghe, Guy, *The Englishman's Boy* (Toronto: McClelland and Steward, 1996).
Veracini, Lorenzo, *Settler Colonialism: A Theoretical Overview* (New York: Palgrave Macmillan, 2010).
Vizenor, Gerald, 'Edward Curtis: Pictorialist and Ethnographic Adventurist', in Nathaniel Lewis, William R. Handley (eds.), *True West: Authenticity and the American West* (Lincoln, Nebraska: University of Nebraska Press, 2004), 180–93.
Vizenor, Gerald, *Manifest Manners: Postindian Warriors of Survivance* (Hanover: University Press of New England, 1994).
Wachhorst, Wyn, 'Come Back, Shane! The National Nostalgia', *Southwest Review* 98: 1 (2013), 12–25.
Wakefield, Dan, 'John Williams, Plain Writer', *Ploughshares* 7: 3/4 (October 1981), 9–22.
Wall, Drucilla Mims, *Identity and Authenticity: Exploration in Native and Irish Literature and Culture*, unpublished PhD dissertation (University of Nebraska, 2006).
Wallace, Jon, 'Speaking Against the Dark Side: Style as Theme in Thomas McGuane's *Nobody's Angel*', *Modern Fiction Studies* 33: 2 (Summer 1987), 289–98.
Wallach, Rick, 'Theater, Ritual, and Dream in the Border Trilogy', in Hall and Wallach (eds.), *Sacred Violence*, 159–74.
Walts, Robert (ed.), *The American Southwest: Cradle of Literary Art* (San Marcos: Southwest Texas University, 1979).
Waters, Frank, 'Notes on Alan Swallow', *University of Denver Quarterly* 2 (Spring 1967).
Weber, Bruce, 'Richard Ford's Uncommon Characters', *New York Times* (10 April 1988).
Webb, W. E., *Buffalo Land* (E. Hannaford and Co., 1872).
Weiss, Daniel, 'Cormac McCarthy, Violence and Borders: The Map as Code for What is Not Contained', *The Cormac McCarthy Journal* 8: 1 (Fall 2010), 73–89.
Welter, Barbara (ed.), *The Woman Question in American History* (Hinsdale, IL: The Dryden Press, 1973).
Weltzien, Alan, 'Annie Proulx's Wyoming: Geographical Determinism, Landscape, and Caricature', in Hunt (ed.), *Geographical Imagination*, 99–112.
Werden, Douglas, '"She had Never Humbled herself": Alexandra Bergson and Marie Shabata as the "Real" Pioneers of *O Pioneers!*' *Great Plains Quarterly* 7: 1 (2002), 199–215.
Westling, Louise, *The Green Breast of the New World: Landscape, Gender, and American Fiction* (Athens: University of Georgia Press, 1996).
Westrum, Dexter, 'Review of *Keep the Change* by Thomas McGuane', *Western American Literature* 25: 2 (Summer, 1990), 174.

Westrum, Dexter, *Thomas McGuane* (Boston: Twayne, 1991).
White Jr., John H., 'Hunting Buffalo from the Train: Buffalo, Iron Horses, and the Path Toward', *Railroad History*, 201 (Fall-Winter 2009), 42–9; https://www.jstor.org/stable/43525228 [accessed 10 October 2020].
White Jr., Lynn, 'The Historical Roots of Our Ecological Crisis', *American Association for the Advancement of Science* 155: 3767 (March 1967), 1203–5.
White, Richard, 'Frederick Jackson Turner and Buffalo Bill', in Grossman (ed.), *The Frontier in American Culture*, 7–65.
White, Richard, *It's Your Misfortune and None of My Own: A New History of the American West* (Norman: University of Oklahoma Press, 1991).
Whyte, Kyle, 'Settler Colonialism, Ecology, and Environmental Injustice', *Environment and Society* 9 (2018), 125–44.
Wilkinson, Charles, 'Paradise Revised', in Riebsame and Robb (eds.), *Atlas of the New West: Portrait of a Changing Region* (New York: Norton, 1997), 15–44.
[Novels] Williams, John, *Augustus* (1971) (London: Vintage, 2003).
Williams, John, *Butcher's Crossing* (1960) (New York: NYRB, 2007).
Williams, John, *Nothing but the Night* (1948) (Fayetteville, London: University of Arkansas Press, 1990).
Williams, John, *The Tent*, incomplete typed manuscript part handwritten, John Williams Papers: MC716: Box 29, folder 2.
[Essays appearing in Periodicals] Williams, John, 'Henry Miller: The Success of Failure', *The Virginia Quarterly Review* 44: 2 (spring 1968), 225–45.
Williams, John, 'The "Western": Definition of the Myth', in *The Nation* XLIII: 17 (18 November 1961), 401–6. Reprinted in Irving Deer and Harriat A Deer (eds.), *The Popular Arts: A Critical Arts* (New York: Charles Scribner's and Sons, 1967).
[Unpublished Academic Essays]
'The Cowboy', typed manuscript with handwritten corrections, John Williams Papers, MC716: Box 22, folder 4.
Williams, Terry Tempest, *Refuge: An Unnatural History of Family and Place* (New York: Vintage, 1991).
Williams, William Carlos, *In the American Grain* (Norfolk, CT: New Directions, 1940).
Wilson, Alex and Jenifer L. Uncapher (and members of the Rocky Mountain Institute), *Green Development: Integrating Ecology and Real Estate* (New York: Wiley and Sons, 1998).
Wilson, Rob, and Wimal Dissanayake (eds.), *Global/Local: Cultural Production and the Transnational Imaginary* (Durham, North Carolina: Duke University Press, 1996).
Wister, Owen, 'The Evolution of the Cowboy', *Harpers* 91 (September 1895), 602–17.
Wister, Owen, *Out West: His Journals and Letters*, editied by Fanny Kemble Wister (Chicago: University of Chicago Press, 1958).
Wister, Owen, *The Virginian* (1902) (Oxford: Oxford University Press, 1998).
Witschi, Nicolas (ed.), *A Companion to the Literature and Culture of the American West* (Oxford: Wiley-Blackwell, 2011).
Woodward, Richard B., 'Cormac McCarthy's Venomous Fiction', *New York Times* (19 April 1992).

Wolfe, Patrick, *Settler Colonialism and the Transformation of Anthropology: The Politics and Poetics of an Ethnographic Event* (London: Cassell, 1999).

Woolley, Bryan, 'Interview with John Williams', *The Denver Quarterly* 20: 3 (1985–6), 11–31.

Wrobel, David, *The End of Exceptionalism: Frontier Anxiety from the Old West to the New Deal* (Lawrence: University of Kansas Press, 1993).

Wypijewski, JoAnn, 'A Boy's Life: For Matthew Shepard's Killers, What Does it Take to Pass as a Man?' *Harper's Magazine* (September 1999) https://abrahamson.medill.northwestern.edu/WWW/READINGS/10-05_Toolbox/Wypijewski_Boys_Harpers_Sept1999.pdf [accessed 12 August 2020].

Young, Alex Trimble, 'The Rhizomatic West, or, The Significance of the Frontier in Postwestern Studies', *Western American Literature* 48: 1/2 (Spring, Summer 2013), 115–40.

Young, Alex Trimble, with Lorenzo Veracini, '"If I am Native to Anything": Settler Colonial Studies and Western American Literature', *Western American Literature* 52: 1 (Spring 2017), 1–23.

Yueh, Norma N., 'Alan Swallow Publisher 1915–1966', *The Library Quarterly* 39: 3 (July 1969), 223–32.

INDEX

Abbey, Edward 60, 107
Adams, Robert 16
Alexie, Sherman, *Lone Ranger* 111–12, 153, 173
Allard, William, *Vanishing Breed, Photographs of the Cowboy and the West* 16–17
Allmendinger, Blake 61
All the Pretty Horses (McCarthy) 54–69
   Blood imagery 55, 59
   comparison with McMurtry 57, 58
   maps in 60–1
   Native Americans in 56–7
   women in 57–8, 63–4
Altman, Robert, *McCabe and Mrs Miller* 40, 156, 205
Anderson, Sherwood 15, 17, 96
Annales school 14, 115, 119
Arendt, Hannah 10
Arthur, Jay, *Default Country, The* 70, 149
Arthur, Penn 156
Audiard, Jacques, *Sister's Brothers, The* 130, 194
authenticity 33, 48, 96, 147
   Cody and 3, 97, 200
   cultural 71, 105
   and heritage 106
   and kitsch 75, 125, 159
   and Native Americans 146, 150, 173, 200
   and nostalgia 79, 111, 170
   notional 15, 99, 129, 155
   postmodern anxiety 54, 62, 74, 77
Avedon, Richard, *In the American West* 105, 133

Bailey, Charles 55
Barry, Sebastian
   Days Without End 185, 201–5
   Temporary Gentlemen, The 204
   Thousand Moons, A 203
Baudrillard, Jean 4, 74
Beauvoir, Simone de 10, 41–2
Big Sky (Guthrie) 10, 159
Billy the Kid 3, 11, 48, 58, 66
blood imagery 55, 59
Blood Meridian (McCarthy) 47–54
   Butcher's Crossing, comparison 49, 50, 56, 59, 66, 69, 82
   comparison to *The Englishman's Boy* 199, 201
   comparison with McMurtry 52, 55
   Darwinism 47, 50, 53–4, 71
   Essay on Man, Pope 47, 49–50
   Moby Dick 48
   optics and eyes 49–51
   Turnerian influence on 53
Boag, Peter 87, 136
   Re-Dressing America's Frontier Past 87, 136, 202
Bold, Christine, *Frontier Club, The* 3
borders 2, 12, 17, 54, 72, 103, 149
   Campbell's 'third space' 49
   cultural 40
   of identity 31, 69, 85, 185
   linguistic 70
   McCarthy's. *See* McCarthy, Cormac
   Tex/Mex 8, 11, 48
Bowles, Samuel, *Our New West* 2
Brace, Charles, *New West, The* 2
Brautigan, Richard, *Trout Fishing in America* 177
Bredahl, A Carl Jr. 12
Brenner, Jack 35

'Brokeback Mountain' (Proulx)
126–38
  Ang Lee as director 127
  comparison with *Border Trilogy*
    130
  film soundtrack 129–30, 134–5
  influences on 127, 131
  Kinsey report in 132
  Matthew Sheppard 134
Brooks, Xan 208 n.5
Brown, Dee, *Bury My Heart at Wounded Knee* 194, 200
Butcher's Crossing (Williams)
  archetypes in 25, 27, 29, 33, 36, 38
  comparison to *The Tent* 25, 37
  Emersonian influence on 26–8, 34, 35, 37, 38
  existentialism in 25, 27, 31, 33–6
  identity in 27, 31, 34, 36, 37, 40, 43
  landscape in 26, 29, 30, 34, 36, 38
  Native Americans in 32
  relationship to Anthony Mann's *Westerns* 30
  sexuality in 25, 37–42
Butler, Judith 62

Cadence of Grass, The (McGuane) 18, 181–8
  comparison with Proulx 182–3, 186
Calamity Jane 18, 38, 157, 161, 166, 202, 207
Calvinism 9, 10, 158
Campbell, Neil 13, 47
  Cultures of the American New West, The 6
  Rhizomatic West 6, 17
  thirdspace 14, 49
Camus, Albert 10
Cather, Willa, *My Antonia* 107, 149, 173, 205
Cawelti, John 32
Chamberlain, Samuel, *My Confession: Recollections of a Rogue* 48
Clark, Alex 202
Cody, Bill 3, 4, 39, 97, 150, 197, 199–200
Coen brothers, *True Grit* 196–7
Comer, Krista 5, 107, 128

commodification 5, 146, 150, 166, 173
Cook-Lynn, Elizabeth 70
Costner, Kevin, *Dances with Wolves* 111, 112
Country and Western music 125, 129, 135, 155, 170, 179, 183, 193
cowboy
  anti-cowboy 81, 88
  cinema 4, 169, 193–5
  counter-culture cowboy 146–7
  dislocated cowboy 145
  kitsch 6, 14, 18, 121–2, 152, 157, 165–6, 170–1
  masculine model 3, 8, 125, 149, 183–4
  performance 12, 17–19, 29, 57, 59–66, 74, 76–8, 81, 99, 105–6, 113, 129, 154, 162–5, 207
  sexuality 37–8, 82–8, 127–30, 132–3, 155–6
  symbol and myth 10, 12, 16, 30–1, 42, 54, 56, 58, 69, 77, 80, 89, 96, 98, 102, 117, 125, 158, 168, 175–6, 178, 182
Cronon, William, *Trouble with Wilderness, The* 120
cross-dressing 18, 87, 114, 185, 202
Crossing, The (McCarthy) 69–78
  borders in 69–70
  comparison with *Lonesome Dove* 77
  Native Americans in 70–1, 75
  performance in 74–6

Darwinism 3, 47, 50, 53, 54, 71, 77, 106, 116, 169, 182, 206, 207
Deadrock (McGuane) 17, 19, 145, 147, 157, 159, 171
  Deadrock novels 16, 18, 147, 148, 156, 162, 174
Deloria, Philip, *Playing Indian* 57
Deloria, Vine Jr. 112, 171
D'Emilio, John, *Intimate Matters* 132
Dickstein, Morris 11
Dime novels 3, 38, 48, 87, 96, 195
  Deadly Outlaw, The 195, 196
Disneyland 120–2
Dunlap, Thomas 6

Earle, Steve, *Devil's Right Hand, The* 135
Eco, Umberto, *Travels in Hyperreality* 166
Eden
    Adam in 2, 3, 33, 38, 55, 69, 114, 117
    creation of 69
    destruction of 33, 55, 114, 115
    discovery of 2, 15, 98, 107, 114
    Eve in 18, 38, 117, 181
    expulsion from 34, 55, 129
Ellis, Brett Easton 11
Emerson 10, 26–8, 34, 38, 48–50, 53, 70, 158, 177, 188
    Nature 9, 26, 35, 37
    transparent eyeball 26–9, 34, 36–8, 48, 49, 146
Erkkila, Betsy, *Missouri Breaks, The* 155, 156
Estes, Nick, *Our History is the Future* 119
Etulain, Richard 3
existentialism 9, 12, 25, 27, 48, 113. *See also* outsider
    absurdity 51
    anxiety 69, 171
    crises 160, 173
    French 10, 36, 41
    journey 30–3
    landscape 89
    malaise 16
    terror 34
    treatment 35
    Western 10, 12, 35

Faulkner, William 71
feminine 79, 130, 180, 183
    femininity 18, 84, 100, 123, 134, 203
    feminist 5, 7, 181
    performance of the 86–8, 100–1, 134
    threat to cowboys 12, 58, 124
Fenimore, David 99
Fiedler, Leslie 2, 11, 56
Flanagan, Mary 95
Ford, John 35, 85, 95, 130, 154, 193

Ford, Richard, *Rock Springs* 16
Freedman, Estelle, *Intimate Matters* 132
Frontier 76, 87, 128, 137, 148, 161, 174, 187
    crossing 37
    Fiedler's 56
    Frontier Club 3
    gender fluidity on 185, 202
    justice 151, 161, 204
    settlement 27, 42
    Turner's thesis 2–7, 12, 50, 120
    women on 39, 98–103

gender 3–4, 103, 120, 133, 156
    fluidity 85, 185, 194–5, 199, 202–3, 206
globalization 15, 113
Gottlieb, Robert 201, 205
Grey, Zane 3, 63, 88
Guthrie, A. B. 8, 16

Hamilton, Amy 1
Hamlet 17, 152
Hardy, Thomas, *Return of the Native, The* 16
Heilman, Robert 27
Hemingway, Ernest 16, 97, 101, 167, 178, 179
Henderson, William Haywood, *Native* 129, 131
Holloway, David 93 n.58
homoeroticism 85, 88
homophobia 135, 158
homosexuality 100, 127–9, 132, 135–7
Houston, Pam, *Cowboys Are My Weakness* 183
Hubbard, Tasha 32
Hunt, Alex 109, 116–17, 141 n.56
Hutchison, Anthony 28
hyperreal 4, 14, 15, 96, 111, 121, 138, 170

Indianness 56, 70–1, 200

Keep the Change (McGuane) 158–68
    comparison with Proulx 160, 162, 164

comparison with the South 163
filial bonds 158–9
kitsch 161
Kerouac, Jack, *On the Road* 5, 108
King, Meg 56
Kingsolver, Barbara, *Animal Dreams* 16
Kinsey, Robert 132
Kittredge, William 7, 98, 103, 107, 112, 115, 174, 176
Kollin, Susan 58, 70
Kosofsky Sedgewick, Eve 94 n.69

landscape 15, 17–19, 73–4, 89, 97, 100, 107–10, 117, 167
La Von, *Rural Compendium* 110, 113–15
Levi-Strauss, Claude 4
Limerick, Patricia 5, 7, 13, 99, 111, 118
Little House on the Prairie, The 39, 203
London, Jack, *Call of the Wild* 71
Lopez, Barry, *Home Ground: Language for an American Landscape* 70
Lott, Milton 33
Lynch, Tom 7, 70, 115, 149

McCarthy, Cormac
 Cities of the Plains 78–82
 cowboy's and sex in 57–8, 64, 82–9
 eyes and vision in 49–51, 56–8, 70–2, 77
 and Melville 11, 48, 51
McDonagh, Martin, *Three Billboards Outside Ebbing, Missouri* 193, 208 n.5
McGuane, Thomas
 Bushwhacked Piano, The 146–7, 151, 155
 'Cowboy, The' 175–6
 cross-dressing in 185–6
 Crow Fair 182
 'Father, Son and Holy Permit' 179
 Longest Silence, The: A Life in Fishing 177–9
 'Long View of the West, A' 182

 Missouri Breaks 155–6
 Rancho Deluxe 145
 'Small Streams in Michigan' 179
 Tom Horn 156
MacKenzie, David, *Hell or High Water* 193, 208 n.4
Maclean, John, *Slow West* 205–7
McMurtry, Larry 13, 15, 55, 58, 126, 127
 with Diana Ossana 'Brokeback Mountain screenplay' 126–7, 130
 Horseman, Pass By 55
 Lonesome Dove 8, 52, 57, 77, 91 n.18, 126
Mangold, James, *3:10 to Yuma* 195, 196
Manifest Destiny 3, 7, 8, 11, 28, 32, 98, 102, 107, 114, 115, 171, 199, 200, 202
Mann, Anthony
 Man from Laramie, The 30
 Man of the West 30
maps 1, 2, 7, 109, 110, 114
 Albert's expectations 109–14, 117, 138
 in *Butcher's Crossing* 31
 in *The Crossing* 60
 deep 112
 Frank's collection 170
 Grady's 60
 military 109
 oil company 60, 61
 topographical 163
Marx, Leo 55
masculinity 14, 16, 71, 100
 acculturation 48, 158
 archetypes 4, 38, 89, 124, 133, 194–5
 codes 82, 85, 99, 125–6, 128, 130, 202
 culture of 84, 101, 117, 129
 hyper 3, 17, 18, 66, 159, 202
 identity 19, 76, 159, 181
 symbols and rituals of 87, 122, 134, 154, 167–8, 176
 toxic 181
 violence 56, 86
 white 5, 58 87, 128, 149, 193

Melville, Herman, *Moby Dick* 9–11, 29, 34, 48, 51, 91 n.20
Mexico 48, 64, 69, 72
   cliché 61, 67, 115
   maps of 60–1, 109
   as Old West 8, 12, 66–9, 76–7, 80, 102, 115, 162
   revolution 65, 76
   symbol of effeminacy 87, 136
Miller, David, *Lonely are the Brave* 59–60, 102
Milton, John, *Minneapolis Sunday Tribune* 35
Mitchell, Lee Clark 58, 65
Mundik, Petra 91 n.15, 91 n.20

Native Americans
   in Barry, Sebastian 201–4
   in *Butcher's Crossing* 32–3, 36
   'Cowboys and Indians' 3, 10, 16
   on film 5, 21 n.25, 194, 199–200
   in McCarthy 32, 51–2, 56–7, 70–1, 74–5
   in McGuane 146–54, 160–1, 167, 171–4, 182, 188
   in Proulx 96–7, 110–13, 199–200
   vanishing 17, 32, 56, 69, 70–1, 172–3
   Vizenor, Gerald on 56–7, 70, 75
New Historians 5–7, 47, 98
New West 122
   fragmented 145, 171, 182–3
   free-floating signifier 5–6, 12, 17, 104
   of Frontier 2–4
   kitsch 121, 147, 150–2, 162, 166–8, 170
   Old West binary 8, 14, 18, 61, 70, 72, 97, 106, 145, 148, 162, 166, 167, 174, 181, 184–5, 195, 204
   as region 1–3, 5–6, 31–2, 61, 95–7, 107–10, 113–4, 117, 148, 169, 177, 180
   settler colonial project 6–7, 15
   trope 1–2
   urban/industrial 4, 12–13, 19, 148, 164
Nobody's Angel (McGuane) 147–58
   comparison with Proulx 150
   Native Americans in 148–50, 152–4
   women in 155–7
Nothing but Blue Skies (McGuane) 169–80
   comparison with Proulx 169
   fishing in 176–80
   Native Americans in 171–4
   soundtrack 170–1

outsider 10, 14, 18, 26, 27, 48, 147, 161, 181, 201. *See also* existentialism
Owens, Barcley 71, 94 n.65
Owens, Louis 71, 173

postmodern 5, 12, 14, 16, 18, 27, 48, 54, 65, 74, 78, 95, 111, 170, 173
poststructuralist 5
postwestern 5, 6
prostitution 103, 151
   cliché of 9, 29
   historical reality 38–9, 42
   in McCarthy 65, 79, 84, 99
   in McGuane 151, 156
   in Proulx 123, 185
   in Williams 37, 39–42
Proulx, Annie 15, 95–7
   annales 14, 115, 119
   Bad Dirt 104, 169
   Barbwire Festival 120, 121
   Bird Cloud 13, 98
   Close Range 95–6, 127
   'Florida Rental' 103–4, 150, 164
   'Governors of Wyoming, The' 107, 111, 122
   'Great Divide, The' 101–3
   'How the West was Spun' 111, 132
   'Indian Wars Refought, The' 150, 199
   Inhabitants of the Margins 104–5
   'Lonely Coast, A' 133
   'Mud Below, The' 123–6
   'Negatives' 105
   'Pair of Spurs, A' 120, 121, 151
   'People in Hell Want a Drink of Water' 123, 126
   Postcards 14, 103, 111, 186

Red Desert: History of a Place 14, 96, 101
'Sagebrush Kid, The' 96–7, 137
Silent Enemy 199
'Them Old Cowboy Songs' 98–100, 125
'Wamsutter Wolf, The' 103–6
Wyoming Stories 16, 18, 95, 96, 122, 133
Wyoming Trilogy 14, 107, 162
psychological novel 10, 12, 30, 58

rhizome 6, 14, 17
Riebsame, William, *Atlas of the New West* 2, 180
Robinson, Sally 56–7
Rockstar group
  Red Dead Redemption 207
  Red Dead Revolver 207
romanticism 17, 18, 28, 30, 67, 78, 89, 95, 103, 112, 162, 164, 168, 170
  Emersonian 9, 70
Roosevelt, Theodore 2, 3, 159

Sander, Jon, *Painted Angels* 38–9
Sandoz, Mari 33
Sartre, Jean Paul, *Being and Nothingness* 10, 36, 41. *See also* existentialism; outsider
settler colonialism 6, 7, 9, 97, 98, 113, 114, 149, 172, 173, 201
Shane
  book/film 7, 59, 84, 122–3, 175, 195–6, 206
  character 19, 85, 126, 138, 166, 207
  longing to be 8, 74–5, 152
Shields, Charles J. 25–6
Slotkin, Richard 3
  concept of regeneration through violence 9, 48, 49, 65, 158
Snyder, Philip 78, 91 n.25
Something to be Desired (McGuane) 158–68
  filial bonds 158–9, 167
  hyperreality 165–6
  kitsch 165
Spurgeon, Sara 47, 51–3, 55, 63

Stegner, Wallace 14, 16, 30, 114–15, 134
History, Myth, and the Western Writer 145
Sense of Place, A 69, 70, 145
Steinbeck, John, *East of Eden* 69, 115–17
structuralism 4, 7, 13, 70, 96, 107, 120, 186
Sullivan, Nell 82, 86, 88

Tarrantino, Quentin, *Django Unchained* 194
Taylor, Joseph 2, 4, 8, 12
That Old Ace in Hole (Proulx) 106–21
  ecocritical text 107
  maps in 109–10
  Native Americans in 110–13
  Old Testament mythology in 114–17
  performance in 113
  rewilding in 118–20
Thoreau, Henry 26, 29
Tompkins, Jane 3–4, 30, 63, 85
Turner, Frederick Jackson 2, 5, 7, 9, 11, 16, 27, 31, 47–51, 53, 64, 75, 76, 98, 202
Turner, Ted 118, 120, 193

Vanderhaeghe, Guy, *Englishman's Boy, The* 199–201
Veracini, Lorenzo 98, 101
Vizenor, Gerald 56, 70, 75

Wallach, Rick 13
Wars of Civilization 199
Westerns
  anti 8, 11
  archetypes in 8–12, 26, 106, 156, 162, 197
  Dime 3, 4, 87
  existential 10, 12, 35
  and gaming 207
  homoeroticism in 85–7, 126–8, 155–6
  meta 205
  Native Americans in 32, 53–5, 206
  neo 111, 193

postmodern 4, 12, 14, 18, 21, 48, 51, 57, 61, 65–6, 74, 78, 95–6, 170
remakes of 39, 150, 194–6
revisionist 7, 11, 13, 38–9, 47, 55, 118, 174
tropes 27, 29–31, 33
women in 38–9, 42, 63, 83–4, 100–1, 148, 155–6
Whitman, Walt 38, 129
Wilkinson, Charles 1–2
Williams, John 7, 8, 25–42. *See also Butcher's Crossing* (Williams)
Augustus 36
Nothing but the Night 10, 41
sexual subplot 40–1
Sleep or Reason, The 25
Tent, The 25, 37
"Western", The: Definition of the Myth 10
Williams, William Carlos 149–50
Wister, Owen, *The Virginian* 122, 151, 162, 194
homoeroticism in 38, 84–5, 87, 126
Wolfe, Patrick 6
Worster, Donald 1
Wypijewski, JoAnn 121

www.ingramcontent.com/pod-product-compliance
Lightning Source LLC
Chambersburg PA
CBHW062138300426
44115CB00012BA/1968